'For those who fear that the world is becoming too inward-looking, *Connectography* is a refreshing, optimistic vision'

The Economist

'Incredible . . . We don't often question the typical world map that hangs on the walls of classrooms – a patchwork of yellow, pink and green that separates the world into more than two hundred nations. But Parag Khanna, a global strategist, says that this map is, essentially, obsolete . . . With the world rapidly changing and urbanizing, [Khanna's] proposals might be the best way to confront a radically different future'

The Washington Post

'Clear and coherent . . . Khanna provides a rare account of the physical infrastructure of globalization . . . Khanna also provides a well-researched account of how companies are weaving ever more complicated supply chains that pull the world together even as they squeeze out inefficiencies . . . [He] has succeeded in demonstrating that the forces of globalization are winning the battle for connected space, building tunnels, bridges and pipelines at an astonishing pace'

Adrian Woolridge, *The Wall Street Journal*

'This is probably the most global book ever written. It is intensely specific while remaining broad and wide. Its takeaway is that infrastructure is destiny: follow the supply lines outlined in this book to see where the future flows'

Kevin Kelly, Senior Maverick, *Wired* magazine

'To get where you want to go, it helps to have a good map. In *Connectography*, Parag Khanna surveys the economic, political and technological landscape and lays out the case for why

"competitive connectivity" – with cities and supply chains as the vital nodes – is the true arms race of the twenty-first century. This bold reframing is an exciting addition to our ongoing debate about geopolitics and the future of globalization'
Dominic Barton, Global Managing Partner, McKinsey & Co.

'From Lagos, Mumbai, Dubai and Singapore to the Amazon, the Himalayas, the Arctic and the Gobi desert steppe, Parag Khanna's latest book provides an invaluable guide to the volatile, confusing worlds of early twenty-first-century geopolitics. A provocative remapping of contemporary capitalism based on planetary mega-infrastructures, inter-continental corridors of connectivity and transnational supply chains rather than traditional political borders'
Neil Brenner, Director, Urban Theory Lab, Harvard University Graduate School of Design

'*Connectography* gives the reader an amazing new view of human society, bypassing the time-worn categories and frameworks we usually use. It shows us a view of our world as a living thing that really exists: the flows of people, ideas and materials that constitute our constantly evolving reality. *Connectography* is a must-read for anyone who wants to understand the future of humanity'
Sandy Pentland, Professor, MIT Media Lab

'*Connectography* is ahead of the curve in seeing the battlefield of the future, and the new kind of tug-of-war being waged on it. Khanna's scholarship and foresight are world-class'
Chuck Hagel, former US Secretary of Defence

'Parag Khanna has vision'   Nassim Nicholas Taleb

Parag Khanna is a leading global strategist, world traveller and bestselling author. He is a CNN Global Contributor and Senior Research Fellow at the Centre on Asia and Globalisation at the Lee Kuan Yew School of Public Policy at the National University of Singapore. In 2008, Parag was named one of *Esquire*'s '75 Most Influential People of the 21st Century' and featured in *Wired* magazine's 'Smart List'. He has travelled to more than one hundred countries and is a Young Global Leader of the World Economic Forum.

www.paragkhanna.com
www.facebook.com/DrParagKhanna
@paragkhanna

By Parag Khanna

*The Second World: Empires and Influence in
the New Global Order*

How to Run the World: Charting a Course to the Next Renaissance

Connectography: Mapping the Global Network Revolution

CONNECTOGRAPHY

Mapping the Global
Network Revolution

PARAG KHANNA

WEIDENFELD & NICOLSON

A W&N PAPERBACK

First published in the United States in 2016
by Penguin Random House
First published in Great Britain in 2016
by Weidenfeld & Nicolson
This paperback edition published in 2017
by Weidenfeld & Nicolson,
an imprint of the Orion Publishing Group Ltd,
Carmelite House, 50 Victoria Embankment
London EC4Y 0DZ

An Hachette UK company

1 3 5 7 9 10 8 6 4 2

A CIP catalogue record for this book
is available from the British Library.

ISBN 978-1-474-60425-3

Printed and bound by CPI Group (UK) Ltd, Croydon, CR0 4YY

www.orionbooks.co.uk

To Ayesha,
the only compass I need

CONTENTS

Prologue   *xv*
A Note About Maps   *xix*

PART ONE: CONNECTIVITY AS DESTINY

CHAPTER 1   FROM BORDERS TO BRIDGES   3

A Journey Around the World   3

Bridges to Everywhere   7

Seeing Is Believing   12

From Political to Functional Geography   14

Supply Chain World   19

Balancing Flow and Friction   29

CHAPTER 2   NEW MAPS FOR A NEW WORLD   35

From Globalization to Hyper-Globalization   35

The Measure of Things   41

A New Map Legend   45

BOX: From Diplomacy to "Diplomacity"   *58*

PART TWO: DEVOLUTION AS DESTINY

CHAPTER 3   THE GREAT DEVOLUTION   63

Let the Tribes Win   63

Growing Apart to Stay Together   69

From Nations to Federations   73

CHAPTER 4   FROM DEVOLUTION TO AGGREGATION   79

Geopolitical Dialectics   79
The New Grand Trunk Road to *Pax Indica*   84
From Sphere of Influence to *Pax Aseana*   87
From "Scramble for Africa" to *Pax Africana*   92
From Sykes-Picot to *Pax Arabia*   99

BOX: *The Israeli Exception?*   105

CHAPTER 5   THE NEW MANIFEST DESTINY   111

United States or Tragedy of the Commons?   111
The Devolution Within   116
Pacific Flows   121
Oil and Water Across the World's Longest Border   125
The North American Union   128

BOX: *A South American Union*   132

PART THREE: COMPETITIVE CONNECTIVITY

CHAPTER 6   WORLD WAR III—OR TUG-OF-WAR?   137

An Ancient Metaphor for Postmodern Times   137
Was Orwell Right?   139
The Calm Before the Storm?   142
War by Other Means   147

CHAPTER 7   THE GREAT SUPPLY CHAIN WAR   151

Trading Atoms and Bits   151

BOX: *Printing, Sharing—and Trading*   156
Horizontal + Vertical = Diagonal   158
Resource Genes and Data Centers for Food   163

BOX: *The "Supply Circle"*   166
Coming Home—but Only to Sell at Home   167
A Longitudinal World?   170

CHAPTER 8   INFRASTRUCTURE ALLIANCES   172

    Getting Grand Strategy Right   172

    Post-Ideological Alliances   178

    BOX: Piraeus: China's European Gateway   184

    From Sanctions to Connections   186

    Beware Friendship Bridges   189

    Oil Is Thicker Than Blood   192

CHAPTER 9   THE NEW IRON AGE   196

    Iron Silk Roads Across the Heartland   196

    BOX: "Mine-Golia": Where (Almost) All Roads

        Lead to China   201

    Kublai Khan's Revenge: The Return of Sino-Siberia   204

    Iran: The Silk Road Restored   210

    North Korea: An Iron Silk Road Through the Hermit

    Kingdom   214

    The Supply Chain Strikes Back   220

CHAPTER 10   HOPSCOTCH ACROSS THE OCEANS   226

    An Empire of Enclaves   226

    "Mobile Sovereignty"   229

    Sovereigns of the Sea   234

    Escaping the "Malacca Trap"   237

    The Maritime Silk Road   241

    Atlantic Cities   245

    The Capital of the Arctic   248

PART FOUR: **FROM NATIONS TO NODES**

CHAPTER 11   IF YOU BUILD IT, THEY WILL COME   259

    Dubai: Home to the World   259

    First Port of Call   271

    BOX: Lagos: Africa's Global City   276

CHAPTER 12   GETTING ON THE MAP   279

Pop-Up Cities   279

From Exclave to Enclave   283

China's Supersize SEZs   285

Master Planning for Megacities   291

City Building as State Building   293

Leapfrogging to Hybrid Governance   298

CHAPTER 13   SUPPLY CHAINS AS SALVATION   300

Who Runs the Supply Chain?   300

Beyond the Law?   305

To Move or Not to Move?   308

BOX: *Getting Beyond Corruption?*   310

The Global Underclass Revolt   312

Spend Now, Gain Later   316

The Financial Supply Chain   319

PART FIVE: **TOWARD A GLOBAL SOCIETY**

CHAPTER 14   CYBER CIVILIZATION AND ITS DISCONTENTS   327

Invisible Infrastructure   327

Walled Gardens or Bumps on the Information
Superhighway?   331

The Digital Identity Buffet   337

Spreading the Connective Wealth   340

The Global Digital Workforce   343

CHAPTER 15   THE GREAT DILUTION   346

A Mongrel Civilization   346

BOX: *China: Imperial Nation-State*   356

Global Passports   357

Global Citizens   362

Citizenship Arbitrage   364

CHAPTER 16   WHEN NATURE HAS ITS SAY,
                         GET OUT OF THE WAY   367

         Retreat from the Water's Edge?   367

         BOX: Rivers over Borders   369
         How to Negotiate with Nature   370

         BOX: Measuring the Supply Chain's Footprint   377
         Location, Location, Location   378

CONCLUSION: FROM CONNECTIVITY TO RESILIENCE   381

         A New Moral Compass   381
         Networks That Run Themselves   386
         Building a Borderless World   389

         Recommended Sites and Tools for Mapping   393
         Acknowledgments   403
         Notes   413
         Bibliography   423
         Map Credits and Sources   445
         Index   449

PROLOGUE

THE NATURAL CONSEQUENCE OF ANY OBSESSION IS PASSING IT on to one's children. I've been collecting globes, maps, and other geographic artifacts since my itinerant childhood. Thus it is hardly a coincidence to have been writing portions of this book while methodically assembling a thousand-piece world map with my daughter. The map is a Mercator projection, named for the sixteenth-century Flemish geographer who sought to make maps more useful for navigation but in the process massively distorted the scale of the extreme latitudes. Hence my daughter exclaiming, "Greenland is so big!" (While also wondering why it was colored orange.) Africa was the easiest continent to piece together: With fifty-four countries, each little jigsaw shape was full of clues such as contrasting national colors and city names. We left the vast oceans for last—a truly frustrating slog, with hundreds of featureless pieces differentiated only by shades of blue. We passed the time discussing where the oceans are deepest, where the largest underwater mountain ranges are, and how people survive on remote islands.

When the entire puzzle was complete, we carefully wrapped it with a roll of wide, transparent tape and stuck it on her wall. Taking a step back, I could easily envision how neatly all the continents were once joined together as the supercontinent Pangaea and begin to imagine how over the next fifty to a hundred million years they will again cluster together (around the Arctic), fusing into another supercontinent scientists call Amasia.

But what if we are already connecting all the continents together today? What will our planet look like once we have built seamless transportation, energy, and communications infrastructures among all the world's people and resources—when there is no geography that is not connected? A better term for it might be "Connectography."

THIS BOOK IS ABOUT the staggering consequences of connectivity on almost every facet of our lives. It completes a trilogy on the future world order. The arc began with *The Second World,* a tour of the new geopolitical marketplace in which multiple superpowers compete for influence in major regions rife with instability and divisions. I argued, "Colonies were once conquered; today countries are bought." And yet smart states practice a shrewd multi-alignment of being friendly with all great powers at the same time to extract maximum benefits without committing to deep alliances. The sequel *How to Run the World* examined the increasingly neo-medieval global landscape in which governments, companies, civic groups, and other players all compete for authority yet collaborate in a new kind of mega-diplomacy to tackle global challenges. It ended with a call for "universal liberation through exponentially expanding and voluntary connections" as the path to a global Renaissance. *Connectography* is about how we get there—literally and intellectually.

The road map of this book follows several interconnected thrusts. First, connectivity has replaced division as the new paradigm of global organization. Human society is undergoing a fundamental transformation by which functional infrastructure tells us more about how the world works than political borders. The true map of the world should feature not just states but megacities, highways, railways, pipelines, Internet cables, and other symbols of our emerging global network civilization.

Second, devolution is the most powerful political force of our age: Everywhere empires are splintering and authority is dissipating away from central capitals toward provinces and cities that seek autonomy in their financial and diplomatic affairs. But devolution has an important counterpart: aggregation. The smaller our political units get, the more they must fuse into larger commonwealths of shared resources in order to survive. This trend is playing out around the world from East Africa to Southeast Asia as dynamic new regional federations take shape through common infrastructures and institutions. North America too is growing into a truly united supercontinent.

Third, the nature of geopolitical competition is evolving from war over territory to war over connectivity. Competing over connectivity plays out as a tug-of-war over global supply chains, energy markets, industrial production, and the valuable flows of finance, technology, knowledge, and talent. Tug-of-war represents the shift from a war between systems (capitalism versus communism) to a war *within* one collective supply chain system. While military warfare is a regular threat, tug-of-war is a perpetual reality—to be won by economic master planning rather than military doctrine. Around the world, thousands of new cities or special economic zones (SEZs) have been constructed to help societies get themselves on the map in the global tug-of-war.

Another way this competitive connectivity takes place is through infrastructure alliances: connecting physically across borders and oceans through tight supply chain partnerships. China's relentless pursuit of this strategy has elevated infrastructure to the status of a global good on par with America's provision of security. Geopolitics in a connected world plays out less on the Risk board of territorial conquest and more in the matrix of physical and digital infrastructure.

Connectivity is a major driver of the deep shift toward a more complex global system. Economies are more integrated, populations are more mobile, the cyber domain is merging with physical reality, and climate change is forcing seismic adjustments on our way of life. The significant—and often sudden—feedback loops among these phenomena remain almost impossible to decipher. And yet even as connectivity makes the world more complex and unpredictable, it also offers the essential pathways to achieve collective resilience.

It is precisely in such times of uncertainty that people most want to know what's next. The best we can do, however, is scenarios. During the Cold War, scenarios became an important way to examine how stability could suddenly mutate and escalate into hostility, how peace could give way to war. Today we build scenarios to depict what the world might look like if energy abundance is achieved or if resource competition intensifies, if global migration surges or if restrictions are enforced, if financial flows flood emerging markets or if policy shifts force capital to retrench, if inequality generates widespread political unrest or if governments recommit to delivering jobs and welfare. It's easy to find evidence pointing in all directions.

Good scenarios therefore are about not predictions but processes: the greater the diversity of perspectives, the richer the scenarios that result. At a time when both the "death of globalization" and the "age of hyper-globalization" are heralded with equal confidence, assembling an accurate view of the future is less a matter of binary choices—a rosy versus a gloomy scenario—than of constructing a mélange of several visions. Today we don't get to choose between a world of great power competition, globalized interdependence, and powerful private networks; we have all three at the same time.

In this book, I have combined elements from hundreds of scenarios along with my own research and observations from two decades of traveling to every corner of the world and analyzing global affairs. Thanks to phenomenal improvements in data visualization, some of these findings are depicted in the unique maps and graphics included herein and in the accompanying *Connectivity Atlas* available online at https://atlas.developmentseed.org/. Whatever shape the world takes in the coming decades, there is still no substitute for a good map.

A NOTE ABOUT MAPS

THE FIRST KNOWN MAPS OF THE WORLD—THE ANCIENT BABYlonian *Imago Mundi* and the Greek philosopher Anaximander's circular map centered on the Mediterranean—date to the sixth century B.C.E. The Greek astronomer Ptolemy subsequently developed the full grid of latitude and longitude to enable more precise positioning of coordinates. But for many centuries thereafter, Byzantine and Islamic maps remained oriented around holy sites; they were as much about theology as geography. Through the Crusades and expansion of the Eurasian Silk Road, European scholars strove for greater accuracy about geography and climate, producing approximately a thousand *mappa mundi* that contained cities, towns, and animal species but also biblical allegories. The maps of the fifteenth-century Italian polymath Leonardo da Vinci added the relief elements of today's modern atlas, with colors and shading to capture elevation and landscapes.

Even as mapmaking techniques developed, however, the knowledge to fill them was still limited. In the decades following Ferdinand Magellan's circumnavigation of the world five centuries ago, many maps continued to feature sketches of sea monsters and the Latin phrase *hic sunt dracones*—"Here be dragons"—over East

Asia. Mid-seventeenth-century European maps of Africa were still filled with vague sketches of monkeys and elephants, underscoring Westerners' dearth of knowledge about the precolonial societies of the Southern Hemisphere. Almost nothing was known in the West about Hawaii and the South Pacific islands until James Cook's voyages in the mid-eighteenth century. At the time, the most important notations on maps were arguably the oceanic currents that guided maritime navigators.

Today's maps have evolved to correct the distortions of their predecessors. The Gall-Peters and Hobo-Dyer projections, for example, use equal area scaling techniques to render the size of continents such that, for example, Greenland doesn't appear as large as Africa because, in reality, Africa is fourteen times larger. But beyond providing more accurate scale and locations, these maps do little to represent the reality of place.

This is especially true of today's political maps, to which we ironically ascribe such sacred veracity even though they are one of history's foremost propaganda tools. Maps are seductive but also dangerous. Competitive cartography is a centuries-old duel as mapmakers promote nationalistic versions of reality. What we put on a map has iconic power to shape how people think. Israel's maps show its borders as legally codified, while its neighbors either don't show Israel at all or label Palestine as "Occupied Territories." In 2014, even the publisher HarperCollins released an edition of its *Middle East Atlas* that omitted Israel entirely to cater to the sensitivities of its Arab market. India and China continue to issue conflicting maps as to the precise location of their border in several different sectors where their armies continue to skirmish. Google Earth has heretofore made its maps outside national dictates, depicting disputed areas as such without taking sides. When it mistakenly ceded a disputed portion of the San Juan River to Costa Rica in 2010, however, Nicaragua almost declared war—on one of the only countries in the world that has no army!

Amusingly, borders change so constantly that they are themselves the best reminder that there is nothing permanent about maps. Indeed, over time even the most basic cultural labels that we associate with the compass directions evolve in meaning. A quarter century ago, "East" meant the Soviet Union; the Cold War was often referred to as the "East-West conflict." Yet today nobody would place the label "East" over Russia. The *real* "East" is China-centric Asia that contains over half the world's population and represents one-third of the global economy. Similarly, "West" used to refer to only the Judeo-Christian countries of western Europe, or more expansively the members of the transatlantic NATO alliance. But today when we speak of the "West," we mean the European Union's almost thirty members as well as North America and even the entire South American continent, the third pillar of the Western world.[1] And indeed, with many countries of the erstwhile "South" (meaning "third world") such as India growing faster than the West, the diplomatic bloc of the Southern Hemisphere has all but dissolved. "Old World" once meant Europe, and "New World" referred to the Americas. Now the West has become the "old," while Asia is the "new." As the reality of Asia's hyperdevelopment sank in for a recently arrived Western journalist in Singapore, he mused during our first conversation, "Modernity now begins in the East and flows west." And in the coming generation, one identity that never really existed—"Northern"—is being born in the Arctic region as the zone of the earth's sphere above 66° north latitude becomes more populated as temperatures rise.

Maps are the original—and still most commonly used—infographics. But pre-infrastructure maps are increasingly irrelevant in today's world. The corporate strategist Kenichi Ohmae thus claimed that maps are "cartographic illusions" because of how little they reflect our ability to overcome geographic distance through technology. In polite society, sins of omission are regarded as lies; the same should be true of maps. Concluding his exhaustive and eloquent survey of the history of cartography, the British historian Jerry Brotton sagely points to the paradox that "we can never know the world without a map, nor definitively represent it with one."[2] Yet still we must try. A complex world needs maps more than ever, but it needs better ones. Maps have graduated from art and theology to commerce and politics; now they need to better reflect demographics, economics, ecology, and engineering.

During the early Cold War, America's Sixty-Fourth Topographic Engineer Battalion surveyed rugged terrain such as jungles and minefields from Liberia to Libya and Ethiopia to Iran to help the United States produce more accurate maps for military operations and munitions targeting. By the time of the Vietnam War, it was phased out and replaced by satellites. There is a revolution under way in cartographic technology that is enabling us to reinvent the map, making it a living, moving image of the world. Rather than static 2-D on paper, we can now view the world, and the trends and relations transpiring within it, in dynamic and digital 3-D, on digital screens or holograms. Cartography is making the leap from X-ray to MRI.

The best maps juxtapose physical geography with man-made connectivity. They are constantly updated snapshots reflecting ground realities and virtual gravities. Each time we "refresh," they should depict new natural resource discoveries, infrastructures, demographic movements, and other shifts. The GeoFusion flight tracker, available to passengers on British Airways, uses real-time WorldSat data to show with precise detail the brown-green granularity of farmland, the jagged counters of mountain ranges, and the wide gray patches of cities, with touch-screen navigation of scale and elevation. All kids should have this app on their iPads. For one thing, they would see right away that the world is round rather than flat.

When one pilots through GeoFusion, it also becomes obvious that dividing the world into political units is utterly secondary to the fact that mankind is becoming a dense coastal urban civilization. By 2030, more than 70 percent of the world's people will live in cities, with most of them located within fifty miles of the sea. While human settlement along fertile river plains and oceanic coasts is an ancient pattern, the demographic concentration, economic weight, and political power of today's coastal megacities makes them—more than most states—the key units of human organization.

If we are an urban species, then producing data-driven cityscapes—mapping cities from *within*—is as important as capturing their scale. In the 1980s, GPS technology firms began painstakingly driving and geo-coding roads all over the world, building up databases for the suites of navigational tools that are now in almost every new car's dashboard. Google soon joined the fray, adding more satellite imagery and street views. Today every individual can become a digital cartographer: Maps have gone from *Britannica* to *Wiki*. OpenStreetMap, for example, crowdsources street views from millions of members who can also tag and label any structure, infusing local knowledge and essential insight for everything from simple commuting to delivering supplies during humanitarian disasters.* We can now even insert updated imagery from Planet Labs' two dozen shoe-box-size satellites into 3-D maps and fly through the natural or urban environment.

All of this is coming to the palm of your hand. Google Maps is already by far the world's most downloaded app; it represents the "ground truth" far better than Rand McNally. With the rise of the global sensor network dubbed the "Internet of Everything" (Internet of Things + Internet of People), our maps will perpetually update themselves, providing an animated view into our world as it really is—even the five thousand commercial aircraft in the sky and the more than ten thousand ships crossing the seas at any given moment.† These are the arteries and veins, capillaries and cells, of a planetary economy underpinned by an infrastructural network that can eventually become as efficient as the human body.

The cartographic revolution will leave almost nothing to the imagination. Underwater cameras now provide precise images of

---

* Maptitude, StatPlanet, and iMapper are also programs that allow us to insert cultural or economic data into maps. With Google's Tango project, our mobile phones will become 3-D mapping tools that constantly scan our immediate environment and even "see" through walls.

† Eventually, we may not need satellites at all for positioning and navigation with the advent of lower-cost but extremely accurate Quantum-Assisted Sensing that determines location by measuring the impact of the earth's magnetic field on atoms.

the ocean's ridges and trenches, mineral deposits and reef systems, rapidly augmenting the less than 0.05 percent of the ocean seabed that has been surveyed to date. Lidar, which uses lasers to detect and survey changes in the atmosphere and identify mineral deposits deep underground, also allows us to produce precise maps of natural resources.

When we combine demographic data, climatological forecasting, and seismic patterns, we can see that more than half the world's population is clustering on the Pacific Rim of Asia along the Ring of Fire, the zone in which three-quarters of the world's 450 active volcanoes lie, more than 80 percent of the world's largest earthquakes occur, and sea levels are rising the fastest. As dramatically as any Hollywood film, we can animate the future and potentially our own self-inflicted destruction.

Mapping the complex dynamics among the three greatest forces shaping our planet—man, nature, and technology—will require a whole new kind of geographic literacy. From the depths of the Amazon rain forest to the middle of the Taklamakan Desert of China, there are places where the best guides are still "living maps": elderly tribal folk or nomads who have developed an intuition for sensing the growth of the jungle or the shifts of the sand dunes. As their skills fade with them, however, we rely ever more on technology. This new generation of maps and models is thus more than a collection of pretty digital guides. They should be the focal point for the synthesis of environmental science, politics, economics, culture, technology, and sociology[3]—a curriculum curated through the study of *connections* rather than *divisions*. We shouldn't be using static political maps any more than we would cling to QWERTY keyboards when we have voice recognition, gestural interfaces, and instant video communication.

Today's "digital natives"—also known as millennials or Generation Y (and Z)—need this new tool kit. There are more young people alive today than ever in history: Forty percent of the world population is under the age of twenty-four, meaning an even larger percentage has no personal memory of colonialism or the Cold

War. According to surveys by Zogby Analytics, these "first globals" identify connectivity and sustainability as their prime values. They aren't automatically loyal to the establishment at home or feel secure behind the borders that separate them from "others" abroad. In America, Latin millennials were in favor of full normalization of ties with Cuba; South Korean millennials are for reunification with the North. They believe their destiny is not only to belong to political states but to connect across them. By 2025, the whole world's population will likely be connected to mobile phones and the Internet. As life becomes more connected, we must adjust our maps accordingly.

PART ONE

CONNECTIVITY
AS DESTINY

CHAPTER 1

FROM BORDERS TO BRIDGES

A JOURNEY AROUND
THE WORLD

Let's take a journey around the world—without ever getting on a plane. If we get an early start in Edinburgh, Scotland, we'll arrive at London Euston station around noon, stroll quickly past the British Library, and have a quick lunch at the masterfully renovated Victorian-era St. Pancras station, from which we'll board the Eurostar train, travel under the Dover Strait to Paris, followed by a high-speed TGV to Munich and a German ICE to Budapest. An overnight train along the Danube River brings us to Bucharest, Romania, and another overnight along the Black Sea to Istanbul. Where once a creaky ferry was the fastest way to cross from Europe to Asia across the Bosporus Strait, today we can glide over one or the other suspension bridge or continue by train through the newly opened Marmaray tunnel and onward to Iran. We could also catch the revived Hejaz Railway through southeastern Turkey, stopping in Damascus and Amman before continuing to Medina or across Israel and the Sinai to Cairo, from which we might ultimately descend through Africa all the way to Cape Town on a sturdy upgrade of the "Red Line" British colonialists began in the late nineteenth century. From Tehran, we'll head eastward on a new Chinese-built railway

Map 1, corresponding to this chapter, appears in the first map insert.

through the rugged Asian steppe, cross Turkmenistan and Uzbekistan to Kazakhstan's commercial hub of Almaty. Several times per week, we can cross into China's largest province of Xinjiang to its capital, Urumqi, and onward via Xi'an to Beijing.

Back in Paris, we might have opted for an overnight sleeper to Moscow, from which we could catch the fabled Trans-Siberian Railway to Vladivostok—and carry on to Pyongyang and Seoul—or branch off a bit earlier toward Beijing, via either Manchuria or Mongolia. Either way, if we opt for the tropical route, we'll speed southward along the world's most extensive high-speed rail network into mountainous Yunnan and its capital, Kunming. From there, we can cross directly into Laos and take in Vientiane before crossing into Thailand toward Bangkok, or take a coastal route along the South China Sea via Hanoi and Ho Chi Minh City in Vietnam and through Phnom Penh in Cambodia to Bangkok. Now the options narrow with the geography: we speed on down the Malay Peninsula to Kuala Lumpur and Singapore, the southernmost point on mainland Asia.

But water hasn't stopped us so far, so let's continue by train through a tunnel under the strategic Strait of Malacca onto Indonesia's largest island of Sumatra, then over the Sunda Strait bridge to reach the capital, Jakarta, on Java, the world's most populous island with more than 150 million people. Just a bit farther and we're on the beaches of Bali, from which we can catch a cruise ship to Australia. If we choose the fastest routes and don't miss any connections, we will have traversed the entire Eurasian landmass—Scotland to Singapore, and then some—in about a week.

And yet we're only halfway done. Instead of the Antipodes, from Beijing we should actually head north through Vladivostok and eastern Siberia. If you fancy sushi, we could take a bridge to Sakhalin Island and pass through a 45-kilometer tunnel to Japan's northernmost Hokkaido Island, passing seamlessly southward across Japan's major islands on high-speed Shinkansen trains. When we reach Kyushu, we'll loop back through a 120-kilometer undersea tunnel to Busan, zipping northward through the Korean peninsula back toward Siberia to continue our next 13,000-kilometer segment that takes us parallel to the volcanic Kamchatka Peninsula and through a 200-kilometer tunnel under the Bering Strait that emerges in Alaska and takes us to Fairbanks. From there, of course, it's straight south to Juneau and Vancouver, Seattle and Portland, San Francisco and Los Angeles. California, Texas, Illinois, and New York all want more Acela Express high-speed rail (though it's planned to hit only about two hundred kilometers per hour, about half as fast as the Japanese). Still, we'll make it from Pacific to Atlantic across the Lower 48 in two days. All that's left is to catch a zippy but smooth hovercraft to London, followed by any of the more than twenty daily trains headed to Edinburgh. A journey around the world—as promised.

One could fly almost seamlessly along this itinerary, drive much of it too except for the oceans, and indeed eventually do it the old-fashioned way on iron railroads.* Many of these routes already exist, and all of them will in due course. The more connections there are, the more options we have.

"GEOGRAPHY IS DESTINY," one of the most famous adages about the world, is becoming obsolete. Centuries-old arguments about how climate and culture condemn some societies to fail, or how small countries are forever trapped and subject to the whims of larger ones, are being overturned. Thanks to global transportation, communications, and energy infrastructures—highways, railways, airports, pipelines, electricity grids, Internet cables, and more—the future has a new maxim: "Connectivity is destiny."

Seeing the world through the lens of connectivity generates new visions of how we organize ourselves as a species. Global infrastructures are morphing our world system from divisions to connections and from nations to nodes. Infrastructure is like a nervous system

---

* Should a Bering Sea tunnel be constructed, one could walk from South Africa through the Middle East and across Eurasia and south through North America to South America's Cape Horn. This is sometimes referred to as the New Eurasian Land Bridge.

connecting all parts of the planetary body; capital and code are the blood cells flowing through it. More connectivity creates a world beyond states, a global society greater than the sum of its parts. Much as the world evolved from vertically integrated empires to horizontally interdependent states, now it is graduating toward a global network civilization whose map of connective corridors will supersede traditional maps of national borders. Each continental zone is already becoming an internally integrated mega-region (North America, South America, Europe, Africa, Arabia, South Asia, East Asia) with increasingly free trade coupled with intense connectivity across their thriving city-states.

At the same time, maps of connectivity are *also* better at revealing geopolitical dynamics among superpowers, city-states, stateless companies, and virtual communities of all kinds as they compete to capture resources, markets, and mind share. We are moving into an era where cities will matter more than states and supply chains will be a more important source of power than militaries—whose main purpose will be to protect supply chains rather than borders. *Competitive connectivity* is the arms race of the twenty-first century.

Connectivity is nothing less than our path to collective salvation. Competition over connectivity is by its nature less violent than international border conflicts, providing an escape hatch from historical cycles of great power conflict. Furthermore, connectivity has made previously unimaginable progress possible as resources and technologies move much more easily to where they are needed, while people can more quickly relocate to escape natural disasters or to cities for economic opportunity. Better connectivity allows societies to diversify where their imports come from and where their exports go. Connectivity is therefore how we make the most of our geography. The grand story of human civilization is more than just tragic cycles of war and peace or economic booms and busts. The arc of history is long, but it bends toward connectivity.

BRIDGES TO EVERYWHERE

*The central fact of the age we live in is that every
country, every market, every medium of communication, every natural resource is connected.*

—SIMON ANHOLT, THE GOOD
COUNTRY PARTY

Connectivity is the new meta-pattern of our age. Like liberty or
capitalism, it is a world-historical *idea,* one that gestates, spreads,
and transforms over a long timescale and brings about epochal
changes. Despite the acute unpredictability that afflicts our world
today, we can be adequately certain of current mega-trends such as
rapid urbanization and ubiquitous technology. Every day, for the
first time in their lives, millions of people switch on mobile phones,
log on to the Web, move into cities, or fly on an airplane. We go
where opportunity and technology allow. Connectivity is thus more
than a tool; it is an *impulse.*

No matter which way we connect, we do so through infrastructure. While the word "infrastructure" is less than a century old, it
represents nothing less than our physical capacity for global interaction. Engineering advances have made new infrastructures possible that were the dreams of previous generations. Over a century
ago, crucial geographic interventions such as the Suez and Panama
Canals reshaped global navigation and trade. Since the nineteenth
century, Ottoman sultans aspired to construct a tunnel that would
connect Istanbul's European and Asian sides. Now Turkey has both
the Marmaray tunnel that opened in 2013 and freight railways and
oil and gas pipelines that are strengthening its position as a key corridor between Europe and China. Turkey has been called the country where continents collide; now it is the country where continents
connect. The early twentieth-century Japanese emperor Taisho also
sought to link Honshu and northern Hokkaido Island, but only in

the 1980s did it complete the Seikan Tunnel, which traverses fifty-four kilometers (including twenty-three kilometers under the seabed) and carries Shinkansen high-speed trains.* Once the tunnels to Sakhalin and South Korea are complete, Japan won't truly be an island anymore.

We are in only an early phase of reengineering the planet to facilitate surging flows of people, commodities, goods, data, and capital. Indeed, the next wave of transcontinental and intercontinental mega-infrastructures is even more ambitious: an interoceanic highway across the Amazon from São Paulo to Peru's Pacific port of San Juan de Marcona, bridges connecting Arabia to Africa, a tunnel from Siberia to Alaska, polar submarine cables on the Arctic seabed from London to Tokyo, and electricity grids transferring Saharan solar power under the Mediterranean to Europe. Britain's exclave of Gibraltar will be the mouth of a tunnel under the Mediterranean to Tangier in Morocco, from which a new high-speed rail extends down the coast to Casablanca. Even where continents are not physically attaching to each other, ports and airports are expanding to absorb the massive increase in cross-continental flows.

NONE OF THESE MEGA-INFRASTRUCTURES are "bridges to no-where." Those that already exist have added trillions of dollars of value to the world economy. During the Industrial Revolution, it was the combination of higher productivity *and* trade that raised Britain's and America's growth rates to 1–2 percent for more than a century. As the Nobel laureate Michael Spence has argued, the internal growth of economies would never have reached today's rates without the cross-border flows of resources, capital, and technol-

---

* Similarly, after twenty straight years of blasting, drilling, and boring, the third and most complex of Switzerland's trans-Alpine Gotthard tunnels opens in 2016, reducing freight rail transport times between Germany and Italy, and passenger train travel between Zurich and Milan, decongesting the roads of heavy trucks and reducing carbon emissions.

ogy. Because only one-quarter of world trade is between countries that share a border, connectivity is the sine qua non for growth both within countries and across them. Connectivity itself—alongside demographics, capital markets, labor productivity, and technology—is thus a major source of momentum in the global economy. Think of the world like a watch whose battery is constantly charged through kinetic energy: The more you walk, the more power it has. For all the effort we expend calculating the value of national economies, therefore, it is time to devote as much attention to the value of connectivity between them.

There is no better investment than connectivity. Government spending on physical infrastructure—what is known as gross fixed capital formation—such as roads and bridges, and social infrastructure, such as medical care and education, is considered investment (rather than consumption) because it saves costs in the long run and generates widespread benefits for society. Large-scale spending on infrastructure was relatively low for most of the nineteenth century, accounting for about 5–7 percent of England's GDP and peaking at 10 percent on the eve of World War I.[1] The United States ramped up its infrastructure investment to almost 20 percent of GDP from the late nineteenth century through World War I, enabling it to double Britain's growth rate and become the world's largest economy. Even though the major American and Canadian canal and railroad companies went bankrupt at the turn of the twentieth century, they left the country with an extensive transportation network that enabled continental-scale commercial expansion right up to the present.

The influential British economist John Maynard Keynes strongly argued for such public works investment as a tool of creating jobs and boosting aggregate demand, policies adopted by President Roosevelt during the Depression. From World War II onward, fixed capital formation rose like a west-to-east wave from under 20 percent of GDP to over 30 percent. Germany's 1950s *Wirtschaftswunder* (economic miracle), Japan's 1960s 9 percent growth rates, the "Asian Tigers" of the 1970s and 1980s (South Korea, Taiwan, Singapore, and Hong Kong), and then China starting in the 1990s, where it topped 40 percent of GDP and powered sustained growth of close to 10 percent for the past three decades. China embraced Keynes like nobody's business.

The past several decades prove beyond any doubt that connectivity is how regions move from economies valued in the billions to the trillions. Furthermore, infrastructure is a foundation of social mobility and economic resilience: Urban societies with ample transportation networks (such as southern China) rebounded much faster from the 2007–8 financial crisis, with people able to move efficiently to find work. Spain was among the hardest hit by the eurozone recession but thanks to its high-quality infrastructure is today Europe's fastest-growing economy. As global debt surges to record levels while interest rates remain at historical lows, the world's finances should be directed toward underwriting productive connectivity rather than ethereal derivatives.

For a massive country such as America to live up to its self-proclaimed destiny, it too must spend much more on connectivity. Historically, U.S. infrastructure spending has returned almost $2 for every $1 invested, but investment has been tailing off for decades.[2] Today America's clogged roads and tunnels cause wasteful congestion, its crumbling bridges cause accidents and delays, and its ailing ports and refineries lack both the efficiency and the capacity to meet global demand. Since the financial crisis, dozens of prominent economists including Yale's Robert Shiller have advocated infrastructure-led investment as a way to create jobs and boost economic confidence. The American Society of Civil Engineers has called for $1.6 trillion in spending for an overhaul of America's transportation system. Only now—and just before it is too late—is such a national overhaul near the top of America's agenda with proposals for the creation of a national infrastructure bank.

The same is true across the world: The gap between the supply and the demand for infrastructure has never been greater. As the world population climbs toward eight billion people, it has been liv-

ing off the infrastructure stock meant for a world of three billion.*
But only infrastructure and all the industries that benefit from it can
collectively create the estimated 300 million jobs needed in the coming two decades as populations grow and urbanize. The World Bank
argues that infrastructure is the "missing link" in achieving the
Millennium Development Goals related to poverty, health, education, and other objectives, and infrastructure has been formally included in the latest Sustainable Development Goals ratified in 2015.[3]
The transition beyond export-led growth toward higher value-added
services and consumption begins with infrastructure investment.

We are finally witnessing a massive global commitment to infrastructure. Cities and highways, pipelines and ports, bridges and
tunnels, telecom towers and Internet cables, electricity grids and
sewage systems, and other fixed assets command about $3 trillion
per year in global spending, well over the $1.75 trillion spent annu-
ally on defense, and the gap is growing.[4] Infrastructure outlays are
projected to rise to $9 trillion per year by 2025 (with Asia leading
the way).[5]

The global connectivity revolution has begun. Already we have
installed a far greater volume of lines connecting people than dividing them: Our infrastructural matrix today includes approximately
64 million kilometers of highways, 2 million kilometers of pipelines, 1.2 million kilometers of railways, and 750,000 kilometers of
undersea Internet cables that connect our many key population and
economic centers. By contrast, we have only 250,000 kilometers of
international borders. By some estimates, mankind will build more
infrastructures in the next forty years alone than it has in the past
four thousand. The interstate puzzle thus gives way to a lattice of
infrastructure circuitry. The world is starting to look a lot like the
Internet.

---

* While the Americas have a combined population of about one billion, and Europe,
the Middle East, and Africa together about two billion, the Asia-Pacific region contains
four billion people—more than half the world total.

SEEING IS BELIEVING

Astronauts in low Earth orbit (about 215 kilometers high) have snapped stunning pictures of our majestic planet. They've captured natural features like oceans, mountains, ice caps, and glaciers, and even caught glimpses of man-made structures. It turns out that the Great Wall of China and the Great Pyramid of Giza in Egypt are rather difficult to discern without high-performance zoom lenses, but more modern engineering such as megacities, ultra-long bridges, and straight desert highways are easy to spot. The Kennecott copper mine in Utah and the Mir diamond mine in Siberia stretch several kilometers across, making their stepped terrace structure noticeable as well. The two hundred square kilometers of greenhouses in Almería in southern Spain, where up to half of Europe's annual demand for fresh fruits and vegetables is grown, is unmistakable, especially as sunlight reflects off their plastic roofs.

What about borders? How many of those are physically robust enough to see? Many political borders are formed by natural environmental features, reminding us of nature's fundamental role in shaping human settlement and cultural differentiation. The border between North and South Korea is best seen when the sun goes down, when the bright lights of the South contrast with the darkness of the North. The most visible border between any two large countries is undoubtedly between India and Pakistan. Stretching diagonally for twenty-nine hundred kilometers from the Arabian Sea to Kashmir, it also stands out from space at night due to the 150,000 floodlights that form a bright orange blaze.

The maps hanging in our classrooms and offices would lead us to believe that all borders were as robust as the Indo-Pakistani border. Yet North America's two major borders mask the deeper reality of growing connectivity. The three-thousand-kilometer U.S.-Mexico border crosses beaches and deserts and along the Rio Grande River but also between cities that have the same name on either side such as Nogales, Naco, and Tecate. Even with haphazardly patrolled security fencing on the American side, it is still the most frequently traversed border in the world, with over 350 million legal crossings annually (more than the entire population of the United States). The U.S.-Canada border that stretches from the Arctic to the Pacific to the Atlantic Ocean is the world's longest at almost nine thousand kilometers, but 300,000 people and over $1 billion in *daily* trade traverse the almost twenty major border crossings.

There are many places where borders are stiffening: Israel's security barrier, the fifteen-kilometer Évros River fence in Greece, and the two-hundred-kilometer Bulgarian barbed-wire fence aimed at curbing illegal immigrants, among others.* And yet all of these borders—and even more unfriendly ones—remain porous. And indeed, almost all such fences are terribly costly and ineffective responses to problems that borders cannot solve.

If borders are meant to separate territories and societies, then why are ever more populations clustering along them? It is a particular irony that our maps show mostly political borders rather than border demographics and economics, which are the embodiment of the *anti*-border nature of many border regions. Most of Canada's population lives near the U.S. border and benefits from proximity to the American market. Since 2010, *both* the Mexican *and* the U.S. populations on their border have grown by 20 percent.[6]

Even more ironic: The best place to see how connectivity fundamentally changes relations from hostility to cooperation is borders. The thriving business between India and Pakistan and many other pairs of antagonists is a reminder that borders are rarely the solid lines we see on maps but rather porous filters for exchange. In these and dozens of other cases, we increasingly work around our borders—and build straight across them—more than we bow to them.[7] Ultimately, from the Great Wall of China and Hadrian's Wall to the Berlin Wall—and eventually the Cypriot Green Line and the

---

* Russia unrolled a barbed-wire border fence around South Ossetia after its 2008 war with Georgia, and India is deploying a sixteen-hundred-kilometer fence along its northeastern border with Myanmar aimed at preventing drug smuggling, people trafficking, and other illicit trade. Tunisia is installing a fence on its Libyan border to prevent migrant spillover, as is Saudi Arabia on its border with Yemen.

Korean demilitarized zone—forces far more powerful than these barriers prevail. As Alexandra Novosseloff has written, "A wall ends its life as a tourist attraction."[8]

In today's world, territorial boundaries don't even really capture the geography of borders: Airports may be far inland but contain borders within them, while cyber-security forces patrol technology infrastructures that stretch far across borders. Even if political borders remain physically robust, the world has still become more borderless as countries eliminate extraneous visa requirements, currencies are exchangeable in real time at ATMs, content from almost anywhere can be accessed online, and the cost of phone calls drops to zero due to Skype and Viber. The more societies trade and communicate—and depend on each other for food, water, and energy—the less we can pretend that borders are the most important lines on the map.

The absence of the full panoply of man-made infrastructure on our maps gives the impression that borders trump other means of portraying human geography. But today the reverse is true: Borders matter only where they matter; other lines matter more most of the time. Hardly anywhere are they a more significant factor in the fate of nations than what crosses them. We are building a new world order—literally.

FROM POLITICAL TO FUNCTIONAL GEOGRAPHY

Geography matters intensely, but it does not follow that borders do. We should never confuse geography, which is paramount, with *political* geography, which is transient. Unfortunately, maps today present natural or political geography—or both—as permanent constraints. Yet there is nothing more numbing than unyielding circular logic: Something *must be* because it *is*. Reading maps is not like reading palms, as if each line presents an immutable destiny. I am a deep believer in the profound influence of geography but not in its caricature as a monolithic and immovable force. Geography may be the most fundamental thing we *see*, but understanding cause and effect requires complex thinking about the interplay of demographics and politics, ecology and technology. It is precisely the great geographic thinkers such as Sir Halford Mackinder who a century ago urged statesmen to appreciate geography and factor it into their strategies but not to become slaves to it. Geographic determinism runs no deeper than blind faith in religion.

A deeper study of all the ways in which we modify geography thus begins with realizing how we have already filled the world with our presence: There is no undesignated space; every square meter is being surveyed and mapped. And the skies are cluttered with airplanes, satellites, and increasingly drones, layered with CO_2 emissions and pollution, and permeated by radar and telecommunications signals. We don't just reside on earth but colonize it. The environmental scientist Vaclav Smil elegantly captures how impressed we should be by the "magnitude and complexity of the global material edifice erected by modern civilization since the middle of the nineteenth century, and no less so by the incessant material flows required to operate and maintain it."[9]*

Mega-infrastructures overcome the hurdles of both natural and political geography, and mapping them reveals that the era of organizing the world according to *political* space (how we legally subdivide the globe) is giving way to organizing it according to *functional* space (how we actually use it). In this new era, the de jure world of political borders is giving way to the de facto world of functional connections. Borders tell us who is divided from whom by political geography. Infrastructure tells us who is connected to whom via functional geography. As the lines that connect us supersede the borders that divide us, functional geography is becoming more important than political geography.

Many of today's existing and planned transportation corridors track to ancient passages hewn by geography, climate, and culture.

---

* Smil also makes an important distinction between resources, which are often immeasurable, and reserves, which are the measurable and fungible quantities of resources that supply chains move from one place to another.

Large segments of the rail itinerary that opened this chapter are built atop the 1960s "Hippie Trail" from London to India (and on to Bangkok), which in turn followed ancient Silk Road routes across Eurasia. Stretching from Chicago to Los Angeles, America's historic Route 66—also known as the Will Rogers Highway—followed ancient trails of the Native Americans (and today passes through their reservations in Arizona) as it paved the way for Americans fleeing the midwestern dust bowl after the Great Depression. Today we know it as Interstate 40, the route taken by those giving up on the Rust Belt in search of a better life in the fast-growing Southwest.

But whereas the ancient Silk Roads were dirt paths or rough tracks, today we have asphalt highways, iron railways, steel pipelines, and Kevlar-wrapped fiber Internet cables—stronger, denser, broader, faster. These infrastructures are laying the foundation of our emerging global system. They connect whichever entities lie on either end or along the way, whether empires, city-states, or sovereign nations—all of which may come and go, while the logic of the pathway persists.

For this reason, connectivity and geography are not opposites. To the contrary, they very often reinforce each other. The United States and Mexico share a continental geography, but it is their deepening connectivity that transforms their political division into a mutually structured space. Connectivity is thus about not detaching from geography but making the most of it. It morphs our perception of what constitutes "natural" regions.* Europe is often spoken of as a continent simply because it is culturally distinct from the two-thirds of the Eurasian landmass east of the Ural Mountains. But as trans-Eurasian connectivity grows, references to "Europe" in geographically exclusive ways should disappear. It is connectivity that makes Europe's Eurasian destiny meaningful rather than coincidental. Indeed, the Chinese-funded Silk Road

* The geographer Harm de Blij has identified twelve physical realms, each with multiple subregions: Europe, Russia, North America, Central America, South America, Sub-Saharan Africa, North Africa/Southwest Asia, South Asia, East Asia, Southeast Asia, Australasia, and the Pacific Islands.

Economic Belt is the largest coordinated infrastructure initiative in the history of the world.

Here are two more specific examples of functional geography superseding the political. Linked by the dual highway-railway Øresund Bridge, the economies of Denmark's capital, Copenhagen, and Sweden's Malmö have become so connected that many now refer to them as KoMa. Copenhagen airport is now closer for Malmö residents than their own, and Swedish taxis have their own stands there. Baltic nations tried to form an entente shortly after World War I but were split by Soviet expansionism. A century later, the much larger Baltic Union has emerged from Norway to Lithuania and is directly connected to western Europe by the Øresund Bridge. In China's Pearl River delta—where cities such as Hong Kong, Macau, and Zhuhai have very different legal arrangements with Beijing—a Y-shaped bridge (over artificial islands and through a six-kilometer tunnel) set to open in 2017 will connect all three cities, cutting the passage across the southern mouth of the delta from four hours to one hour. The entire delta region is becoming one giant urban archipelago despite differences in political status.

The answer to which lines matter most challenges our deepest assumptions about how the world is organized. When countries think functionally rather than politically, they focus on how to optimize land, labor, and capital, how to spatially cluster resources and connect them to global markets.[10] Connective infrastructures across sovereign borders acquire special properties, a life of their own, something more than just being a highway or a power line. They become common utilities that are co-governed across boundaries. Such connective infrastructures thus have their own essence, a legitimacy that derives from having been jointly approved and built that makes them more physically *real* than law or diplomacy. The Yale professor Keller Easterling calls this infrastructural authority "extra-statecraft."

Infrastructures transcend their original masters. The world is undergoing not only a major infrastructure build-out but also a major new wave of infrastructure privatization as governments try to generate cash to balance budgets and make new investments. Governments worldwide are thus handing over infrastructure management to private companies or third parties that operate them according to market forces. Then there are times when infrastructure built by a foreign country (or company) gets expropriated and taken over by its local host. Even when Russian state-owned companies build pipelines and railways, they want to keep infrastructure passages open despite boundary disputes. Think about it: Unless infrastructure is active and operational, it hardly generates value to anyone. Tensions that arise over revenue sharing, maintenance costs, or illicit smuggling are all fundamentally about who gains the most *from* connectivity.

Connectivity is thus intensely geopolitical even as it changes the role of borders. When we map functional geography—transportation routes, energy grids, forward operating bases, financial networks, and Internet servers—we are also mapping the pathways by which power is projected and leverage exercised. American officials speak about accommodating China's rise as if the global system has an entrenched essence that prefers American leadership. But the system wants only one thing: connectivity. It doesn't care which power is the most connected, but the most connected power will have the most leverage. China has become a welcome and popular power in Africa and Latin America because it has sold them (and often built for them) the foundations of better connectivity. Ethereal concepts such as "soft power" are a pale substitute for the power of connectivity.

Depicting the world's growing infrastructure connections is no less real or important because they are not sovereign borders. To the contrary, they represent the lines we are installing *now* rather than the many contingent or arbitrary lines drawn in the past. As the famed architect Santiago Calatrava has said, "What we build today will last centuries." That is more than one can say about most nations. Yet today many scholars still hold political boundaries to be the most fundamental man-made lines on the map out of a bias toward territory as the basis of power, the state as the unit of political organization, an assumption that only governments can order life within those states, and a belief that national identity is the primary source of people's loyalty. The march of connectivity will bring all these beliefs to collapse. Forces such as devolution (the fragmentation of authority toward provinces), urbanization (the growing size and power of cities), dilution (the genetic blending of populations through mass migration), mega-infrastructures (new pipelines, railways, and canals that morph geography), and digital connectivity (enabling new forms of community) will demand that we produce maps far more complex.

SUPPLY CHAIN WORLD

It's time to reimagine how human life is organized on earth.

There is one—and only one—law that has been with us since we were hunter-gatherers, outlasted all rival theories, transcended empires and nations, and serves as our best guide to the future: supply and demand.

Supply and demand is more than a market principle for determining the price of goods. Supply and demand are dynamic forces in search of equilibrium in all aspects of human life. As we approach universal infrastructural and digital connectivity, the supply of everything *can* meet demand for anything; anything or anyone *can* get nearly anywhere both physically and virtually. The physicist Michio Kaku believes we are headed toward such "perfect capitalism."[11] There is another term for this scenario: "supply chain world."

Supply chains are the complete ecosystem of producers, distributors, and vendors that transform raw materials (whether natural resources or ideas) into goods and services delivered to people anywhere.* Whether you are awake or asleep, scarcely a moment of our

---

* A more formal definition of supply chain is the systems of organizations, people, technology activities, information, and resources involved in moving products and services from producers to customers. "Global supply chain" and "global value chain" are often used interchangeably, with the latter sometimes preferred to emphasize the value-added processes not inherent in simple supply-demand terminology. Others speak of value webs or value networks to capture the wide range of participants involved in supply chains and their interdependent and mutually beneficial nature.

daily lives—sipping morning coffee, driving a car, talking on the phone, sending an email, eating a meal, or going to the movies—doesn't involve global supply chains.

And yet as universal as they are, supply chains are not things in themselves. They are a *system of transactions*. We do not *see* supply chains; rather, we see their participants and infrastructures—the things that connect supply to demand. What we can see, however, by tracing supply chains link by link is how these micro-interactions add up to large global shifts. We are witnessing the full consequences of Adam Smith's free markets, David Ricardo's comparative advantage, and Émile Durkheim's division of labor: a world where capital, labor, and production shift to wherever is needed to efficiently connect supply and demand. If "the market" is the world's most powerful force, supply chains bring markets to life.

Supply chains and connectivity, not sovereignty and borders, are the organizing principles of humanity in the 21st century. Indeed, as globalization expands into every corner of the planet, supply chains have widened, deepened, and strengthened to such an extent that we must ask ourselves whether they represent a deeper organizing force in the world than states themselves.[12] Supply chains are the original worldwide webs, enveloping our world like a ball of yarn. They are the world's plumbing and wiring, the pathways by which everyone and everything moves. Supply chains are self-assembling and organically connecting. They expand, contract, shift, multiply, and diversify as a result of our collective human activity. You can disrupt supply chains, but they will quickly find alternative pathways to fulfill their missions. It is as if they have a life of their own. Does this sound familiar? It should: The Internet is just the newest kind of infrastructure upon which more supply chains are built.

The World Wide Web was born in 1989, the same year the Berlin Wall fell, which feels like an appropriate turning point to mark the shift from the Westphalian world to the supply chain world.* The

---

* I use "supply chain world" or "supply-demand world" or "supply-demand system" or other variations interchangeably.

seventeenth-century Thirty Years' War represented a transition from the fragmented medieval disorder to the modern system of nation-states in which European monarchs agreed to respect each other's territorial sovereignty. Today we remember the 1648 Peace of Westphalia not so much for who won (basically no one!) as for ushering in the system of sovereign states that has framed international relations for nearly four centuries.

But there is nothing immutable about this system, and its reality has rarely lived up to its (theoretical) ambitions. Instead, supply-demand dynamics have always driven our social organization. For fifty thousand years since the end of the last ice age, the human diaspora has been organizing itself into polities of ever-shifting shapes and sizes that combine vertical authority across horizontal territory, from empires and caliphates to duchies and chiefdoms. Cities and empires have been the common denominators of history, not states. Furthermore, the notion of Westphalia as a birth moment for a universal system of sovereign equals betrays both Western and non-Western history. In Europe, medievalism gave way to nation-states as kings built stronger fortifications to assert greater control over dispersed populations and agricultural resources while protecting their borders from invasion. But European empires persisted both on the Continent and globally until the twentieth century. Colonialism codified foreign territories, but it certainly did not make them sovereign. Only with decolonization after World War II did a worldwide system of sovereign states come into effect, and yet, of course, the notion that they are equal remains an utter fiction.

The past quarter century has been a Goldilocks period of great power stability during which infrastructure, deregulation, capital markets, and communications have accelerated the rise of a global supply chain system. Globalization has compromised national sovereignty from above as governments shift from creating national regulations to enforcing global ones and undermines it from below as devolution, capitalism, and connectivity strengthen the autonomy and influence of key cities that—like corporations—pursue their own interests across increasingly permeable state boundaries.

And as government institutions unbundle and privatize, supply chains take over as the new service providers. The supply chain doesn't eliminate polities; this is not about the "end of the state." It reconfigures states as market regulations and authorities become co-governors and resizes them as substate cities and provinces compete within and beyond states.[13]

THE DELINEATION OF STATES makes the world seem orderly, but they are not what make the world function. Rather, infrastructure and supply chains are how we function *despite* our dysfunctional political geography. As the economist Robert Skidelsky reminds us, wars and borders are what keep capital scarce, while stability and openness unlock it.

Smoothing the path for supply chains brings enormous benefits to the world economy. According to the historian Marc Levinson, the advent of the shipping container in the 1950s "made the world smaller and the economy larger." Simply standardizing the size of one box facilitated and accelerated global supply chains. Today, according to the World Economic Forum, reducing international customs barriers to even half the leading standard would raise world trade by 15 percent and global GDP by 5 percent. By contrast, eliminating all the world's import tariffs would raise GDP only by less than 1 percent. Companies such as DHL lend their expertise pro bono to customs agencies across the developing world to speed up their border clearance procedures; adopting electronic documentation in the air cargo industry alone could save $12 billion annually as well as prevent almost all the paperwork that delays airfreight. When we reduce border holdups, producers can get on with the business of selling to global markets rather than holding large inventories. In a supply chain world, inefficiency is the enemy.

Because supply chains link diverse players across vast distances who may not have any trusted personal relationships among them, they impose what managers call "one version of the truth," the need for real-time and accurate data sharing so that everyone in the network can know where all things are at all times.[14] Walmart's CEO, Douglas McMillon, has said he runs a "tech company," one that perpetually communicates sales and stock volume data digitally with suppliers like Procter & Gamble. Unilever constantly reads local demand conditions and taps into its global production system to more flexibly deliver goods across its markets. M.B.A. programs now consider supply chain management a core competency due to its high demand by employers in retail, defense, information technology (IT), and other sectors.[15]

Outside the boardroom, the movements of ordinary people in search of a better life are the best evidence that we have entered a supply chain world. In 1960, only 73 million people lived outside their country of origin; today the number of expatriates is 300 million and growing rapidly since the financial crisis. Migrants span the entire length of the global economic ladder—from the top multinational executives to the bottom third world laborers—circulating temporarily or permanently outside their country of origin. And whereas migration has previously been considered a largely South-to-North phenomenon, today half of all international migrants are moving *across* developing countries following growth rates and job opportunities. Africa's and India's massive youth cohorts are fanning out across the postcolonial world to rebuild failing nations, with the Arab Gulf countries having most benefited from Asian labor. Wherever construction workers, maids, child and elder caregivers, and other essential service functions are required, borders come down to allow supply to meet demand.

Americans have joined this global expatriate horde. More than six million Americans now live abroad, the highest number ever recorded, and surveys suggest that the percentage of Americans planning to move abroad has risen from 12 percent to 40 percent for youth aged eighteen to twenty-four. It is no longer just investment bankers, exchange students, journalists, and Peace Corps volunteers but members of a wide cross section of American society who have become economic migrants, especially since the financial crisis.

Where supply chains don't come to people, people move to supply chains. From San Francisco to Johannesburg, nineteenth-century discoveries of gold deposits turned villages of homesteads into bustling cities. In the past decade, fifty thousand Canadians have moved to Fort McMurray, a new oil boomtown in Alberta, to work in the rugged tar sands. In Africa's extractive industry, hundreds of thousands of miners flock to jobs extracting tungsten, coltan, and other minerals essential for mobile phones, even if they have to work like slaves. The supply chain is a potential escape from state failure in Africa's largest country of Congo and the smaller nations surrounding it. Decades from now, we will all still live *within* the nominal borders of states, but more important, almost the entire world population will also live *along* infrastructure corridors and supply chains, physical and virtual.

URBANIZATION IS ALSO EVIDENCE of the shift toward a supply chain world. As Harvard's Neil Brenner and NYU's Solly Angel have documented, urban land area is expected to triple over the course of this century. Most of the world's population already lives in cities, and approximately 150,000 people per day—or the equivalent of one Los Angeles per month—are moving in, especially in developing countries where at least two billion more people are expected to shift to cities by 2030. Measuring urbanization is even more revealing than measuring international migration, for new arrivals in cities join the ranks of the billions employed in industry or service supply chains despite not crossing a border.

Indeed, though most of the world's population never physically leaves their nation of birth, urbanization significantly boosts their degree of connectedness *despite* their location. The lives of any two people in cities across Europe and Asia are increasingly more similar than the lives of fellow citizens living in rural areas. In terms of access to basic services, people in Jakarta have more in common with those in London than they do with their countrymen on the remote Maluku Islands. Even those in the slums of Dharavi in Mumbai or Kibera in Nairobi earn far more than the landless peasantry they left behind.

A world where people have more in common across geography than within it is a telltale sign of a supply chain world. As the Columbia University professor Saskia Sassen has shown, globalization has enabled a proliferating set of networks—what Sassen calls "circuits"—that have a life of their own. Financial investors in New York and London and the capital pools they deploy in Asia, Swiss and Singaporean commodities brokers and the resource deposits they control in Africa and Latin America, Silicon Valley and Bangalore programmers and their global customers, German and American carmakers and their factories from Mexico to Indonesia—these are all cross-border circuits connected by way of supply chains. It is not countries as a whole that ascend value chains but such circuits of people who are attached to global nodes. Gradually, places such as garment production centers in Dhaka and Addis Ababa begin to feel almost detached from their own country even as they become key drivers of its growth; they belong as much to the global supply chain as to their nation.

So synchronized are global supply chains that they serve as a seismograph of our amplified connectivity. Like earthquakes causing equally powerful aftershocks, the financial crisis of 2008 contracted world trade five times more severely than it did world GDP. First the credit crunch created a demand shock, meaning a huge slump in purchases of durable goods. Then the adjustment in inventories cascaded horizontally as the velocity of trade in most goods slowed in unison, shrinking industrial production cycles from Germany and Korea to China. The same phenomenon occurred when oil prices collapsed in 2014, causing new investments in oil fields to shrink from Fort McMurray to Malaysia. Even the oil-rich sultanate of Brunei now talks about austerity. Supply chains are transmission lines: They affect everyone connected but dissipate the pain throughout the system.*

---

* In his book *Antifragile*, Nassim Taleb demonstrates through the convexity principle that the degradation effect (harm) diminishes across a range of smaller units as opposed to a larger one of size equal to the sum of the smaller units.

———

SUPPLY CHAINS ARE THE GREATEST BLESSING and the greatest curse for civilization. They are an escape from the prison of geography, creating economic opportunities where none existed, bringing ideas, technologies, and business practices to places that lack the advantages of good climate and soil or other propitious variables. As the Princeton economist and Nobel laureate Angus Deaton lucidly captures in *The Great Escape,* billions of people have joined the global marketplace by building connectivity despite "bad" geography and institutions. It is no longer foreordained that tropical countries will suffer unproductive agriculture and labor, nor that landlocked countries must underperform: Singapore and Malaysia are thriving modern economies near the equator, while Rwanda, Botswana, Kazakhstan, and Mongolia are landlocked countries enjoying unprecedented growth and development. A country cannot change where it is, but connectivity offers an alternative to the destiny of geography.

Supply chains are thus a form of salvation for the bottom billions in developing countries, whose governments now bend over backward to attract them. To that end, the rise of special economic zones—districts or cities designed to attract investment into specific industry clusters—is the single most significant innovation in how dozens of countries are run since the creation of modern states. SEZs are both local anchors and global nodes. It is yet another sign of the shift from a political to a supply chain world that cities are increasingly named not after people or scenery—think Jefferson or Ocean View—but instead for what role they play in the global economy: Dubai Internet City, Bangladesh Export Processing Zones Authority, Cayman Enterprise City, Guangzhou Knowledge City, Malaysian Multimedia Super Corridor, and about *four thousand* more.

According to conventional maps, I've spent the past half decade visiting dozens of places that don't exist. Whether industrial parks or "smart cities," these supply chain nodes are popping up so quickly that most are not yet on our maps. Such zones used to be places where people just went to work; now they are communities in which people *live*. For hundreds of millions of workers and their dependents, the supply chain has become a way of life, an all-encompassing existence in the service of the global economy and their society's desire to be connected to it. The fastest-growing category of city in the world is with populations of around one million, usually built around one major company or industry. These are the new "factory towns" of a supply chain world, pop-up cities that are the best hope to productively engage the world's masses and spread growth like no aid program could ever imagine.

Now for the bad news: Supply chains are also how the market rapes the world. They are the conduit for plundering the world's rain forests and pumping emissions into the atmosphere. From Arctic natural gas to Antarctic oil, lithium deposits from Bolivia to Afghanistan, forests from the Amazon to central Africa, and gold mines from South Africa to Siberia, scarcely a natural resource will remain untouched in the supply chain world. Governments have not protected what is "theirs." Instead, they have been willingly complicit in sacrificing nature. The oceans too are being overharvested through trawling, both for fish and for seabed minerals, while also being polluted by oil spills and industrial waste. Supply chains are also the conduit for the illicit smuggling of drugs, weapons, and people, and there are more people trafficked today than ever in history. The five largest criminal syndicates—Japan's Yakuza, the Russian Bratva, Italy's Camorra and 'Ndrangheta, and Mexico's Sinaloa—have globalized the reach of their operations and rake in an estimated $1 trillion per year as they bridge the supply and demand for rhino horns, counterfeit currency, synthetic drugs, and prostitutes. Without the markets, infrastructures, and agents who operate supply chains for *everything,* it would be harder for us to exploit each other and nature on a global scale. The fate of human society is inextricably linked with how we manage our supply chains.

———

THIS GLOBAL SUPPLY CHAIN system has replaced any particular superpower as the anchor of global civilization. Neither America nor China alone props up this new order, nor is either the final authority capable of shutting it down. Instead, they compete in a Great Supply Chain War that will redraw twenty-first-century maps as much as the Thirty Years' War did in the seventeenth century. The Great Supply Chain War is a race not to conquer but to connect physically and economically to the world's most important supplies of raw materials, high technology, and fast-growing markets. The Great Supply Chain War is not an event, nor an episode, nor a phase. It is a semipermanent condition in a world where great powers consciously seek to avoid costly military confrontations that could be self-defeating, for they would disrupt these essential supply chains. In the Great Supply Chain War, infrastructure, supply chains, and markets are as crucial as territory, armies, and deterrence. The largest power does not always win; the most connected one does.

Does America understand the new geography of the Great Supply Chain War? As the past president of the American Geographical Society Jerry Dobson has coolly pointed out, "America abandoned teaching geography after WWII and hasn't won a war since."[16] Now it must grasp not just the territorial frame of traditional geopolitics but also the commercial lens of geoeconomics, a battlefield far more subtle and complex.

Questions we used to traditionally call on governments to answer—relationships among great powers, balance between public and private sectors, the future of economic growth and inequality, and the fate of our ecosystem—are best explored by following the world's supply chains. Doing so will reveal that while twentieth-century territorial geopolitics was inspired by Mackinder's twentieth-century dictum "Who rules the Heartland rules the world," there is a revised mantra for the twenty-first century: "Who rules the supply chain rules the world."

In a supply chain world, it matters less who *owns* (or claims) ter-

ritory than who *uses* (or administers) it. China is harvesting minerals far from its own borders in terrain too far to steadily rule. It thus
prefers de facto maps to de jure ones—the world as it can rearrange
it, rather than the world international law sees. The long-standing
mantra of the de jure world is "This land is my land." The new
motto of the de facto, supply chain world is "Use it or lose it."

BALANCING FLOW
AND FRICTION

The seventeenth-century philosopher Thomas Hobbes, hailed as
the godfather of modern international relations, saw the world as
functioning according to fairly simple mechanical laws. All phenomena, he believed, could be reduced to the interaction of bodies
in motion. Since that time, the discipline of geopolitics has acquired
the status of the unalterable foundation of world order, the ultimate
logic on which all other human activity rests: The control over territory trumps all else. When forces collide, one must give way.

But the physics of classical geopolitics is being superseded by the
physics of complexity. Our times are analogous to a century ago
when quantum mechanics shook up the neat rationalism of Isaac
Newton's classical physics with its findings: Units are difficult to
quantify and in perpetual motion; invisible objects can occupy
space; gravity matters more than location; there are no causal cer-
tainties, only probabilities; and meaning is derived relationally
rather than from absolutes.

It is time for geopolitics to have its own complexity revolution.
To make sense of today's world, we must simultaneously grapple
with accumulating forces beyond seventeenth-century sovereignty
such as eighteenth-century enlightenment, nineteenth-century imperialism, twentieth-century capitalism, and twenty-first-century
technology. A young, urban, mobile, and technologically saturated
world is far better explained through the concepts of uncertainty,
gravity, relationality, and leverage than the centuries-old logic of anarchy, sovereignty, territoriality, nationalism, and military primacy.

One of the most important quantum insights is that the nature of change itself changes. We are living through such a "change in change": not merely a shift in *structure* from one superpower to multiple, but rather a far deeper shift from a state-based order to a multi-actor *system*. The ancient world of disjointed empires gave way to the disorderly medieval world, followed by the modern order of sovereign states and now the transition to a complex global network civilization. Structural change happens every few decades; systems change only every few *centuries*. Structural change makes the world complicated; systems change makes it *complex*. International relations among states are complicated, while today's global network civilization is complex. Financial feedback loops destabilize markets, and corporations can be more influential than countries, while ISIS, Occupy Wall Street, and WikiLeaks are all quantum in nature: everywhere and nowhere, constantly metastasizing, capable of sudden phase shifts. If planet Earth had a Facebook account, its status should read "It's Complex."

Connectivity is the main cause of this complexity. Globalization is almost always written about in terms of how it operates *within* the existing order rather than how it creates a *new* one. Yet connectivity is the change emerging from within the system that ultimately changes the system itself. Its networks are not merely conduits of connections, but the power of the network itself increases exponentially as the number of nodes increases (Metcalfe's law).

No superpower is robust enough to stand outside the system. It is telling that in the *Global Trends 2030* report of the National Intelligence Council (NIC), the United States is no longer characterized as a predictable stabilizer but fingered as an uncertain variable. How much power will America have in 2030? Will it have its domestic house in order? Will it be capable of projecting power worldwide? None of these can be taken for granted, for America does not fully control its own fate. In a complex world, even America is a price taker.

There is another conceptual dynamic we should borrow from

physics: *flow* and *friction*.* There are many kinds of flows in the connected global system: resources, goods, capital, technology, people, data, and ideas. And there are many kinds of friction: borders, conflict, sanctions, distance, and regulation. Flows are how we distribute the great energy of our ecosystem and civilization—whether raw materials, technologies, manpower, or knowledge—and put them to work across the planet. Frictions are the barriers, obstacles, and breakdowns that get in the way such as wars, plagues, and depressions. In the long run, flow wins out over friction. Supply connects to demand. Momentum triumphs over inertia.

This proposition is not revolutionary but evolutionary. As the Duke University mathematician Adrian Bejan explains in his brilliant exposition *Design in Nature,* the fundamental property of all systems is to maximize *flow:* allowing all parts of a system to connect to all other parts. This basic principle of physics explains everything from the shape of trees to biological evolution to the best layout of airport terminals to the arc of globalization. The history of our emergent global network civilization is the story of flow and friction on an ever-expanding scale.

Flow and friction are the yin and yang of the world: They complete each other and keep each other in balance. They are in perpetual negotiation, constantly calibrated to suit strategic goals. In order to attract more foreign investment into its ailing infrastructure, the United States has had to ease certain restrictions that had blocked Chinese capital into sensitive sectors. For China to globalize the renminbi, or RMB, it must further liberalize its capital account. In both cases, less friction to enable more flows.

But greater flows can amplify risks: Migrants can be terrorists, *hawala* networks sending remittances to the poor can also fund organized crime, travelers and livestock can carry pandemics, emails can spread viruses, and financial investment can stoke bubbles. The

---

* Solids, liquids, and gases experience flow and friction when moving in the open or in contained spaces. In fluid mechanics, friction takes the form of viscosity, meaning a material's resistance to changing its form.

tipping point by which any of these flows topples the system can be as unpredictable as the precise location of a lightning strike.*

These are all serious daily realities, yet rarely is the solution to "put up borders." Taken too far, frictions can be self-defeating. For example, America's restrictive immigration policy has frustrated Silicon Valley's efforts to recruit highly skilled programmers from abroad. Similarly, when Mexico in 2013 decided to raise corporate taxes on mining profits, several global companies declared they would no longer make major investments there, undermining the country's mining boom by depriving it of essential foreign capital and technology.

Countries will fail unless they are open to flows, but they need sensible frictions to gain the upside while minimizing the downside: capital controls on speculative investment, limited liberalization to ensure domestic industrial competitiveness, radiation scanners at ports, immigration quotas to avoid overburdening public services, passport scanners cross-checked with Interpol databases, Internet Service Providers (ISPs) scanning for computer viruses, and other measures. Governments should think of borders like traffic lights, calibrating the colors to manage the flows in and out of the country. China wants energy and mineral inflows from Myanmar but not its drugs; it wants copper and lithium from Afghanistan but not Islamist radicals. Europe wants to export goods to the Middle East and Africa but not import its poor and persecuted refugees. The trained dogs that sniff baggage four times before you are allowed to exit Auckland airport are essential to catch pathogens before they wreak havoc on New Zealand's agricultural economy. Singapore's strict controls on narcotics are equally sensible given how much crystal meth flows out of Thailand and North Korea.

We are getting better at managing some of the riskiest flows. Consider how the fourteenth-century Black Death traveled west-

---

* Indeed, the rate of ionization of air (in which negatively charged ions destabilize the air's molecular structure) that conducts the path of lightning can be calculated only through quantum mechanics.

ward along the Silk Road and wiped out half of Europe's population, while the influenza of 1917–18 killed fifty million people. By contrast, in 2003 the SARS virus spread to twenty-four countries but then disappeared. In 2014, Ebola spread from West Africa to Europe and America along ever more frequent airline routes but was quickly contained. The effective use of friction such as medical checks, quarantines, and surging treatment to the source of outbreak helped limit the damage. Similarly, the precautionary principle dictates that we implement macro-prudential safeguards in high-risk areas of the world economy: separating commercial and investment banking, restricting the re-securitization of collateralized debt obligations and swaps, requiring banks to invest their own capital with client trades, and so forth. Such measures protect the financial system as a whole against the spread of contagion despite its growing integration and are superior to allowing all activities while attempting in vain to micromanage them.

Our world will continue to be rife with friction, but the friction of the future is to control flow. We will fight less over the lines that divide us than over the lines that connect us. It is precisely because almost all the world's international border disputes are being settled—either peacefully or aggressively—that future conflicts will be no longer about laying down more borders but instead about controlling connections. That is why all countries practice some form of "state capitalism" today, whether subsidizing strategic industries, restricting investments in key sectors, or mandating financial institutions to invest more at home. Such industrial policies are part of a cautious search for balance between local needs and global connectedness. Brazil, for example, now requires foreign car manufacturers to invest in local renewable energy research and has implemented capital controls to stem "hot money." Countries such as Indonesia have stood their ground in raising corporate taxes and fees yet remain investment magnets because they ultimately control their geographic resources. India welcomes free trade in software services because it has a cost-effective and talented IT workforce but is more cautious about liberalizing agricultural imports that might undermine its farmers.

We will likely never have a global free market but rather have a world where the expanding global economy becomes ever more a strategic battleground. Indeed, economies are opening but not necessarily according to the same rules. Still, a consensus is emerging that endorses such sensible if also self-serving frictions that generate home-country advantages and preserve essential local foundations of industry and employment even if they don't perfectly optimize cost efficiencies.

Free-market purists denounce such measures as protectionism, but countries cannot be value-added participants in the world economy unless they take steps to enhance their vitality. Consider this: Most of the Brazilian electronics industry has been lured to a free trade zone in Manaus deep in the Amazon rain forest. Why? Because it creates jobs for locals who might otherwise take jobs in the logging industry. As a result, Brazil has moved up the value chain and curbed deforestation at the same time. African governments protecting infant industries to promote jobs and avoid being wiped out by cheap Chinese imports, and blocking full foreign ownership of natural resources to prevent their being siphoned off in foreign-funded landgrabs, are examples of smart friction, not antiglobalization. As the saying goes: all things in moderation.

CHAPTER 2

NEW MAPS FOR A NEW WORLD

*Arguing against globalization is like arguing
against the law of gravity.*

—KOFI ANNAN, FORMER UN
SECRETARY-GENERAL

FROM GLOBALIZATION TO
HYPER-GLOBALIZATION

THE ADVANCE OF A GLOBAL NETWORK CIVILIZATION IS THE
surest bet one could have made over the past five thousand years.
Globalization began in the third millennium B.C.E., when the city-
states of ancient Mesopotamian empires started regular trade with
each other and as far as Egypt and Persia. At its peak in the mid-first
millennium B.C.E., the Achaemenid Empire of the Persian king
Cyrus the Great had made itself the midway point of an imperial
network whose reach spanned from Europe to China, connections
built upon by the Greek and Roman commercial expeditions along
the Eurasian Silk Road. Connectivity spread riches and religion in
all directions. As the sociologist Christopher Chase-Dunn has
shown, today's world civilizational network has expanded through
the interactions of once discrete regional and cultural systems, with
waves of deepening connectedness launched by the confluence of
new technologies, sources of capital, and geopolitical ambitions.
Both the Arab conquerors of the mid-first millennium C.E. and the

---

Maps 2, 3, 4, 5, 6, 7, 8, 9, 10, 11, and 13, corresponding to this chapter,
appear in the first map insert.

Mongols of the thirteenth century leveraged their organized mobility to establish vast empires. The Crusades and the Commercial Revolution of the late Middle Ages enabled the flourishing of maritime commerce and set the stage for centuries of European colonialism during which most of the world's territory was mapped and claimed.

Globalization surged as empires expanded their connections: the fifteenth- and sixteenth-century Iberian (Spanish and Portuguese) voyages and the seventeenth-century Dutch and eighteenth-century British East India companies. The mills and factories that emerged in Britain through the nineteenth-century Industrial Revolution required ever more cotton and other raw material taken from far-flung colonies. Textiles and agriculture gave rise to global supply chains and the global slave trade. Germany's and America's huge increase in steel production and industrial output in the late nineteenth century together with the expansion of colonial European railway and shipping networks created an interconnected global economy as had never before been seen.

Describing those halcyon days in his famous 1919 treatise, *The Economic Consequences of the Peace,* John Maynard Keynes wrote, "The inhabitant of London could order by telephone, sipping his morning tea in bed, the various products of the whole earth, in such quantity as he might see fit, and reasonably expect their early delivery upon his doorstep. . . . [He] regarded this state of affairs as normal, certain, and permanent, except in the direction of further improvement, and any deviation from it as aberrant, scandalous, and avoidable."[1]

The pre–World War I period was indeed a golden age of globalization—but only for those in charge of it. The mercantile dynamics of borderless imperialism appropriated resources at little or no cost from Latin America, Africa, and Asia and returned them to Europe. African slaves and indentured Asian coolies were shipped around the world to work in plantations and mines from Cuba to the South Pacific islands. Continents were turned into dependencies, which upon independence remained subservient in a world of great power blocs. Globalization's Western dominance a century ago also made it vulnerable: World War I, trade barriers, immigration restrictions, financial retrenchment, and political nationalism caused the geopolitical crises of the 1930s that culminated in World War II.

Yet while war has indeed been globalization's greatest nemesis, it has only slowed its expansion, never stopped it. Despite the fourteenth-century Black Death, twentieth-century world wars, and early twenty-first-century financial crisis, mankind's migratory explorations, capitalist instincts, and technological innovations continue to create a worldwide system of interactions that gets bigger (global in scale), faster (instantaneous in speed), and more resilient (capable of recovery) over time. Today, globalization is radically more dispersed, with far more engines and participants, robust, and inclusive—and thus more stable—than ever before.

The word "globalization" gained wide usage only in the late 1980s—just before the end of the Cold War. Despite the radical expansion of worldwide connectivity since that time, globalization has been pronounced dead three times in just the past decade or so. First came the 9/11 terrorist attacks on New York and Washington in 2001. It was claimed that the erosion of trust between the West and the Arab world, increased security at borders, and the geopolitical disruptions of the wars in Iraq and Afghanistan could grind the global economy to a halt. Then came the collapse of the World Trade Organization (WTO) Doha round of negotiations in 2006, when it was argued that without an agreement on a single overarching global framework of rules, global trade would unwind, retrench, or contract. And most recently with the financial crisis of 2007–8, exports slumped, international lending diminished, and the Anglo-Saxon model of capitalism came under attack, all cited as evidence of "de-globalization." A fourth front of "end of globalization" hyperbole is now under way as American interest rates rise, Chinese growth slows, and cheap energy and advanced manufacturing technologies together enable the near-shoring and automation of production.

But I argue that globalization is entering a new golden age. Driven by the confluence of strategic ambitions, new technologies, cheap money, and global migration, globalization continues to widen and deepen in almost every conceivable dimension. Since 2002, total exports (of goods and services) have risen from 20 percent to more than 30 percent of world GDP, with some estimates pushing the ratio to well above 50 percent in the years ahead. America's share of exports to GDP has also risen: America's hardware, software, automobile, pharmaceutical, and other companies all depend more than ever on sales abroad for their growth; 40 percent of the S&P 500's revenues are international.

The ancient and medieval trade networks that once linked the thriving Africa, Arab, Persian, Indian, Chinese, and Southeast Asian civilizations are also being resurrected. Today the trade in goods, services, and finance across emerging markets represents a quarter of total global flows but is growing faster than any other category.* Between any two pairs of high-growth regions—China and Africa, South America and the Middle East, India and Africa, Southeast Asia and South America—trade volumes have risen by anywhere from 500 percent to 1800 percent (yes, four digits) in the past decade. While starting from a low base, the China-Africa trade volume of more than $250 billion per year is now almost double U.S.-Africa trade and projected to catch up to EU-Africa trade.

As airline fleets expand to include long-haul aircraft and Internet cables span all the oceans, the lower cost of intercontinental travel and connectivity will enable even small and medium-size companies across South America, Africa, and Asia to rent supply chain services. Anyone can do business with anyone, anywhere.

Foreign investment volumes have also climbed to more than one-third of world GDP. America's outbound investment has continuously risen to more than $5 trillion in 2013, the same year in which

---

*   Since 2000, the volume of financial data transfer facilitated by the inter-bank SWIFT network has risen steadily at more than 20 percent per year chiefly on the back of cross-emerging market transactions.

foreign direct investment (FDI) inflows into the United States rose to nearly $3 trillion. As of 2012, FDI into developing countries was more than half the world's total foreign investment—exceeding investment into developed countries. Even with the 2014–2015 slump in emerging market performance, China is quickly becoming the world's largest cross-border investor as measured by foreign exchange reserves, portfolio capital, and FDI, with its total overseas holdings projected to reach $20 trillion by 2020. The Cambridge scholar Peter Nolan has written that the West is still more "in China" than China is "in the world,"[2] but that is changing quickly. Indeed, more capital now flows out of China than into it.[3]

Globalization has become a multidirectional series of tsunamis that surges across the oceans and undertows continents into the collective currents. Chinese banks lending in Latin America to promote exports across the Pacific, Indian tractors exported to boost African commodities exports to Asia, European banks financing companies to expand machinery production in Southeast Asia for sales in China, American software companies developing apps in Japan for Asian markets, and eventually nonstop flights between any two major cities on any continent.

There is no meaningful precedent for the scale, depth, and intensity of today's multipolar and multi-civilizational order in which all regions are important and reaching out to each other at the same time. After five centuries of Western geopolitical and economic dominance, postcolonial regions have the opportunity to engage on a more level playing field, selling in a global marketplace rather than giving away resources at gunpoint. Monthly summits bring together Latin Americans and Chinese on agriculture, Africans and Arabs on infrastructure services, Europeans and Southeast Asians on free trade, Americans and Africans on power development, Chinese and Europeans on the Arctic, and many other combinations of global complementarity. If this is the "clash of civilizations," we need much more of it.

It is tempting to believe that globalization has reached its peak, but the only significant area of decline in cross-border capital flows since 2008 has been bank lending, owing almost entirely to the financial crisis within Europe.[4] Globalization is no longer the same as Americanization, either. Rather it is the American economy whose dependence on globalization continues to grow with respect to inflows of talent and investment and outflows of goods, services, and capital seeking high returns—especially in Asia. Globalization no longer has to be underwritten by Wall Street and the U.S. Fed. Hong Kong and Singapore rival New York and London among the world's leading financial centers as Asia's markets expand, assets under management grow, and foreign exchange transactions increase. You pick the metric—international travelers and migrants, cross-border mergers and acquisitions, volume of data transfers, and more—they are all going up.

In a connected world, a reduction in one type of flow is often replaced—at even greater volume—by another, more stable kind. For example, America's gradually rising interest rates have reduced outbound portfolio capital to emerging economies, but deepening Asian bond markets simultaneously attracted growing inflows from American pension funds. America's energy revolution has meant dropping U.S. oil imports, but it has also encouraged massive new inflows of European and Asian capital into the country for high-tech fracking operations, oil refineries, and chemical plants—*more* globalization. Inbound FDI into China has begun to decline, but China's outbound FDI has skyrocketed as its currency has appreciated (even exceeding inbound FDI as of 2014). Smart global investors don't treat trends in isolation but look at the full picture and play the second- and third-order consequences.

America's efforts to bring back home 1 or 2 million manufacturing jobs pale in comparison to the nearly *100 million* manufacturing jobs that are flowing out of China and recirculating to Myanmar, Bangladesh, Ethiopia, and other low-wage, low-skill countries. By 2020, almost all new entrants into the global workforce will come from other developing countries across Asia and Africa. As infrastructure improves in these frontier markets, manufacturers can rapidly switch locations, making competition more ruthless than ever. There is always going to be "the next China" to take on labor-intensive, low-wage manufacturing, hence a Chinese company such as Huajian Shoes, one of the world's largest apparel makers, is relocating production from China to SEZ "apparel cities" in Ethiopia.[5] Flows are shifting, but there is no doubt that they are surging as well.

Trade theorists, investment bankers, and tech companies all call this the age of hyper-globalization. If globalization were a balloon, it would still be in the early puffs of expanding to its full capacity. The shortsightedness that dominates Western discourse utterly confuses internationalization—which varies dramatically depending on industries and cycles—and globalization, which is our relentlessly growing *capacity* for global interaction. Globalization is deeper than any one statistic. The *volume* of transactions—whether currency trades, shipping tonnage, or export receipts—can be perpetually volatile, but the system's capacity for global activity is a much better indicator of where globalization is headed. There is actually little reason to speak of globalization in the future tense—only degrees of connectivity.

THE MEASURE OF THINGS

A decade ago, voices from India and Africa spoke about how "one billion people can't be ignored," presuming that their demographic size alone denotes importance, such as the right to have a seat on the UN Security Council. But the world can and does very well ignore a billion people when they are poor and destitute, disconnected and disenfranchised. Only when one billion Africans and one billion Indians are connected to the global economy are their nations truly taken seriously.

Strategic importance has traditionally been measured by territorial size and military power, but today power derives from leverage exercised through connective reach. The paramount factor in determining the importance of a state is not its location or population but its connectedness—physically, economically, digitally—to flows of resources, capital, data, talent, and other valuable assets. Consider how China and India both have populations of approximately 1.5 billion people, but China represents 10 percent of world imports while India only 2.5 percent. China is the top trade partner for more than a hundred countries (more than the United States), while India is the top trade partner of only Nepal and Kenya. According to research by J. P. Morgan, a 1 percent decline in China's GDP correlates to a 10 percent decline in oil prices. From the rest of the world's point of view, there is scarcely a country in the world for which India is nearly as significant as China—even as its population becomes larger than China's.

But even as China's GDP surpasses that of the United States and its currency joins the dollar in the IMF's reserve basket, America still commands the most connected financial system, responsible for close to half of the world's total financial assets of nearly $300 trillion. The U.S. dollar represents the lion's share of global currency reserves, the U.S. government Treasuries market of about $12 trillion is by far the world's largest, America's equity markets are valued at half the world total of approximately $70 trillion, and America also has the world's deepest corporate debt market (while also dominating euro-currency corporate bond issuance). Foreign governments, banks, companies, and citizens worldwide are more invested in America's financial system than any other.

Measuring connectedness helps correct for the mismatch of geographic size and perceived influence. Russia is the largest country in the world but by far the least connected of major economies.[6] Its economy depends almost entirely on commodities exports, but as oil and gas supplies rise worldwide, Russia's influence beyond its so-called near abroad of former Soviet republics will continue to fade.

Russia is an important example, however, of how less connected countries tend to be less predictable and more volatile. Iran, North Korea, and Yemen, as well as isolated but violent countries such as Niger and the Central African Republic, rank very low in connectivity but very high as sources of danger. This suggests that rather than isolating countries further, we should engage them in more positive forms of connectivity. Afghanistan, for example, has been a major exporter of drugs and terrorist violence but has the potential to become more constructively connected by exporting copper and lithium and serving as a Silk Road conduit between Central Asia and the Arabian Sea and from China to the Middle East.

The most connected nations have traditionally been Western states whose centuries of far-flung colonial ties, dense regional relations (through the EU and the transatlantic community), deep capital markets, and technological prowess have built up over centuries. According to the McKinsey Global Institute's Connectedness Index—a measure of the density of flows of goods, finance, people, and data—the trading powerhouse Germany has a flow intensity (the value of economic connectedness relative to the size of GDP) of a whopping 110 percent, indicating how crucial connectedness is to the world's best-run large country. (The United States and China, owing to their massive internal markets, have lower but still substantial flow intensities: the United States at 36 percent and China at 62 percent.) Connected states are respected states. Germany ranks at the top of both the McKinsey Connectedness Index and the Pew/GlobeScan survey of the world's most admired countries.

The primacy of connectivity allows smaller states to have far greater gravity than their size would suggest. Singapore and the Netherlands have high flow intensity because they depend more on the in- and outflow of goods, services, finance, people, and data than large countries. Norway is a relatively small and geographically remote Arctic country, but its oil-generated sovereign wealth fund is the world's largest and controls 1 percent of global stock exchange value and 3 percent in Europe. As it expands its emerging market portfolio allocation to 10 percent, its leverage over hundreds of major international companies will grow as well.[7]

More connectivity means more growth and more flows. Already 40 percent of global GDP (as well as 25 percent of global growth) depends on the flows of goods, services, and capital across borders,[8] while knowledge-intensive flows such as digital services are already worth $13 trillion annually (about half the value of all flows) and rising rapidly—a reminder that viewing globalization only from the standpoint of manufacturing tells us ever less about its full trajectory.* In the standard "gravity model," trade grows in proportion to the size of communities and inversely to the distance between them. But with digital connectivity, the supply chain is physically unchained: Once the hard wiring of the Internet is in place, the marginal cost of delivering services falls to nearly zero. Between digitally connected societies, the only distance is political and cultural.

Mapping software that shows connectivity overcoming geography thus becomes a useful explanatory tool. The Worldmapper research consortium and Pankaj Ghemawat's CAGE program, for example, allow the visualization of countries and regions based on their economic size, trade partners, and other metrics and vectors, emphasizing globalization's depth, distribution, and directionality. This way one can easily see how Africa, despite its enormous geographic size, appears very slender in terms of economic weight but balloons again based on its natural resource endowments. One can also track how Germany's exports within the eurozone have fallen from over 50 percent to under 35 percent of its total, while its exports to Asia are taking off. Rather than presume that one's closest economic relations are with neighbors, we can now toggle between geographic distance and functional proximity, highlighting industry-specific supply chain linkages that show, for example, how closely tied Bangalore's software industry is to America. Distance is not dead, but it is certainly compressed.

---

* Knowledge-intensive flows are represented by high-tech products (for example, semiconductors, computers, software), pharmaceuticals, automobiles, machinery, and business services (for example, accounting, law, engineering), as well as foreign investment that transfers management and expertise, payments for royalties and patents, business traveler spending, and international telecom revenue.

A NEW MAP LEGEND

All maps have a box in the corner—called the legend—where one finds the symbols, colors, arrows, lines, dots, and other markings to help us decipher differentiations in landscape. In order to produce an atlas for the supply chain world, we'll need a much more sophisticated glossary of power.

The first step is to map authority and connections rather than only states and their divisions. We should highlight the most coherent units, the most concrete connections, and the strongest gravities of influence. As a rule of thumb, these fall into one of the "Five Cs": territorial *countries,* networked *cities,* regional *commonwealths,* cloud *communities,* and stateless *companies.*

Countries

The biggest mistake our traditional maps make is to portray countries as unified wholes, equating political geography with sovereign authority—as if having a country means you actually control it. Instead of mapping de jure sovereignty, we should be mapping de facto authority.

Some countries are so culturally and politically diffuse that only geography holds them together. India, for example, is united much more by geology than democracy: A peninsula is hard to escape. In northern Kashmir and northeastern states such as Manipur and Nagaland, secessionist movements have raged intermittently. Other countries are so fragmented geographically that they are united only in name. Poor island archipelagoes such as Indonesia lag desperately in the transportation and communications infrastructure necessary to maintain cohesion. Many of its fourteen thousand islands are scarcely governed by Jakarta at all but rather drift into Singapore's or Malaysia's orbit. Natural boundaries thus make for good political borders but also divide countries in ways that require added effort to maintain unity.

Countries that are not physically united find it hard to remain politically united. The Democratic Republic of Congo, the largest country in Africa, has barely one thousand kilometers of paved roads. No wonder leading scholars have bluntly stated that while Congo is legally a state, it literally "does not exist." What better captures the life of Congo's seventy-five million people are the tugboats and barges loaded with merchants, families, refugees, livestock, palm oil canisters, cars, and clothing that take weeks to migrate the one thousand kilometers along the Congo River between Kinshasa and Kisangani. Physically united states stay together; unconnected spaces drift and dissipate.

Distance is a double-edged sword: It gives countries large geographic buffers to defend their core populations but also requires far greater investment to maintain unity. When Stalin took control of the Soviet Union after Lenin's death in 1924, his immediate concern was the country's infrastructural backwardness, prompting the launch of an intensive modernization campaign including a major railway from Novosibirsk in Siberia to Tashkent in Uzbekistan. Yet much like the Ottoman Empire's, the Soviet Union's vast internal inequality across diverse ethno-geographies led to its inevitably falling apart. Today Russia is still the world's largest state but has barely invested in knitting what remains together; hence its subregions gravitate toward far larger and more densely populated Europe and China. As I've learned driving across Russia, a road atlas often reveals more than a political map.

According to Vaclav Smil, China consumed more cement between 2010 and 2013 than America did in the entire twentieth century. Yet many of the largest developing countries in the world are far more fragmented than they appear on our maps precisely because they lack the essential infrastructure that promotes unity. Just four of them—Brazil, Indonesia, Nigeria, and India—represent approximately two billion people, yet each performs as far less than the sum of its parts because many of its parts are barely connected. In such countries, the gradient of governability often diminishes drastically with distance from the main capital city.

Taking the present map at face value would lead one to believe that Congo, Somalia, Libya, Syria, and Iraq actually exist as meaningful states rather than the geopolitical black holes they truly are. Why not lighten their shade on the map, fading toward white, to depict their weakness? Some state-like entities—such as Kurdistan and Palestine—are not on our maps but should be even as their political geography is in flux. There are also "states within states" such as Lebanon's Hezbollah, Nigeria's Boko Haram, and the Taliban straddling Afghanistan and Pakistan that hold more sway in certain geographies than the governments of the states in which they are located. ISIS is not a recognized state but holds territory and has aggressively expanded across the pseudo-states of Syria and Iraq. Middlebury Institute of International Studies professor Itamara Lochard has identified thirteen thousand armed militias—sixty-five times more than the number of "sovereign" countries. Wouldn't it be nice to know their effective area of operation?

While some governments' influence extends not far beyond the capital, a few can assert themselves far *beyond* their nominal borders. Indeed, what Washington, Brussels, and Beijing say and do shapes the world more than any other capital cities. In fact, we should depict their radius of influence in ways that don't misrepresent them merely as national capitals. If we map cross-border infrastructure investments, for example, we would be able to see how China, while nominally accepting the political borders set during the Qing dynasty, actually operates a robust and growing set of tentacles penetrating deep into almost all of its neighbors—and China has more neighbors than any other country in the world—using them to re-create the tributary model of civilizational empire that is far more characteristic of Asia's history over the past three thousand years.

And yet even the central political authority of America and China—two powerful and vertically commanded empires—betrays a far more fragmented ground reality underneath. Large countries are meant to provide stability through scale, but the United States,

China, India, Brazil, Russia, Turkey, Nigeria, Indonesia, Bangladesh, and Pakistan—the ten largest countries in the world by population (minus exceptionally modern Japan)—are also the most unequal countries in the world. Precisely the policies essential to mitigating inequality—universal access to quality education and health care, flexible labor markets combined with worker protections, and widespread access to capital—are lacking and seemingly unattainable in many large countries. Far too much national wealth is concentrated—or hoarded—in one or two cities, leaving little for the masses. It is in those same cities where we can see firsthand the narrow economic base on which "national" growth has been built. Places close together may actually be worlds apart. There is a big difference between the emerging markets that have made major capital investments in infrastructure and social mobility such as China and Colombia and those that have been driven by cheap consumer credit growth such as Brazil and Turkey. Indonesia's productivity figures outside Jakarta are so low as to be almost immeasurable. The expression "Cairo is Egypt" may sound romantic, but it is not healthy. It is precisely because such inequality plagues almost every nation that we need more nuanced maps that distinguish *within* countries between their connected and disconnected populations.

We should map *all* countries' economic disparities in much more detail such as by shading cities and provinces according to their wealth. Choropleth maps (which overlay thematic data onto geography) that show the concentration of wealth and talent in New York City and Silicon Valley give a much more accurate rendering of the true nature of the American economy, as they do for China, where coastal cities are as wealthy as South Korea and remote inner provinces as poor as Guatemala. Extreme inequality challenges the notion of coherent national units. It is a world where median income tells us much more than average income, and in America median real incomes are stuck at 1980s levels.

Cities

More than one hundred countries together represent only 3 percent of world GDP; they are basically small and relatively poor cities surrounded by variously sized hinterlands. These states thus resemble atoms: The nucleus (capital) represents a small fraction of the atom's (state's) size but almost all the mass (weight). In a world where connectivity matters more than size, therefore, cities deserve more nuanced treatment on our maps than simply as homogeneous black dots.

Cities are mankind's most enduring and stable mode of social organization, outlasting all empires and nations over which they have presided. For example, although the Byzantine and Ottoman Empires are long gone, Constantinople—now Istanbul—survives as a center of commerce and culture whose geographic radius of influence stretches far beyond that of its imperial predecessors, even though it is no longer the capital of Turkey. Cities are the truly timeless global form.

Cities in the twenty-first century are mankind's most profound infrastructure; they are the human technology most visible from space, growing from villages to towns to counties to megacities to super-corridors stretching hundreds of kilometers. In 1950, the world had only two megacities of populations larger than 10 million: Tokyo and New York City. By 2025, there will be at least forty such megacities. The population of the greater Mexico City region is larger than that of Australia, as is that of Chongqing, a collection of connected urban enclaves spanning an area the size of Austria. Cities that were once hundreds of kilometers apart have now effectively fused into massive urban archipelagoes, the largest of which is Japan's Taiheiyo Belt that encompasses two-thirds of Japan's population in the Tokyo-Nagoya-Osaka megalopolis. China's Pearl River delta, Greater São Paulo, and Mumbai-Pune are also becoming more integrated through infrastructure. At least a dozen such megacity corridors have emerged already. China is in the process of reorganizing itself around two dozen giant megacity clusters of up to

100 million citizens each.* And yet by 2030, the second-largest city in the world behind Tokyo is expected not to be in China but to be Manila.

America's rising multi-city clusters are as significant as any of these, even if their populations are smaller. Three in particular stand out. The East Coast corridor from Boston through New York to Washington, D.C., contains America's academic brain, financial center, and political capital. (The only thing missing is a high-speed railway to serve as the regional spine.) From San Francisco to San Jose, Silicon Valley has become one continuous low-rise stretch between I-280 and U.S.-101 that is home to over six thousand technology companies that generate more than $200 billion in GDP. (With a San Francisco–Los Angeles–San Diego high-speed rail, California's Pacific Coast would truly become the western counterpart to the northeastern corridor. Elon Musk's Tesla has proposed an ultra-high-speed "Hyperloop" tunnel system for this route.) And the Dallas–Fort Worth Metroplex, the largest urban cluster in the American South, houses industry giants such as Exxon, AT&T, and American Airlines in an economy larger than South Africa's and is actually building a high-speed rail (well, only 120 kilometers per hour) called the Trans-Texas Corridor that could eventually extend to the oil capital Houston based on plans rolled out in 2014 by Texas Central Railway and the bullet-train operator Central Japan Railway.

As populations, wealth, and talent concentrate in global cities, they gradually supersede countries as the world's key gravitational centers. Cities today are ranked by their influence in global networks, not by their territorial possessions. Global cities amass finance and technology, diversity and vibrancy, and seamless connectivity to growing numbers of their counterparts. As Christopher

---

* Some of these are Chuanyu, which includes Chongqing, Chengdu, and thirteen other cities of Sichuan; the Capital Region megalopolis (also known as the Bohai Rim) that combines Beijing, Tianjin, and other cities of Hebei province; and the Yangtze delta region encompassing Shanghai, Nanjing, Hangzhou, Suzhou, and others totaling 88 million inhabitants.

Chase-Dunn has pointed out, it is not population or territorial size that drives world-city status but economic weight, proximity to zones of growth, political stability, and attractiveness for foreign capital. In other words, connectivity matters more than size—and even more than sovereignty. New York, Dubai, and Hong Kong are not national capitals, but they rank in the top five cities in the world in terms of the flows passing through them.

Demographic and economic weight gives cities greater policy-making leverage, allows them to maneuver for greater autonomy, and enables their direct diplomacy—what I call "diplomacity"— with other cities. Great and connected cities, Saskia Sassen argues, belong as much to global networks as to the country of their political geography. They are disembedded assemblages of circuits; the more they belong to, the more resilient they are as they reconfigure their infrastructure and reallocate resources based on global patterns. Today the world's top twenty richest cities have forged a super-circuit driven by capital, talent, and services: They are home to more than 75 percent of the largest companies, which in turn invest in expanding across those cities and adding more to expand the intercity network. Indeed, global cities have forged a league of their own, in many ways as denationalized as Formula One racing teams, drawing talent from around the world and amassing capital to spend on themselves while they compete on the same circuit.

The rise of emerging market megacities as magnets for regional wealth and talent has been the most significant contributor to shifting the world's focal point of economic activity. McKinsey Global Institute research suggests that from now until 2025 one-third of world growth will come from the key Western capitals and emerging market megacities, one-third from the heavily populous middle-weight cities of emerging markets, and one-third from small cities and rural areas in developing countries. Because prices for goods are so much lower in second- and third-tier cities of China and India, they have hundreds of millions of citizens who have become sizable aggregate consumers well before reaching the $8,000 per capita GDP (in purchasing power parity terms) projected as the baseline beyond which consumption takes off. No wonder companies target high-growth cities as their main product destinations, while investors look at municipal debt as a key metric of national economic health.

There are far more functional cities in the world today than there are viable states. Indeed, cities are often the islands of governance and order in far weaker states where they extract whatever rents they can from the surrounding country while also being indifferent to it. This is how Lagos views Nigeria, Karachi views Pakistan, and Mumbai views India: the less interference from the capital, the better. Especially when capital cities have been designed to occupy more central geography to assert their statewide authority—such as Brasília and Abuja—they have inadvertently marginalized themselves as the world economy privileges populous and connected coastal cities.

It is, of course, very difficult if not impossible to neatly disentangle the interdependencies between city and state, whether territorially, demographically, economically, ecologically, or socially. That is not the point. Across the world, city leaders and their key businesses set up SEZs and directly recruit investors into their orbit to ensure that their workers are hired and benefits accrue locally rather than nationally. This is all the sovereignty they want. To that end, entire new districts (sometimes called aerotropolises) have sprung up around airports to evade urban congestion and more efficiently connect to global markets and supply chains. From Chicago's O'Hare and Washington-Dulles to Seoul's Incheon Airport, such sites have become the fastest-growing economic geographies, underscoring the intrinsic value of connectivity. For companies moving their headquarters into an aerotropolis, the airport is the gateway to world markets while the nearby city, no matter how large, is just another sales destination.

Commonwealths

The more cities connect to other major hubs in their regions, the more regions become collective forces rather than tectonic coincidences. Per the U.S. National Intelligence Council's *Global Trends 2030* report, "Megacities and regional groupings [such as the EU, the North American Union, and Greater China] will assume increasing powers whereas national governments and global multilateral institutions will struggle to keep up with the rapid diffusion of power."[9] Regional commonwealths are a more realistic way to share capacities and organize collective action than far-off and centralized global institutions. They help to modernize weaker members, as the EU has done for eastern Europe and the Balkans through its more than $300 billion worth of funds for infrastructural upgrading, human capital investments, digital transformation, and other areas. Becoming EU members has made these countries investment grade and more attractive for supply chains through giving them clear and reliable laws. The same is now happening with the ASEAN Economic Community of Southeast Asia and the pan-Asian Regional Comprehensive Economic Partnership, where economies are opening at their own pace to protect their comparative advantages and boost employment. The infrastructural and market integration under way within regions today makes them far more significant building blocks of global order than nations. Importantly, the geographies *not* knitting themselves together into collective functional zones—the Near East and Central Asia—are also generally where one finds the most failed states.

Mega-regions are not monolithic blocs but what scholars call "composite empires," informal and transactional rather than formal and institutionalized. They feature nominal central authority but substantial autonomy for various provinces within. The Roman, Byzantine, and Ottoman Empires were geographically vast, militarily dominant, and economically wealthy, but they were also highly unequal, politically devolved, and culturally fractured. Yet even weak regionalism is a crucial antidote to imperialism. If one cause of the outbreak of warfare is the uncertainty surrounding proxy rivalries (as occurred on the eve of World War I), then strong regional groupings that guard against external manipulation are a welcome development.

Such commonwealth regions are larger, more coherent, and more powerful than the ethereal cultural communities mapped by the late Harvard professor Samuel Huntington in his book *The Clash of Civilizations and the Remaking of World Order*. Catholics may look to Rome and Orthodox to Moscow, but they don't act as a united geopolitical agent. The more violence undertaken by radical groups in the name of Islam, the more divided the so-called Islamic world becomes; just witness the ground held by ISIS and its attacks on Sunni regimes in the Near East. Islam's internal borders are far bloodier than those with its neighboring civilizations.

The reality of economically integrated mega-regions is far more persuasive. The North American Union spans across Western and Latin cultural boundaries, the EU's empire effectively subsumes parts of Arab, Orthodox, and Turkic civilizations, and China's growing sphere of influence is spreading deeper into Southeast Asia's indigenous cultures, encroaches on the ancient Japanese and Korean civilizations, and reaches into the Orthodox and Turkic realms as well. As Fernand Braudel foresaw in his exhaustive studies, the "Greater Mediterranean" region is not so much divided by sea as united around it. Anyone who has met a Lebanese Sunni from Beirut or a merchant from Tripoli knows he identifies more with Phoenician history and Mediterranean culture than with Islam. Civilizations connect far more than they clash.

Communities

It is just as important to capture how individual identities and loyalties transcend geography. The best example of this is ethnic diasporas. Diaspora relationships have historically been just a simple two-way street: cultural transmission from the motherland to far-flung diaspora members and remittances back in the other direction. The $583 billion worth of remittances logged in 2014 is reason enough to take notice of how diasporas can be powerful change agents in countries they might have left more than a generation ago. But now diasporas are a perpetual multidirectional flow of finance, communications, and political networks across dozens of national boundaries: Chinese not China, Indians not India, Brazilians not Brazil.

Mapping diaspora networks shows us what force multipliers they are. The Indian diaspora across North America, the Middle East, East Africa, and Southeast Asia is an internally lubricated commercial realm (which I have dubbed Bollystan) that finances real estate, schools, factories, and gold mines across the former British colonial universe with no directives from India itself. Yet governments are increasingly taking advantage of connectedness to their diasporas as a source of loyal, long-term capital. India, Israel, and the Philippines offer financial products to the savvy diaspora such as infrastructure bonds that target specific projects and have transparent progress tracking. At the same time, after decades of migrating outward for education and never returning, diasporas are also resettling at home in record numbers as the quality of life improves, creating a "brain gain." Such "re-pats" are accelerators of innovation because they bring Western ideas back to more rigid societies and dilute traditional power structures; indeed, diaspora figures have taken prominent political roles in each of these countries and numerous others.

The great Sinosphere of over fifty million ethnic Chinese spanning Asia and spreading across the oceans is also a gravitational field unto itself. In the 1980s, Deng Xiaoping tapped the ethnic Chinese industrialists of Taiwan, Hong Kong, Malaysia, and Thailand to fund the country's nascent SEZs. If Beijing were to offer dual citizenship to some of its forty million members, it might lure many more overseas Chinese, bringing in fresh talent and replenishing the aging population. While diasporas are often resentful of the political systems they have left behind, several generations on from the Chinese Civil War and great exile they increasingly act as opportunistic nodes in a global Chinese civilization.

Diasporas are a leading harbinger of a world moving from vertical to horizontal authorities, communities that occupy mind share if not territory. These are not nation-states but *relational* states: Neither their physical footprint nor their number of members matters as much as their capacity to act across the virtual and real worlds. As the Internet rose to prominence in the 1990s, the sociologist Manuel Castells distinguished between the "space of places" and the "space of flows."[10] Today the two are blending together as never before. The intersection of demographic and technological flows creates new opportunities for Facebook groups and other cloud communities to emerge more rapidly, globally, and in greater number, generating flash mobs of allegiance that force us to evolve our political concepts beyond states. Social networks provide the tools for people to shape their welfare by motivating members, financing activities, and sparking political action. The WikiLeaks founder, Julian Assange, argues that the Internet enables connected groups to anneal into empowered collectives that can act on their principles. The taxonomy of influential actors is thus expanding to include terrorist networks, hacker units, and religious fundamentalist groups who define themselves by *what* they do rather than *where* they are.

Global connectivity gradually undermines national roots and augments or replaces them with a range of transnational bonds and identities. Imagine a world where people are loyal to cities and supply chains rather than nations, value credit cards and digital currencies over citizenship, and seek community in cyberspace rather than country. As John Arquilla, an expert on emerging patterns of warfare at the Naval Postgraduate School, has observed, such networks are now taking on nations the way nations took on empires. They draw their strength from compelling narratives and use technologies to build cohesion. A micro-blog is not just a communications medium but the seed of a virtual community of belonging that challenges government writ and state identity.

Companies

Corporate superpowers are also becoming autonomous players in the supply chain world. Whereas multinational corporations of the Cold War era were strongly rooted in home markets, today a growing class of companies have elevated themselves above national boundaries, avoiding overdependence on any one market, investor, headquarters, or location of employees. After the financial crisis, massive corporate bailouts and a raft of new financial regulations were meant to rein in Wall Street. But according to the Financial Stability Board's annual list of the most "systemically relevant" financial institutions (based on their size and breadth of exposure), more than thirty banks have consolidated assets of more than $50 billion *each*—meaning greater financial weight (and certainly global reach) than two-thirds of all the countries in the world. Even as their operations have been curtailed and more closely monitored, they continue to restructure themselves through overseas mergers and tax arbitrage: HSBC has considered shifting its headquarters from London to Hong Kong. Glencore Xstrata in commodities, DHL in logistics, Accenture in professional services, and Academi (formerly Blackwater) in private military services are other examples of companies that, even if they are listed and traded on exchanges, have fragmented themselves into global partnerships of locally owned joint ventures. They view countries not as sovereign masters to be obeyed but as jurisdictions to be negotiated.

The more connectivity we have, the more such companies can make their mastery of it their competitive advantage. Even Silicon Valley's technology companies increasingly make their products— and keep their money—in the cloud. There are fewer than five countries in the world whose GDP is larger than the more than $200 billion of liquid cash Apple Inc. holds in securities worldwide, meaning Apple could buy many countries' combined output (minus their debt). Having sold almost two billion products to over one billion people, Apple not only has more money but also occupies greater mind share than most nations.

Countries run by supply chains, cities that run themselves, communities that know no borders, and companies with more power than governments—all are evidence of the shift toward a new kind of pluralistic world system. The ranks of such global authorities that belong on our maps of connectivity are rapidly growing, a reminder that the map itself is never finished in a world of constant change.

FROM DIPLOMACY TO "DIPLOMACITY"

When scholars began to study the geography of global connectedness, they began with cities. As the historian Peter Spufford points out, Europe's urbanization in the thirteenth and fourteenth centuries drove its capitalist expansion through the growing use of credit and insurance for merchants' participation in international trade fairs. The European Commercial Revolution also linked the Continent's key urban markets to Asian trade centers such as Constantinople and Calicut. It is precisely because globalization has reduced national borders that cities can more fluidly cooperate internationally.

Today's activities are orders of magnitude more impactful. Since New York City set up its first mission abroad in 1953, over two hundred U.S. state and city offices have opened around the world. Massachusetts signed its first international agreement with Guangdong in 1983 and has since established more than thirty direct partnerships with foreign countries through its Office of International Trade and Investment. Non-capital cities such as São Paulo and Dubai have large international affairs offices and formal bilateral relations with countries including the United States, the U.K., and Germany. The Economic Development Authority of Fairfax County, Virginia, has offices in Bangalore, Seoul, and Tel Aviv to lure companies to the Washington, D.C., suburbs.

No empire is a large enough substitute for the benefits of direct global access. Even Chinese cities actively forge their own international economic ties based on comparative advantages with little regard for geopolitical relations. Sichuan province's largest trading partners—the United States, Europe, and ASEAN—represent about $10 billion in annual trade each; thus it wants to remain as connected as possible to each of them. Commercial diplomacy among cities represents this broader turn toward a functional world rather than a political one.

Even capital cities such as London can simultaneously act like independent states. In order to keep England united in the early thirteenth century, King John acceded to special provisions in the Magna Carta that preserve special rights for the one-square-kilometer City of London (now known as the City of London Corporation). Today, twenty-four thousand companies elect its executives and lord mayor, who travels like a statesman from Brazil to China securing financial arrangements, all with the full support of the U.K. Foreign Office and the mayor of Greater London. Unlike Britain's populist politicians who use anti-EU rhetoric to gain votes from an equally ignorant electorate, London City's leaders know all too well their economy needs to trade and invest with the eurozone—and in dollars, yen, and renminbi—to survive and underwrite the entire rest of the country.

There is a reason more former mayors are currently serving as heads of state than ever in history. On the great issues of our age such as climate change, cities are doing as much as or more than national governments. Forty of the largest cities in the world have launched their own greenhouse gas emissions reduction scheme (called C40) that circumvents intergovernmental negotiations that produce nothing but hot air. China's mayors and city officials farm out to Copenhagen, Tokyo, and Singapore to learn how to combine innovation with livability to gain an edge on each other. (Indeed, much of the substance of European diplomacy with China today is direct interactions between the business associations of major cities and the trade in commercial technology that increases China's efficiency and sustainability.) To learn how to get arguably the world's top priority of sustainable urbanization right, you go to the World Cities Summit in Singapore or the Smart City World Congress in Barcelona—or visit the many online portals where experts, activists, and managers from hundreds of cities share information—not the UN General Assembly. "Diplomacity" is already embodied in organizations such as the United Cities and Local Governments and more than two hundred other inter-city learning networks that together already outnumber all the international organizations in the world.[11] Because cities define themselves in part by their connectedness rather than their sovereignty, one can imagine a global society emerging much more readily from intercity relations than international relations.

PART TWO

DEVOLUTION
AS DESTINY

CHAPTER 3

THE GREAT DEVOLUTION

It's the Second Law of Thermodynamics: Sooner or
later everything turns to shit. That's my phrasing, not
the Encyclopedia Britannica.

—SALLY, IN WOODY ALLEN'S
HUSBANDS AND WIVES (1992)

LET THE TRIBES WIN

THE MOST POWERFUL POLITICAL IMPULSE PROPELLING US TOWARD
a connected world is precisely the one that points in the opposite
direction: devolution. Devolution is the perpetual fragmentation of
territory into ever more (and smaller) units of authority, from empires to nations, nations to provinces, and provinces to cities. Devolution is the ultimate expression of the tribal, local, and parochial
desire to control one's geography, which is exactly why it drives us
toward a connected destiny.

Devolution is the geopolitical embodiment of the second law of
thermodynamics that all systems tend toward maximum entropy.
Large-scale devolution has been under way for centuries: America's
independence from Britain was a major milestone in the dismantling of Europe's global empires, followed by the early nineteenth-
century independence from Spain of major Latin nations from
Mexico to Colombia. Historically, wars of conquest have created
larger imperial societies, but the decolonization era since World

Maps 12 and 14, corresponding to this chapter,
appear in the first map insert.

War II was dominated by wars of independence and secession across Africa and Asia. The collapse of the Soviet Union was the last great devolutionary act of the twentieth century, creating more than a dozen new nations whose identities most Westerners were not aware of until 1991. Collectively, these tides of devolution have raised the membership of the United Nations from approximately 50 members in 1945 to close to 200 today. We could have 250 independent states by mid-century. If there is any destiny in politics, it is devolution, not democracy.

International relations are so preoccupied with threats to sovereignty from the outside, and yet sovereignty is most visibly unraveling from *within*. Indeed, the growing power and connectivity of provinces and cities are driving devolution in the twenty-first century as significantly as decolonization did in the twentieth century. Devolution rests on irrevocable trends: the spread of capitalism and markets, the growing breadth of transportation and communications, the universality of access to information, and the rise of popular movements for self-rule. Cities no longer need their national capitals to filter their relations with the world, every place can compete as an investment destination, and central governments no longer control knowledge of how money is spent. The test of devolution is not sovereignty but authority, not legal independence but autonomy to pursue one's own interests. Whether mayors or rebels, there are many ways to circumvent the prison of imposed nationhood. Maps of sovereign states thus betray the far fuzzier reality of hundreds of relatively autonomous nodes.[1]

Over the span of two centuries, nation-building efforts have failed to amicably hold even culturally similar peoples of diverse ethno-linguistic communities together. When Italy was unified in 1861, only 10 percent of the country actually spoke Italian. (Italy's first king, Victor Emmanuel II, spoke dialects of French.) The mid-twentieth-century Spanish dictator, Francisco Franco, tried to create a single national "personality" through language as well. But this "odious homogenization" (as the Harvard economist Alberto Alesina calls it) inevitably causes backlash where minorities (or even majorities) are forcibly integrated.[2] From the Scots and Basques to the Catalans and Venetians, David is winning the long battle against Goliath.

Daily headlines from the Middle East are also a constant reminder that the end of colonialism three generations ago continues to bring forth bitter struggles to rectify hastily drawn borders. Yet if there is a silver lining to the hundreds of thousands of people who have perished in Iraq and Syria, it is that they represent the tail end of a major era in world history in which the primary conflicts were over the definition of political boundaries. Indeed, devolution has been the main driver of designing away traditional interstate warfare. It is no accident that the rate of decline in international conflict (and deaths from such conflicts) coincides with the post–World War II doubling of the world's nations through decolonization. What reason is there for anticolonial wars when colonization has ended? Since the Cold War, significant international conflict has continued to decline toward nearly zero. Almost all international border disputes are either settled or in stalemate, and few that remain are over genuinely strategic geographies. Tribal separation is thus a far more pragmatic approach to preventing additional loss of life in the futile hope of maintaining multiethnic harmony. Settlement does not equate to appeasement; rather it paves the way for the cartographic stress of hostile borders to be replaced by the urgent priorities of domestic state building. Newly created and fragile states simply have less capacity to pursue international conflict, especially while they are getting their own houses in order.[3] At the same time, intensive diplomacy and peacekeeping can keep a lid on conflicts and police boundaries as they have in Central America, the Balkans, and Africa. Giving each tribe its own nation is the surest path to international peace.

Devolution is also proving to be a far more important driver of global stability than democracy. Democracy prioritizes elections, while devolution establishes the boundaries for political stability. Without the latter, the former can simply lead to polarized ethnic politics and renewed conflict—as we continue to witness in Iraq. In the rush to democratize societies, we have forgotten to get the dimensions of the polity right first. What democratization has done, though, is fuel devolution. It has given people the voice to express their dissatisfaction and agitate for more self-rule. Whether Bosnia or Ukraine, Nigeria or Sudan, India or Pakistan, few things cause as much cartographic stress as holding on to territory whose population wants independence or to join a neighbor instead. National elections, provincial plebiscites, and other political maneuvers have forced each of these countries to accede to devolutionary pressures. In Ukraine, devolution is the only weapon Kiev has against Russian-backed separatists in the country's eastern provinces to keep them in the national orbit.

Devolution may not immediately lead to democracy as small newborn states such as South Sudan focus on internal stability. But it does remind us to see the trees rather than just the forest. It corrects for the tendency of states, as the Yale professor James Scott has elegantly pointed out, to ignore local context and impose inappropriate national preferences. Devolution is thus as important a check on the abuse of authority as democracy, if not more so.

Devolution is now more important than ever to stop the bloodletting in the many other civil wars that cost over 300,000 lives annually from Nigeria and Sudan to Syria and Iraq. Anthropologists of warfare such as John Keegan correctly remind us that conflict is a social activity intrinsic to human nature. A century ago in World War I, only 10 percent of fatalities were civilians, whereas since the Cold War 90 percent of casualties have been civilian and only 10 percent have been battlefield deaths.[4] Furthermore, close to fifty million people are internally displaced or international refugees, the highest number since World War II. As the contrarian strategist Edward Luttwak argued almost two decades ago, we should actively encourage partitions to defuse violent conflicts and accelerate the process of reconciliation.[5] However, rather than being haphazardly imposed from outside, as was the case between India and Pakistan in 1947, partition in more recent cases such as Yugoslavia and Iraq could have been preemptively negotiated—if not for the mythology of harmonious multiethnic democracy that reigned in Western capitals while populations on the ground were actively cleansing each other in the name of sectarian purity.

A century after Woodrow Wilson's Fourteen Points that called for the self-determination of peoples, devolution is needed more than ever. The traditional tool kit of aggressive military action often makes things worse: Where genuine desires for autonomy or federalism are ignored and suppressed, violent secessionist movements will likely follow. Secessionists are willing to give up their voice in one state for the sake of speaking to the world on their own terms; they won't be cheated out of their legitimate aspirations for self-rule. Indeed, self-determination should be seen as "pre-legal" in the sense that it reflects the will of peoples rather than the international law's bias toward existing states. Yet because of the political and logistical inconveniences of state birth, many diplomats and scholars seem to believe more in nations as they are rather than the nationalism that makes them possible. That is a mistake. Attempting to freeze the world's political map as it is now without correcting past mistakes is both reactionary and hypocritical. Two major remaining boundary disputes—Palestine and Kashmir—hail from mismanaged British mandates. How can we look back and not see that granting independence to both in the late 1940s would have averted decades of bloodshed and suffering? Whether one celebrates nationalism or finds it odious, it will decline as a force in politics only once more states are born.

The world of nation-states makes maps appear neat and tidy, but a map that appreciates legitimate differences would be far more humane. Sudan and Indonesia have ruthlessly suppressed provincial minorities, leading to the secession of South Sudan and East Timor. The fact that a violent power struggle ensued among South Sudanese factions upon its independence in 2011 does not mean that it should have remained in the clutches of genocidal leaders such as Sudan's Omar Bashir, nor does the fact that East Timor remains poor mean that it would have been better off remaining strangled by Jakarta. And then there is Kurdistan, whose people were tortured and gassed by Saddam Hussein but who have been quietly building their autonomy since the first Gulf War of 1990. It goes without saying that they deserve their own state.

Self-determination is a sign not of backward tribalism but of mature evolution: Remember that territorial nations are not our "natural" unit; people and societies are. We should not despair that secessionism is a moral failure, even if it recognizes innate tribal tendencies. A devolved world of local democracies is preferable to a world of large pseudo-democracies. Let the tribes win.

And yet the more nations there are, the smaller they are. Today almost 150 countries have populations of fewer than ten million people. They are more like city-regions than robust states. How could they possibly survive without connectedness? They have autonomy but not autarky: Basic agriculture and a modest army won't cut it in the twenty-first century. Even the extreme scenario of mapping hundreds—if not thousands—of autonomous cities and provinces would give the impression that political frictions have triumphed when in fact the opposite is true. That is why we must map the networks among them to truly appreciate the emergence of a connected world. Fragmentation is thus not the antithesis of globalization but its handmaiden.

This is the radical paradox at the heart of our increasingly borderless world: It has the maximum number of borders. Not a single border needs to "disappear" for the supply chain world to emerge. Rather, it is precisely the growing number of political borders that makes functional connectivity more necessary than ever.*

---

* Studies by the New England Complex Systems Institute (NECSI) underpin this "good fences make good neighbors" approach by which clear boundaries between linguistic and ethnic groups lead to more stability than forced coexistence. For example, the cultural communes of Switzerland's cantons have historically been separated from each other by rivers, mountains, and lakes—except for the canton of Jura, where French Catholics felt neglected by the dominant German Protestants, leading to arson and mild but regular political disturbances until the canton was split in 1979. And yet Switzerland's seamless infrastructure enables hundreds of thousands of Swiss who live in any canton to commute daily for work in another. Some predict that after several decades of internal harmonization, the number of cantons could (again) reduce itself from more than two dozen to just a few.

Devolution brings us much closer to the optimal scale of states than our present political maps suggest. In an ideal world, each political unit would be geographically contiguous (to avoid the added transportation burdens of operating separate exclaves), have a viable population size of anywhere from five to twenty million people (representing a sufficient internal market size), contain multiple well-built and populous cities with robust connectivity between them and to neighboring states, have diversified access to natural resources, and have efficient and accountable governance that enforces property rights and the rule of law. There are already city-states such as Singapore or cities-states such as Switzerland, Israel, and the United Arab Emirates (U.A.E.) that meet these criteria. Nations such as Estonia, Slovenia, and Uruguay also thrive despite their small populations and size due to their ethnic homogeneity, good governance, and international connections. Countries such as Lebanon and Bosnia have become too small and religiously mixed to fracture further; while they are certainly not role models of amicable ethnic coexistence, their principal cities, Beirut and Sarajevo, are good examples of the emerging urban-centric interdependence among small states. The connected world thus has an ironic rallying cry: The more borders, the better!

GROWING APART TO
STAY TOGETHER

Paradoxically, some of the largest countries in the world—either by size or by population—will hold together only if they pursue greater devolution. Whether India, Nigeria, Pakistan, or Myanmar, the most intractable and seemingly incurable internal violence— triggered by terrorism, assassination, external invasion, or ethnic secessionism—is fundamentally about how to geographically organize ethnic groups within postcolonial boundaries. With the exception of 9/11, the world's casualty count from terrorist violence year after year overwhelmingly stems from such local ethnic or sectarian grievances and territorial disputes.* The list of countries suffering the highest incidence of terrorist violence tellingly overlaps with the many unsettled ethno-geographies: the Ogaden and Ogoni in Nigeria, the Baluchis and Sindhis of Pakistan, Kashmiris in India, the Hmong and Rohingya in Myanmar, and other groups clamoring for a voice.[6] Few of these ethno-separatist groups could survive on their own. At the same time, none of the large countries they are in will become role models of multiethnic democracy either. Devolution is the only way they will succeed: Greater autonomy will bring greater stability.

The Kurds of Iraq, the Shia of Saudi Arabia, and the Arabs of Iranian Khuzestan are yet more suppressed minorities—with the added complication of sitting atop vast natural resources. As the Oxford economist Paul Collier has pointed out, such cases are simultaneously about identity, resources, and territory; they are about maps. Where decades-long civil wars have been ended through one-sided and often brutal imposition—Colombia, Angola, Sri Lanka—infrastructure has been crucial to stabilization and subsequent economic growth (if not yet widespread equitable development). Colombia struggled to get the upper hand in suppressing the FARC narco-insurgency during its decades-long civil war until it paved through mountainous jungles and built out a substantial road network for the army and police to assert themselves. Afghanistan won't enjoy national stability until it does the same. That is why President Ashraf Ghani is pushing for fifteen new border crossings with Pakistan and a transportation network to "connect South Asia to Central Asia."

Governments of frail multiethnic societies often fear that infrastructure will reinforce fissiparous tendencies inherent in the legacy of neglect, emboldening minorities to chart their own course. Yet these are precisely the conditions under which the devolution and development combination has helped two major Asian countries—

---

* Countries perennially experiencing the highest number of terrorist incidents include India, Pakistan, Palestine, Iraq, Nigeria, Yemen, and Somalia.

the Philippines and Indonesia—achieve territorial settlements and improve the fastest on the Fragile States Index.

The Philippines government, unable to defeat the Muslim Moro insurgency centered on the southern island of Mindanao, granted autonomous status to a swath of southern regions under the new name of Bangsamoro in 2012, knowing that investors were keen to access the region's rich deposits of coal, iron, and other minerals. Such federalism allows minorities to become provincial majorities and feel more secure within the country's federation and encourages them to demobilize while claiming their fair share of value from natural resources while paying less tax. Now it is the Bangsamoro government that has to deliver stability in order to benefit from investment and diminish its reliance on Manila, which still provides almost its entire budget. Similarly, the secession of East Timor from Indonesia in the late 1990s was a wake-up call, after which the government realized that the restive Aceh province of Sumatra would also break free unless it promised a larger share of revenue from forestry and other extractive sectors to the province. Indonesia's current modernization wave may yet hold the sprawling archipelago together as a collection of interconnected supply chain nodes.*

Large multiethnic states such as India, Pakistan, and Myanmar will also succeed only if they can harness resources, represent collective interests, and redistribute economic wealth to minimize separatist impulses. The Naxalites of eastern India, the Baluchis and Pashtuns of Pakistan, and the Kachin and Karen tribes of Myanmar regularly bloody the noses of the far more powerful governments that nominally rule them. These countries' numerous resource-related rebellions and insurgencies similarly require devolutionary compromise combined with infrastructure development. India

---

* One other civil war in the region, on the island of Bougainville in Papua New Guinea, was resolved in similar fashion. In the 1970s, Bougainville had the world's largest copper mine (then run by Rio Tinto) but descended into two decades of civil war. Only in the early years of the twenty-first century did a successful peace process result in a combination of cease-fire and greater autonomy for the island.

should know this well: Its number of states has more than doubled since independence in 1947 from fourteen to twenty-nine. The lesson from all these cases is that holding countries together generally requires political devolution, infrastructure investment, and the mutually beneficial exploitation of resources.

The same holds for large transition societies such as Russia. As the Soviet Union crumbled in the early 1990s, some provinces briefly began issuing their own passports. All eyes were on oil-rich and Muslim-populated Tatarstan, whose agitations have been a feature of Russian history for centuries. In their search for a racially pure motherland, Russian ethno-nationalists also called for the expulsion of such minority-populated republics. But with Russia in demographic free fall and nearly one-fifth of the country Muslim, Russia needs neither more Chechnya-style separatism nor the loss of large population centers. The interim solution is that Tatarstan has its own Moscow-approved president, Rustam Minnikhanov, and substantial economic autonomy. Minnikhanov travels the world like the president of his own country, with a retinue that includes bodyguards, translators, and key business figures including the heads of its burgeoning special investment zones who have already recruited Western car companies to set up plants and distribution centers there.

Tatarstan's proximity to Moscow means it will never become independent; its capital, Kazan, is a fabled city to Russians of all religions. Yet it is becoming a crucial node on the Eurasian "Iron Silk Road": In October 2014, Russia and China agreed to make Moscow-Kazan the first stretch on which to build a high-speed rail that will eventually continue all the way to Beijing. Remember the world's largest country's official name: Russian Federation.

FROM NATIONS
TO FEDERATIONS

Under the strongman Josip Broz Tito, Yugoslavia was a stable multiethnic federation and an important nonaligned Cold War swing
state. Upon his death, the manipulation of ethno-religious identity
and ensuing genocidal civil war ripped the country apart, leaving
behind Humpty Dumpty fragments. But there is a new ending to the
story. Once hypernationalistic Serbs and Croats have realized they
can no longer survive alone. Instead, two decades after its brutal
war of dissolution, this is what the former Yugoslavia has become:
a "Balkan free trade zone (FTZ)" of twenty million residents spanning six countries. Highway and rail projects are now connecting
central Europe to the south Balkans. One by one, each former Yugo-
slav republic is joining the eurozone and the EU. Ideally, they would
have leapfrogged to this solution, but political logic had to run its
course for functional logic to take over.

Still the task is not yet done. Bosnia today remains a precarious
multiethnic federation; its confusing, three-member, ethnically defined presidency is as much a reminder of its bloody civil war as an
escape from it. Proper stability and democracy seem unlikely until
basic ethnic and territorial grievances are sorted out. Jettisoning
the Serbia-leaning Republika Srpska and corresponding Croatia-
leaning western flank including scenic Mostar to join their more
favored nations would help qualify Bosnia to become an EU member (as Croatia is) or on the short-term path to it (as Serbia is) while
leaving Bosnia's Muslims to finally get their house in order without
ethnic politics hijacking yet another decade. Boundary agreements
are rarely perceived as fair by both sides, and yet they have the virtue
of bringing settlement and stability and the infrastructure and commerce that transcend those same borders.*

---

* The testiest border remains between Serbia and Kosovo, but a novel solution is now
in place: Kosovo taxes the imports that are usually smuggled through the Serb-populated
northern region but places the revenues in a special development fund for those same
Serb municipalities that is chaired by both countries' finance ministers and the EU.

Conflict resolution efforts of the past had different end states in mind such as maintaining multiethnic democratic unity within a single state. But today there are new horizons that emerge from giving each his own: more borders but more borderlessness at the same time.

Since the end of the Cold War, devolution in Europe has continued largely peacefully (the Ukraine-Russian war being the exception). Czechoslovakia experienced a "velvet divorce" in 1993, with both successor states subsequently joining the EU. In Spain's Basque Country and British Northern Island, devolution has come hand in hand with demobilization—laying down one's arms—leading to both disarmament and political stability. Belgium scarcely exists as a united country but is rather dissolving into linguistic kinships as its Dutch-speaking provinces gravitate toward the Netherlands, French-speaking regions drift toward France, Flemish craft their own identity and diplomacy, and Brussels serves as the EU's capital.

The archetype of the modern Western multiethnic, liberal democratic nation-state is being chipped away as cities and provinces make concrete cost-benefit calculations in their engagements with rent-seeking capital cities. Nations are becoming federations of powerful local administrative centers. In recent years, the Catalans and the Scots have also moved decisively toward greater autonomy, gaining the substance of independence without (yet) the style. They have achieved "dev-max"—maximum devolution. The center cannot win. When federal governments give an inch—as Tony Blair did by granting Scotland its own parliament in 1997—the Scots continue to want a full yard. When it suppresses the will of the people—as Madrid did by rejecting Catalunya's request for only the same degree of autonomy enjoyed by the Basques—it fuels waves of resentment. Before votes were even cast in Scotland's 2014 referendum, the British prime minister, David Cameron, and his team were so worried by sentiment swinging toward Scottish independence that they promised a raft of additional powers to Edinburgh (and Wales and Northern Ireland) such as the right to set its own taxes— granting even more concessions than Scotland's own parliament had demanded. Scotland won before it lost. Then only six months later in the British general election, the Scottish National Party nearly swept the entire parliament, guaranteeing maximum devolution on most policy matters while also continuing to expand its own international commercial strategies to draw investment. The best London can hope for is a more cooperative federalism in which responsibilities and ideas are shared across the union.

Londoners used to feel a divine right and privilege to run the entire country to which they belonged. Now they would just as soon divorce from it. London's gross value added per capita to the U.K. economy is more than $150,000 per year, more than triple that of the next largest contributor: Edinburgh. The more Scotland withdraws from the U.K., the more London will shoulder the burden of propping up England's depressed and depopulated regions—especially because 80 percent of all new jobs created in the U.K. since the financial crisis have been in London, which is growing by one million people per decade. More than half of all British university students head for London upon graduation. For Londoners (old and new), it doesn't seem a price worth paying. Several years ago at a dinner of British journalists, diplomats, and intellectuals, I was struck by how many of them viewed the rest of Britain as a liability sapping London's finances rather than a strategic asset. An informal statement headlined the evening: "Resolved: London should secede from the U.K."

The more peripheral areas witness—but don't partake in—the success of the center, the more they will push to seize control of their own affairs. Since the 1980s, conservative British governments packed up and sold off national industry to cheaper markets, with Scotland particularly harmed. And in the decade before the financial crisis, the top five British banks lent 84 percent of their portfolios to property and financial services centered on London, neglecting the entire rest of the country. Under the rubric of "Big Society," London's new devolution plan provides infrastructure loans to cities such as Manchester and Sheffield to develop their own urban regeneration plans and skills programs. But these are loans, *not* grants or investments; they must be paid back. The former Goldman Sachs executive Jim O'Neill has called for the creation of a super-region called "ManSheffLeedsPool" that would invest these funds into connective rail corridors between them while pushing for Scotland-like autonomy.

Demographics further ensure that devolution will continue to remap Britain, even in areas it has fought for decades to control. Northern Ireland's latter twentieth-century "Troubles" (which pitted the militant IRA against British counterterrorism forces) peaked when Protestants made up the majority of the population. Today, however, Catholics are overtaking them. This spells far greater autonomy for Northern Ireland if not outright independence or merger with Ireland. Even if the U.K. holds together, it is much more as a devolved kingdom.

The triumph of transparency, particularly over how tax revenue is distributed and spent, intensifies the devolutionary struggle. Since Philip II moved his royal court to Madrid in the sixteenth century, Madrid has been accustomed to seeing itself as the center of the universe, drawing in all the profits of empire before sharing them. A modern equivalent is to try to make sure flights arrive in Madrid first before connecting to Barcelona or Bilbao. But neither has any interest in being a second-class city given its own rich heritage. Instead, they use devolution as a tool of economic slipstreaming: Having maximized the benefits they get from Madrid, the Basque and Catalunya regions have also become the wealthiest in Spain. Flush with tourism revenues, Catalunya contributes almost double to federal coffers what it gets in return. In 2014, the province held a referendum in which 80 percent of the people supported independence, and in 2015 pro-independence groups claimed nearly half the seats in Catalunya's parliament. The Harvard- and MIT-trained brain trust of Catalonian economists that spearheads Catalunya's independence bid calls itself the Col·lectiu Wilson (Wilson Initiative). Another postmodern tool of devolution, of course, is to popularize the usage of Internet domains such as dot.cat for the Catalans and dot.eus for the Basques.

Secession is unconstitutional in both Spain and Italy, even if pursued through fully enfranchised provincial plebiscites. But devolution and connectivity enable such networked cities to reclaim their independent heritage. During the Middle Ages, Venice ran its own trading empire along the Adriatic coast, developed strong economic ties with the Byzantine Empire, and sent two hundred ships to capture the Syrian coast. Along with many other great European city-states of the premodern world, Venice was eventually subsumed into the nation-state order. But today, with Italy's national economy in shambles, little is stopping Venice from going it alone. In 2014, the province of Veneto in Italy actually declared independence, calculating that it receives only 5 euros in government services for every 7 it pays to Rome in taxes.

Italy's Northern League is also agitating for greater freedom from Rome's defunct political leadership, leaving the capital with little choice but to grant yet more devolution. In 2014, Italy began reorganizing into fourteen new jurisdictions called "metropolitan cities," each effectively an autonomous province responsible for pooling revenues and administering block grants from Rome. (France too began in 2015 to reorganize its administrative regions based on economic viability rather than historical and cultural pride.) The autonomous Italian island of Sardinia finds Italy so economically unsatisfying that a campaign has been launched to secede and offer itself to Switzerland as its twenty-seventh canton—Canton Marittimo—giving the landlocked Alpine country pristine Mediterranean beaches and strategic maritime geography.[7]

Devolutionary movements—whether for greater autonomy or outright secession—shrewdly seek to ensure that taxes and revenues are spent on the local population rather than transferred through corrupt capitals to less efficient regions. But they also tacitly seek the security of larger unions that spare them the costs of defense spending. Throughout the 1990s and the first decade of the twenty-first century, the question of Quebec's separatism hung existentially over all Canadians; passionate pleas were made to hold the world's second-largest country together. Yet by 2012, 50 percent of Canadians said they "don't care" what happens to Quebec. Having lost razor-thin independence referenda on multiple occasions, the Quebecois have been contented to act like their own Francophile nation but with diminished appetite for leaving the state. In western Canada and Western Australia, there is no question of independence: It's all about the money. Oil-rich Alberta and gas-rich Western Australia (the country's largest province responsible for half its exports) have set up their own wealth funds to retain resource revenues before sharing them with the national capitals, Ottawa and Canberra, respectively.

After centuries of bloody wars, Europe's devolutionary dynamic has even evolved into a form of commercial geographic arbitrage. Because the EU offers a larger institutional framework for new states to join, devolution is just the first step toward something larger. The EU is in this sense a giant Germany: a loose federation of multiple powerful centers. It strengthens member states' provinces through its shared parliament in Strasbourg while weakening national capitals by centralizing functional authorities in Brussels. But Europe has been able to recombine into a giant multistate society only because it is breaking down into nearly the maximum number of smaller units that have no other choice than peace with their neighbors. It goes without saying that an independent Scotland or Catalunya would join the EU after "leaving" the U.K. or Spain. The entire European Union is thus a reminder that local independence movements are not the antithesis of lofty post-national globalism but rather the essential path toward it.

CHAPTER 4

FROM DEVOLUTION TO AGGREGATION

GEOPOLITICAL DIALECTICS

D EVOLUTION HAS BECOME A UNIVERSAL PHENOMENON, DRIVEN by identity, urbanization, fiscal transparency, and other factors. But so is its opposite—aggregation—which advances through infrastructure connectivity, economic integration, labor migration, political reconciliation, and more fundamental trends. Devolution embodies local nationalisms in the short term, but itself brings about aggregation in the long term. The devolution-aggregation dynamic is thus a dialectic in the sense that the German philosopher G. W. F. Hegel truly meant: progression through opposites toward transcendence. Devolution-aggregation is how the world comes together by falling apart.

Aggregation is the next phase of history beyond political division. Every region of the world is proceeding through this accordion of fragmentation and unification. Eighteenth-century Europe had four major powers subsuming many far smaller principalities. The nineteenth-century post-Napoleonic Concert of Europe featured five major powers balancing each other and maintaining relative stability until World War I. After World War II, imperial efforts to singularly dominate Europe gave way to dismantling empires while

---

Maps 15, 16, 17, 18, and 19, corresponding to this chapter,
appear in the map inserts.

fusing nation-states such that Europe today has more than forty independent states while also aggregating into a single supranational European Union.

Africa's historical dynamic also illustrates cycles of fragmentation and integration. Before European colonization, Africa had approximately two dozen tribal kingdoms. By the nineteenth century, the entire continent was controlled by just five European powers. Since decolonization, Africa's map splintered again into fifty-four sovereign countries. But many of them are now finding ways to reconsolidate such that the continent's true functional map today boasts just four subregional groupings. African heads of state have announced plans for a continent-wide free trade zone by 2017.

Before colonialism, Southeast Asia was also dominated by several major indigenous empires such as the Sumatran Srivijaya, the Thai Ayutthaya, and the Khmer, after which the British came to control South Asia while the French and Dutch established large colonies spanning Indochina and Indonesia. Today, Southeast Asia is divided into a dozen separate countries yet is rapidly integrating both infrastructurally and institutionally into the single ASEAN group with EU-like aspirations.

In the new dialectic of devolution and aggregation, each region of the world is at various points along the arc from violent postcolonial separation to collective functional integration. Geopolitical evolution should be measured by this progress toward aggregation: Europe today is both the most legally devolved *and* the most supranationally integrated region, while Africa is still splintering in some areas while coming together in others. Eventually, every region of the world may arrive at a similar end state—functional geography over political geography—even if they take very different paths to get there.

There are two kinds of remapping going on in the world: exclusive and inclusive. We are most familiar with *exclusive* remapping, in which borderlines are shifted or new lines are demarcated. When secessionist groups carve out their own territory—such as Kosovo, East Timor, or South Sudan—a new nation's gain is a former master's loss. When one country unilaterally seizes another's territory for its own exploitation—such as Russia's annexation of Ukraine's Crimea or seizure of South Ossetia from Georgia—that too is exclusive remapping.

Particularly Russia's effective dismemberment of Ukraine raised alarm bells that the world is retreating into zero-sum territorial logic. The former Soviet space certainly presents other live cases: From Estonia to Moldova to the Caucasus and Central Asia, Russia constantly manipulates ethnic Russian minority populations with passports and propaganda. In the Caucasus, Armenia and Azerbaijan's violent confrontation over the disputed Armenian exclave of Nagorno-Karabakh within Azerbaijan also continues to fester. But even the volatile former Soviet space presents strong counterexamples: Georgia and Azerbaijan have moved from cultural condescension to shared growth due to the major Baku-Tbilisi-Ceyhan (BTC) pipeline linking them.*

While Ukraine is a reminder that the re-sorting of the post-Soviet space may drag on for decades, it is *inclusive* remapping that is far more the norm worldwide and is far more significant for the future geopolitical order. Inclusive remapping is occurring as countries use shared infrastructure, customs agreements, banking networks, and energy grids to evolve from political to functional spaces.

Europe has become the archetype of inclusive remapping. It took almost thirty years during the mid-nineteenth century for the German *Zollverein* (Customs Union) to evolve into the modern German state and a similar amount of time for the European Community to crystallize out of the wreckage of postwar Europe. Particularly since the end of the Cold War, Europe has focused much more on building bridges and tunnels than walls and trenches. There are no more military checkpoints on the German-French border; in fact, as you drive full speed on the Autobahn, the only official indication that one has crossed one of history's bloodiest international battle-

---

* Because Armenia was not included on the BTC route, there is no connective infrastructure reducing its ongoing territorial conflict with Azerbaijan over Nagorno-Karabakh.

fields is an EU flag and a *Bienvenue* sign. Similarly, instead of British and French navies patrolling the Strait of Dover, we have a "Chunnel" underneath with hourly high-speed rail service from London to Paris—and Amsterdam and Brussels.

EU countries are functionally inseparable, an egg that cannot be unscrambled. Their monetary system, transportation routes, energy grids, financial networks, and manufacturing supply chains are all heavily integrated. Each state is an administrative unit within a common framework of rules that supersede its national sovereignty, and each would benefit more from advancing the collective union further. Greeks may resent German stringency in bailing out its economy, but Greece's citizens can also move to Germany to find work. European countries' recent political bickering over sharing the costs of bailing out Mediterranean countries misses the longterm reality that connective integration propels them toward far greater collective growth than they would have achieved as discrete national economies. And indeed, Europe is actually still in the process of integration. It has learned that partial integration of monetary but not fiscal affairs leads to structural stagnation, while the emerging Banking Union, Capital Markets Union, and Digital Single Market will increase Europe's collective liquidity, market depth, and global leverage.

Across the world's regional clusters, the legacy of the tireless activist-diplomat visionary Jean Monnet, founding father of the European Union, is carrying the day: All are healing internal divisions and paving over borders through cross-border infrastructures backed by shared functional institutions; they are choosing flow over friction. The more connected states become, the less we can untangle them simply by pointing to their borders. Even maps that show a fully devolved political landscape are therefore utterly misleading, for they ignore the formation of regional commonwealths that allow countries, like atoms, to fuse into larger compounds.

The shift from sovereign space to administrative space is actually the logical consequence of the whole world being divided up into irreducible political units. Once borders are settled, countries search for optimal service areas for power and water utilities, telecoms and Internet cables, roads and railways. By creating overlapping functional zones, economies scale beyond their geographic limitations.

Especially in so-called frozen conflicts where exclusive remapping remains a continuous threat, inclusive strategies can diminish tensions: using shared infrastructure to enable both sides to benefit from connectivity. For example, today both the Greek and the Turkish populations of Cyprus want greater mobility across the barbedwire Green Line that divides the capital, Nicosia. Even though a far stronger Turkey will never give up its grip on the island's (unrecognized) North, both sides could massively gain from jointly pursuing a larger Mediterranean transshipment port to capture the surging volumes of Asian cargo bound for both Europe and North Africa. Kashmir is similarly divided into Indian- and Pakistani-controlled sectors by a contested Line of Control, yet trade is multiplying across their main border crossing. Even dangerous borders can be transcended.

In the end, even exclusive remapping leads to inclusive remapping. Indeed, often we need the former to get to the latter. Unresolved territorial tensions, arbitrary colonial border demarcations, and nationalist rivalries, often dating back centuries, continue to plague the Middle East, the Far East, and other regions as well. As some states disintegrate, others are born. The sooner misalignments are corrected and borders are settled, the sooner these regions can—as Europe has done—graduate from exclusive to inclusive remapping, focusing less on territorial frictions and more on connective flows. The two paths eventually lead to the same destination.

Inclusive aggregation is particularly visible today in the postcolonial regions that represent most of the world's countries and population. After World War II, decolonization brought freedom but also the intense insecurity of being thrust into self-reliance.* Since that time, a discernible pattern has emerged particularly in former

---

* As the Yale political scientist Bruce Russett has demonstrated, conflict is highest in regions such as the Middle East and Central Asia where there is low intra-regional trade and despotic rule.

British colonial regions such as Southeast Asia, South Asia, East Africa—and even hesitatingly in the Middle East: The first generation of independence-era leaders is nationalistic and suspicious of its former colonial brethren, jealously guarding its territory and fearful of encroachment. The second generation is more deferential, settling differences and cautiously engaging across borders where necessary. By the third generation, historical animosities have faded from memory, and few are alive to remember independence-era anxieties. Divisions are blamed on the British, while leaders push ahead with cross-border infrastructure projects, trade and investment agreements, and other cooperative projects. Generational change gives this gradual evolution from hostility to fraternity an organic inevitability. Instead of pushing problems off onto future generations, the new attitude is not to burden future generations with the threat of conflict. Once political geography is resolved, functional geography takes over. Flows become the solution to problems that frictions alone don't solve.

THE NEW GRAND TRUNK ROAD TO *PAX INDICA*

The Grand Trunk Road is no longer the world's most majestic road trip. The portion from Kabul to Jalalabad, while now a paved section of Afghanistan's new highway system, has endured more than a decade of suicide bombers attacking NATO convoys. Heading east from Jalalabad through the spectacular Khyber Pass, one enters Pakistan's restive tribal areas, where the government is struggling to build roads, power lines, and irrigation canals in a landscape beset by feudal rulers and Taliban insurgents. Another day of driving past the capital, Islamabad, and four hundred kilometers south to the cultural hub of Lahore brings you to the heavily armed Indian border at Wagah, famous for its goose-stepping daily flag-lowering ceremony. India is the longest stretch, and while the government has upgraded the northern flank of the "Golden Quadrilateral" from Delhi to Kolkata, much of the fifteen-hundred-kilometer route remains a morass of belching trucks, rickshaws, and stray cattle. Beyond the tedious border crossing into Bangladesh lie the final five hundred kilometers of swerving traffic and broken-down trucks to the port of Chittagong.

Over the years that I've driven the Grand Trunk Road's various national segments from the Hindu Kush Mountains to the Bay of Bengal, I've been on the lookout for archaeological and architectural reminders that this trade route predates the nations it crosses by more than two thousand years. From the ancient Mauryan Empire to the colonial British, the Grand Trunk Road has been upgraded and renamed every few centuries. Whatever name it goes by, across all of South Asia everyone knows it simply as the GT Road. Kipling had a more elegant term for this great artery: "a river of life."

Even if you merely fly this route, you can look down and see the slanted Radcliffe Line separating India and Pakistan just east of Lahore that so blatantly (and senselessly) bisects a perfectly organic natural geography. Lahore and Karachi, Delhi and Kolkata, Dhaka and Chittagong, lie in three separate countries, but uniting their harvests across the fertile Indo-Gangetic Plain would create the world's largest breadbasket. Given the existential dependence Pakistan, India, and Bangladesh all have on this corridor's agricultural productivity, resurrecting the Grand Trunk Road—and all the commercial linkages, water-sharing agreements, and cultural strength it represents—seems a better investment than endlessly guarding arbitrary colonial boundaries.

India was once the jewel in the British imperial crown, the heart of London's imperial Raj stretching from the Persian Gulf to the Strait of Malacca. Before partition, lengthy railways connected the whole subcontinent, with the famous Frontier Mail line running from Bombay to Peshawar. Today it stops at Amritsar and never crosses the border. Despite their track records as abusers of religious fundamentalism, both Pakistan's Nawaz Sharif and India's Narendra Modi have acted like economic and diplomatic pragmatists, pledging to extend existing rail connections from Karachi to Ahmedabad and open new ones. The most frequent current route, known as the Friendship Express, connects Delhi to Lahore. Given both countries' chronic energy shortages, yet more steel lines will be laid across their border in the coming years: gas pipelines from Iran and Turkmenistan. Five thousand years after the Indus valley civilization arose during the Bronze Age, a new *Pax Indica* is gradually emerging.

The Grand Trunk Road need not stop in Bangladesh. South Asian nations are so insurmountably hemmed in by the Indian Ocean, the Himalayas, and the Hindu Kush Mountains that even India can scarcely project power beyond the immediate region. Building through its neighbors is the only way to reach crucial energy supplies and markets in Central and Southeast Asia. Myanmar has thus become the site of jockeying for foreign influence as the country reduces the lock China has long held on its trade and investment. The mostly Buddhist nation of over fifty million was actually part of the British Raj until just before World War II and could in the not too distant future host an extended Grand Trunk Road down to Yangon. Indo-Burmese connectivity plans also include a gas pipeline stretching from Sittwe on the Bay of Bengal through India's northeastern states of Mizoram and Tripura and across central Bangladesh to Kolkata.

Myanmar also reveals how the perception of Indian-Chinese zero-sum competition in Southeast Asia won't necessarily play out as high-altitude warfare amid a nuclear backdrop. Instead, there is another major connective artery emerging to connect South and East Asia: the Stilwell Road, a crucial zigzagging supply route for the Chinese Nationalists of Chiang Kai-shek. Today the adjacent corners of northeast India, northern Bangladesh and Myanmar, and southern China are among the poorest areas of all four countries, comprising a patchwork of Buddhist, Muslim, and animist tribes whose neglect has fueled alienation and resentment of distant national capitals. But all four governments recently formed a BCIM*

---

* The unoriginal name BCIM (Bangladesh, China, India, Myanmar) is an acronym arranged to avoid sounding like the ICBM missile.

forum to invest in a multimodal corridor connecting over two thousand winding kilometers from Kolkata via Bangladesh's Sylhet
province and Mandalay in Myanmar to Kunming, bringing desperately needed investment to the deprived and isolated communities—
especially better roads, as drivers in the inaugural BCIM Kolkata to
Kunming Car Rally learned in 2013.

Two thousand years ago, monks traversed this mountainous terrain spreading Buddhism from India across East Asia. Today these
ancient and organic connections are reemerging, some sturdier than
ever. It takes several generations for colonial scars to heal, but the
end point is not merely accepting arbitrary postcolonial boundaries
but rather transcending them in favor of connective infrastructures.

FROM SPHERE OF INFLUENCE
TO *PAX ASEANA*

The former British colonies Singapore and Malaysia have become the
leading crucible of postcolonial fraternity replacing independence-
era hostility. In the 1960s, Singapore's Lee Kuan Yew pursued "independence through merger" with Malaysia—strength through size.
But after their acrimonious 1965 divorce, the two countries spent
several decades as rivals. Singapore's fear of a Malaysian invasion
motivated its strict, Israel-like military service requirement. But as
Singapore rose up the value chain and Malaysia modernized through
harnessing its oil deposits and forests, the two countries have graduated from suspicion to cautious interdependence to infrastructural
density to commercial integration. They failed to remain a political
federation fifty years ago but are becoming a functional federation
today.

Running right through the middle of Singapore is the narrow
twenty-kilometer Green Corridor of tall grass and weeds. Every few
kilometers are evidence of the erstwhile colonial unity of the Malaysian peninsula, starting with the art-deco-style Tanjong Pagar
railway station to rusted old train tracks and dilapidated wooden
shacks that served as waiting areas. While the Tanjong Pagar sta-

tion is now a museum, Singapore and Malaysia's twenty-first-century integration continues apace. Soon three major bridges will link Singapore to peninsular Malaysia to accommodate the growing numbers of businesspeople and shoppers shuttling back and forth to the thriving border province of Johor—with rapid digital clearance smoothing the journey.

Three times the size of Singapore, Johor is the perfect place for Singapore's property developers to build the large suburban developments and amusement parks there is little room for on their own side of the border. As of 2013, Singapore allows retirees to spend their pension funds on lower-cost health care in Malaysia as well. The Johor model has expanded northwest to Batu Pahat, where over $50 billion in investment since 2006 has boosted industries such as textiles, food processing, and electronics. The Batu Pahat–Malacca corridor is slated to get a large new technical university, upgraded port, and new airport. Development spreads along connective corridors.

Singapore and Malaysia have begun to include Indonesia in this axis through the creation of the Growth Triangle spanning Singapore, Johor, and Indonesia's Riau Islands of Batam and Bintan. It took a generation after Indonesia's first modern president Sukarno's militaristic *Konfrontasi* policies for the three countries' leaders to think less about borders and more in terms of land, labor, and capital. Singapore is an order of magnitude wealthier per capita than Malaysia, which in turn is far wealthier than Indonesia—though the total size of their economies was until very recently arranged in the reverse order. But Singapore is too small for the large-scale factories and shipyards that have instead been located on much larger Batam, just forty-five minutes away by ferry. Every New Yorker knows the phenomenon: As Manhattan has gotten crowded and expensive, offices and people have relocated to New Jersey. Offshore industrial zones also allow Singapore to fill labor shortages without adding to its social liabilities. And yet they catapult development in ways neither Indonesian dictatorship nor democracy has. When I cycled around Batam in late 2014, I saw rows of colorful, private two-story condominiums under construction for families of workers who just a few years earlier came from huts in Sumatran villages.

Singapore doesn't have a natural hinterland, but now it can buy and build one. Much like Hong Kong's integration into the Pearl River delta, the more investment, production, and other services become integrated across the three countries, the more they coordinate their master planning of infrastructure to maximize flows. When countries are willing to sell, trade, or open their territory to foreign governance at such large scale, it is a sign of the shift toward a supply chain world where optimizing economic geography supersedes preserving territorial sovereignty.

All of Southeast Asia is now aggregating according to the same logic. The regional diplomatic grouping called ASEAN was founded four decades ago on the mantra "Prosper thy neighbor," but Cold War politics prevented any such camaraderie. Since the region's hammering in the 1997–98 Asian financial crisis, however, the ASEAN Economic Community has risen to become the world's fifth-largest economic area with a GDP of over $2 trillion (behind the EU, the United States, China, and Japan) and attracts more FDI than China due to its youthful 650 million people. Even as it competes with China, ASEAN helps Asia strengthen its grip on global supply chains.[1] From 1990 to 2013, Asia's share of global manufacturing rose from 25 percent to 50 percent and will rise even further in the coming decade.

Disparity is an opportunity. The wealthiest tier of Asian economies (Japan, South Korea, coastal China, Singapore) can offshore production to the second tier (Vietnam, Thailand, and Malaysia), third tier (the Philippines, Indonesia, and India), or fourth tier (Cambodia, Laos, Myanmar) to save on labor costs while creating jobs and building regional markets. Toyota makes 20 percent of its vehicles in Thailand but has also expanded to produce in Indonesia, where it already has half the car market.* The Hong Kong–based

---

* Toyota's twin innovations of simplifying the number of components and accelerating toward just-in-time delivery ushered in a new era of lean management in global

Esquel, the world's largest cotton shirt manufacturer, makes its higher-end shirts in China and standard ones in Vietnam. A "single window" point-of-entry system is being deployed to allow traders to operate seamlessly across the region. By discovering and leveraging one another's comparative advantages—Myanmar's food production, Thailand's manufacturing, Indonesia's raw materials and cheap labor, Singapore's corporate governance and cash—they are finally becoming a whole greater than the sum of their parts. Each country even has a nickname in the emerging division of labor: Myanmar the "garden," Thailand the "kitchen," Laos the "battery," and so on. Even when they outsource to each other, therefore, Asia still wins.

Importantly, ASEAN countries are also integrating their capital markets to deepen the liquidity needed for long-term investments and avoid the whiplash that occurs when Western portfolio capital flows out as quickly as it flows in. Asians no longer need to make "round-trips"—investing in American money managers who then reinvest back in their economies. As their stock exchanges move toward multi-city listings, Ho Chi Minh City, Manila, Kuala Lumpur, and Jakarta—to say nothing of Singapore—have all built up central business districts that increasingly resemble Frankfurt, funneling capital into companies and projects across the region. Infrastructure, finance, and supply chains are the drivers of *Pax Aseana*.

If you live in Southeast Asia, not a week goes by without a news item related to the region's advancing cross-border railways. China now leads the world in high-speed rail construction and is actively extending railways southward just as it has to its north and west. A Kunming-Bangkok line has been approved cutting through Laos—a $6.2 billion project worth more than the entire Laotian GDP—to be built by fifty thousand Chinese workers erecting half a dozen bridges

---

supply chains. But since the Taiwan earthquake in 1999 and the Japanese tsunami of 2011, companies learned not to over-concentrate the production of critical components in a single geography that, if suddenly lost, would send shock waves through the system. Japanese and Taiwanese companies now ensure that they distribute their industrial capacity to include backup areas in the event of natural disasters.

and carving seventy-six tunnels.* Laos, like Kyrgyzstan or Mongolia, is another country whose political map tells us ever less about how it's actually run. The Mekong River with Thailand and the Annamite mountain range with Vietnam are natural boundaries, but as rail networks and power lines from giant foreign-financed hydroelectric stations crisscross this once isolated sliver of a nation, the country will be a crucial electricity supplier to Thailand, which is desperate to avoid the rolling blackouts of the past decade as it struggles to pump out nearly two million cars per year for almost all the major auto manufacturers. Once the Kunming railway crosses Laos and reaches Bangkok, it will smoothly connect to another high-speed linkage to Kuala Lumpur and Singapore, or toward Myanmar, to both Yangon and its port so that it can serve as the conduit for transit from the Andaman Sea back through Thailand to China.

This north-south rail artery eventually connecting Asia's southernmost tip at Singapore to its northeast Asian hubs of Shanghai and Beijing will be the vertical axis of eastern Eurasia—the industrial counterpart to the Mekong River that flows southward from Tibet to Vietnam. This Greater Mekong Subregion of six countries—with Bangkok as its effective capital—covering an area one-third the size of the United States now has over 700,000 kilometers of roads and 15,000 kilometers of railways and a GDP nearing $1 trillion. East-west corridors crisscrossing from Myanmar to Vietnam funded by the Asian Development Bank will further deepen Indochina's organic unity.

China's downstream mission remains unchanged: to alleviate Southeast Asia's bottlenecks both to extract resources from smaller neighbors and to cut through them to the Bay of Bengal and the Andaman Sea. After decades under intense global sanctions, Myanmar has gone from walled off on three sides to opening to China, Southeast Asia, and India in rapid succession. As the first power to engage when Myanmar's border trade was legalized in the 1980s,

---

* China could have paid for Laos's portion but instead issued it a loan that will have to be paid back through mining concessions. China will also provide substantial financing and construction for a high-speed railway line in Indonesia.

China has capitalized on what is a centuries-old history of Sino-Burmese seasonal migration, especially in provinces such as Shan State where China and Myanmar blur together. Chinese companies operate mines in Shan, pipelines cross through it, the yuan can be used as currency there, and mixed marriages are rising.* Carving through Southeast Asia is no longer about borders but about the management of flows and frictions.

ASEAN's businesspeople, workers, students, and tourists now ferry across the region in record numbers on the back of low-cost carriers such as AirAsia, which has done as much for regional integration as any diplomatic body. Demographic shifts guarantee that Asia's blending will continue: The erstwhile "Asian Tigers" such as Singapore and Taiwan—to say nothing of much larger China and Japan—are aging, while Indonesia and the Philippines are full of youthful labor. Over 250,000 Burmese live in Thailand alone, without which the micro-economy would grind to a halt just as many American cities and towns would without Mexicans. As in Europe, a generation of post-national Southeast Asians is being born.

FROM "SCRAMBLE FOR AFRICA" TO *PAX AFRICANA*

Unscrambling Africa

Everyone seems to have a one-word answer to the plight of African nations today: "democracy," "secession," "micro-credit," "literacy," "vaccines." But African states won't survive at all without basic physical infrastructure. What will make the difference between celebrating independence and achieving success in Africa is not just political nation building but physical state building—both within and across borders.

Africa has never had a time-out period to pause and decide how to best organize itself without outside interference. Its geopolitical

---

* China has also been accused of backing the ethnic Kokang rebels of the United Wa State Army operating along their border.

complexity is the result of the layering of two centuries of European colonialism, a dozen major independence movements after World War II, the Cold War maneuverings that supported some of them while thwarting others, and the globalization of its commodities industries, which has brought in powerful foreign supply chain operators.

Many of Africa's interstate boundaries are visible only if one overlays the geometric grid of latitude and longitude, which European colonialists used rather than any sensible respect for cultural geography to draw the continent's many straight-line borders. Colonial powers only haphazardly cobbled together African states; they didn't knit together cohesive societies. The considerations that should guide the design of administrative space—natural geography, demographic commonality, and economic viability—were mostly ignored in Europe's nineteenth-century "Scramble for Africa." As a result of divide-and-rule colonialism, its 850 partitioned ethnic groups suffer a far higher incidence of civil wars and conflict spillover than unified national groups.[2] The Masai, for example, are two-thirds in Kenya and one-third in Tanzania; the Anyi are 60 percent in Ghana and 40 percent in the Ivory Coast; the Chewa are split across Mozambique, Malawi, and Zimbabwe; the Hausa across Nigeria and Niger. Mali and Burkina Faso, Senegal and Gambia, and other sets of African states exhibit how poor demarcation and divided populations cause chronic cartographic stress that diverts attention from development. Somali tribes have been divided by three different colonizers—Italy, Britain, and Ethiopia—and are now spread across Somalia, Kenya, Eritrea, and Djibouti, leading both to irredentist movements for a Greater Somalia and to Somalia's internal chaos spilling over into neighboring Kenya. There are traditional border wars as well, such as Ethiopia's clinging to territory recently awarded to Eritrea by a tribunal.

More than one dozen African states are landlocked—unable to access the sea—the most of any continent. Africa's ethnic and territorial fracturing is only compounded by its lack of navigable rivers that would promote cross-border trade, making it much more a collection of disparate subregions than a coherent continent. An accurate portrait of Africa is thus far more diffuse than today's map of fifty-four nominally independent countries suggests. Congo, the continent's largest country, is widely described as a "hole in the middle of Africa." Its ground reality more resembles isolated enclaves than a coherent place.

African states are either large and weak or small and weak. But make no mistake: All fifty-four of them are weak. In the seventy years since decolonization, infrastructure has decayed while populations have tripled. Fifteen of the twenty most fragile states in the world are in Africa. The continent's old power brokers—South Africa, Libya, and Egypt—have degenerated or collapsed since the end of the Cold War, while its new drivers—Nigeria, Angola, Rwanda, Kenya, and Ethiopia—are each vulnerable to ethnic, sectarian, resource, or political conflict. It says something about Africa that two small and poor countries—Chad and Rwanda—have staged military interventions in two of the largest, Nigeria and Congo.

The only way to overcome the contingencies of history is through the one-two punch of foreign investment and infrastructure development, which together boost productivity and export efficiency. In the past decade, high commodities prices catapulted seven resource-rich sub-Saharan African states such as landlocked Rwanda, Botswana, and Zambia, as well as coastal Ghana and Angola, into the top ten fastest-growing countries in the world. In all cases, inserting themselves into global supply chains has made the difference. Now Kenya, Mozambique, and Tanzania are also tapping large offshore energy reserves that will quickly deepen their ties across the Indian Ocean to thirsty Asian customers.

As many postcolonial states disintegrate, they will not be magically replaced by functional democracies. Instead, functional pockets such as special economic zones are popping up on an unprecedented scale. They are governed less by national capitals than by the domestic-foreign, public-private supply chain. Postcolonial suspicions and trade barriers have meant that Africa has been trading more with the rest of the world than with itself. But as in

Asia, building supply chains is leading to commercial integration. African states can be stronger if they leapfrog toward such larger agglomerations beyond their postcolonial boundaries. Africa is so large, though, that this will happen not all at once but in subregional clusters. Africa will achieve a broad renaissance only if its many micro-economies fuse into just a few. Infrastructure is transforming Africa's map into what it should be.

From China with Love

For centuries, European colonial powers sought an edge in their African maneuverings by financing infrastructure projects. Today it is China's turn to cultivate Africa's resources while finding ways to mitigate its own risks. Already in the 1970s, China built a nearly two-thousand-kilometer railway linking Dar es Salaam on Tanzania's Indian Ocean coast to landlocked Zambia. Now it is financing and building Sudan's Merowe Dam, a railway and pipeline from South Sudan to the Indian Ocean, and rebuilding Kenya's railway to Lake Victoria (which British Indian labor laid down a century ago). What look like big-ticket resource and infrastructure deals are effectively barter arrangements: Chinese construction services in exchange for millions of tons of raw materials. Africa's fragile states need Chinese-built (and often Chinese-financed) infrastructure to modernize their societies, cope with demographic stress, and aggregate their economies. Despite the World Bank's legacy of financing postwar reconstruction, in the 1960s it shifted its aid focus away from infrastructure, leaving basic irrigation, transportation, and electrification systems underdeveloped. China has stepped in as a new and symbiotic partner. China is therefore not "buying the world" per se but *building* it in exchange for natural resources.

Today China is the greatest force evolving Africa beyond its artificial European colonial borders because it is paving over them with sturdy infrastructures reaching deep into landlocked countries such as Congo and Zambia (or digging under them to install a fiber-optic cable grid across West Africa). Rail lines that were cut by independence-era strongmen are being restored with the full muscle of Chinese overseas industrial support. The most ambitious is the Chinese-financed Lamu Port–Southern Sudan–Ethiopia Transport Corridor that will crisscross Kenya and create a multi-country railway web north to Addis Ababa, south to Juba, and west into Uganda to export its newfound gas reserves. And yet China is not a new colonialist: It wants neither useless territory nor more hungry mouths to feed. It is a new mercantilist: It wants the supply chain and only the supply chain.

Even if the next railroad from Cairo to Cape Town is built by China instead of Britain, it may still serve to bring about a genuine Africa for Africans—a *Pax Africana*. Good infrastructure and institutions are the only cure for bad geography. Kenya, Uganda, and Rwanda have become like the Benelux (Belgium-Netherlands-Luxembourg) states of Africa, building an integrated core that extends tethers into neighbors and draws them closer together as well. A commercial-diplomatic-legal division of labor has emerged where countries take the lead on collective issues such as the location of ports, formation of investment promotion boards, and structuring of a potential monetary union. Rwanda and Burundi are now hubs for major railway, pipeline, and inland waterway projects (known as the Northern and Central Corridors) across Kenya and Tanzania that will bring their minerals—and those of Congo's far eastern Kivu province—to the Indian Ocean. The Mombasa-Kampala-Kigali railway stretches over fifteen hundred kilometers through four countries, mostly Tanzania, where the Australian-run Mkuju River Project is making Tanzania one of the largest uranium producers in the world. As African resources from the interior accelerate toward the Indian Ocean coast, ports such as Mombasa and Dar es Salaam must rapidly modernize to cut their costly on- and off-loading delays.*

---

* South African ports are also intolerably backlogged even though 96 percent of the country's exports exit the country on ships, which is why starting in 2010 the Ngqura port on the eastern cape set up the Coega Industrial Development Zone and has hired more than twenty-five thousand people in its upgraded logistics clusters.

What begins as one country trading and transiting goods via neighbors until they reach the sea has leapfrogged to a new plane. From railways to power grids, East African infrastructure is becoming regional rather than national. The Pan-African Infrastructure Development Fund has begun channeling a planned $50 billion per year into airports, dams, and highways, as well as cross-border transport linkages and electricity, agriculture, and manufacturing supply chains, each with its own public-private planning, fundraising, and execution strategy. Continent-wide, Africans now rank only behind Europeans as the largest source of investment across Africa. The African Development Bank has launched close to $10 billion in public-private infrastructure projects since 2008 and a Nasdaq-listed infrastructure fund in 2014. The coming decade will witness dozens of new multilateral projects that will remap the face of Africa. Ethiopia's Renaissance Dam could generate up to six thousand megawatts of power, tripling the country's electricity supply. The Great Inga Dam on the Congo River could generate forty thousand megawatts (more than China's Three Gorges Dam) and provide electricity to several hundred million people.

Connectivity corridors merge transportation and electricity networks into a single system that is co-owned by all parties—as well as foreign investors and operators. China is thus not so much conquering Africa as enabling it to aggregate and become more attractive to global investors, including China. Bringing down borders also makes Africa more attractive to tourists, a crucial source of hard revenue: In the Chobe River region where Zambia, Zimbabwe, Botswana, and Namibia converge, border crossings have been alleviated so that visitors can focus on pursuing wild elephants rather than getting visas stamped.

Try to imagine Ethiopia's nearly 100 million people today without Chinese investment and supply chains. While Ethiopia successfully warded off any long-term colonization by Europeans, it is a landlocked country with the continent's second-largest population and ranks among the lowest in human development. As China makes the country its bridgehead into Africa, however, it has built a

780-kilometer railway connecting Addis Ababa to the Port of Djibouti to speed up exports. China's spending on Ethiopia's roads has further given it a functional transportation network that benefits farmers and food distribution to malnourished citizens while helping tourists spread outside Addis Ababa to Axum and other sites of millennia-old rock-carved Orthodox Christian churches. Thanks to the combination of foreign investment, infrastructure development, job creation, and progressive leadership, the country that was once the poster child for African starvation is touted as Africa's next economic powerhouse.

But Africa will graduate from supplier to market only if it further builds out road networks China has begun, trains more youth in infrastructure management from ports to railways, and spends resource revenues on sustainable development. Supply chains, then, are where Western demands for good governance and Asia's demand for resources come together. Chinese connectivity makes Western political goals possible.

After beginning to smooth African supply chains, China is now searching for ways to protect them. Already China funds and contributes to major African peacekeeping operations, and dozens of private military companies protect China's resource installations across the continent as well. But in recent years, there has been an uptick in the kidnapping and murder of Chinese workers from Nigeria to Sudan. In Angola, home to an estimated 300,000 Chinese workers, low oil prices combined with almost nonexistent job creation for locals could lead to wanton violence against those perceived as being a self-serving foreign horde. If anti-Chinese blowback takes hold, African countries may evict the Chinese and emerge as champions of newly acquired, Chinese-built, cross-border roads, railways, and pipelines. It is too soon to tell whether Africa will pull together or succumb to another round of divide and rule. The answer will reveal itself only by watching the supply chain tug-of-war.

FROM SYKES-PICOT
TO *PAX ARABIA*

While embedded with U.S. Special Operations Forces in 2007, I witnessed firsthand America's incredible ability to apply technology to the battlefield. The digital map layered on Iraq's topography was rich with satellite feeds, drone surveillance, heat maps of local violence, real-time situation reports from troops on the ground, and other forms of human and signals intelligence. With about two hours' notice, special ops teams could strike anywhere in the country. During the so-called surge, the "op tempo" was relentless, and yet the coalition's ability to hold Iraq together was fleeting at best. One cool and cloudy night, while walking around Balad Air Base northwest of Baghdad with a senior commander, I asked him point-blank, "Are all these gizmos necessary because you can't speak Arabic?"

Political goals imposed on a complex cultural geography from halfway around the world stand little chance of surviving even a year. To their credit, American commanders did not bat an eye during my briefings that debunked the Bush administration's blind faith in the inevitability of a unified, multiethnic, democratic, pro-American Iraq. Sitting in the middle of a country that didn't really exist, they were as keen to understand alternative scenarios as they were to play "whack-a-mole" against al-Qaeda and other insurgent groups.

The Arab Spring and sudden state collapse across the region were shocks to many Middle Eastern countries. Decades of corrupt rule, infrastructure neglect, burgeoning populations, and social decay exposed arbitrary regimes—and the state itself—to be fragile fictions.* Even the so-called deep state of military and intelligence elites has withered, leaving behind a power vacuum filled either by chaos and radicalism or by political cockfighting. It is precisely be-

---

* Four-fifths of all civil wars since 1970 have occurred in countries with a median age below twenty-five, precisely the Arab world's demographic profile.

cause Libya has ceased to be a coherent state that its map requires more explanatory detail about the location of its still-functioning oil terminals, which tribes and militias actually hold sway in which cities and towns, and which neighboring countries rebels and migrants are passing from.* In both Libya and Yemen, the U.S. military has negotiated with the rebels to maintain safe passage for oil tankers. The supply chain outlasts the state, and controlling the supply chains determines who controls what is left of it.

It is important to note that most of the world's Muslims live not in the Middle East but in the South Asia and Pacific regions—from Pakistan to Indonesia—with no religious violence as grotesque in magnitude as the Arab world's current degeneration. Both the problem and the solution, therefore, lie as much in political geography and governance as in religion. Indeed, the region's sectarian divisions are far more political than theological, with barely understood and doctrinal differences inflated to mask nakedly political and territorial objectives.

The disintegration of major Arab states from Libya to Syria and Iraq is an invitation to rethink the principal lines that define the Middle East's geography. With hundreds of thousands of casualties from the civil wars in Iraq and Syria, and neighboring states such as Lebanon and Jordan pulled into the vortex, the current Arab convulsions have been likened to Europe's Thirty Years' War. Arabs are now more concerned with their internal stability than external threats, and establishing their next map may take several decades. Indeed, Libya, Syria, and Iraq are still so chaotic that they cannot yet be sensibly partitioned. But given the experience the Arab world already has with Islamic caliphates, foreign colonization, imperial suzerainty, insecure statehood, fitful pan-Arabism, tragic civil wars, and now widespread state collapse, it would be wise to learn from the past rather than repeat it.

The Arab world is ripe for reorganization. Rather than the futile

---

* In 2015, Tunisia began construction of an approximately 120-kilometer fence on its Libyan border.

pursuit of artificial national pillars under corrupt strongmen, the region must recover its historical cartography of internal connectivity. So dire is the decay of the region's postcolonial system that even many Arabs—not just Turks—speak yearningly of the Ottoman Empire. As the historian Philip Mansel has documented, for three centuries the Ottoman Empire was the *anti*-clash of civilizations, a polyglot and multireligious domain of mosques, synagogues, and churches. From Egyptian Alexandria to Turkish Smyrna (now Izmir) to Beirut, "dialogue trumped conflict, deals came before ideals."[3] Though allusions to Ottoman-era openness intrinsically imply Sunni dominance, this is not incompatible with broader regional peace. Since the early eighteenth century, Ottomans and Persians coexisted within the framework of an Islamic *ummah,* and in 1847 the Ottomans and Qajar Iran signed the Treaty of Erzurum that codified long-lasting peaceful relations. Boundaries were perpetually negotiated for centuries, but they remained open. Imagine this past as a guide to dealing with Iran today. Rather than decades of a failed isolation policy focused exclusively on nuclear weapons and terrorism—one that has witnessed Iranian influence actually *increase* in Lebanon, Syria, and Iraq, while its nuclear program continues—greater openness could enable far more commerce across the Arab and Persian worlds and build mutual understanding. The virtues of tolerance and coexistence will come to the Middle East through a combination of "to each his own" cartographic remapping and supply chain interdependence.

A similar paradigm for the future—a *Pax Arabia*—would consciously build such fluid connectivity among urban oases to collectively enrich the region. Recall that it was Phoenician city-states such as Tyre in present-day Lebanon that sent forth merchants and explorers to settle colonies on Aegean and Mediterranean islands such as Sicily, in southern Spain, and at Carthage in North Africa. Indeed, from Tunis and Beirut to Damascus and Baghdad, some of history's most successful trading centers have been Arab cities, a reminder that the Arab world is almost entirely urbanized. Its natural map *is* that of commercially oriented city centers with ties to the

European, Turkic, and Persian realms—a legacy far richer than what the past century has produced.

Exactly a century ago, the Sykes-Picot (1916) and San Remo (1920) agreements carved up the Middle East, turning Ottoman protectorates into feeble Western client states, after which they became strongman dictatorships. But Lebanon's civil war, the Iran-Iraq War, the U.S. invasion of Iraq and its aftermath, the Arab Spring, Libya's dissolution into anarchy, Shia control of Basra and sectarian cleansing of Baghdad, Kurdistan's moves toward independence, and Syria's civil war have all fractured the real map of the region beyond recognition. In 2014, then Iraqi prime minister, Nouri al-Maliki, proposed the creation of four new provinces to appease Turkmen and Christians—both of whom within a year found themselves under sustained attack by ISIS. With or without sovereignty, ISIS quickly became as functional a state as any number of its Arab neighbors, raising capital, issuing its own currency and passports, and broadcasting its propaganda worldwide to millions of adventure-seeking or marginalized youth, thousands of whom have flocked to join its cause from as far away as America and Australia. Sectarian conflict and the radicalized jihad diaspora could continue to spread across the region and bring down weak states such as Jordan, and a Saudi-Iranian proxy war in Iraq could destroy what little is left of that country.

ISIS demonstrated how borderless the Arab world is by rapidly conjoining Syria's Deir al-Zor and Iraq's Anbar provinces into a rump "Syriraq," with further ambitions to capture all of the historically amorphous *Al-Sham* (Greater Syria). In Afghanistan, it declared an equally vast and border-spanning Khorasan province. ISIS aspires to establish a state-like caliphate, but its strategy is to control infrastructure—dams, pipelines, refineries, and roads—while cutting off supplies such as water to Iraqi cities. The map of ISIS-held areas looks not like a two-dimensional patch but like an octopus of tentacles extending along the "jihad highways" it controls extending outward from its strongholds in Anbar province. The Sykes-Picot map has given way to the National Geospatial-

Intelligence Agency's real-time plotting of satellite feeds of oil trucks and financial data on black-market oil sales to capture the shifting of ISIS's supply lines. We cannot know today whether Anbar will remain an ISIS stronghold, return to Iraqi control, become an annex of Saudi Arabia's Northern Borders province—or whether ISIS will succeed in partitioning Saudi Arabia as well.

As borders collapse, demographics blend. From the half a million Palestinians in Kuwait to the one million Egyptians in Libya, the fluidity of the Arab labor force has been crucial to physical state building across the region. But the past decade's implosions of Iraq and Syria have created a refugee crisis that the UNHCR director has described as "not an increasing trend, but a quantum leap."[4] There are at least 15 million refugees or internally displaced people from Syria and Iraq. With one-third of its 6 million population already of Palestinian descendant and close to 1 million refugees from Syria and Iraq, Jordan is effectively a giant refugee camp where people are "warehoused" in stateless administrative areas that have become semipermanent cities. Zaatari in northern Jordan houses over 100,000 Syrians, making it the fourth-largest city in the country. The World Food Programme head remarked, "We don't look at Zaatari as a camp anymore, but as a municipality or a town."[5]

The space in between the region's civilizational anchors—Turkey, Saudi Arabia, Egypt, and Iran—is now up for grabs. Iraqi nationalism is meaningless, and Syria is an artificial failed state. Given its sectarian diversity and rugged topography, it is destined to devolve further, with Damascus and Aleppo remaining autonomous commercial hubs. The entire region is experiencing Lebanonization: sectarian towns at various distances from more multiethnic capitals. The Middle East, it has long been argued, is but a collection of "tribes with flags." Today tribes such as the Kurds that have no state have far more meaningful nationalism than Jordanians or Lebanese who do. Indeed, tribal states that hold their ground such as Kurdistan and Israel are the anchors of the region's future map.

Erbil, one of the oldest continuously inhabited cities in the world, now stands as the central hub of the Kurdistan proto-state.

While Kurdistan's political geography remains confined to the KRG region of Iraq, its effective sphere of influence stretches outside these borders into Kurdish-populated areas of Turkey, Syria, Iraq, and Iran. This does not mean that Kurdistan will seek to further expand. To the contrary, Kurdistan has dug ditches along its Syrian border to prevent Syrian Kurds from taking a greater share of the border smuggling business via Turkey and to maintain leverage over them. Kurdistan has outlasted its most recent colonizer, Saddam Hussein's Iraq, and expanded control over the rich oil deposits of Kirkuk. Even before formally getting Baghdad's approval, the Kurds signed numerous oil deals with Western majors such as Exxon and now export oil from Kirkuk to the junction of Kurdistan, Syria, and Turkey, from which it flows onward to the Mediterranean port of Ceyhan. Seeking a buffer between itself and Arab turbulence, Turkey has actually become Kurdistan's patron despite decades of officially denying the existence of an independent Kurdish identity (Kurds were referred to as mountain Turks). Kurdistan remains a landlocked territory, but one with self-governance and two outlets for its oil reserves: Turkey and Iraq. It shares a nation with neither but supply chains with both. Preserving these corridors matters more than statehood—for now.

The Humpty Dumpty states of the Arab world will not be put back together again: The region is on course for more devolution, but aggregation is still far away. Getting from the current apocalypse to a higher stage of Arab self-organization will therefore be a marathon. At present, only the Gulf Cooperation Council (GCC) core of petro-powers has begun the integration process. Even though Saudi Arabia has effectively annexed Bahrain* and tried to block the construction of a bridge linking Qatar to the U.A.E., major projects such as a planned high-speed rail link along the entire southern Gulf perimeter and the Dolphin pipeline from Qatar to Oman are

---

* With a Sunni minority ruling over a Shia majority, Bahrain has been the only one of the wealthy Arab Gulf countries to face a major violent uprising since the Arab Spring began in 2011.

all moving forward alongside greater labor mobility, speedier customs clearance, and an eventual monetary union. With their own stability threatened by the chaos in Syria and Yemen, GCC countries also anchor the nascent pan-Arab military force while manipulating political factions and militias in Egypt as well as Lebanon and Syria.

Even with its political geography in flux, Arab civilization has the cultural commonalities and wealth to advance a new functional connectivity. Jordan, Syria, and Iraq have served as the eastern edge of the Roman Empire, the seat of great caliphates, and the site of European competition for spheres of influence, but they have only ever been powerful when unified. Unlike the caliphate eras, however, the future *Pax Arabia* should have multiple capitals such as Cairo, Dubai, and Baghdad—a borderless archipelago of connected urban nodes. If one rule of counterinsurgency is to find, protect, and build stable enclaves, that is also the right bottom-up approach to replacing Arab colonial cartography with a more legitimate order of urban hubs and their trade routes. The Ottoman era Hejaz Railway, which stretched from Istanbul to Mecca, with branches to Cairo and even Haifa in present-day Israel, is precisely the intercity model that should guide our thinking. Arabs reject a restoration of Turkish or Persian hegemony, but if they ever want to recover the vast geographic strength they enjoyed a millennium ago, it will have to be through connective cartography.

THE ISRAELI EXCEPTION?

Ever since claiming its territory and achieving independence in 1948, Israel is the one country that has constantly tried to escape its geography, whether through its diaspora in the West, alliance with the United States, membership in European associations, and now energy linkages across the Mediterranean. But infrastructure, demographics, and economics paint a more complex picture of how Israel is becoming more embedded with its neighbors rather than less. Indeed,

Israel's tentacles across the region include $500 million in software exports and agricultural and medical equipment to the GCC countries (to which it has also opened a "virtual embassy"), strong backing of Kurdistan's energy infrastructure, and $7 billion in railway investments intended to eventually extend through Jordan, Egypt, and even Lebanon.

The Israeli-Palestinian dynamic also embodies this complex flow and friction. The nearly impenetrable security barrier through the West Bank represents the fortification of Israel's core. But what can't be crossed over ground has been crossed underground through dozens of so-called terror tunnels, with Hamas in Gaza (and Hezbollah in Lebanon) digging their way under the Israeli border to attack and kidnap Israel Defense Forces soldiers. And yet the security barrier is by no means meant to represent a future border. To the contrary, in 2014, Israel passed a bill declaring the country an exclusive nation-state of Jews, with the fence serving as an internal security mechanism rather than an international boundary—so much for the two-state solution.[6] Within this Greater Israel, however, there are new passages that promote flows such as Jerusalem's expanded light-rail that runs along the 1948 Green Line through settlements and past holy sites, carrying a mélange of Orthodox Jews, Palestinian youth, and Israeli soldiers. The city's business-oriented mayor sees transportation infrastructure as a tool to promote decent treatment and equal opportunities for Palestinians. In the West Bank, Israel builds not only controversial settlements but also entirely desirable industrial zones that do food packaging, textiles, and furniture assembly serving both the Israeli and the Palestinian economies and workers.[7] The Palestinian capital, Ramallah, feels increasingly like the proper administrative center of a nation, even if not an independent one, with a new low-cost residential and commercial development called Rawabi under construction.

If the Palestinians' own factionalism prevents them from

pursuing independence, they can still pursue infrastructural connectivity in the form of the "Arc" of roads and railways connecting West Bank towns north to south from Jenin through Nablus, Ramallah, East Jerusalem, Bethlehem, and Hebron and crossing Israel to Gaza, where the Palestinians could have an airport and seaport. Such a functional passage would not only strengthen the Palestinian economy despite its legal limbo but also enable a broader Arab cartographic contiguity from Egypt via the Sinai through the Palestinian territories to Jordan.

In 1845, when the French colonial government in Algeria agreed with Morocco to demarcate their border, they stopped 165 kilometers south of the Mediterranean because "a territory without water is uninhabitable, so boundaries are superfluous." And indeed they are: Even after the fruitless "Sand War" of 1963, the two countries continued to share the Tindouf region's iron ore revenue. By 2006, they had reciprocally removed visa requirements. Even the bitterest Arab rivals eventually learn to cooperate.

Arab nations' geologic characteristics are more important than their political ones: They are either oil rich, oil poor, water rich, or water poor. With water scarcity threatening the very survival of countries like Yemen and Jordan, Arabs and their neighbors must build more water canals, pipelines, and railways rather than military checkpoints. For example, Israel, Jordan, and the Palestinians all favor a Red Sea–Dead Sea canal running along the Israel-Jordan border to provide potable water and irrigation. (A canal from the Mediterranean to the Dead Sea is also under study.)

In the 1940s, the Trans-Arabian Pipeline built by Standard Oil and Chevron was the world's longest, stretching over twelve hundred kilometers from Abaqiq in eastern Saudi Arabia to Lebanon. Over the decades, it became a symbol of the Arab world's own bickering and inability to cooperate as sovereign brothers, with Syria cut off over transit fee disagreements in the 1970s and Jordan in 1990 over its support for Iraq in the Gulf War. And yet today a new south-north pipeline from Saudi Arabia to a post-Assad Syria would be crucial to revive the northern Levant. Turkey, meanwhile, could also become a far greater source of hydroelectric power and also infrastructure investment for Syria. Already Turkish construction companies have taken the lead in building up Kurdistan's infrastructure and support Kurdish pipelines flowing through Turkey to Ceyhan, from which oil is put on tankers and shipped to Europe as well as Israel's port of Ashkelon despite Baghdad's objections.* Qatar, which on paper is the world's richest country per capita, produces almost no food, while its three desalination plants provide only enough water reserves for a single day. As it buys up agricultural land across Jordan and Syria, it should also subsidize modern desalination plants and irrigation systems for them to boost food production. In all these ways, infrastructure connectivity creates the essential contiguity that political borders by definition inhibit.

New infrastructures also bring the strategic resilience great powers seek. China is increasing its naval presence in the Mediterranean to ensure minimal supply chain disruptions for its cargo vessels crossing to and from the Indian Ocean. In 2014, China Harbour Engineering Company began construction of a new Israeli port at Ashdod capable of handling larger vessels than Haifa, and Israel has promised a new freight railway between Ashdod and Eilat on the Red Sea (the "Red-Med Link") that can bypass the Suez Canal in case of shutdown.

At Israel's southern tip, Israelis can easily see Jordan, Egypt, and Saudi Arabia at the same time. Eilat, this scenic yet strategic Red Sea gateway on the Gulf of Aqaba, is becoming the focal point of new energy connections that will reshape the region's geopolitics. Since the 1950s, the Trans-Israel pipeline has linked Eilat to Israel's Mediterranean port of Ashkelon, but rather than transporting Iranian oil to Europe as it did for two decades until the 1979 revolu-

---

* In 2015, it was reported that more than 75 percent of Israel's oil imports came from Kurdistan.

tion, it now transports Russian oil to Asia in the opposite direction.*
Soon it will also serve to complete a circular pipeline network that
includes Iraq and provides oil and gas for its energy-starved neighbors such as Jordan. Until recently, Jordan got all its electricity from
power stations fueled by the Arab Gas Pipeline that runs from
Egypt's Mediterranean terminal of Al-Arish to Aqaba and then
north through Jordan and Syria. But persistent attacks by the Sinai's
disgruntled Bedouin have meant severe fuel shortages for both
Egypt and Jordan, forcing them to spend several billion dollars just
on diesel and heavy oil.

Risk-taking companies are also crucial to regional energy stability. The Houston-based Noble Energy has invested $3.5 billion in
operations in the eastern Mediterranean capable of accessing an estimated 800 billion cubic meters of natural gas from the adjacent
Tamar and Leviathan fields. Tamar gas already powers half of Israel's electricity generation, and Noble has begun gas sales to Egypt,
Jordan, and the Palestinian Authority. Electricity plants near Ashkelon currently produce enough power to begin export to all of Israel's neighbors as well. And yet Noble's rig sits in vulnerable waters
that can be attacked by rockets fired from shore or speedboats,
meaning Israel has to defend its maritime gas supply as intensely as
its precarious borders.[8]

Before Mubarak's ouster in 2011, Israel was actually Egypt's best
customer for gas exports via the much shorter Arish-Ashkelon pipeline, but now Egypt finds itself in the position of needing to import
gas from Israel via reverse flow from the same pipeline. And fortunately for both Jordan and Egypt, Iraq is about to repay the favor of
Aqaba being its main supply line during the 1980s Iran-Iraq War.
Seeking alternatives to Persian Gulf gas export routes, Iraq is building a gas pipeline from Basra to Aqaba to serve the Jordanian market while also allowing excess gas to continue into Egypt via the

---

* Iran is promoting the development of a new gas pipeline across Iraq and Syria to the
Mediterranean Sea to supply European markets. Some call this project the "Islamic
pipeline" and view it as a competitor to the planned Nabucco pipeline that would carry
gas from Azerbaijan to Austria.

Arab Gas Pipeline. Basra, which holds over 80 percent of Iraq's oil, may well advance its own devolution agenda similar to Kurdistan's. Meanwhile, as Jordan's only seaport, Aqaba is equally strategic for Jordan and indeed as important as the capital, Amman, itself. Since 2000, Aqaba has been run as a special economic zone shielded from excessive interference from Amman as it pursues plans for a nuclear power station, a large-scale desalinization facility, an expanded airport connecting two dozen destinations, and additional pipeline routes across the country. The Basra-Aqaba energy axis between two quasi-autonomous port cities is thus more significant than any border in the entire region.

Crossing the Red Sea from Egypt's Sinai to Jordan is a tedious affair: long hours on slow ferries and abusive security checkpoints. For two countries that need each other so much and are separated by so little, it is just another shame of sovereignty trumping common sense. In the 1950s, Arab dictators formed short-lived ideological mergers such as the Egyptian-Syrian United Arab Republic and the Iraqi-Jordanian Arab Federation. Today, thanks to the emergence of shared infrastructures, these mergers are more real than symbolic.

The space between the Mediterranean Sea and the Tigris River can still earn its place on the emerging Silk Roads between Europe and Asia. Arabs will need connectivity as a driver of long-term growth if for no other reason than that both the United States (already) and China (eventually) are diversifying away from Arab oil and gas supplies. They will have to become thriving urban hubs connecting and servicing all the continents on their periphery, including Africa. Westerners hesitate to draw any more maps (publicly, at least) for the region they so cravenly carved up last century, while the Arab regimes left standing are too busy manipulating local forces to put forth a collective long-term vision. But if Sykes-Picot has failed them and chaos is engulfing them, they must draw their own maps of *Pax Arabia* to have something to aspire to.

CHAPTER 5

THE NEW MANIFEST DESTINY

UNITED STATES OR TRAGEDY OF THE COMMONS?

HERE ARE SOME STARTLING FACTS ABOUT HOW AMERICANS relate to their own country: Sixty percent believe the American Dream is out of reach for themselves and their children, and 40 percent of Americans aged eighteen to twenty-four believe they will need to migrate abroad in search for work. Many of those surveyed in 2014 belong to a baby boomer generation whose retirement savings were wiped out in the 2008 financial crisis, while the subsequent financial repression (resulting from ultralow interest rates) slashed any hope of what's left of their pensions recovering value. Record numbers of elderly are moving to Mexico, Panama, and elsewhere seeking more affordable sunset years. Yet more emigrants come from America's unskilled youth who make up 50 percent of the unemployed. (Some American scholars have even suggested that the United States should export its structurally unemployed so they can reduce demands on the government.) The combination of deindustrialization and the sub-prime meltdown has created severe internal dislocation as well, with droves of unemployed or homeless migrating to America's 350 major metro areas in search of jobs at any wage.

Maps 20, 21, 22, and 23, corresponding to this chapter, appear in the second map insert.

Higher up the value chain, America's wealthy and talented not only share ambivalence about remaining at home but act on it. The United States ranks only behind France, Britain, and Spain as a net loser of LinkedIn members to emerging markets, while each year as many as four thousand Americans renounce their U.S. citizenship or permanent residency ("green cards"). A record nine million Americans now live abroad: They have voted with their feet and wallets, seeking a better quality of life, especially lower taxes and better work opportunities, outside the United States. When being American becomes a liability, American companies take flight as well, uprooting themselves and their profits. As of 2014, a record $5 trillion in cash was being held abroad by U.S. companies avoiding high repatriation taxes and instead funding overseas mergers, corporate relocations, and share buybacks that further insulate them from American regulatory pressure.

America used to represent the richest, safest, most technologically advanced society in the world. But one should never confuse the fortuitous combination of circumstances with destiny. Much of what was true for the period after World War II need not hold much longer. Remaining the world's pivotal superpower guarantees only that America has preserved its empire, not that its system and way of life have triumphed. Indeed, recent years have exposed both the fragility of America's global status and the efficacy of its governance model. Both will continue to be severely tested in the decades ahead as America becomes even more dependent on foreign investment from and exports to the same rising powers, financial centers, and corporate hubs that compete with it in global markets.

Imagine this rosy scenario of 2020: America's military is mostly anchored at home after two decades of foreign policy disasters, more oil and gas is captured from shale deposits than is produced by Russia and Iran, and California's tech titans produce breakthrough applications that propel the world's first trillion-dollar company. The economy cruises at a steady 3 percent growth rate, and more inclusive mortgage standards allow a record 70 percent of Americans to own their own homes.

Does restored growth mean that American citizens and corporations return home with their cash and loyalty? Does the energy boom in Texas and the Dakotas mean that wealth is shared with depressed states? Does a thriving technology sector mean that enough Americans are qualified for the best jobs? The answers to these questions will reveal whether America rises as a whole or whether it degenerates into a tragedy of the commons, whether it merely continues as a great but crumbling empire or restores itself as a truly United States. One thing is for sure: In the hypercompetitive supply chain world, just being American is no longer enough.

The 2013 bankruptcy of Detroit, once America's richest city, was not merely an event but a symptom of the reality that residing in a world-class competitive country doesn't assure the competitiveness of the city. America's unraveling—by which some cities, companies, and communities thrive while others languish—is symptomatic of its devolutionary tendencies, both positive and negative. New York, Miami, Dallas, Los Angeles, San Francisco, Chicago, Boston, and Atlanta are national anchors, regional magnets, and even global hubs to various degrees. They belong to global circuits, whether academia, technology, finance, or energy. California is more populous than most countries; under Governors Jerry Brown and Arnold Schwarzenegger, it sent extensive trade delegations abroad to boost exports and attract investment. Other states too are crunching numbers to determine exactly how many jobs are created by exporting to which countries and then targeting them directly to boost their commercial connectivity.

But many American states and cities are the embodiment of the downside of devolution: They get authority from Washington but not money and can't generate enough investment on their own, because they are too small. (America is the least urbanized of major Western states.) For such cities, the prospects are bleak. A 2013 report declared that Cleveland is "Balkanized," describing it as "cut off from the global flow of people and ideas."[1] In Buffalo, once-bustling factory buildings producing Otis elevators and Wonder bread are now hollow, rotting carcasses. Experts predict a much wider wave of municipal bankruptcies across the Rust Belt of Michigan, Ohio, Pennsylvania, Illinois, New York, and even some New England cities that are losing talent, business, and investment to Boston. For a large empire such as America, failing cities are its own version of failing states.

While many blame outsourcing to low-wage car plants in China as the cause of Detroit's decline, the Motor City has a counterpart in China as well: Dongguan. Dubbed one of the "Four Little Tigers" in China's southern Guangdong province, Dongguan specialized in electronics manufacturing, ranking only second to Shenzhen in total trade volume.[2] But the 2008 financial crisis crushed its exports as well: Factories closed, and workers vacated. The newly opened New South China Mall, twice the size of Minnesota's Mall of America, lay stillborn and vacant.

But Dongguan has several advantages Detroit doesn't. Its population is over eight million, with workers able to quickly commute or relocate to other large nearby cities and find work while riding out the export slump. Its infrastructure is relatively new and can be quickly repurposed for companies packaging food, requiring logistics centers, or making high-quality appliances and tools. Also, its services sector (such as restaurants and hotels) is a larger share of the economy than manufacturing. At its peak, Dongguan's prostitution industry alone—from massage parlors to karaoke bars—employed more people than the entire population of Detroit. Today the New South China Mall is operating at nearly full capacity.

One other crucial difference between the two cities is that unlike Detroit Dongguan was not fleeced by the financial markets. China's municipal debts are exorbitant and its state-owned enterprises badly need restructuring, but both are backed by the $4 trillion of the People's Bank of China. Meanwhile, days before its bankruptcy, Detroit paid out $250 million to UBS and Bank of America on debts inflated due to interest rate swap agreements, leaving it with pennies to cover almost $20 billion in pension and health-care obligations.

Does China have a better model for managing central government relations with cities than America? China has embarked on economic liberalization far more quickly than political democratization, but what is proving to be equally important for its long-term stability is how it manages devolution. Beijing is the captain of China's urban tug-of-war team: It promotes experimentation but backstops failure. The country is becoming a confederation of megacities that compete with each other for investment, industries, talent, and visibility, generating a dynamism the country needs to ensure broad-based stability. Even Beijing, Shanghai, Tianjin, and Chongqing—all directly controlled politically by the party—have growing latitude to build their own economic plans. Though Beijing appoints provincial governors and mayors, they are, in the words of Daokui Li of Tsinghua University, the "chairmen of holding companies that have wide latitude in allocating capital and attracting investments" and recruit foreign investors much as New York and Los Angeles do. Shanghai recently opened a free trade zone to allow foreign firms to more flexibly operate across multiple currencies. The former Communist Party Secretary of Chongqing Bo Xilai's meteoric rise and subsequent scandalized removal is an example of how autonomous a major city and public figure can become—as well as how Beijing can tolerate only so much devolution. No wonder the old adage is so often quoted today: "The hills are high, and the emperor is far away."

China wants to make sure that it thrives both in an era of strong states *and* in an era of strong cities. Unlike the "warring states" period of ancient China, where the central government was reduced to symbolic powers, today Beijing provides support to the provinces and regions the way the Song dynasty did. Each of China's more than two thousand counties (with populations ranging from under fifty thousand to over three million) jockeys to find a place for itself in Beijing's five-year plans, whether as a district of a megacity or in piloting subsidized schemes to reduce factory emissions. With as much as 70 percent of China's budget consumed by local government expenses, many scholars argue that China is already de facto federalized and should become more formally so.[3] Indeed, the central government no longer sets or rewards growth rate targets for provinces, indicating they are expected to determine economic strategies for themselves.[4] Inland provinces are thus leveraging China's improved infrastructure to draw companies from the high-wage coastal cities toward the lower-wage interior.

Meanwhile, a "race to the bottom" competition for manufacturing jobs is playing out in America today reminiscent of Asia in the 1980s. Tennessee is reimbursing much of the up-front cost South Korea's tire maker Hankook will incur to set up its first U.S. plant in Clarksville, where it will become the largest employer in the city. On the other side of Nashville is Smyrna, a town that barely existed until Nissan came in 1983, after which the population quadrupled to more than forty thousand. Today Nissan subcontracts labor to an American company that demands overtime work without extra pay, requires long weekend shifts, and provides no benefits. Yet Mike Sparks, a Tennessee state representative, feels the state has no choice but to play along. If the United Auto Workers union were able to rally support in Nissan's factories, "they'll go to Alabama, they'll go to Georgia, they'll go to Mississippi."[5]

In the supply chain world, American states compete as much with each other as with those in Mexico, Thailand, and China. But there are fewer than twenty million manufacturing jobs left in America, and nothing that Michigan and Tennessee do today can keep them from being gone tomorrow.

THE DEVOLUTION WITHIN

America has leaders in the supply chain war, but it isn't winning it. Silicon Valley is a wealthy high-tech node, New York a world financial center, and Houston an energy powerhouse. But while America's geography is an asset, its vast scale can be a liability. Highways and bridges are crumbling, railways too slow or nonexistent, and broadband connectivity insufficient. Then there is the soft infrastructure: education levels in decline, immigration policy failing to recruit enough talent, and severe economic inequality between the connected haves and the disconnected have-nots. Banks and companies don't want to invest in or lend to stressed states and communities, leaving them to form their own credit unions and lending clubs.

America is increasingly divided between its key global nodes and its Rust Belt backwaters. Already it is inaccurate to think of America as "united" when in fact Americans belong—or don't belong—to vastly different global supply chain circuits. The divides are not just red state versus blue state but urban versus rural. Voter preferences align much more according to professional circuit—factory worker, teacher, management consultant, banker, farmer—than to geography.

Cities with three to eight million residents and diverse economies are far better at withstanding shocks than smaller mono-industry cities such as Detroit. America's largest cities with the densest districts—New York and Los Angeles—have rebounded from recessions, crime waves, and industrial competition to retain world-leading concentrations of high-earning talent. Their resilience lies in their size and constant creation of new opportunities to shift gears, train for new careers, and move up the value chain without ever leaving the city. Hence New York City has become a tech magnet since the financial crisis, and the once dilapidated Playa Vista area of Los Angeles has become an advanced aerospace and media complex.

Major cities account for 85 percent of America's GDP, with New York City alone almost 8 percent of the economy. However, much as the gap between first-tier cities and the rest is growing, so too is the gap *within* cities. New York City's income inequality has become as severe as that in many third world countries. Dallas–Fort Worth (whose airport alone is the size of Manhattan) is America's fourth most populous city, and as Mayor Michael Rawlings confesses, it is the "poorest rich city"[6] in the country. Rich cities, however, can grow even while they go broke. Under Rahm Emanuel, Chicago has pursued a massive debt-driven regeneration campaign, but its excessive spending has dropped the state's economic outlook to near the bottom of the fifty states while pushing up taxes for individuals and businesses that may ultimately drive them away.

Illinois thus reveals how anachronistic the idea of politically (rather than economically) defined states is today. As the longtime *Chicago Tribune* columnist and urban expert Richard Longworth has written, "Midwestern states make no sense as units of government."[7] Kansas City is shared by Kansas and Missouri, but the two states battle to get companies to relocate across State Line Road rather than uniting against global competition. Indiana's municipalities are also engaged in a Tennessee-style race to the bottom to attract low-wage jobs, undermining Indianapolis's effort to become a high-wage tech hub.

Some second-tier cities have managed to stay afloat by effectively privatizing themselves. The Port of Corpus Christi, for example, was the first American territory to be granted a foreign trade zone license by the Department of Commerce in 1985, making it a self-governing private entity independent of the city with the same name and taking no federal, state, or city tax revenues.* After decades of service as a key port for oil imports and almost zero exports, it has become a major gateway for outbound shale oil exports from the Eagle Ford formation only a hundred kilometers away.† In 2009, it began a $1 billion joint venture with Tianjin Pipe Corporation, which hails from China's leading port, to produce 500,000 tons per year of seamless pipe essential for oil and gas wells. The largest Chinese manufacturing investment in the United States, it has already created hundreds of construction jobs with more to follow in the factory itself—the only delay being the shortage of qualified local personnel who can speak Mandarin with the factory owners. Still, with its flexibility to capitalize rapidly on rising global energy demand, Corpus Christi has made itself America's gold standard in how to become a valued global node in short order.

Other cities cannot self-finance or capitalize on global energy

---

* FTZs are permitted for general multipurpose functions such as warehousing and storage, while subzones are granted on a company-specific basis.

† Shipments out of Corpus Christi have doubled every year since 2011 to almost 130 million barrels in 2013, bound first for a string of refineries along the Gulf Coast and then around the world.

markets as readily. American banks were so reluctant to finance Denver's downtown redevelopment that the city turned to Canadian banks. But the more private financing middle-tier cities require to survive, the more they come to resemble SEZs where services from education to security are effectively outsourced to private corporations. In return for building new stadiums, museums, and railways inside the Denver Enterprise Zone, companies get tax credits and special authority to add auxiliary charges for everything from "membership packages" for parks to "facility fees" for hospital beds. Colorado's other option: legalizing medicinal and recreational marijuana, which is now heavily taxed to raise revenue for education—antidrug education.

An even deeper irony is what Denver's corporatization reveals about the future of American politics. America's cities are largely run by Democratic mayors. Dallas, Houston, and Austin are "blue" Democratic cities surrounded by "red" Texas. Yet by voting in referenda to fund social infrastructures that are then governed by private companies, they inadvertently act like Republicans. In 2015, Dallas even sold its name and city logo to a sewage waste insurance company for $500,000, leading to confused (and angry) citizens receiving corporate mailers that looked like official communications. America's post-partisan consensus is indeed about putting aside differences and getting things done, but is it of, by, and for the public?

America's devolution into self-governing enclaves of various shapes and sizes is destined to continue, meaning America should learn from other countries that remain greater than the sum of their parts. German cities have great football stadiums too, but not at the price of privatized public services. Each has an *economic* master plan made jointly by government officials, corporate leaders, and the educational establishment to constantly calibrate the trade and investment strategy and train the workforce to capitalize on the latest technologies and global opportunities. This is why China seeks to emulate Germany more than it does America, for its combination of many robust economic hubs, world-class infrastructure, export-worthy goods, and socially oriented policy. Germany has more millionaires (and billionaires) per capita than any other country, yet with lower inequality than other large industrial powers. What Germany—and Japan and South Korea—have that America doesn't are policies that promote solidarity *despite* devolutionary competition among cities. The name of the tax that has improved eastern Germany's infrastructure standards to beyond the levels of western Germany in the twenty-five years since reunification says it all: *Solidaritätszuschlag*.

But such solidarity is in short supply in America, where rich cities and states would rather spend on themselves than share the wealth.* Indeed, the same Data.gov movement that is meant to make Washington more responsive and efficient also empowers New York and Los Angeles—like Barcelona and Venice—to know exactly where their tax money goes and how it is spent. As a result, California, Texas, New York, and other states are keeping what they can and building their international connections while leaving Washington to prop up the welfare cases: a mix of the geographically largest, demographically smallest, or economically poorest states across Democratic and Republican divides such as South Dakota, Arizona, New Mexico, Louisiana, Alabama, and Maine.[8]

A new American map is emerging, one defined by functional gravities of commerce and talent rather than nominal state lines. According to the urbanist Joel Kotkin, America resembles not so much fifty united states as seven distinct nations (clustered around cities such as San Francisco, Dallas, Houston, Chicago, Washington, Denver, and Atlanta) and three quasi-independent city-states (Los Angeles, New York, and Miami). Each is the capital of a regional economy, whether oil, agriculture, industry, or technology, while the city-states have global demographics, economies, and connectivity. Additional mega-regions foreseen by urban geographers include the Arizona Sun Corridor from Phoenix to Tucson, the Cascadia belt from Portland through Seattle to Vancouver, and

---

* The billionaire venture capitalist Tim Draper is petitioning to split California into six states, both to maximize California's overall vote in Washington and to minimize Silicon Valley's burden.

the Piedmont Atlantic cluster from Atlanta to Charlotte. This map of America's functional mega-regions tells us how America actually works and how to improve it through greater connectivity.*

PACIFIC FLOWS

So what happens to Detroit? There is no single template for urban revival—or survival. Loyal Detroit billionaires such as Dan Gilbert of Quicken Loans have bought up downtown office space, financed a light-rail project, and are paying for the removal of residential and industrial blight. Such piecemeal steps rejuvenate the city's shrunken urban core, making it tidy and livable for the fraction of the original population that remains while demolishing both the glorious and the miserable past. Far more radical proposals have been offered to restore the city to its previous size and sense of purpose: making it a tax-free zone, creating a Detroit-only visa for hardworking Latin and Asian immigrants, and giving Detroit to Canada, which provides a much larger federal share (approximately 20 percent) of city budgets than America does (less than 10 percent).

Dozens of other cities are also on life support, in deep debt, and without viable business models. Fiscal stress makes municipal welfare a token gesture at best. Many of these cities are also so deeply divided by wealth and race that they have become tinderboxes—the 2014 Ferguson, Missouri, riots were only the most widely reported episode. They are so poor and unequal they should be treated like underdeveloped countries.[9] Washington is haphazardly helping them pay for police officers and commuter buses, backing bonds to cover pensions, and offering investment rebates and tax credits for job creation and business start-ups. But creating a few jobs isn't a sustainable economic strategy. Making investments in desperately needed infrastructure upgrades and globally competitive industries is. For example, Detroit has reached its peak as an automobile town,

* Hillary Clinton has called for a "flexible federalism" that "empowers and connects communities."

but its many underemployed entrepreneurs should immediately have been redeployed into transportation engineering systems such as high-speed railcars America itself ought to install. The U.S. solar industry now employs more than 200,000 people and is growing 20 percent per year. The Commerce Department's SelectUSA program is sending delegations crisscrossing the world from Poland to Indonesia to lure investment into business-friendly American cities, making it one necessary—but gravely underfunded—effort to systematically do what used to come so naturally: make America the world's most attractive investment destination.

America therefore needs a large-scale employment strategy built around enabling workers to boost skills and move to where the jobs are. As the authors of the Cleveland study argue, "Migration is economic development." The city is offering incentives to tech start-ups and is trying to lure college degree holders away from Austin and Seattle. With its cluster of research labs centered on Carnegie Mellon University, Pittsburgh similarly embodies the phenomenon of populations shrinking due to industrial decline while incomes are growing in sectors such as software, biotech, and advanced materials. Skilled engineers are also to be found in Michigan—but western Michigan—where companies such as Gentex make not cars or airplane parts but optical products with embedded electronics and sensors, a segment of the supply chain too advanced for China— for now at least.

America may be losing jobs to Asia, but it can still keep an edge in the tug-of-war by capturing capital flowing in the opposite direction. China doesn't just export things; it exports capital and people too. The China Development Bank has pledged close to $2 billion in investment with Lennar Corporation, America's largest home builder, to finance two long-stalled real estate projects in San Francisco (Treasure Island and Hunters Point Shipyard) that would create thousands of jobs constructing over twenty thousand homes as well as new office and retail space. San Francisco could become affordable again—ironically through Chinese money, which along with tech and financial wealth has turned San Francisco (and New York) into a London-like enclave for the world's moguls.

Altogether, Chinese companies are investing up to $13 billion per year across American cities. After losing its glass industry to China, Toledo, Ohio—once known as America's Glass City—began soliciting Chinese buyers for its hotels and factories and set up university partnerships and art exchanges, emphasizing its cost competitiveness and proximity to Chicago (which has also launched a campaign to brand itself America's most China-friendly city). China has also developed state-by-state plans to build Shenzhen-like SEZs to locate the final assembly portion of its industrial supply chains inside American borders to avoid import tariffs. Sinomach has proposed a fifty-square-mile self-sustaining technology zone near Boise airport with manufacturing facilities and housing for its workers. Such Chinese commercial bridgeheads may become common across America in the coming years, and many states will welcome them. As Idaho's lieutenant governor, Brad Little, says, "Asia is where the money is."[10]

It is also where the people are. The financial crisis, mounting education debts, and other factors have combined to make America a nation of smaller households and in need of more immigrants to work in every sector from elder care to high-tech start-ups. America's neglected southern states are lucky that some people will go anywhere to start anew. Chinese citizens are hedging against their own real estate bubble and anticorruption crackdown by buying more homes in America than any other country's nationals, even Canada. They are also the largest investors in the EB-5 program, which grants green cards in exchange for $500,000 in investment in federally approved (but not guaranteed) projects.* EB-5 centers have popped up across the American South in Louisiana, Mississippi,

---

* Chinese investment of approximately $22 billion per year represents about 50 percent of the total EB-5 pool so far. Similar to the Chinese, investors from Mexico, Nigeria, France, and Korea have put up $1 million each for a Houston property developer to build them a luxury condo that will create about one thousand construction jobs.

and other hard-hit states to attract foreign cash. Investors scarcely check the value of the assets that got them entry into the United States in the first place: All they want is an American passport—especially for their unborn second child.*

Yet it is Canada that receives the wealthiest Chinese immigrants by more than a factor of ten: around six thousand Chinese EB-5 applications per year versus approximately sixty thousand for Canada's Immigrant Investor Program.† And Canada shrewdly requires $1.6 million in investment per family—or a visa for every $1 million invested in a Canadian technology start-up fund. The British Columbia government also offers RMB-denominated bonds to deepen its financial ties to the Chinese mainland. "Hongcouver," as many now call Vancouver, is the leading port of call for Chinese "yacht people" (a far wealthier type of migrant than Asia's twentieth-century "boat people"), who have driven real estate prices to stratospheric levels and pushed locals into the suburbs. Eventually, Vancouver's complexion, like its skyline, will more resemble Hong Kong than Toronto. As the Chinese proverb goes, "A smart rabbit has at least three holes to live in."

The Asianization of the West Coast embodies the massively expanding flows of capital and people across the vastest of the earth's oceans. Only China's ongoing crackdown on capital flight and American and Canadian immigration restrictions could stem these trends. But China's currency liberalization will make preventing Chinese money from flowing out of the country harder, and the Chinese passport now gets red-carpet treatment: Red is the new green.

---

* Though the one-child policy was formally lifted in 2015, Chinese families have been lining up in droves and paying up to $120,000 to have California surrogates give birth to their children.

† This is also more than double the total number of Chinese participating in similar schemes in Australia, Britain, and the United States combined.

OIL AND WATER ACROSS THE
WORLD'S LONGEST BORDER

For centuries, natural resource supplies have lured waves of economic migrants seeking work and fortune. Today, Fort McMurray in Alberta, Canada, is one of those towns to which migrants have flocked in search of North America's new "oil rush" riches. Canada only seriously tapped its oil sands (a patch larger than England) after the OPEC embargo of 1973. Suddenly Fort McMurray found itself properly incorporated as a city for the first time, and its population more than tripled to thirty thousand by 1980. In just the past ten years, the population has shot up again to eighty thousand.

But that's just the official population. The world of transient mobile laborers normally associated with Filipinos or Pakistanis in Dubai has come to Fort McMurray, where outside the city perimeter, on land owned and operated by oil companies, fifty thousand live in trailers and work tedious shifts as "rig pigs," electricians, truckers, cafeteria servers, bartenders, prostitutes, and any other chore needed to keep energy levels high and oil pumping—even during the frigid winters.* The falling oil price has slowed Fort McMurray's momentum but not its trajectory. Today it is the world's new Wild West, but eventually it will have a stable population, gated communities, a larger airport, and other amenities befitting a major new global supply chain node.

Fort McMurray has also become a metaphor for how western Canada—where the oil sands, potash, diamonds, and other minerals are—is gradually replacing the east as the country's economic center of gravity. (Farther north, the diamond-mining hub of Yellowknife has a per capita income of $100,000.) Canada has moved west: For the first time, more Canadians live west of Ontario than east of it. Yukon, Alberta, Saskatchewan, Manitoba, and British Columbia are all getting more seats in parliament. Canada's prime

---

* Fort McMurray's twin in the Southern Hemisphere, Rincón de los Sauces, near Argentina's giant Vaca Muerta shale formation, is similarly evolving into a gas industry hub with rapid growth in demographics and debauchery.

minister from 2006 to 2015, Stephen Harper, is from Alberta, and it seems almost obvious that Naheed Nenshi, the Muslim-Indian-Tanzanian mayor of Calgary, will one day rise to the same office.

Americans should get to know the names of these large Canadian provinces, because that is where their water might be coming from. America's water, agriculture, and demographic ecosystem is increasingly fragile—especially in the fastest-growing southwestern states such as Arizona and Nevada to which waves of retirees and "Rust Belt to Sun Belt" migrants have flocked. Phoenix already has over four million residents, and like other surging urban patches such as Las Vegas, Scottsdale, and even Baja, Mexico, it depends on water from the Colorado River that is first consumed by thirsty California, whose ongoing drought coupled with low reservoir levels has crippled agricultural output other than fruits and nuts. California's population is growing even as it is running out of precious water, which it increasingly uses to fight raging forest fires made worse by the drought. Nearby, Lake Mead (created by the Hoover Dam) has shrunk to near-record low levels, forcing major water rationing for twenty million people. "Without Lake Mead, there would be no Las Vegas," a city official has said.[11]

When Lake Mead finally runs dry, even Canada's ample sales of bottled water to America won't be enough. Water may indeed be the "oil of the twenty-first century," but Canada has been reluctant to price it as such for fear of commoditizing such a precious resource. The Great Lakes Compact, signed in 2008 by eight American states and two Canadian provinces, prohibits any diversion of Great Lakes water, leaving even once water-rich towns such as Waukesha, Wisconsin, in a lurch as its community size and industrial activity grow. Without Canadian water, it is hard to imagine the United States continuing to produce one-third of the world's corn and soybean exports—especially as America's own corn subsidies have encouraged the rapid draining of the Ogallala aquifer (which provides one-third of all irrigated water in the Great Plains) while polluting it with pesticides, and American cities continue to overconsume water allocated by volume rather than priced by usage.

Even the two dozen desalination plants under construction from California to Florida will not be enough to cope with the rising mismatch between water supply and demand.

The time has come to dust off schemes such as the renowned Canadian engineer Tom Kierans's Great Recycling and Northern Development Canal and the ill-fated 1970s North American Water and Power Alliance (NAWAPA), both of which borrow from Dutch and Chinese experience to use dikes and canals to capture river runoff as far north as Canada's Yukon and Hudson Bay and channel it through the sixteen-hundred-kilometer Rocky Mountain Trench and the Great Lakes into man-made reservoirs and interbasin canals that could both replenish the Ogallala aquifer and feed the Colorado River. As the final remaining glaciers of Montana's Glacier National Park melt away in the coming two decades, channeling their new runoff patterns will also be essential to prevent flooding and potentially deliver more water southward.

These schemes are the hydrological equivalent of the Interstate Highway System, both in scale and in cost. The United States will have to become a "hydraulic civilization"—the term coined by Joseph Needham to describe ancient Chinese canal and aqueduct building practices—installing water pipes as long as oil pipelines to reach Texas and Arizona, and even Georgia and Florida, where rapid groundwater depletion has led to saltwater substitution. NAWAPA even foresaw using nuclear explosions to forge underground trenches and reservoirs and nuclear power stations to pump water across the continent. As mass urbanization coincides with existential levels of water scarcity, there could be no more sensible use of nuclear weapons and power today.

Water supplies are only the newest reason why North Americans will come to view their continent far more geologically and less nationally. Energy is another. Since the 2003 electricity blackout that plunged the Northeast region from Toronto to Baltimore into darkness, Canadian companies have been deploying underwater and underground power lines to deliver Quebec's vast hydro and wind power across New England. There are already over three dozen oil and gas pipelines across the U.S.-Canada border, and dozens more have been proposed, most notably TransCanada Corporation's controversial Keystone XL pipeline, which would connect Alberta via Nebraska to Texas, provide additional oil supply for the United States, accelerate South Dakota's shale oil flow southward, and allow Canadian oil to be exported across the Atlantic from terminals at Port Arthur near Houston, which has already surpassed Los Angeles and New York to become America's busiest port. Connectivity is profitable no matter what the energy price: Kinder Morgan, the continent's largest pipeline operator, has amassed an empire of oil and gas transportation and storage networks and is valued at over $150 billion.

Much as every Saudi citizen takes pride in the name Ghawar, still the world's largest oil field, Americans are wisely becoming fluent in the geography of shale rock formations: Eagle Ford in Texas, Permian between Texas and New Mexico, and Bakken spanning Montana and North Dakota in the United States and Saskatchewan and Manitoba in Canada. Though regulations differ, the political divisions across the 49th parallel separating the United States and Canada matter far less than the output of the underlying formations that unite them.

THE NORTH AMERICAN UNION

Resource independence is not a quest "America" is on alone; rather, it is a goal sought collectively with and through continental neighbors. The two-decade-old NAFTA is graduating toward a European-style empire of city-regions that many are calling the North American Union. As North America's resources unite, the continent's geopolitical weight stacks up differently than the United States does alone. While Russia and the United States produce approximately the same volume of natural gas per year, the United States also imports more than half of Canada's production. At the same time, the United States serves Mexico's electricity-hungry market by exporting gas southward. In 2015, Mexico's national oil company, Pemex, signed a deal with the U.S.-based BlackRock and First Reserve to build new gas pipelines from the United States to central Mexico. Eventually, Mexico's energy market liberalization will boost its oil and gas production such that it will join the United States and Canada in exporting to Europe and Asia. This is exactly what China wants as well: more North American energy clear of geographic bottlenecks like the Strait of Malacca. And unlike before the financial crisis, China's efforts to invest in North American energy production face far less friction today.* North America should make the most of its edge in horizontal drilling and hydraulic fracking before Asian production catches up: Estimates suggest that China has up to 50 percent more recoverable shale gas reserves than even the United States.

North America's *internal* stability also hinges on pursuing a more integrated union. American policies such as corn subsidies have indirectly driven Mexican farmers to abandon their crops and join the drug cartels whose narco-insurgency has killed close to 100,000 people since 2007. In 2014, General John Kelly of U.S. Southern Command made headlines arguing that the flow of drugs, weapons, and migrants from particularly El Salvador, Honduras, and Guatemala through Mexico into the United States makes it an "existential" national security risk. Giant fences, armed border patrols, drone surveillance, and mass deportations have reduced the number of migrants, but the larger story is of Mexicans voluntarily leaving America seeking to capitalize on the growing economy back home. The smartest thing America can do is to send job-creating and socially stabilizing supply chains with them: near-shoring jobs once outsourced to China back home and to Mexico.

Foreigners are already investing there. Between 2009 and 2014, $19 billion in investment has come to Mexico just from German, Korean, and Japanese carmakers, doubling the country's output to

---

* Whereas CNOOC's bid to buy Unocal in 2005 was scuttled due to uproar over generic national security concerns, its acquisition of a $2.2 billion stake in Chesapeake Energy in 2010 encountered minimal resistance, as did its 2013 acquisition of Canada's Nexen for $15.1 billion.

more than three million cars per year. With more than fifty thousand new auto-industry jobs created, the province of Aguascalientes has become the new Detroit. It was not wages alone that brought this investment to Mexico but also Mexico's aggressive free trade policy that gives Mexican exports better access than American firms have to huge markets such as Brazil. More American production in Mexico thus means not only lower-cost manufacturing but also more exports to the rest of Latin America. And while Mexico has taken American and Canadian autoworker jobs, it has required that foreign carmakers purchase at least two-thirds of their parts from North American suppliers, including major American ones. In a supply chain world, America's neighbors' competitiveness is its own too.

Canadian, American, and Mexican cities thus view each other as essential allies. Trade in North America is dominated by two dozen pairs of interdependent cities—such as New York and Toronto, San Jose and Mexico City, Seattle and Montreal—that together power major industries from cars and planes to electronics and pharmaceuticals.* Even proximate cities with violent histories have swapped suspicion for collaboration. San Diego and Tijuana now view the border between them as a hindrance costing $2 billion in lost revenues. Their new mantra is "Dos ciudades, pero una región." San Diego's mayor has a satellite office in Tijuana and envisions a bridge linking their airports and a joint Olympic bid for 2024. Crime, illegal immigration, and narco-trafficking have fallen drastically there not because of a more rigid border but because of more investment and job creation *across* the border.

As pipelines, water canals, freight rail corridors, electricity grids, and other infrastructures link hundreds of key economic hubs across the continent's borders, America should come to think of itself as the heart of an integrated North American supercontinent.

---

* There are twenty-five pairs of North American cities whose annual "bilateral" trade exceeds $1 billion each. Trade between major U.S. and Canadian/Mexican metropolitan areas represents 58 percent of the $885 billion total trade across the three countries. See Brookings's Metro Monitor 2013.

Indeed, America has for 150 years been all but cut off physically from its largest state, Alaska, but now a railway is planned to augment the Pan-American Highway and connect Valdez to Fort Mc-Murray and a new liquefied natural gas (LNG) pipeline from the North Slope into Canada, both embedding Alaska deeper in the regional energy and transport architecture while boosting its oil and gas exports to Asia as well.

The infrastructural, economic, cultural, and strategic blending of North America has become an irreversible fact. Canada has oil and water but few people; America and Mexico have 400 million people that lack water but offer huge markets. As climate change thaws the vast Canadian Arctic, some believe Canada could one day be home to as many as 100 million people (up from only 30 million today), with Asians and Latinos representing almost all of the new labor essential for harnessing arable land and shale oil and colonizing the increasingly livable northern Canadian bounty.

The melting of the polar ice caps is giving birth to new nations such as Greenland, whose ice sheet melt is ironically most responsible for rising sea levels. Greenland is set to become the first country born of climate change when it votes for independence from tiny Denmark and becomes an Arctic power in its own right with abundant quantities of uranium and other rare earth minerals.* The fact that Greenland's and Canada's Inuit populations are related hints at how the island's geographic meaning is evolving from colonial European legacies toward eventual membership in the North American Union.

When, in 1867, the American secretary of state, William Seward, purchased Alaska from Russia, he envisioned a united hemisphere from Greenland to Guyana, with a second capital in Mexico City. And if America's nineteenth-century "Manifest Destiny" is finally

---

* Greenland has already attracted major investment interest from far-off countries that are expert suppliers of mining technology (Australia) and major consumers of mined resources (China) and begun to issue licenses for oil and gas exploration in the fields located between itself and Canada's Baffin Island. European engineering firms have explored towing Greenland icebergs to provide freshwater to Africa.

becoming a reality—through integration rather than conquest—it doesn't seem ambitious enough. After the Cold War ended, the former Nixon administration interior secretary and Alaska governor, Walter Hickel, proposed linking Alaska to Russia via an eighty-kilometer tunnel under the Bering Strait. A quarter century later, the Russian Railways president Vladimir Yakunin proposed a superhighway from London via Moscow and Siberia to Alaska and eventually New York. While Russia can't afford such a grand scheme, China can, proposing to fully fund construction of a thirteen-thousand-kilometer (longer than the Trans-Siberian Railway) high-speed railway that would begin in eastern China and into Siberia, then enter a two-hundred-kilometer tunnel (four times longer than the U.K.-France Chunnel) under the Bering Strait to Fairbanks, Alaska, and south through Canada to the United States—a scenic route for Chinese traveling to Vancouver, no doubt.

A SOUTH AMERICAN UNION

South America, too, is experiencing a functional reconfiguration. For the first time since Spain and Portugal carved it up five hundred years ago, the once "lost continent" is free from exploitative colonialism, Bolivarian nationalism, revolutionary socialism, or right-wing anticommunism. Rather than fighting left-wing guerrillas and denouncing American imperialism, the continent's leaders are focused on reforming subsidies, attracting investment, and raising energy output. Like in North America, resource-based regionalism is the best way to take advantage of South America's massive biodiversity. Cross-border infrastructure investment is overcoming the continent's two overwhelming features: the Amazon rain forest and the Andes Mountains. The Interoceanic Highway project will connect Brazil's Atlantic coast to Peru's Pacific ports (as will a Chinese-financed railway), cutting one week off shipping time from Brazil to China. Hence its nickname: the "Road to China." Peru has given landlocked Bolivia rights to build its own Pacific port at Ilo, and a giant tunnel through the Andes will give Argentina efficient access to Chile's ports to boost exports across the Pacific. The upgraded Pan-American Highway traverses the north-south axis from Colombia's Darien Gap to Argentina's Tierra del Fuego. This emerging *Pax Latina* even has a nascent continental parliament and a new EU-sounding institutional umbrella: the Union of South American Nations.

PART THREE

COMPETITIVE
CONNECTIVITY

CHAPTER 6

WORLD WAR III—OR TUG-OF-WAR?

AN ANCIENT METAPHOR FOR
POSTMODERN TIMES

THE WORLD'S OLDEST TEAM SPORT—WHOSE LEGACY IS RECORDED in ancient stone etchings from Egypt to Greece to China to Guinea—is tug-of-war. Often conducted in resplendent royal ceremonies, tug-of-war was used by the soldiers of great armies to build strength in preparation for combat. In the eighth century, the Tang dynasty emperor Xuanzong was known to pit over five hundred warriors on each side of a rope over 150 meters long. In the early twentieth century, tug-of-war was officially included in five successive Summer Olympics, with European countries (such as Sweden's team comprising members of Stockholm's police force) faring best in the medal count.

The *Oxford English Dictionary* defines tug-of-war as a "severe contest for supremacy," and indeed it is. Tug-of-war is utterly excruciating: Victory requires the utmost strength, endurance, and willpower. Even brief moments of rest (called "hanging") are arduous; the body truly gets no respite. And yet tug-of-war is the world's most brutal *non*contact sport. In thousands of years, almost no one has ever died in tug-of-war. It is an apt metaphor for our times.

Maps 28 and 29, corresponding to this chapter,
appear in the second map insert.

Thousands of years of history have witnessed large-scale mobilizations of armies for territorial conquest and self-defense. Today's world too is full of tension, strife, and hostility: cross-border invasions, nuclear standoffs, terrorist insurgencies, collapsing states, and tragic civil conflicts. But even this significant violence, with all of its casualties, neither defines nor dominates the nature of competition across the world. In fact, very few societies are at war today, either internally or externally. But *all* societies are caught in the global tug-of-war.

Tug-of-war is where geopolitics and geoeconomics come together. War among states is declining while war over supply chains is rising. Tug-of-war, however, is fought not over territory but over *flows*—of money, goods, resources, technology, knowledge, and talent. These flows are like the rope in tug-of-war: We compete over them, yet they connect us. The global tug-of-war is about pulling the world's supply chains toward oneself, to be the largest producer of resources and goods and gain the maximum share of value from transactions.

Britain's elite Royal Military Academy Sandhurst publishes a manual of strategies for success in tug-of-war, pointing out that a good team "synchronizes its movements to the point that their pull feels like it comes from a single, unified being." Does America act like this? Do Washington politicians, Wall Street bankers, Texas oil companies, and the other players on America's team act like a single, unified being whose whole is greater than the sum of its parts? Or does China do it better?

Tug-of-war requires sustained tension in the rope: Slack destabilizes everyone, while excessive strain might snap the rope and slice off fingers and hands. A key strategy isn't to deploy brute strength alone but to skillfully build leverage while maintaining balance. Too big a step by one competitor could knock his team off balance and allow the opponents to heave the rope over to their side of the line. Game over. Think of an analogy to today's geostrategic environment. Should the United States yank back millions of manufacturing jobs from China through the combination of cheap energy and automation, or would that weaken the Chinese economy to which America seeks to boost exports and lead to a sell-off of dollars and a spike in interest rates for Americans? Tug-of-war is thus won slowly and carefully. Smart teams dig in their heels to hold ground and tire out opponents while collectively taking small steps to ultimately gain control.

The future of global stability hinges on whether great powers think and act in terms of sovereignty or supply chains, war or tug-of-war. The protagonists of war are militaries and allies; in tug-of-war, they are cities and companies. Governments are owners, coaches, and funders—and rig the rules of the game—but the quality of the players is ultimately decisive.

Tug-of-war is still war without end, a marathon without a finish line. New opponents emerge constantly and from all directions—as if pulling multiple ropes at the same time. Indeed, twenty-first-century tug-of-war feels like a massive multiplayer game in which countries, cities, companies, and various other communities all compete in an all-encompassing struggle. Winston Churchill once advised that it is always better to "jaw-jaw" than to "war-war," meaning diplomacy is preferable to conflict. Today's world is a hybrid of the two: It is an endless tug-tug.

WAS ORWELL RIGHT?

Witnessing the negotiations that carved up Eurasia into spheres of influence during the early years of the Cold War, George Orwell was seized with a sense of inevitability about perpetual war between the world's rival blocs—especially after the testing of atomic weapons. A keen witness to the homogenizing rigidity of both European colonialism and Soviet communism, Orwell portrayed all three of the mega-continental superstates in his landmark novel *1984*—Oceania, Eastasia, and Eurasia—as totalitarian regimes intolerant of dissent.

There is a stunning prescience to the map corresponding to *1984*. If we correct for continental Europe not having been conquered by the Soviet Union and cede it to Oceania (America), it accurately depicts the three-pillared Western constellation of North America, South America, and the European Union (with London and New York as twin regional capitals). Meanwhile, Russia (Eurasia) retains sway over the "Mongolic" mass of northern Eurasia, while "death-worshipping" Eastasia (China) expands and subsumes Japan, Southeast Asia, and Central Asia.

Orwell's world was one of perpetual stalemate, with no single power—or even alliance of two against the third—able to dominate the planet.* However, in a perverse twist Orwell never could have imagined at the time of his death in 1950, the superstates' primary mode of interaction is not the conquest of each other's territory but the pursuit of access to each other's resources and markets. Precisely because they cannot conquer each other, they wage not war but tug-of-war.

In supply chain geopolitics, the notion of discrete geographic blocs becomes untenably twisted, displaced by the physical glue of infrastructures and the institutional glue of treaties. For example, the United States and Europe are in the midst of forming a Transatlantic Trade and Investment Partnership (TTIP) that will eliminate almost all regulatory frictions across the Atlantic and deepen what is already the world's largest investment pool. Already the United States and Canada are each other's largest trade partners, and the EU is by far the largest source of investment into the United States. With TTIP, transatlantic exchange would rise even further above its $3 billion of *daily* trade. TTIP is therefore as close to a merger as two continents can get without fusing together.

At the same time, the United States so desperately needs to export energy, goods, and services to the ravenously growing Asian markets that it has championed *both* the TTIP negotiations across the Atlantic and the Trans-Pacific Partnership (TPP) agreement across the Pacific, which will phase out tariffs and set common

---

* The regions they are warring over, those squeezed in between these continental mega-powers, are the ones I explored in *The Second World: Empires and Influence in the New Global Order*.

standards among a dozen countries totaling 40 percent of world GDP. Building economic ties with one's rivals—or one's rivals' neighbors—is a crucial tool of strategic influence, but this kind of competitive liberalization is waged over supply chains, not territory. TPP's goal is thus not to exclude China but to build up leverage to further *open* China.* American exports to China grew fivefold from 2000 to 2010, and China's exports to the United States are rising as well; indeed, China is overtaking Canada as America's largest trade partner. Even with a bailout from Washington, General Motors, a market leader in China, would never have survived the financial crisis if not for its overseas revenues. Furthermore, neither the United States nor the U.K. can meet its goal of doubling exports without attracting hundreds of billions of dollars more investment into its factories, refineries, and other facilities—especially from China.

It would appear that the larger China's and Asia's economies grow—and grow together—the more the United States and the EU must join forces to maintain leverage. But America's anxieties about China are not shared uniformly within Oceania, as evidenced by the deepening connectivity between Europe and China across Eurasia's Ural Mountain divide. Unlike America, Europe doesn't view China as a security threat. It has no role in America's deepening military cooperation with India, Australia, and Japan in the Indian and Pacific Oceans. Instead, Britain, France, and Germany are China's leading source of advanced defense technologies. As the RMB appreciates and the euro weakens, Europe is the main beneficiary of China's surging overseas asset binges into everything from real estate to clean energy.† EU-China trade will soon surpass EU-U.S.

---

* There is an ongoing debate as to whether China itself might join TPP if it agrees to adhere to the standards of protecting intellectual property and ending preferential treatment for state-owned enterprises. At the same time, as rules-of-origin requirements are reduced, China may simply invest in the minimal required amount of production in an actual TPP member country and qualify nonetheless for duty-free exports across the TPP membership, including the United States.

† Xi Jinping's October 2015 state visit to the U.K. was hailed as the laying of the foundation for a "global comprehensive strategic partnership," including nearly $50 billion in bilateral trade and investment deals.

trade in volume. Bottom line: Connectivity across Eurasia now competes with culture across the Atlantic.

Collectively, the world's three largest economic areas and trading powers—Europe, China, and America—represent the vast majority of world GDP, investment, and trade, especially with each other. Conflict, cooperation, and competition thus overlap in a complex interplay where relations become a subtle mix of cooperation on some issues (containing North Korea's nuclear program, confronting climate change, expanding bilateral trade) and competition on others (reserve currency, regional influence, cyber regulation)—rather than an all-or-nothing proposition. When Presidents Obama and Xi held a 2014 summit at Sunnylands in California and spoke of aspiring toward "a new kind of great power relationship," that was a reflection of the current reality—not a future scenario. As the University of Virginia political scientist Dale Copeland has demonstrated, interdependence forestalls conflict if leaders expect its benefits to continue—if they learn the benefits of fighting tug-of-war instead of the real thing.

THE CALM BEFORE THE STORM?

In the 1990s, as the dust settled on the Cold War, Pentagon strategists were already worried about World War III. Geopolitical history suggested that it would take place in the region of most rapidly concentrating power (Asia) between a declining hegemon (America) and a rising power (China). The answer to what they would fight over was unanimous: Taiwan. Yet fast-forward twenty-five years and almost nobody believes World War III will take place over Taiwan. What happened to defuse what once seemed inevitable?

Deterrence, of course, played an important role. After four decades of American arms sales and security guarantees, Taiwan's military has become a formidable force, even as China's huge investments in modernizing the People's Liberation Army (PLA) give it the ultimate advantage. At the same time, relations between Taiwan and the People's Republic of China have evolved from the dogma of "no contact, no compromise, no negotiation" to something that resembles "one China, two interpretations." There are more than three hundred weekly flights between Taiwan and the mainland, many carrying the droves of Taiwanese who are moving to the mainland to capitalize on higher growth. China has even proposed the construction of a 120-kilometer tunnel across the Taiwan Strait from Fujian province. China is by far the largest destination for Taiwanese exports, earning the island a trade surplus of over $100 billion per year. Eighty percent of Taiwan's foreign investment goes to China as well; think of Foxconn, the Taiwanese company that makes (in China) most of the world's iPhones and iPads. The supply chain on which Taiwan—and American consumers—depend is very much a Chinese supply chain as well.

Even though former president and Kuomintang leader Ma Ying-jeou and Chinese president Xi Jinping held a historic meeting in 2015—the first between the leaders of both sides since the end of the Chinese Civil War in 1949—there are plausible scenarios whereby the gradual rapprochement toward peaceful reunification stalls or even reverses. The more nationalist Democratic Progressive Party (DPP) could push for its platform of Taiwan becoming the country's official name instead of the confusing "Republic of China" and assert greater sovereignty in island disputes. Then there is Foxconn, whose chairman, Terry Gou, wants to relocate his factories—and install docile robots instead of restless humans—to Indonesia to save on costs. If Taiwanese businesses begin to unlink their supply chains in China while the DPP asserts independence, reunification will seem far from inevitable. None of this means that war will ensue, but it guarantees that the tug-of-war will continue.

Can we forever transmute war into tug-of-war? Each day we wake expecting to hear that Israel has attacked Iran, China has sunk Japanese warships, Russia has annexed another former Soviet republic, or North Korea has launched an invasion of the South. World War III should have broken out ten times over by now, yet not one of these major geopolitical tensions has erupted. In every case of severe military escalation over the past two decades, not only have leaders stood down from the brink, but as with China and Taiwan the underlying dynamic of steady integration advances as well. (Today's most tragic conflicts, by contrast, such as the collapse of Iraq and Syria and the Russia-Ukraine war, were scarcely predicted by anyone.)

Since their simultaneous independence in 1947, India and Pakistan have fought three major wars, built substantial nuclear arsenals, skirmished in the Himalayan Mountains, and continue to dispute the status of Kashmir. But in recent years, they have opened their borders to more regular commerce in textiles, pharmaceuticals, and other goods, eased visa restrictions for each other's citizens, approved more direct airline routes, and granted each other most favored nation trading status.

India and China also fought a major war in 1962 along their still disputed border, and India is home to the Dalai Lama and Tibetan exile community whom China considers dangerous separatists. And yet trade between China and India has skyrocketed to over $100 billion per year and climbing. During his state visit in 2014, Xi Jinping signed $3.5 billion worth of investment deals, including the construction of a new industrial park in Narendra Modi's home state of Gujarat, and during a reciprocal visit to China in 2015 $22 billion worth of new deals were inked covering energy, logistics, entertainment, and other areas—and crucially the installation of a hotline linking military commanders.

Strategic discourse on South Asia over the past several decades has focused on simple geometric assertions such as the "strategic triangle" of India, Pakistan, and China, with the latter two teaming up to contain the former, while India gradually joins forces in a "global NATO" with the United States, Japan, and Australia to encircle China. This is the kind of antiquated stratagem that sounds deep and grave but reveals an almost cultivated unwillingness to appreciate more complex realities.

The fact that there are now three cross-border trading posts between India and China has not slowed China from stationing two armored brigades and motorized infantry at Xigaze in Tibet, where its chosen successor to the Dalai Lama resides, nor India from stationing an equivalent number of tanks across the recently opened Nathu-La Pass on the high plateau of Sikkim, training a new army mountain division, and locating a new combat air wing at nearby airfields in Assam. In a reversal of conventional wisdom that China always has time on its side, in this case it is India that has youth and growth, swelling pride and surging military spending.

While the two Asian giants have far more to gain from friendly ties than from fighting over literally 0.1 percent of their combined territory, it would still be entirely unsurprising if Chinese infiltration of a narrow protrusion of northern Sikkim near a strategic Tibetan highway (known as the Finger), or a political crisis surrounding the Dalai Lama's succession, created a fait accompli for China to occupy India's Tibetan-populated Arunachal Pradesh (which China claims as "South Tibet") on the other side of Bhutan.* But after the dust has settled, the ice has melted, the wreckage has been cleared, the bodies have been counted, the treaties have been signed, and the borders have shifted, the "Southern Silk Road" from India to China would thrive again.

If any single historical row has replaced Taiwan in terms of geopolitical fatalism, it is China and Japan's dispute over the Senkaku/Diaoyu Islands, a string of uninhabited rocks equidistant from Japan, China, and Taiwan—the latter two in agreement that the islands belong to Taiwan, while Japan traces its claim to victory in the 1894–95 Sino-Japanese War. When China and Japan agreed to normalize relations in 1945, it was agreed that the islands would not be militarized and the dispute would be put off for future generations. The next generation has arrived. With the discovery of large potential oil reserves under the islands, the dispute has heated up dramatically: Coast guard and naval warships jostle in overlapping zones of declared control, and fighter jets scramble to patrol and

---

* During the 1962 war, the PLA briefly occupied the spiritually significant Tawang Monastery.

escort commercial planes crossing the skies above. The slightest miscalculation is an invitation to war. In 2014, Japan's prime minister, Shinzo Abe, made major speeches around the world to rally attention to China's aggression, and in 2015 the Japanese parliament lifted the long-standing ban on overseas military operations. But whether Chinese actions or Japanese nationalism is to blame for the current bout of antagonism, the constant references to history show that they have learned something from it: Deterrence massively raises the stakes of conflict, and the economic incentives align more with the status quo and integration than with escalation.

Indeed, while daily newspapers report about China impounding Japanese cargo ships and demanding war reparations, street protests and boycotts of Japanese carmakers, Japanese coast guard ships ramming a Chinese fishing trawler and imprisoning its skipper, and China banning the export of rare earth minerals to Japan, there are also the delegations of Japanese executives given red-carpet treatment by China's commerce minister and vice-premier, a huge rebound in sales of Japanese cars in China (Toyota sold a record number of cars in China in 2015), and over $340 billion in annual trade.[1] Japan needs China's market, and China needs Japan's technology.

Asia abounds in other high-risk war scenarios. China and Vietnam skirmish over the Paracel Islands, while the Philippines clings to the Scarborough Shoal amid Chinese blockades. North Korea has a limited nuclear weapons stockpile and is perennially testing ballistic missiles with little warning. America's rebalancing of forces to East Asia means even more bases, ships, jets, maneuvers, and flash points, intended or accidental. The Pentagon strategists of the 1990s were certainly correct that if World War III happens, it will surely be in Asia: The current dynamic between military escalation and economic integration may just be a prelude in the shadow of an inevitable slide into major war.

Indeed, China's rapid rise and growing assertiveness are reminders that Asian political institutions remain immature, leaving commercial integration as the main brake on military escalation. Ideally, the U.S. military presence in Asia can serve to maintain a strategic balance in the Pacific such that diplomatic bodies can rise to the occasion as they did in postwar Europe when America's security umbrella enabled political integration to advance. The French foreign minister Robert Schuman wisely foresaw that once the French and German commodities markets were integrated through the European Coal and Steel Community, the two countries would jointly own a merged supply chain and could never fight again. Not only are Asian supply chains deeply integrated across China, Japan, South Korea, and Southeast Asia, but Asia is also the locus of many joint U.S.-Chinese supply chains. This is why Admiral Samuel Locklear, former chief of U.S. Pacific Command, has said that the United States and China converge on 80 percent of everything.

The commonsense truth is that while leaders talk about "red lines" for public consumption, and navies come dangerously close to trading direct fire, the stock markets churn forward, knowing that there are two kinds of mutually assured destruction at play: military and economic. Military maneuvers don't tell us enough about what drives leverage among great powers nor what they are willing to fight over. The tangled complexities of today's system force leaders to think beyond borders and make functional calculations about the cost-benefit utility of their strategies—knowing full well that supply chain warfare involves not just an enemy "over there" but also one's own deep interests "over there." Waiting for World War III thus reminds us of Samuel Beckett's *Waiting for Godot,* in which Vladimir and Estragon resolve to hang themselves if Godot does not arrive—so they simply sit endlessly. Their would-be savior, Godot, of course never comes, but the protagonists never actually commit suicide either.

WAR BY OTHER MEANS

It is easy to detect where the conditions for conflict are ripe and proclaim that war is at hand. Especially in 2014, the centennial of the outbreak of World War I, media and academic chatter was replete with such historical analogies. It is no doubt unwise to argue that World War III is a passé risk. However, as the French scholar Raymond Aron argued, nuclear deterrence and the benefits of hindsight are crucial in warding against the uncontrolled escalations of the twentieth century or even harrowing episodes such as the Cuban missile crisis. Furthermore, China's neo-mercantilism today is quite different from the zero-sum European colonial mercantilism of centuries ago: It is the pursuit of catch-up modernization rather than global hegemony. China seeks foreign raw materials and technology, not foreign territory.

In our haste to make analogies between today's global dynamics and pre–World War I Europe, most observers have missed the enormous differences. European nations traded heavily across each other prior to World War I, but they did so as vertically integrated mercantile empires exploiting raw materials from their own vast colonies. They traded in finished goods and didn't outsource production to each other; we did not have today's international manufacturing networks in 1895. The nineteenth and twentieth centuries brought trade interdependence; in the twenty-first century, we have complex supply chain dispersal as well.

The growing depth of global cross-border trade and investment makes tug-of-war much more complex than in previous geopolitical eras. This evolution of economic integration from the nineteenth to the twenty-first century is best captured in the progression from the ideas of David Ricardo to those of Ricardo Hausmann. The English political economist David Ricardo is best known as the champion of comparative advantage over mercantilism, advocating industry specialization and free trade among nations. Today's world economic structure goes far beyond Ricardo's wildest imagination. As the Harvard economist Ricardo Hausmann maps out in his pathbreaking *Atlas of Economic Complexity,** the global economy is like a game of Scrabble with millions of pieces (letters) distributed

---

* The *Atlas* is now installed as a widget of multicolor boxes appearing on every country's *Wikipedia* entry, visualizing the specific roles it plays in the global economic division of labor.

across countries (players) who work in teams to combine the pieces to make products (words). We don't just trade in goods; we "trade in tasks" along the supply chain. Hausmann's data comes mostly from the production and trade of goods, yet it applies in spades to the expanding supply chain of global financial and digital services.

Both Ricardos have won the day. In numerous sectors such as automobiles and electronics, the import quantity of exports hovers near 50 percent, meaning much of what we sell to each other is made from things we've bought from each other. Furthermore, the biggest companies of generations past were less dependent on exports for financial survival than General Motors and Apple, 60 percent of whose gadgets are sold outside the United States. The West depends more than ever on the rest for its bottom line and for jobs: Forty million American jobs alone are directly linked to exports. Even though America's imports have declined due to its shale gas reserves, America is very much still a trading nation because services are a far larger component of America's economy—and its trade—than manufacturing. America's services aren't shipped but zipped to giant consumer markets in Asia.

Under a Cold War geopolitical paradigm, rivals wouldn't invest in each other either; the United States and the Soviet Union certainly didn't. But today's robust flows of global investment among friends *and* enemies—"frenemies"—further highlight how we have shifted from a Westphalian world to a supply chain world. The world's leading powers have become financially integrated, with investment linkages as important as trade relations. This comes in the form of both the trillions of dollars of assets invested in each other's currencies and equities and the tangible, productive capital—factories, real estate, banks, agriculture—they have bought and built inside others' territory to efficiently and profitably access each other's markets. Supply chains thus diminish the incentives for conflict, while decoupling from them raises the potential for antagonism to escalate.

Those who believe globalization can be switched off so quickly also inadvertently make the logic of war more likely. American warships patrol the Strait of Hormuz, while Chinese vessels circle disputed islands in the Pacific Ocean, and India modernizes its nuclear arsenal and navy. It does not follow, however, that interstate conflict is the natural order of things. How else could it be that despite a century of world wars, followed by a decade of civil wars and a decade-long "war on terror," globalization continues to widen and deepen? Warfare is an event; network building is a process.

A hyper-connected multipolar world is uncharted territory, but the paradox of tug-of-war may be that the longer it goes on, the more everyone wins. Economic coercion precedes military hostilities in today's geopolitical maneuvering. Even though interdependence can be weaponized through financial sanctions, cyber-attacks, and supply chain disruptions, escalation is far costlier for both sides today than a century ago because they immediately harm one's own businesses operating in the rival country. Clausewitz's dictum that "war is the continuation of politics by other means" must be updated: War is the continuation of tug-of-war by other means.

CHAPTER 7

THE GREAT SUPPLY CHAIN WAR

TRADING ATOMS
AND BITS

THE MORE YOU TRY TO UNTANGLE GLOBAL TRADE, THE MORE quantum it becomes. The path by which so many even simple products are put together is so complex that there is no clear answer as to where something is "made." Manufacturing supply chains began to unbundle almost fifty years ago, shifting a massive share of the production of everything from electronics to clothing to the Asian Tigers (Hong Kong, Singapore, South Korea, and Taiwan), China, Thailand, Mexico, and eventually other pockets of low-wage and semiskilled workers in India, Indonesia, and beyond. Components and inputs from screws and bolts to dyes and paints to copper and glass circulate for assembly, finishing, packaging, and more tasks along the supply chain. Like data packets routed through servers around the world before arriving at your neighbor's computer, there is no avoiding the radically dispersed nature of supply chains.

Global value chains are becoming one complex but comprehensive whole. European companies have software development in the United States, manufacturing in Asia, back-office work in the Middle East, and joint ventures with local partners for after-sales services such as repair and insurance in every market they sell in.

Maps 24, 25, and 26, corresponding to this chapter,
appear in the second map insert.

America's import content of exports is relatively low at only 15 percent, but it is actually 40 percent if one takes a full-cycle view of downstream distribution and sales. WTO chief economist Patrick Low describes the emergence of such "hybrid value chains" in somewhat quantum terms: "The physical and the digital, the manufacturing and the services, and the value-added from intangible factors such as competence and reputation are simply not captured by today's statistical methods."[1] Products should start carrying the label "Made Everywhere."

Beware simplistic calls for corporate America to "return home": Globalization is *not* the one-way outbound flow of jobs portrayed by populist politicians. American multinationals have added over two million jobs across Asia and Latin America and cut nearly one million jobs at home, but they have also created many new high-skill jobs domestically in engineering, consulting, and finance.* Furthermore, the more jobs and wealth American companies create abroad, the more foreigners buy American goods: U.S. exports to emerging markets doubled from 1990 to 2012. Cutting off American investment (and thus profits) overseas will therefore lead to reduced investment at home too. Remember tug-of-war: Be careful when untangling the rope.

Even what looks like de-globalization is actually still globalization. Apple is a perfect example of these complex realities. The Berkeley economist Enrico Moretti estimates that Apple is substantially responsible for sixty thousand jobs in Silicon Valley, only twelve thousand of which are employees in its Cupertino headquarters. "In Silicon Valley," Moretti claims, "high-tech jobs are the *cause* of local prosperity, and the doctors, lawyers, roofers and yoga teachers are the *effect*."[2] What appears a thriving community is primarily

---

* American multinationals have generated 11 percent of the jobs created in the United States since 1990, 19 percent of current private sector jobs, and 25 percent of total private sector wages. Almost half of American exports are created by multinationals, and 90 percent of intermediate goods produced in America are bought by American multinationals. Three-quarters of America's private sector R&D comes from multinationals. See McKinsey Global Institute, "Growth and Competitiveness in the United States: The Role of Its Multinational Corporations" (June 2010).

the result of corporate innovation and global growth—*not* public investment. Apple is now taking its passive provision of goods a step further by strategically relaunching the production of one iMac line in Texas. As the CEO, Tim Cook, said in December 2013, "I don't think we have a responsibility to create a certain kind of job. But I think we do have a responsibility to create jobs."[3] The distinction is important, because even though Apple will invest $100 million in repatriating assembly, Apple products are still largely made from foreign parts such as Samsung chips and Sharp screens that will have to be *imported,* and its longtime manufacturing partner, Taiwanese Foxconn, has facilities in Texas already. Even the most advanced economies cannot create good exports without good imports.

The lesson applies in spades to emerging markets that cannot become more competitive without acquiring the latest technologies and techniques from abroad. China imports 34 percent of all the world's electronic components, without which it could not have become the largest exporter of finished information and communications technology (ICT) goods, which represent 27 percent of its total exports. (Worldwide, at least two-thirds of the value of goods and services is generated by such intermediate inputs.)

The difference between winners and losers in this global tug-of-war is not rich versus poor but *new versus old.* Because China needs the latest technology products to move up the value chain, in 2015 it accepted a WTO-brokered agreement to liberalize trade in over two hundred crucial tech components. Even as labor costs rise, foreign electronics, textiles, and chemical companies report that China's higher-quality workers and integrated supply chain offerings make it a sticky investment destination. By contrast, countries that restrict imports through unnecessary tariffs and customs hurdles shoot themselves in the foot by raising the costs to local producers of getting the quality inputs they need to make better exports.*

Because such measures do more harm than good, supply chain

---

* For example, Brazil's rules-of-origin requirements for supplying to the oil giant Petrobras has hampered its ability to get the best technology while also tarnishing its— and the country's—reputation.

tug-of-war isn't just protectionism in new clothing. Instead, it operates within a far more powerful code: reciprocity. Reciprocity is the
most powerful bulwark against excessive economic nationalism.
When President Obama imposed tariffs on Chinese tires in 2009
while bailing out automakers to protect workers in Michigan and
Pennsylvania, China struck back with a 20 percent tariff hike on
Cadillacs—and for good measure on Hondas and BMWs made in
the United States but sold in China—until the United States backed
down. Similarly, the WTO's rulings against China's 2011 ban on the
export of rare earth minerals allowed other countries to retaliate in
kind until China reversed course. The WTO's dispute resolution
mechanism not only is the most influential arbitration tool but also
prevents countries from hoarding resources for themselves by compelling them to share through markets. It thus moves us further
from a world of nations and borders toward a supply-demand
world.

Reciprocity makes protectionism self-defeating, even senseless.
Indeed, far from the Depression-era Smoot-Hawley tariffs, the four
hundred protectionist measures enacted by countries in 2013 alone
affect a total of only 1 percent of global merchandise goods imports. Eighty percent of world trade takes place within and among
the supply chains of global multinational firms and their affiliates—
why would they want to pay more to supply themselves?*

Smoothing the physical flow of trade matters even more than
reducing tariffs. With the Bali Trade Facilitation Agreement of 2013,
the harmonization of customs administration (cutting red tape)
could add $1 trillion to world GDP and create twenty million jobs. A
study undertaken by the World Economic Forum and Bain estimates
that further aligning supply chain standards would boost world
GDP by an enormous 5 percent, while implementation of all current
WTO accords would deliver only 1 percent growth. The Ethereum

---

* Even currency devaluations between the dollar, the euro, the RMB, and the yen have
effectively negated each other while stimulating both imports and exports, a reminder
that the major economies' relations are so dense that they are better served calibrating
their currencies rather than competing with them.

blockchain platform will allow for standardized and transparent contracts between trading parties beyond any single jurisdiction and, when combined with real-time data sharing on supply chain transactions, can substantially reduce the cost of insuring trade.

Open trade and open borders further reorganize the world into functional circuits. Despite widely divergent geography and wealth, Canada, Argentina, South Africa, Indonesia, Australia, and other countries coalesced into the Cairns Group to push for free trade in agriculture: They are the "farm circuit" of global trade. Five Latin American countries—Mexico, Costa Rica, Colombia, Peru, and Chile—representing a larger and faster-growing economic club than Brazil, have formed a Pacific alliance to boost their cargo volumes to Asia, indicating how important connectivity is to them despite prohibitive geography. High-tech exporters such as the United States and Germany want to pry open protected markets, and thus team up to promote "behind-the-border" issues such as intellectual property protection, labor and environmental standards, removal of investment caps, foreign investor protection, and privatization of state enterprises. Indeed, the "free market" does not yet include major areas of government procurement such as defense, health, education, and infrastructure that amount to almost one-third of the world economy, but as each of these becomes an ongoing service, they too will be subject to global market competition.

With global services trade doubling every five years, commerce is increasingly conducted more on digital waves than across oceanic ones. Services already account for more than 60 percent of the total value of world trade and more than half the world's workforce (with agriculture and industry representing almost equally the remaining half). Banking, insurance, software, programming, consulting, design, architecture, accounting, legal contracts and litigation, health care, and education are all intangible but highly lucrative sectors. More than 30 percent of American and European GDP is generated from portable services, meaning even more work can be performed and delivered anywhere and must be if companies can hope to profit from faster-growing markets.

Multinationals are thus deeply connected and exposed to the emerging markets that have become their main competitors. According to a BCG survey, 73 percent of American companies believe their profits will grow in Asia over the next five to ten years, but only 13 percent believe they will retain an edge over local rivals. China's telecom market used to be dominated by Japan, Germany, Sweden, and France, but all of them now compete for shrinking market share against giant domestic rivals such as China Mobile and handset makers such as HTC and Xiaomi, which earned a valuation of $40 billion in 2014 after only two years of operation. The only way to retain market share in such a scenario is to team up with the competition through more mergers and joint ventures. If you can't beat them, buy them.

Eventually, as countries become wealthier, they import more high-value goods from luxury clothing to iPhones. Thus as China moves up the value chain from sunset industries such as state-owned manufacturing toward tradable services such as telecoms and software, it too will favor openness over protectionism. Indeed, it is precisely the Chinese companies most aggressively expanding internationally that most seek a level commercial field. In 2014, Ericsson managed to block a popular Xiaomi model from sale in India due to a patent infringement. That same year, Huawei sued fellow Shenzhen-based ZTE in a German court for the same reason!

PRINTING, SHARING—AND TRADING

The biggest threat to current patterns of global trade comes from the combination of 3-D printing (which allows more products to be manufactured locally at "home") and the sharing economy (by which fewer goods are purchased but existing goods are consumed as services). Local prototyping and mass production together could bring about a severe long-term contraction in global shipping, inventories, and warehousing. If DHL's largest clients—the U.S. military and hardware companies such as HP—suddenly printed all their components on-site at bases or client facilities, the courier business could go bust. Furthermore, as emerging market companies face greater time pressure from their own customers, they cannot wait weeks for equipment to be delivered or repaired. Instead, airlines, appliance vendors, computer hardware retailers, and many other sectors want access to the full life cycle of production, with replacement parts proximately located through local joint ventures.

But technology doesn't eliminate supply chains; it morphs them. Remember that to "print" objects at a large scale requires major inputs of raw materials—whether organic matter or plastics—most of which might still need to be imported to "feed" 3-D printing devices, which also may be made in and made from components from around the world. Some supply chains may compress, but others will expand. It is not likely that shipping will decline; rather, *what* is shipped will change. An object may be designed in one place, but the design is then zapped to factories near its customer across the world where it is printed using materials that are harvested in one place and loaded into cartridges in another place. Manufacturing will have global dimensions no matter how radical the technology. Don't confuse physics and logistics.[4]

American firms would profit far more from worrying less about the "where" of the hardware than the lucrative value-added "what" of the design of complex products. Google's Ara project epitomizes this trend by creating the equivalent of an app store for modular hardware components that people can design, create, sell, and ship to anyone anywhere so they can assemble a customized mobile phone. The same is happening in medical prosthetics and driverless cars: It matters far less where artificial limbs or composite car parts are printed than whose software and design lead the market. An Australian company producing medical equipment for use in surgeries in China found it easier to print the parts in China rather than manufacture them in Australia using titanium components. The intellectual value chain thrives through collaborative design even as the physical supply chain shifts.

HORIZONTAL + VERTICAL = DIAGONAL

There is just one formula one needs to understand the Great Supply Chain War: Horizontal + Vertical = Diagonal. Competitors want to be horizontal nodes of production and distribution and vertical hubs of value creation—together propelling themselves diagonally up the ladder of economic complexity.

For example, America's harnessing its enormous shale energy reserves has been nothing less than a giant dose of steroids for North America's tug-of-war team, while the resulting collapse in oil prices has imposed enormous fiscal strain on Arab and African petro-states. Even resource-less countries can become key horizontal tug-of-war players: Singapore is a small market with no raw materials yet is a top transshipment port, refined petroleum exporter, and commodities trading hub. It doesn't fight over the supply chain but generates massive profits simply from smoothing it for others.

In horizontal tug-of-war, extortion can be an effective tool of state building. For example, just as the West imposed sanctions on Russia over its invasion of Ukraine in 2014, Indonesia demanded that the foreign mining companies Newmont and Freeport-McMoRan pay higher royalties to access its raw materials and also that they build smelters, refineries, and processing plants to strengthen Indonesia's local value added and profits. Russia tacitly encouraged the move because the dispute temporarily froze Indonesia's nickel exports, raising global prices just as its own mining giant Norilsk came under sanction. More recently, Indonesia has tried to ban the purchase of foreign ships and secondhand clothing to strengthen its shipbuilding and garments industries while also threatening to cancel investment treaties with dozens of countries unless they agreed to new contracts that did not allow for international arbitration in cases of expropriation.

The shipping and commodities industries in combination capture both the arms race and the complexity of tug-of-war resource geopolitics. Rio Tinto and BHP Billiton, which produce most of Australia's iron ore, have dominated China's iron ore imports (even though China itself is the world's largest producer of iron ore). To better compete with Rio and BHP in meeting Chinese demand, the Brazilian mining giant Vale has commissioned a fleet of Valemax ships capable of carrying 400,000 deadweight tons of iron ore under Africa's cape to Asia. But China's iron ore shippers have lobbied against allowing the Valemax to dock at Chinese ports, whose current capacity limit is 250,000 tons per ship. Seeking to keep an edge over their Brazilian rival, Rio and BHP of course side with the Chinese—not least because Chinalco is one of Rio's largest shareholders. At the same time, both BHP and Rio have been the subjects of politically motivated anticorruption witch hunts in China. Meanwhile, in late 2014, Vale opened a major transshipment center on Malaysia's western coast to break down cargo size and remix the iron ore to various grades and spread it across multiple ships bound for China, Japan, and other markets. Collectively, Rio, BHP, and Vale tacitly share an interest in surging production at the risk of creating global oversupply so they can squeeze out smaller players (including those in China) and maintain a big-three cartel that has greater price-setting leverage over China. While China resists such maneuvers, it also knows that the only way to neutralize Australia's alliance with America is to make it a supply chain ally.

Tug-of-war is just as fierce higher up the value chain. The Eastwood City Cyberpark in Manila is home to a bustling high-rise cluster of offices with thirty thousand call center workers varying their shifts by the global time zone they serve—much the same way as the Indian call center workers in Bangalore used to do before the Filipinos took their business. The intense competition among circuit nodes is a reminder that the global economy shapes how we work more than geography or daylight. The former Citicorp CEO

Walter Wriston once wrote, "Time zones matter more than borders,"[5] and indeed some economists have recently proposed that the United States reduce to just two time zones.[6]

If horizontal tug-of-war is resource mercantilism, then vertical tug-of-war is innovation mercantilism: grabbing the most technologically sophisticated and financially profitable segments of strategic industries. In vertical tug-of-war, value matters more than volume. China exports more than twenty times as many watches as Switzerland, but each Swiss watch is worth on average three hundred times more. Germany captures 60 percent of the revenue from its value-add to exports, while China gets only 30 percent.

Vertical tug-of-war is how one's biggest customer also becomes one's largest competitor. Since the 1950s, Asians have been on the receiving end of America's innovative edge in core technologies such as semiconductors, but Asian countries have steadily climbed the value chain through a combination of outsourcing and technology transfer. Japan and South Korea emerged as major electronics and automotive exporters in the 1960s and 1970s. IBM started chip production in Asia in the 1980s; by the 1990s, Japan had captured 70 percent of the computer memory chip industry. South Korea's and Taiwan's massive semiconductor foundries have made them global players in processors, while China is taking over photovoltaic solar cells.

Throughout the first decade of the twenty-first century, Japan, Korea, Taiwan, and China continued massive spending on boosting innovation ecosystems through R&D, subsidies, and guaranteed purchases of companies' output.[7] A typical example is Japan's backing of NEC's satellites to boost its market share against American and European firms. Today, Toyota City near Nagoya and Samsung Town in Seoul are vertically integrated ecosystems of research, design, management, and components—hundreds of companies treated as extensions of the mother ship itself.

When countries compete, they do so with their entire supply chains. That includes America: Washington's bailout of General Motors was not only to salvage one company but to prevent its failure from wiping out all its secondary suppliers—and about one million jobs—across the country. Building and retaining strategic industries are crucial for high employment and keeping up worker skills.

Tug-of-war is very much about using market size as a lever to get industrial innovators to sponsor a population's ascent up the value chain. Even though Emirates airlines is armed with a financial war chest, French and German governments both discount and subsidize the airline to purchase dozens of jumbo Airbus planes because of the tens of thousands of jobs their production creates in Europe.* And yet the U.A.E. is pressuring aircraft makers to locate more of their maintenance operations in Dubai so that locals get the jobs and acquire skills and know-how.

China's ascent up the global value chain suggests that it is as strategic—if not more so—about tug-of-war as about traditional war. Industrial policy to protect companies at home has become strategic subsidies to promote exports abroad. China wants not simply to assemble millions of iPhones—earning $8 per unit—but to design its own competitor such as Xiaomi. "Made in China" is becoming "Made by China." From ZTE phones to CRRC railcars to LiuGong mining equipment, China is rapidly displacing foreign incumbents at home and competing worldwide with the same companies whose investments sparked their industries at the outset. After buying IBM's personal computer division, Lenovo is now the largest desktop and laptop maker. China has also become the largest purchaser of advanced industrial robotics to keep manufacturing churning even as its population ages and labor costs rise.†

* Export credit agencies (ECAs) further give home players the added edge abroad. ECAs already receive far more funding than all the world's commitments to multilateral organizations and aid programs, and in times of heightened volatility and competition they play a powerful countercyclical role in keeping companies churning.

† Chinese companies have also been buying European firms for their intellectual property and to get around WTO antidumping measures and China's lack of "market economy" status. Under the terms of its WTO accession protocols, China's recognition as a market economy is foreseen for December 2016.

To catapult up the value chain, China has also deployed an incredibly sophisticated apparatus to steal valuable intellectual property, with theft of terabytes of data on advanced weapons systems such as the F-35 Joint Strike Fighter only one of its many tactical breakthroughs. Soon after a joint venture with Westinghouse began, Chinese hackers helped themselves to its nuclear power plant designs.

China is not alone in the pursuit of shortcuts. Ravi Venkatesan, the former chairman of Microsoft India, points out that Indian companies think of "copyright" as the "right to copy."[8] The lucrative defense sector is India's target as well. Modi has doubled the military's procurement budget to $19 billion, but rather than lavish it on Lockheed, Boeing, and BAE, India demands joint ventures, technology transfer, and local production. India has also planned a quadrupling of its maritime fleet but will build all its new ships at home. "Make in India" is the country's new mantra as well. Nokia once held 75 percent of the Indian smartphone market, but now India's own Micromax holds the top spot. Only one-third of Indians have their own refrigerators—mostly imported from LG, Samsung, and Whirlpool—but Indian brands aim to capture the next two-thirds. Similarly, as Indian pharmaceutical companies have improved their quality control, they not only have come to dominate the domestic market but now account for 40 percent of U.S. generic drug imports. This may dent the profits of Big Pharma, but it is a godsend for ordinary Americans.

Some Western companies have decided to protect their intellectual property by decoupling research and development: Keep the *R* at home, but cooperate on the *D* abroad. But then they risk losing access to the Chinese market. So instead they are doubling down: Daimler has agreed to begin building Mercedes engines in China. The formula for remaining profitable in China over the long term—keeping R&D outside the country, operating independently inside it, or having local partners who have a stake in protecting intellectual property—is not one any Western companies have confidently figured out. To the contrary, in 2015 IBM began to license server and software technology to the Beijing-based Teamsun, a company bent on using IBM's innovations to build indigenous equivalents. Soon Western companies will seek to be part of Chinese supply chains rather than the reverse.

China has enough land, labor, capital, technology, and knowledge to make almost anything and everything. Despite rising wages and growing competition, its manufacturing employment and output continue to grow, while the import share of the components going into its exports is rapidly declining. In other words, it is becoming a more self-reliant manufacturer of higher-value goods. The only way to retain competitive advantage is to make complex products nobody else can (yet). Germany, Switzerland, Finland, Japan, and Singapore rank atop the economic complexity index. Not only has Germany lost very few sectors to China, but its exports *to* China have surged as China requires the advanced chemical products and precision machine tools cranked out by Germany's technically advanced workforces.

In the 1970s, communist East Germany was a role model for Chinese economic planners. Today united Germany is China's icon for its complex goods and export competitiveness. Late nineteenth-century Germany dominated its continental rivals, while twenty-first-century Germany is a high-tech social democracy. China wants to be a giant Germany—both Bismarck's and Merkel's.

RESOURCE GENES AND DATA CENTERS FOR FOOD

The global mineral and food systems are in perpetual flux, with production expanding and contracting based on climate, technology, geopolitics, and other factors. For years, the extraction and processing of rare earth minerals was controlled by a small number of mostly state-owned companies in China—allowing them to rattle the entire electronics supply chain when China temporarily banned the export of rare earth minerals in 2011. But as with the oil shocks of the 1970s, geopolitical risk has spurred the United States,

Canada, India, Kazakhstan, and Australia to invest in excavating new supplies.[9] Just as distributed energy supplies and alternative and renewable energy technologies have ended OPEC's grip on oil prices, it is better to have diverse mineral suppliers as well.

The even more interesting story, however, is not of material competition but of substitution. Scientists are creating synthetic compounds to replace precious rare earth minerals, radically compressing supply chains in the process. MIT's Materials Project uses high-throughput computing to virtually test artificial composites that are then constructed by companies such as the MIT-affiliated start-up Xtalic, whose high-tech metallurgists can manipulate metals at atomic scale. Xtalic has designed and "printed" advanced alloys that serve the functions of gold and can customize compounds such as graphene, which is lighter and stronger than carbon fiber. Singapore-based IIa Technologies makes pure diamonds in "greenhouse labs" with a fraction of the material footprint and none of the human rights violations, supplying a growing share of the luxury and precision tool markets. Advances in such nano-materials could lead to water-free shale gas fracking, enabling more sustainable drilling in shale-rich but water-poor countries such as China.

Our quest for rare earth elements is even taking us to outer space—the eighth continent. China has sent a probe to the moon as an early step toward an eventual lunar supply chain, while the XPRIZE founder, Peter Diamandis, and Google's chairman, Eric Schmidt, have invested in a company that aspires to mine asteroids for valuable minerals. An entire global value chain has emerged around the space economy with satellite components, launchpads, ground monitoring stations, and other necessary systems built, distributed, and deployed across countries and in the stratosphere to access and share data.

The food industry provides another view into complex supply chain networks and the corporate alliances that make them possible. The Norwegian fish farming leader Marine Harvest, which produces one-third of the world's farmed salmon, has expanded through mergers and acquisitions into twenty other countries as far as Chile to meet rising demand for fish. While global production and distribution networks are expanding, new technologies such as more efficient photosynthesis could massively boost local crop yields even in inhospitable climates. (The Gates Foundation recently announced that empowering African farmers to achieve food self-sufficiency would be its top priority until 2030.)

Aquaponics represents another agricultural revolution: data centers for food. These high-tech greenhouses need neither natural light nor soil and only one-third the water of even organic farming, so they don't have to be greenhouses at all. The California start-up Famgro uses LED light in stackable units that look like tarpaulin-covered computing servers and grow food 24/7. They simply insert the spinach, kale, lettuce, basil, alfalfa, or other seeds and program the software. With mist-based fertilizer, plants grow in weeks rather than months. When the trays of crops are removed from the unit, the water is even recycled. Famgro already sells via FreshDirect in California and New York. But the company's biggest market for its hydroponic units will be land-scarce and entirely food-import-dependent countries such as the U.A.E. and Singapore that could locate its production units in giant hangars or underground bunkers.

Aquaponics could produce massively larger volumes of food in places with frigid climate as well. In Iceland, aquaponic greenhouses leverage the country's abundant freshwater (for the plants), hydro-power (for electricity), and geothermal power (for heating) to farm fish and produce tomatoes at the same time. Finland, which imports several tons of lettuce a day for its fast-food restaurants and grocery stores, is gradually replacing this with its own aquaponic output. Does it spell the end of agricultural globalization? Of course not: Spain and Italy will simply sell more lettuce to the 190 other countries that don't grow their own, just as Iceland is selling its surplus vegetables to northern European countries. In any case, shortening the food supply chain could only be a good thing because the food industry—from fertilizer production to transportation—generates an estimated 25 percent of our global greenhouse gas emissions.

THE "SUPPLY CIRCLE"

Tesla cars have no greenhouse gas emissions, but their supply chain isn't necessarily clean. Tesla has to import aluminum for the cars' bodies and copper and lithium for its batteries, which could come from countries such as Bolivia, Afghanistan, and Russia. Even a "homegrown" Tesla still includes elements from Europe, South America, and other regions. For Tesla's supply chain to truly be sustainable, it would have to work with the Dutch companies whose new battery factories in Bolivia safely mine lithium and invest in minimizing the pollution from aluminum smelting—or move away from aluminum altogether as it plans to for its next-generation vehicles.

Only analyzing the full web of production and externalities allows us to accurately price and tax goods based on their true total footprint. Such full-cycle accounting measures both the value and the cost of products end to end: resource extraction and energy used for production; jobs created and fuel consumed by packaging, shipping, and sales; the impact of operation and maintenance on communities and the environment; and the process of disposal and recycling. Governments and companies that assemble and analyze such data often better maintain and upgrade machinery for more efficient performance. In Europe alone, this "supply circle" approach has generated savings estimated at $380 billion as companies recycle, refurbish, and optimize parts like computer hardware.*

There is also an enormous secondary value to the hardware that builds and drives our economies. An efficient

---

* Companies that have the same suppliers and supply lines for components and assembly are also more willing to invest together to preempt disruptions in their common industry. The competitors Exxon, Shell, and BP have formed Canada's Oil Sands Innovation Alliance to share research and technologies across two hundred projects to develop cleaner extraction methods.

1. THE NEW NODES: SPECIAL ECONOMIC ZONES (SEZs) MUSHROOM AROUND THE WORLD

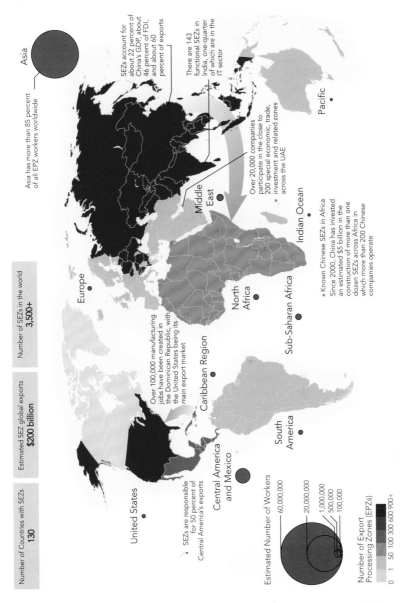

Number of Countries with SEZs	Estimated SEZ global exports	Number of SEZs in the world
130	$200 billion	3,500+

SEZs account for about 22 percent of China's GDP, about 46 percent of FDI, and about 60 percent of exports

There are 143 functional SEZs in India, one-quarter of which are in the IT sector

Asia has more than 85 percent of all EPZ workers worldwide

Over 20,000 companies participate in the close to 200 special economic, trade, investment and related zones across the UAE

Known Chinese SEZs in Africa
Since 2000, China has invested an estimated $5 billion in the construction of more than one dozen SEZs across Africa in which more than 200 Chinese companies operate

Over 100,000 manufacturing jobs have been created in the Dominican Republic, with the United States being its main export market

SEZs are responsible for 50 percent of Central America's exports

Asia
Pacific
Europe
Middle East
North Africa
Indian Ocean
Sub-Saharan Africa
Caribbean Region
United States
Central America and Mexico
South America

Estimated Number of Workers

60,000,000
20,000,000
1,000,000
500,000
100,000

Number of Export Processing Zones (EPZs)

0 1 50 100 300 600 900+

Nearly four thousand special economic zones (SEZs), export processing zones (EPZs), free trade zones (FTZs), and other industrial hubs compete over global supply chains, boosting exports and helping economies climb the value chain.

2. CHINA BUILDS SUPPLY CHAIN COMPLEMENTARITIES ACROSS THE GLOBE

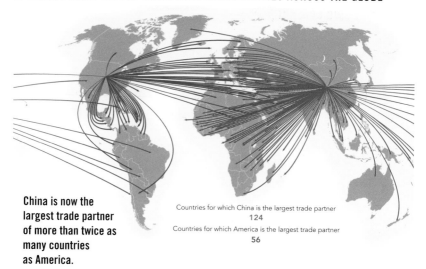

China is now the largest trade partner of more than twice as many countries as America.

Countries for which China is the largest trade partner
124

Countries for which America is the largest trade partner
56

3. INTERNATIONAL TRADE AND INVESTMENT VOLUMES CONTINUE TO CLIMB

Trade in both goods and services is advancing globally and is estimated to reach nearly two-thirds of global GDP by 2020, while the total value of foreign investment is expected to reach one-third of global GDP.

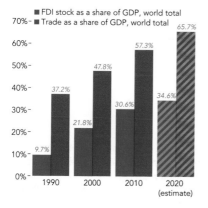

2013 gross bidirectional FDI stock, trillion USD
- 5+
- 1 to 5
- 0.1 to 1
- 0 to 0.1

2013 FDI stock, trillion USD
Inward FDI stock — Outward FDI stock
15
10
5
1

North and Central America

Europe

East Asia

Central and South Asia

Caribbean

South America

Africa

Middle East

Oceania

4. FDI FLOWS AND STOCKS RISING AMONG ALL REGIONS

While the United States, Europe, and East Asia dominate global FDI, growth market regions such as South America, Africa, the Middle East, and South Asia are increasingly attracting investment flows as well.

■ FDI stock as a share of GDP, world total
■ Trade as a share of GDP, world total

	1990	2000	2010	2020 (estimate)
Trade	37.2%	47.8%	57.3%	65.7%
FDI	9.7%	21.8%	30.6%	34.6%

5. GLOBAL TRADE LINKAGES
REVEAL RISING CONNECTIVITY

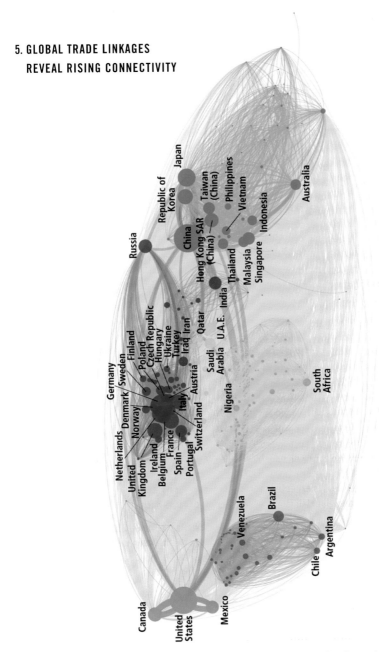

The DHL Global Connectedness Index (2014) captures how Europe remains the world's most connected region but also the increasing centrality of East Asia in supply chains and trade networks. Flows of goods, capital, people, and information are broadening to include the most remote geographies and populations.

6. THE WEALTH OF CONTINENTS

Proportional distribution of total global economic wealth by continent (2013).

7. MORE THAN HALF OF HUMANITY LIVES IN ASIA

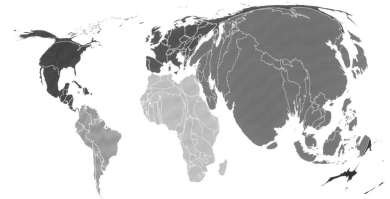

Total world population distribution (2013).

8. WORLD POVERTY CENTERS ON AFRICA AND ASIA

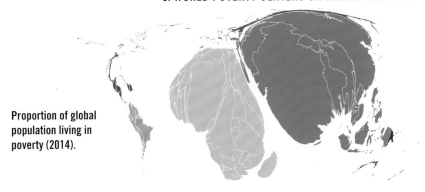

Proportion of global
population living in
poverty (2014).

9. GREENHOUSE GAS EMISSIONS RISING AS POPULATIONS AND WEALTH GROW

Total CO$_2$ emissions from
fossil fuel burning and
cement production (2013).

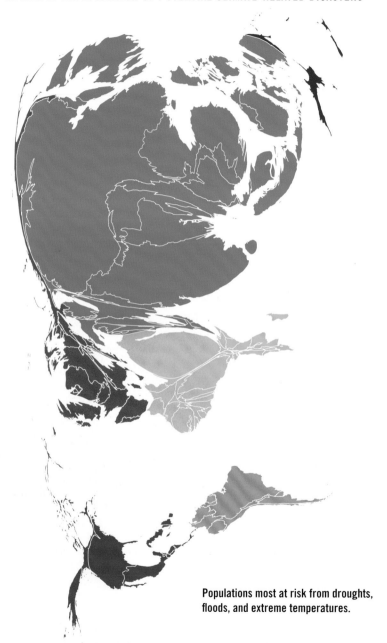

Populations most at risk from droughts, floods, and extreme temperatures.

11. INTER-CITY NETWORKS FLOURISH WITH THE RISE OF "DIPLOMACITY"

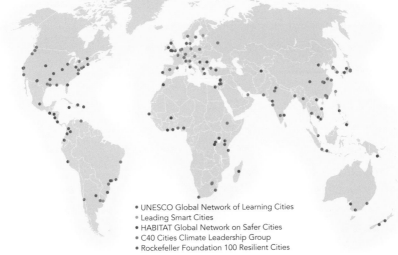

- UNESCO Global Network of Learning Cities
- Leading Smart Cities
- HABITAT Global Network on Safer Cities
- C40 Cities Climate Leadership Group
- Rockefeller Foundation 100 Resilient Cities

Learning networks are proliferating among cities sharing lessons in curbing greenhouse gas emissions, integrating sensor technologies into the built environment, promoting public safety, and enhancing societal resilience to natural disasters. There are more such inter-city networks today than international organizations.

12. EUROPE FRAGMENTS AS IT GROWS TOGETHER

Europe has a substantial number of separatist movements, but even as it devolves, new nations can become members of the collective European Union (EU).

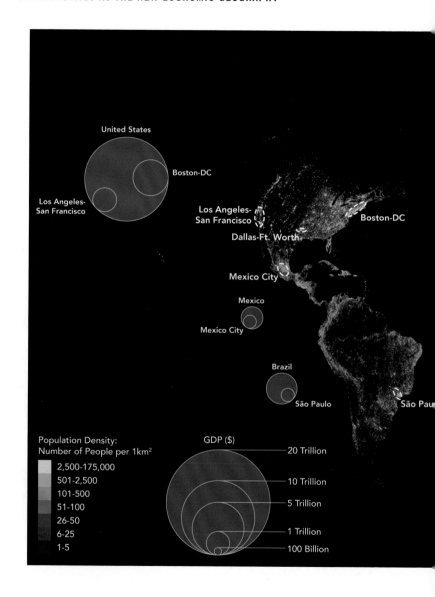

United States

Boston-DC

Los Angeles-
San Francisco

Los Angeles-
San Francisco

Dallas-Ft. Worth

Boston-DC

Mexico City

Mexico

Mexico City

Brazil

São Paulo

São Paulo

São Pau

Population Density:
Number of People per 1km²

2,500-175,000
501-2,500
101-500
51-100
26-50
6-25
1-5

GDP ($)

20 Trillion

10 Trillion

5 Trillion

1 Trillion

100 Billion

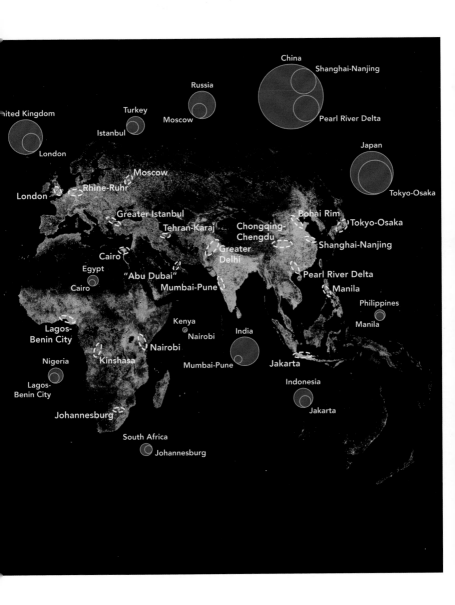

Urban archipelagos represent a growing share of national economies. Moscow, São Paulo, Lagos, and Johannesburg are representative of growth markets where one city dominates the economic landscape.

14. AFRICA'S REMAINING FAULT LINES

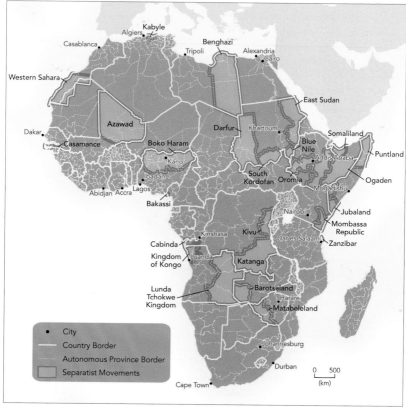

Africa's map still features many separatist movements that could lead to the creation of new states, as well as a large number of effectively autonomous provinces within African countries.

15. SINGAPORE EXPANDS ITS ECONOMIC GEOGRAPHY

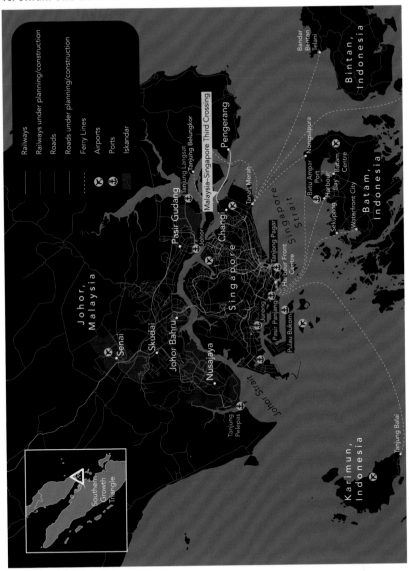

Singapore cannot expand its territory, but its investments in southern Malaysia and Indonesia's nearby islands have given rise to a "Growth Triangle" of expanding industry and land development.

China is leading Asia's westward push to connect the world's largest landmass through energy and transportation infrastructures. These new "Iron Silk Roads" may prove more lasting and transformative than Silk Roads of any previous era.

17. *PAX ARABIA*

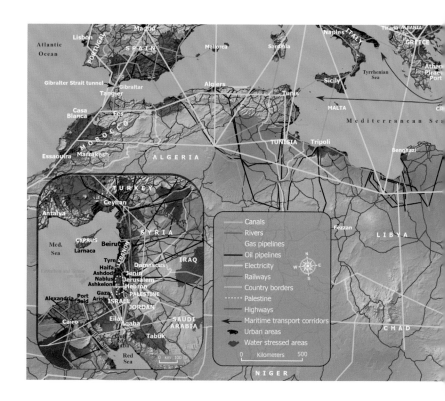

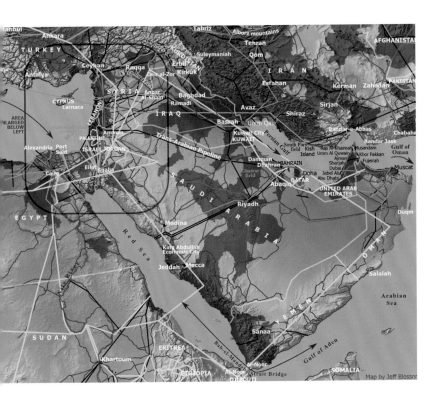

With many states already collapsed, the Arab world is ripe for reorganization. New energy and water infrastructures could promote resource-sharing between resource-rich and resource-poor societies, while improved transportation corridors could transform Arab civilization into a collection of urban oases better connected to Europe, Africa, and Central Asia. Connectivity is also transforming Arab relations with Israel, Turkey, and Iran.

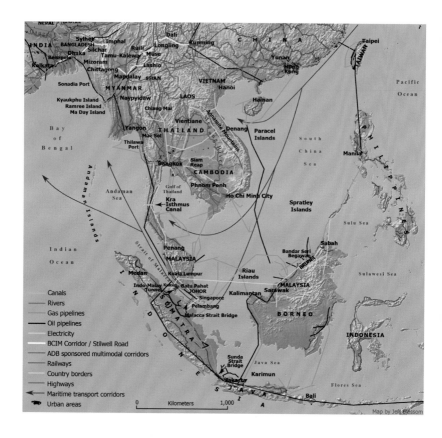

Southeast Asia leads the way among postcolonial regions in evolving toward functional integration through transportation and energy infrastructures, trade agreements, and supply chain complementarities.

supply-demand system would quickly redistribute cranes, pipe layers, and hydraulic lifts from city to city as and when they are needed rather than just manufacturing and selling more such industrial equipment. Similarly, Western cars can be quickly sent abroad to drive for several more years before they are scrapped. A world where everything is commoditized and priced is also a world where recycling trash is an economic opportunity. Lagos is home to one of the largest computer parts "e-waste" dismantling sites in the world. The narrow dirt alleys of Mumbai's two-square-kilometer slum of Dharavi feature among the most organized recycling operations I've ever seen, with collectors fanning out across the city and bringing separated materials to pre-positioned depots for crushing and shipment to other stations for re-purposing. Connectivity allows us to get more usage and mileage, circulation and sharing, out of each tool and product. A new stage has even entered the supply circle before recycling—up-cycling—by which materials are repurposed in higher-value ways: Plastic becomes furniture, tires become boots, shipping containers become two-bedroom homes for dense cities or refugee camps. A supply chain world could be more sustainable if it follows a principle that animates the sharing economy: Unused value is wasted value.

COMING HOME—BUT ONLY TO SELL AT HOME

A half century ago, GE manufactured consumer goods at Appliance Park in Louisville, Kentucky, an SEZ-like town with its own power plant, fire department, and zip code. Rising costs, labor disputes, and outsourcing pushed down its employment from a peak of twenty thousand workers in the 1970s to only eighteen hundred by 2008. But in 2012, GE opened a new assembly line to make water heaters that had previously been made in China, and another one to make refrigerators that were being assembled in Mexico. GE now plans to invest $800 million to ramp up Appliance Park again.

There are many good reasons for near shoring such as creating jobs, maintaining product quality, and protecting intellectual property. And yet America's overall manufacturing output continues to decline, and its share of GDP has fallen below 12 percent. For every job created through near-shoring, a greater number continue to be outsourced.* Because energy is only on average 5 percent of an American manufacturer's costs, while Chinese workers' wages are still less than one-quarter those of Americans, the math still clearly favors arbitrage—producing at the cheapest price and closest to one's customers.

The supply chain is equal parts supply and demand, and the more demanding consumers become, the more companies need to be closer to them. Two-thirds of global manufacturing is already located near final sale destinations, and bringing products closer to customers—through local production and tailored design—might be the only way to compete with rising local rivals. Cadbury, for example, is transporting West African cocoa to newly built chocolate factories in Indonesia where candies will be sprinkled with additional flavors for Asian tastes.

With infrastructure improving, customs harmonizing, transportation costs dropping, and logistics accelerating, market size and access will determine the location of production more than any other factor. Because Europeans have dominated the quality car market, they have always bought more of their own cars than imports. Similarly, Americans are buying more cars made in America, but there will still be as many Toyotas, Hondas, and Nissans on the roads as Fords and Chevys. The question American carmakers face is whether *Asians* will continue to buy American cars across the Pacific as Asians' own production ramps up. As each region's car production quality improves and they all compete for market share

---

* America's trade deficit in manufactured goods has actually grown more than 10 percent since 2010.

worldwide, mergers and joint ventures ramp up to get closer to the action, hence the Fiat Chrysler merger in 2014 (an Italian-American alliance that resulted in an Anglo-Dutch-headquartered conglomerate) and the long-standing Shanghai-Volkswagen and Shanghai-GM joint ventures in China (which together dominate sales in the world's fastest-growing automobile market). Indeed, while GM has spent $16 billion since 2009 on upgrading plants in the United States, it also plans to spend $16 billion in China by 2020.

Ultimately, more companies will be structured like Dell, the world's third-largest PC maker (behind HP and Lenovo) that since the 1990s has pioneered individually customized laptops with regional headquarters, assembly plants, and supply networks within each major longitudinal zone: Americas; Europe, the Middle East, and Africa (EMEA); and Asia-Pacific.[10] As its market share has slipped against local rivals abroad, Dell has worked to further speed up its delivery by expanding local warehouses to stock each region's favorite models. The most successful companies in a supply chain world make the oxymoron of "mass customization" a reality.

Western companies in particular need frictionless investment and trade because most of the world's expanding consumer class already lives outside the West. Especially in the heavy infrastructure categories such as power (think nuclear reactors and wind turbines) and aviation, foreign customers are the only way Western firms will survive. Precisely because Japan's population is shrinking, its high-tech sector depends more than ever on innovations in industrial robotics at home and exports abroad. Moving up the value chain has become an end in itself, both sustainable and lucrative. Whereas China's eleventh Five-Year Plan prioritized oil and shipping, its twelfth plan highlights renewable energy and electric cars—all technologies it seeks to deploy at home and export abroad to other emerging markets.

Antoine van Agtmael, who coined the term "emerging markets," points out that the main driver of corporate strategy remains the "battle for the billions of emerging customers,"[11] especially the two-thirds of the world population that lives in Africa and Asia, where

Chinese and Indian companies aggressively sell at far lower cost than Western firms. Western analysts often miss the rapid globalization of Asian companies precisely because their strategy is to gain a foothold in developing regions outside the United States where competition is less stiff than in America. Huawei's CEO says that being blocked from the U.S. market "doesn't matter" for its bottom line, because it is growing so rapidly everywhere else in the world.

A LONGITUDINAL WORLD?

The paradox of a networked world is that it represents the full flowering of globalization while also amplifying the impact of unforeseeable disruptions. As the supply chain researcher Barry Lynn writes, "Our corporations have built the most efficient system of production the world has ever seen, perfectly calibrated to a world in which nothing bad ever happens."[12] Thus even as the world's economic powerhouses are competing for global market share, they are also trying to insulate themselves from supply shocks by strengthening their own foundations of manufacturing, food production, fuel supplies, and other essentials. In this scenario, the future geopolitical map could still resemble the modified Orwellian pan-regions of the Americas, EMEA, and Asia-Pacific, with each harnessing its natural resources, labor force, and industrial networks cooperatively to produce most of what they need. Will America win the Great Supply Chain War, or will other regions get there first?

Given its rising energy and food production and stable population, the Western Hemisphere is closer to self-sufficiency than the rest of the world. And with its advanced technology and industrial manufacturing potential, America could not only design iPhones but make them all at home as well. That would constitute reaching the pinnacle of the supply chain—dominating high-value production while still exporting worldwide. EMEA could also become more self-sufficient by harnessing Arctic, Russian, Arab, and African energy and food supplies. Meanwhile, Asia is currently the largest importer of Middle Eastern fuel, but from Siberia and China to

Indonesia and Australia rising gas production could diminish its imports in the long term as well.

Emerging technology revolutions could further accelerate local energy production on a scale greater than the shale gas boom. The earth receives eight thousand times more energy per day from the sun than it consumes. If the same $550 billion in annual subsidies that have been spent on the fossil fuel industry were spent on R&D into alternative and renewable energy sources and grids to distribute them, more regions would cross the line toward fuel autarky. Germany's *Energiewende* has already spurred the installation of massive offshore wind turbines in the North Sea; today 27 percent of German energy is generated from alternatives.*

If the major powers and pan-regions had the right mix of energy and technology to truly become self-sufficient, then globalization would become more a longitudinal affair. There would be interdependence but with less momentum toward integration. America and China might become more isolationist, with little reason to intervene outside their geographic blocs. This could be a peaceful "live and let live" world—in which American security guarantees aren't needed in the Middle East and East Asia—but also one where major blocs ramp up arms to defend their regions and expand outward to secure larger markets for themselves.

The irony of a supply chain world is that capital becomes so fungible—even "fixed" assets like factories—investment ceases to be the symbol of long-term mutual trust that it once was: If picking up stakes and planting elsewhere (such as at home) become frictionless, then integration today can evaporate tomorrow. One virtue of industrial policies, then, is that they promote investment stickiness and strengthen the constituencies for cooperation across rivals. The frictions created by demanding joint ventures and technology transfer also enable economic bonds that are harder to untangle when geopolitical tensions rise.

---

* Europe produces 90 percent of all the world's wind power, and China most of the remaining 10 percent.

CHAPTER 8

INFRASTRUCTURE ALLIANCES

GETTING GRAND
STRATEGY RIGHT

Geopolitics has for centuries been synonymous with the conquest of territory, the domination of one's neighbors and rivals. Today the principle could simply be called competitive connectivity: The most connected power wins. States must *protect* their borders, but what matters are which lines they *control:* trade routes and cross-border infrastructures. All great strategists know the importance of the saying "Amateurs talk strategy; professionals talk logistics."

Empires have always focused on infrastructure as a tool of extending influence. The Romans and the Ottomans built sturdy roads stretching far from their capitals and placed these on maps used by armies and traders. From the fifteenth century onward, European colonial empires built standing supply lines and overseas administrative capitals across the Atlantic and Indian Oceans. In the mid-nineteenth century, the British East India Company constructed India's entire railway network, and several decades later Cecil Rhodes attempted (unsuccessfully) to do the same along the East African coast through a single "red line" connection from Cairo to Cape Town. The great British historian Arnold Toynbee argued

---

Maps 13 and 30, corresponding to this chapter,
appear in the map inserts.

against the setting of arbitrary borders in such a system, writing, "The erection of a limes [boundary] sets in motion a play of social forces which is bound to end disastrously for the builders. . . . Whatever the imperial government may decide, the interests of traders, pioneers, adventurers, and so forth will inevitably draw them beyond the frontier."[1]

Connectivity has mattered as much as geography in imperial rise and decline. From the Monroe Doctrine to the Spanish-American War, the United States in the nineteenth century muscled European powers out of the Caribbean basin and Pacific islands in favor of American commercial dominance. Topographical engineering was the complementary strategy on terra firma: surveying terrain, making maps, and plotting the necessary infrastructures to extend influence into the unknown. In 1803, Thomas Jefferson established the Corps of Discovery to study the geography of the Louisiana Purchase and reach the Pacific Ocean. The corps's first leaders were the famed explorers Meriwether Lewis and William Clark, whose 1804–6 Yellowstone expedition was also a reconnaissance mission to establish military outposts up the Missouri River as far as present-day North Dakota to protect America's growing fur trade from the British and the French. America began building its way westward from that moment forward. Because the United States has a greater length of navigable inland waterways than any other country, flowing diagonally and merging across states, natural geography has promoted geopolitical unity rather than hindering it. Infrastructure has been equally important to cementing such advantage: The Chicago River is actually a system of man-made canals 250 kilometers long designed to connect the Great Lakes to the Mississippi River and eventually the Gulf of Mexico. This monument of civil engineering is what made Chicago the most strategic point in interior North America. Again, geography becomes destiny once connectivity makes it so.

It is through such topographical engineering that mega-continental empires such as the North American Union and Greater China have emerged. While the former is stretching north into the

Arctic and south into Latin America, the latter is expanding south into Indochina and northwest into Russia and Central Asia. These supply chain empires represent the alignment of diplomatic, military, and commercial instruments to extend the tentacles of influence. Tracing this connectivity, rather than reading doctrines, reveals the future geopolitical map.

SUPPLY CHAIN MASTERY IS the original driver of geopolitical status—preceding military might. Both nineteenth-century America and twenty-first-century China were supply chain superpowers before they became military ones. They achieved continental dominance, industrialized heavily through import substitution, and became the world's largest economies *prior* to asserting themselves militarily. Good grand strategy is thus multidimensional: Trade, finance, energy, military, governance, and other arenas are all fair game. This is why the domestic and international dimensions of grand strategy cannot be treated as separate priorities. The Yale historian Paul Kennedy calls the present era a "gap between strategic epochs" in which new rules are slowly crystallizing. Yet as his sweeping *Rise and Fall of the Great Powers* underscores, it is economic and technological strength that has always underpinned military superiority, not the reverse. The balance of innovation drives the balance of power.

Successful grand strategies—the long-term doctrines that link means to ends—thus leverage a whole country's resources, public and private. They accurately assess the complex global environment, are realistic about goals, and are efficient in execution. They must also be comprehensive. Diplomats have tended to distinguish between the "high politics" of security, alliances, and arms control—matters of survival to the state—and the "low politics" of economics, rights, and environmental issues. But in a supply chain world, these priorities have become deeply entangled. For example, imposing high standards in trade agreements such as the United States seeks to do with the Trans-Pacific Partnership will determine whether America is able to regain strategic influence in Asia. Almost all our daily headlines can be interpreted through the lens of supply chain geopolitics: Tennessee automobile factories offering to forgo unionization to attract Korean carmakers, thousands of daily cyber attacks to steal corporate and technological secrets, rising trade volumes denominated in Chinese RMB, and more.

The arsenal for tug-of-war thus stresses different elements of power from military conflict. The National Intelligence Council's global power index ascribes sizable weight to nuclear weapons and defense spending, but given the unlikelihood of using the former and the latter's lack of proven effectiveness, other factors such as government revenue and human capital indicate a far earlier ascendance for China than 2030. Remember that power, like wealth, comes in both nominal and real forms. America's nominal power is unsurpassed, but subtract for deterrence, distance, and competence, and its effective power is less formidable than appears on paper. The point should be obvious given how unable more than 200,000 American troops spending over $1 trillion have been to subdue asymmetric enemies in Iraq and Afghanistan.

China too suffers from improvisation in executing its grand strategy and even instances of blatant overreach that cause self-inflicted wounds. Chinese proclamations, like America's, are vague and contradictory, while internal authorities jockey for influence, and success is rationalized after the fact. But China remains ruthlessly clear about one thing: Its power is focused on serving commercial interests and protecting the connectivity on which it depends. A simple equation is usually offered to explain China's clear linkage between domestic and foreign policy: Energy security = economic growth = political stability = continuation of party rule. The formula breaks down without robust global connectivity: inflows and outflows.

By contrast, both the Bush and the Obama administrations have defaulted to military posture as a proxy for influence, forgetting that America's foreign policy failures from Vietnam to Iraq to Afghanistan have come *from* intervening rather than from *not* intervening. The best news for America in the past two decades has been the lucky accident of the shale gas revolution that has nothing to do with military power.

The Iraq War neatly encapsulates the difference between military-focused and supply chain approaches. If the 2003 Iraq invasion was not "for the oil," why did the United States sacrifice 4,000 of its own (and an estimated 100,000 Iraqi) lives? The ultimate winners of the war were certainly not America and Britain but rather China and continental Europe, for they are the ones getting the oil.

There are other instances where the United States claims to do the "heavy lifting" of military intervention or diplomatic leadership but misses out on the prize. For years, the State Department lobbied heavily for International Atomic Energy Agency exemptions for India and the U.A.E. to acquire civilian nuclear technology, but once they were granted, those countries rewarded companies from South Korea and France with reactor contracts. Iran is destined to play out the same way: Under the American-led sanctions, major countries such as Russia, China, India, and Turkey continued to pursue large commercial deals with Iran; once sanctions are completely lifted, they will have a head start on the United States in the Iranian market. Supply chain grand strategy would view such "heavy lifting" as the failure of lightweight strategists.

What passes for grand strategy under Bush and Obama has traced an arc from hegemonic internationalism to deferential retrenchment. Both have claimed to affirm bedrock American values yet with little clarity over what operational principles and policies to pursue. Obama's 2015 National Security Strategy was more a meditation on the past than a vision for the future—more talk than action. A grand strategy premised more on containing than shaping Russia, Iran, and China smacks more of futility than vision, while the minimalism of habitually uttering the need for "restraint" provides no forward guidance. America's top diplomats have forgotten that standing on the shoulders of giants doesn't make one a giant. They have instead been little more than celebrity firemen and fire-women, leaving little dent on the international arena other than the weight of their self-congratulatory autobiographies. So far this century, America's leaders have scarcely nudged history, let alone shaped it.

America needs a strategy for what it wants to do with the rest of this century. War fatigue and fiscal austerity may by default lead to a scenario where the United States only escalates militarily where vital economic interests justify doing so. This would be consistent with supply chain strategy: Only commercially strategic investments such as protecting resource and technology flows merit military action. For rogue states and other hazards, the so-called Powell Doctrine would apply: Only commit large-scale military assets for situations where decisive force is necessary and likely to succeed, where there is a quick exit strategy, and where there is broad American and international support.

After two failed wars and a major financial crisis, it is understandable that Americans want a time-out from global engagement. But foreign policy is not optional in a world where survival depends on connectedness. By this logic, the U.S. "pivot" of greater forces to East Asia should be conceived as an exercise not just in protecting allies from China but in safeguarding America's growing trade volumes across the Pacific. (A quarter of America's exports go to Asia, and 40 percent of its imports come from there.) The U.S. Navy will be mandated to even more vigorously defend commercial supply lines with aircraft carriers, submarines, drones, and other armed chaperones. Their purpose is to protect the supply chain, not any specific ally. Similarly for China, the resources it devotes to expeditionary supply chain protection will matter as much as what it spends on aircraft carriers and submarines for area denial in the Pacific. The Australian navy's "three-ocean strategy" is premised on protecting LNG tankers from piracy and Internet cables from terrorist attacks and warding off ships full of illegal migrants from Indonesia—all mobile or offshore assets and threats.

At the same time, in supply chain grand strategy, the military is only one part of a larger set of tools including industrial policy.

America's massive shale gas reserves have resulted in a slashed current account deficit as energy imports fall, but little has been done to incentivize corporations to invest more at home in gigabit fiber broadband connectivity, high-speed and freight rail networks, and other infrastructures that would truly boost American exports. Equally fundamentally, the United States needs to reboot its educational and R&D apparatus, training the next generation of innovators in everything from robotics to genetically modified seeds so that the United States can occupy both the agricultural and the digital spectrum of global value chains. Controlling the supply chain is immeasurably more useful than controlling any traditional battlefield.

The strategic goal of a supply chain world is not domination, which brings obligation, but leverage, which generates value. Geopolitics now operates on both chessboard and web. On the chessboard, the United States extends its security umbrella to Europeans, Arabs, and Asians in the hopes that they will peacefully integrate regionally and avoid wars with Russia, Iran, or China, respectively. On the web, the United States needs industrial, financial, and commercial connectedness to other key global nodes to build its economic strength at home. If the United States can recognize the primacy of supply chain geopolitics, it would be less likely to undertake costly military interventions that can do more harm than good.

POST-IDEOLOGICAL ALLIANCES

We have just lived through a quarter century of gravely mistaken assumptions about the world, beginning with the "end of history" and the "clash of civilizations." The past decade alone has witnessed the rapid erosion of what was meant to be another century of *Pax Americana*. When scholars and intellectuals seek to define an era by ideologies (rather than conditions), they mistakenly presuppose that there must always be one coherent vision—or two in opposition—of world society in a struggle to assert itself. But a supply chain world is a *post-ideological* landscape. Russia no longer exports communism; America scarcely proffers democracy; China has abandoned Maoism for hyper-capitalist consumerism. From Africa to Asia—the lion's share of the world's population—it's all business, all the time.

From Chile to Congo to Cambodia, the Cold War witnessed perpetual proxy competition between the United States and the Soviet Union to install and protect allies at the helm of otherwise irrelevant countries. For the Soviets, the goal was expanding the network of communist allies, while for America the objective was to prevent liberal regimes from falling like dominoes and to roll back the communist tide.

Today it is not ideology but the promise of privileged access to resources and infrastructure that shapes geostrategic maneuvering. For example, China held out for years in agreeing in the UN Security Council to South Sudan's independence until the latter's proto-government promised to honor its share of China's existing oil contracts with the Khartoum government—as well as tacitly approve a Chinese-built oil pipeline directly from South Sudan across Kenya to the Indian Ocean. Western powers too act more consistently in pursuit of supply chain interests than democracy promotion. From the Cold War through the "war on terror," morally awkward partnerships have been more the rule than the exception: Pakistan, Egypt, Saudi Arabia, Bahrain, Qatar, Uzbekistan, Vietnam, Ethiopia, Uganda, Djibouti, and many others. Furthermore, far from supporting Tibetan separatism as the CIA did in the 1960s or preaching democracy as the Clinton and Bush administrations did for two decades, the recent American ambassador to China Gary Locke actually pressed for more business opportunities for American companies in a province of fast-growing infrastructure investment: Tibet.*

---

* Similarly, in September 2015, British Chancellor of the Exchequer George Osborne became the first British minister to visit China's restive, Muslim-populated Xinjiang province, where he lobbied on behalf of British businesses for deals in industrial parks catering to the emerging Eurasian Silk Roads.

Traditional alliances have been replaced with dalliances, ephemeral partnerships based on supply-demand complementarities. Russia and China are the archetypical case: Russia fears no country more than China, yet together they feign an anti-Western front for media consumption while China buys up growing volumes of Russian resource supplies. Similarly, it is far too lofty to speak of a Confucian-Islamic axis,[2] as Samuel Huntington did, when it is more accurate to simply state, "Asians buy the most Arab oil," and China and India could very conceivably intervene in the Middle East to protect the oil and gas supplies, not to defend so-called allies. Supply and demand explains geostrategic dynamics within the West as well. When the demand for an alliance such as NATO wanes, it flails in search of missions as far as Afghanistan. Hence the mantra from the first decade of the twenty-first century that NATO must go "out of area or out of business." When the demand for alliance protection grows, such as Russia's invasion of Ukraine and intimidation of the Baltic nations, NATO revives. But NATO unity has been exposed as more cheerleading than reality, with many European countries not wanting to even deploy to, let alone fight in, Afghanistan, and economic realities outweighing confrontation with Russia over Ukraine. It is thus a mistake to identify alliance groups as cultural communities. The webs of relations in a post-ideological supply chain world make rigid alliances impossible as each member makes constant cost-benefit calculations about participating in "collective" activities.

Whereas trade relations merely reflect complementarity, investment is a far more serious sign of commitment and thus enhances credibility. Indeed, the strongest predictor of stable relations is not how much two countries trade with each other, nor even the military alliances they participate in. Rather, it is the degree of foreign investment between two nations. America, Britain, and Turkey are all members of the NATO alliance, but the real reason they will never go to war with each other is the number of American multinationals that have headquarters in the U.K. and vice versa and the Western oil companies that have invested in building the oil and gas pipeline infrastructure of Turkey to supply energy to Europe. Their energy supply chain is literally inextricable from their national security. Even in times of cultural strain—such as between the United States and Turkey over how to intervene in Arab civil wars—the supply chain guarantees the alliance. At the same time, Turkey's growing transportation, trade, and energy links to the Turkic-populated former Soviet republics and China have made joining the Shanghai Cooperation Organization (SCO) one of Prime Minister Erdogan's top priorities. Turkey could be the first country to be a member of both NATO and the SCO, demonstrating how its connectivity to both East and West drives its strategic calculations, superseding any desire to join the EU.

Welcome to the age of infrastructure alliances, where the material and the diplomatic are two sides of the same coin. The strength of ties is measured not by color-coding countries according to membership in clubs such as NATO but through mapping connectivity and volumes of flows between them. Infrastructure alliances are more than corrupt deals among autocratic regimes. In fact, they represent job-creating projects that enhance poor and landlocked countries' ability to participate in the global economy. As close examination of traditional Western aid projects has demonstrated, the unrealistic conditions in financing commodities and infrastructure projects have unnecessarily delayed development and failed to create jobs in ways that only these sectors can. Sharing infrastructure is sharing wealth.

Americans have long presumed—largely correctly—that "security" is the most important global public good and that the world looks to America to provide it. After World War II, the U.S. military umbrella over Europe allowed it to peacefully integrate into the world's largest economic region. Today America's military "pivot" to Asia deters Chinese aggression, but China diverts that energy into building more infrastructures with its neighbors (and beyond) to more deeply bind them to China, something America cannot deter. To the contrary, infrastructure provision—and the connectivity it represents—have become global public goods on par with security. They are things countries desperately want, and China is their leading provider. With most of the world's future infrastructure yet to be built, China is out to become the world's largest infrastructure exporter. Many countries still want the American military protecting them, but even more want China's infrastructure finance and low-cost telecom equipment. China sends far larger contingents of construction crews than troops to live on foreign soil.

Europeans and Asians have learned to measure their robustness by their infrastructure spending, while America still measures its strength by its military spending; European and Asian firms (especially from China, Japan, and Korea) dominate the global engineering-procurement-construction nexus, with only Bechtel, Fluor, and KBR as recognizable American names in the field. However, because Asia's global infrastructure contractors heavily utilize technology from GE, Siemens, and Alstom, you won't hear these Western firms grumbling about "China in Africa." Western companies, unlike their diplomats, have long seen China's infrastructure plays abroad as win-win. Indeed, simultaneous Eastern and Western engagement in Africa could be hugely beneficial for the continent. The United States has pledged $30 billion for counterterrorism cooperation alone, about the same amount that China invests in African infrastructure every year. A supply chain world can be one focused on the division of labor more than spheres of influence.

Of course, China is building all this new infrastructure not to be perceived as generous but rather to efficiently access raw materials and bring them back home for the manufacturing and construction industries and then to use export processing zones near major markets to accelerate its throughput. This has become the standard playbook of Chinese neo-mercantilism. In diplomatic circles, China is considered a staunch defender of state sovereignty. Yet as an ancient civilization on a planet populated mostly by young nations, it is understandable how China's mental map of the world places greater significance on the geography of resource supplies than sovereignty. And having had its sovereignty repeatedly violated throughout the nineteenth century, China has little qualm about circumventing such legal fictions in the twenty-first century. Indeed, China views the world almost entirely through the lens of supply chains. It sees New Zealand as a food supplier, Australia as an iron ore and gas exporter, Zambia as a metals hub, Tanzania as a shipping hub, and Greenland as a uranium mine. The Argentine scholar Mariano Turzi calls his country a "soybean republic" in light of the shift in its agribusiness to serve China.[3]

In their first two years at the helm, the Chinese leadership duo of Xi Jinping and Li Keqiang visited more than fifty countries on all continents to sign investment deals. The power of China's supply chain geography lies not in its international military footprint or alliances—which remain relatively limited—but in its ability to exploit mutually beneficial supply-demand axes. In Latin America, China extended long-term contracts to purchase Venezuelan oil, signed currency swaps with Argentina, and supported cross-continental railway projects in Brazil. China has provided Ecuador $11 billion in loans since 2008, with $9 billion more promised in exchange for almost all of Ecuador's oil exports. China is also the main foreign investor in Ecuador's mining sector. Particularly during resource slumps such as that which began in 2013–14, commodities-dependent economies rely more than ever on Chinese loans that are disbursed much faster than the International Monetary Fund (IMF) can and tailored to allow repayment in raw materials if countries can't meet financial terms. Indeed, as Ecuador's debts mount, it is effectively selling one-third of its Amazonian rain-forest region to Chinese oil companies for exploration.

Trade is how China builds complementarity; investment is how it builds leverage. China the trading power benefits from a weak renminbi to boost exports, while China the superpower takes advantage of the strong renminbi to buy more assets abroad. Even if its own commodities imports slow, it wants to own the supplying assets. Acquiring productive (or, until the Chinese takeover, unproductive) assets helps China accelerate market access while also increasing revenues for the local economy. By establishing joint ventures in host countries where it takes a strong (or dominant) fi-

nancial position, China is hedging itself against host-country demands for more local value-added labor and ownership over their
industries (think tug-of-war). Should African countries require that
smelting, refining, manufacturing, assembly, or other production
processes take place on their own soil, China will still be needed to
finance and staff such upgrades while training local workers along
the way and will share handsomely in the new revenue generated
from these offshore exports.

There is a banal pragmatism to this approach. China's attitude
in fact differs little from that of the world's mining and energy companies that think in the long term about extracting resources from
turbulent geographies to supply global markets. Indeed, Rio Tinto's
CEO, Sam Walsh, echoes an old adage of the industry, "God must
have quite a sense of humor to have put so many resources in such
strange places." (That's the polite version of the joke.) Energy companies bet on geology, not governments, knowing their investments
in the former will long outlast the latter. Whether Equatorial Guinea
or East Timor, the state itself matters to the world only insofar as
Marathon, Exxon, Shell, Chevron, Total, or other oil majors are
able to continuously (or not) operate their oil and gas projects. They
fully expect civil wars, expropriation, and other disruptions to their
operations. They roll with the punches in black holes like Congo,
collapsed states like Libya, and bizarre autocracies like Turkmenistan. But they also know that whoever is in charge—now or later—
won't survive long without doing business with them.

PIRAEUS: CHINA'S EUROPEAN GATEWAY

The Greek, EU, and Chinese flags fly side by side, but there
is no doubt who is in charge. Fewer than a dozen Chinese
managers are present in Piraeus, the ancient Greek port outside Athens on the Mediterranean Sea, but inside the conference room of the Piraeus Container Terminal (PCT)
headquarters building, the signage is in Mandarin above English, with large photographs of the Great Wall of China

and the Acropolis on opposite walls. When capital markets abandoned Greece during the financial crisis, it was forced to outsource management of Piraeus to China's COSCO, one of the world's largest bulk shipping and port operators. Since 2010, COSCO has invested more than $600 million in Piraeus, making it the largest foreign investment in Greece.

COSCO offered not just money but a vision for Greece's place in the world that this once proud civilization had lost. The maps hanging inside the PCT offices tell most of the story: From the star marking Piraeus, arrows confidently arc northwest through the Adriatic to central and eastern Europe, westward across the Mediterranean to the Iberian Peninsula, southwest to the North African coast, and northeast through the Aegean and the Black Seas to Russia. Piraeus is China's new gateway to distribute goods across the entire EMEA region—as well as bring them back through the Suez Canal. With the freight railhead beginning inside the port's free zone and heading straight north through the Balkans to the Czech capital of Prague, off-loading at or shipping from Piraeus cuts a full week off the transport time via Europe's dominant ports of Rotterdam and Hamburg. In 2013, HP decided to switch the European terminus point for its Asian shipments from Rotterdam to Piraeus. With its tax-free transshipment and warehousing and customs clearance for all of Europe, the logistics gateway and customs revenue model Piraeus represents now brings in nearly $1 billion per year—paying off COSCO's total investment and then some—inspiring plans to expand the facilities through a new rail corridor right into Athens itself.

Piraeus is just one of a network of logistics hubs COSCO has invested in upgrading on either side of the Suez Canal—for everyone's benefit, not just its own. Indeed, all major global and Asian shipping lines now dock at PCT, while thirty European shipping companies use it as well. Piraeus is now open for business 365 days a year.

Indeed, what also makes Piraeus work, literally, is that it operates according to not just free-zone laws but Chinese rules as well. A monitor in the PCT lobby tracks the progress Piraeus has made since 2010: a nearly annual doubling of warehouse capacity and container throughput, catapulting it back up into the top ten of Europe's busiest ports. One reason for the port's surging productivity is that it is a "strike-free zone": There are no unions. But one also doesn't hear complaints, because salaries for the fifteen hundred new Greek employees are far higher than those at the public Piraeus Port Authority right next door. As I drove right down the strip separating their berths, there was no question as to where Greeks would rather work: rusting and limp orange scaffoldings to the left, and mighty blue COSCO terminals to the right. Thanks to Chinese-financed connectivity, Greeks can once again be proud of their strategic geography.

FROM SANCTIONS
TO CONNECTIONS

There are only two countries in the world where you're not supposed to be able to buy Coca-Cola, but in reality there are no countries where you can't get it. Officially, the ban on exporting Coke to Cuba and North Korea goes back over fifty years. Unofficially, Chinese smugglers have been bringing crates of the world's favorite fizzy soda across the border for years, serving it in high-end restaurants to elites and foreigners; they're told it is "Italian Coke." On my visit to Pyongyang in 2012, Coke was served in almost every restaurant. When Dennis Rodman visited North Korea with the Harlem Globetrotters in 2013, he drank Coke courtside with the young despot Kim Jong Un. (Coca-Cola denies any involvement with unauthorized imports into North Korea.)

Coca-Cola operates one of the world's most sprawling global

supply chains; DHL another—there is literally no corner of the planet to which they cannot deliver something on short notice. DHL is so much more efficient than the U.S. military that it is its largest client—even for mobile battle stations. When a closed-off country like Myanmar signals that it's ready to do business, Coke is there as one of the first foreign companies granted a license to operate under the country's new foreign investment law. All that was required was for Obama to waive sanctions. Once he did, Coke's supply chain came to life. At the Hmawbi Township bottling plant, twenty-five hundred people were immediately employed, with twenty-two thousand more being employed in distribution to over 100,000 vendors across the vast and rugged country. The company's CEO, Muhtar Kent, compares Coke's return to Myanmar after sixty years to the fall of the Berlin Wall.*

A world of competitive connectivity makes a mockery of sanctions only genuinely backed by one power. Recent experience in Iran and North Korea demonstrates how difficult it will be to isolate countries: Even when the American sanctions noose was at its tightest, dozens of countries and companies from oil traders to banks continued to do large business with these so-called rogue states. For example, China used Kunlun Bank of Shenzhen, a China National Petroleum Corporation (CNPC) subsidiary, to make payments for Iranian oil that went to finance the Quds force. The United States has played both carrot (access to the U.S. market) and stick (ability to freeze transactions cleared through U.S. financial institutions or partners). Russians and Iranians have had assets frozen, while Western banks have been fined for laundering their (or Sudanese) money. But overall, America too has shifted to decreasing frictions and increasing flows, as evidenced by its reopening of relations with Iran, reducing sanctions, and unblocking the path for its own companies to compete and build influence there. The same is true of Cuba, where normalizing relations—enabling connectivity—will restore

---

* Coca-Cola is the market leader in Iran as well. Sold by Coke's Irish subsidiary, it is bottled by the local joint venture partner Khoshgovar.

America's geographic gravity over the island that a half century of sanctions undermined.

In a multipolar world, every country has a lifeline. With its enormous dependence on the West for foreign investment in its stock market and currency, Russia's economy suffered tremendously as a result of sanctions imposed after its invasion of Ukraine. But it was not isolated: Russians set up shell companies not named on sanctions lists and continued thriving business with Europeans, while the Kremlin immediately authorized expanded usage of China's UnionPay credit card system. The friction of sanctions blocks some flows while creating new ones.* In a world where every state can play all sides and directions, Russia and China can have their cake and eat it too.

The United States still has no plan of action for a world where it is (rightly) far more reluctant to use military force and where coercive economic measures such as sanctions are of diminishing utility. The gradual de-Americanization of the global financial infrastructure in favor of bilateral and regional arrangements means the United States and its international partners will need new sources of leverage over rogue regimes. Sanctions can still impose pain on countries—unfortunately, more on people than their governments— but their ability to change actual policy is becoming even more dubious. The United States, then, will need to focus more on other tools of economic statecraft. It must think in terms of leverage through engagement rather than containment.

A return to realism rather than false moralism as the underlying principle of diplomacy would go a long way toward expanding global connectivity. Decisions based on cost-benefit calculations rather than rigid ideological principles are more likely to yield accommodation and compromise, coexistence and mutual opening—ultimately achieving the goals sought by moralists more constructively and quickly. Today it is impossible to "corner" large

* Similarly, for every European country that launches a boycott, divestment, and sanctions initiative against Israel on behalf of the Palestinians, some hedge fund or Chinese construction company launches a new investment with it.

countries such as Russia and Iran. Particularly as their commercial connectivity expands, the long-term interests favoring accessing their markets win out over ideological agendas. And yet, as the past quarter century of infrastructure maneuvering between the West and Russia demonstrates, enabling more flows is the best long-term solution to overcoming geopolitical frictions.

BEWARE FRIENDSHIP BRIDGES

When I first traveled to Crimea in 2005, it was on a long bus ride from Kiev crossing one of two narrow land bridges onto the peninsula. Crimea, while mostly populated by ethnic Russians, felt not like Russia (or Ukraine) but rather like a balmy island of craggy cliffs and Black Sea beaches.

Seeking to speed their invasion of the North Caucasus, the Nazis were the first to attempt to physically link eastern Crimea to Russia's Taman Peninsula across the four-and-a-half-kilometer Kerch Strait. The Nazis never completed the bridge, nor did subsequent Soviet efforts. Notably, however, it was between 2010 and 2013, when the EU failed to advance Ukrainian reforms, that Ukraine and Russia formally agreed to make the bridge a joint project to deepen trade and cooperation. The bridge was meant to be a symbol of their friendship.

Now Russia will build the bridge alone—while it has laid land mines on Crimea's northern border. Russia's exclusive engineering has remapped Crimea: Once connected only to Ukraine, now Crimea is functionally cut off from Ukraine and connected only to Russia. Some have called it an "amputation"; that's exactly right.

Crimea is not the only case of infrastructural engineering remapping geopolitics. When the King Fahd Causeway was opened between Saudi Arabia and Bahrain in 1986, and expanded in 2010, it was to accommodate the almost twenty million people per year crossing between the Saudi peninsula and the island monarchy. But by 2011, it was the conduit for Saudi tanks to cross into Bahrain, quash the Shia uprising, and effectively annex the country. Beware of friendship bridges.

Eurasia's geopolitical complexity requires us to examine the deeper and disparate causes of seemingly spontaneous phenomena such as Russia's invasion of Ukraine. In addition to more obvious moves such as Ukraine's push to join NATO, Putin's logic was shaped by seemingly unrelated events such as the Turkish prime minister Erdogan's decision to close the Bosporus Strait (Russia's only naval outlet from the Black Sea to the Aegean and the Mediterranean) to military transit—he says it should be used for water sports—as well as Syria's collapse (which would cut off Russia's access to its naval facility at Tartus).

Russia's actions in Ukraine have thus been more than just a neo-imperialist landgrab but rather a continuation of the historical search for alignment of demographic, functional, and political space. Ethnic Russians in Crimea have been brought (back) into the Russian state (after Khrushchev "gifted" Crimea to Ukraine in 1954 to curry favor with Ukrainians), the status of Russia's naval base at Sebastopol (which itself voted to join Russia as an urban exclave in 1994) has been settled, the mixed Russian-Ukrainian eastern regions will be more federalized, and Russia has claimed lucrative gas fields in the Sea of Azov.

Remapping borders isn't always the end of the tension, however. Even if the fighting aboveground were to cease, the tug-of-war for leverage over the pipelines that unite them underground continues. While many post-Soviet borders are arbitrary and malleable, their fixed, cross-border pipelines are directly connected to deeper hydrocarbon resources. Who owns the soil over (or through) which a pipeline passes is just one dispute. Then there is the pipeline itself, usually built by a multinational corporate consortium sharing costs, revenues, and claims on the asset. Third, there is the volume and value of the oil or gas flowing through it. Territorial sovereignty, asset ownership, and operational control have all become dangerously entangled as Gazprom threatens to cut off flows to Ukraine if it siphons any gas bound for Europe—effectively claiming *extended sovereignty* over pipelines on Ukrainian territory. For Russia, tampering with its gas exports constitutes an act of war, not killing its camouflaged mercenaries operating in eastern Ukraine.*

Russia's dismembering of Ukrainian territory in two places—Crimea and Donbass—is thus ultimately less significant than the supply chain tug-of-war it revealed as tensions unfolded. The United States began by blocking export licenses for the sale of high-tech goods to Russia, but Russia retaliated by limiting the export of rocket engines the United States uses to reach the International Space Station. American and European companies were banned from key investments into Russia, cutting them off from one of their largest customers, while Russia blocked key food imports from Europe, hurting European farmers while raising food prices for its own citizens. The willingness to ratchet up pressure on Russia was in inverse proportion to the degree of supply chain integration with Russia.

The Ukraine crisis is thus more emblematic of twenty-first-century supply chain geopolitics as nineteenth-century territorial conquest, and the long-term outcome from Russia's misadventure will actually benefit the more connected West. Scaremongering commentators always miss the deeper patterns: Even territorial friction creates new flows. The 1970s Sino-Soviet split froze relations between the two great Cold War communist powers but opened a door for the United States and China to build relations that have eclipsed either's ties with Russia in importance. By seizing the economically backward Crimea (which Moscow has had to turn into a tax-free gambling zone to generate revenue) and skirmishing in the postindustrial wasteland of Donbass, Russia gained an inch but lost the real Ukraine, which Kiev has moved westward with a newfound sobriety. Furthermore, Russia's threats to cut off gas supplies have inspired Europe to seek additional energy inflows from the United

---

* Though Ukraine lost Crimea, it still controls Crimea's electricity supply. A series of attacks by Ukranians on power transmission lines in November 2015 plunged Crimea into darkness.

States and North Africa. Ukraine certainly lost a major battle, but Europe is winning the supply chain tug-of-war—one that began a quarter century ago.

OIL IS THICKER
THAN BLOOD

Pilgrims to the annual gathering of the World Economic Forum are familiar with a long stretch of smooth highway and Alpine scenery stretching eastward from Zurich toward the hamlet of Davos. All gas stations along this route have been under the proprietorship of Esso (Mobil) since 1949. Yet within just one year from 2012 to 2013, all 160 Esso stations across Switzerland changed their name to SOCAR—State Oil Company of the Azerbaijan Republic. What are Azerbaijani gas stations doing in the middle of Europe?

When the Soviet Union collapsed, some wondered what would become of the once formidable empire's strongest oil-producing Caucasus region that fell into the hands of the small new republic on the Caspian Sea. Western energy executives wasted little time in finding out. BP and Chevron officials nostalgically recall how they squatted in dilapidated Baku hotels in late 1991 (shortly after its independence vote) while negotiating what became known as the "deal of the century": a $4 billion investment to build the world's second-longest pipeline to transport Caspian oil (including from Kazakhstan and Turkmenistan) across Azerbaijan and Georgia to the Turkish port of Ceyhan on the Mediterranean Sea.

For small and landlocked countries, connectivity *is* strategy. It is precisely because they are stuck in vulnerable geographies that infrastructure and supply chains become their lifelines. Azerbaijan needed the BTC pipeline to escape its dependence on exporting oil through Russia. Now it is also developing the Alyat port into a free zone for trans-Eurasian cargo—also avoiding Russian transit. Since 2006, oil has flowed uninterrupted through the BTC pipeline, a geopolitical victory I described in *The Second World* as the "anti-clash of civilizations" because it irrevocably bonded Shia Muslim Azerbaijan to Orthodox Catholic Georgia, making both crucial links in Europe's energy diversification strategy. Within two months of the book's publication in March 2008, Russia had thrown religious fraternity out the window and occupied the breakaway regions of Abkhazia and South Ossetia and even parts of Georgia itself, but it never touched the BTC pipeline. Russia knew that infrastructure was the real "red line" for its meddling, not Georgia's flimsy borders.

The sight of SOCAR gas stations in Switzerland is a reminder that sometimes it can take decades before one notices, in this case visually, the benefits of strategic infrastructure investments, but they are almost always worth it. Oil proves to be thicker than blood, and oil pipelines the threads that tie civilizations together.

Europe's leaders need to revisit these lessons of the BTC pipeline as they play tug-of-war with Russia for control over energy markets. Gazprom's manipulation of pipeline routes, purchase of downstream assets, bribery of politicians, and rigging of gas prices have made even the NATO and EU members Bulgaria and Romania ambivalent about siding with their Western allies against Russia despite their safe distance from Russia across the Black Sea. And Ukraine's push for NATO membership alienated Russia as much as Georgia's bid—with the result not pretty for either. NATO is now too afraid to bring in either Georgia or Ukraine, leaving it up to the EU to cement Ukraine's Western aspirations. What Ukraine actually needs most is an EU-sponsored industrial overhaul, especially investment in productive sectors such as manufacturing and agriculture that will make it less dependent on crony leaders (and their shared ties to murky Russian-backed energy companies). This would prepare it for eventual EU membership, which Russia has never opposed. Such real investment is money much better spent than the $18 billion in emergency IMF bailout packages issued during the crisis—more than four times the cost of the BTC pipeline but with no economic improvements to show for them.

Ukraine's infrastructure ultimately matters far more to its future than who controls the decaying Donbass region—especially because just as Europe is bailing out Ukraine, it is also accelerating efforts to evade Ukraine altogether as a gas transit middleman. Not only are EU countries boosting gas imports from Algeria and the Arctic; they are also plugging directly into Russia itself via a bundle of new pipelines such as Nord Stream across the Baltic Sea to Germany, which opened in 2011,* and a planned South Stream under the Black Sea to Bulgaria and onward to Serbia, Hungary, Slovenia, and Italy (with branches to Bosnia and Macedonia). Together, North and South Stream could provide about 50 percent of Europe's annual gas consumption. Even if South Stream is canceled due to Euro-Russian antagonisms, another Black Sea "Turkish Stream" would be built and deliver gas to Europe anyway. While Turkey's relevance is growing, Ukraine's will shrink each passing year.

And yet more energy infrastructure may also be Ukraine's savior. North Stream, for example, can provide reverse flows to Ukraine in the event of further Russian gas cutoffs—showing how more flows can actually undermine the supplier's strategic objectives. Indeed, while foreign analysts focus on the maneuverings of Gazprom, it is the silent infrastructure player Transneft—the world's largest gas pipeline company—that is constructing the future Eurasian map through its laying of new trunk pipelines between Russia and the West. Though Transneft is a Russian state-owned monopoly hit by Western sanctions, it has doubled in value as demand for new pipelines surges. In a supply chain world, Transneft is a quiet executor of connectivity—paradoxically helping Europe win the tug-of-war against Russia.

Furthermore, as American LNG terminals switch from gasification to liquefaction to export excess supply across the Atlantic, Europe will soon have a far more resilient energy infrastructure than before the Ukraine crisis. As of 2014, a new floating LNG terminal called Independence has been positioned off the coast of Lithuania, additional LNG terminals are under construction in Poland, and a Danish North Sea terminal can reverse flows to export excess gas

---

* North Stream stretches from Vyborg on the Gulf of Finland to Greifswald in Germany near the Polish border. Nord Stream AG is a Russian-German-owned joint venture incorporated in Switzerland.

imports southward—all of which means that Europe may soon supply more gas to Ukraine than vice versa.

One hundred years ago, there was barely an international energy market and no international oil or gas pipelines; today there are hundreds. Whether between allies or across suspicious neighbors, they are fixed bonds whose flows matter to all countries along the route. Pipelines reconnect feuding siblings and introduce tug-of-war dynamics where otherwise war itself would be the main option. The more pipelines that directly connect Russia to Europe, the more Russia will ensure supply to meet European demand with no reason to choke it off. Eventually, Russia's internal weaknesses and dependence on foreign investment will bring it back on the path of opening to the West, while its fuller role as a global supply state for energy and agriculture, and as a transit corridor across Eurasia, will comprehensively benefit the five billion people on the supercontinent. Buying Russia will prove a more successful strategy than containing it.

CHAPTER 9

THE NEW IRON AGE

IRON SILK ROADS ACROSS THE HEARTLAND

IN 2006, I EMBARKED ON A ROAD TRIP FROM TIBET'S CAPITAL OF Lhasa with a crew cut and clean-shaven face, doing my best to look like a Buddhist monk in training. Almost two months later, after completing an arc to Urumqi in Xinjiang (the equivalent of Texas via California to Minnesota), I had shaggy hair and a beard, fitting in nicely with the Turkic Uighur locals. Yet I had never left China.

My Toyota Land Cruiser lurched across riverbeds, slid down mountainsides, and crawled through rugged landscapes; it took weeks to reach the desolate canyons of western Tibet near the disputed Aksai Chin region adjacent to Indian Kashmir. But as I drove, PLA road crews were working round-the-clock shifts to excavate rocks and lay down asphalt, forge rivers, and span bridges. A decade later, transportation infrastructure has put the most remote places on earth within efficient reach. A sturdy highway is emerging across southern Tibet, while airports are popping up across the punishing terrain. Xinjiang's capital, Urumqi, the city farthest from the sea of any on earth, has become connected by railways and roads across the Taklamakan Desert. Along the way, Tibet and Xinjiang (China's two largest provinces by area) have been politically demoted

---

Map 13, corresponding to this chapter, appears in the first map insert.

from semiautonomous provinces to mere cultural spaces. Their people still have their identity—though even that is being usurped—but little else.

In my first university course on geopolitics, we studied the grand sweep of millennia of imperial expansion and contraction. Modern empires such as the Soviet Union, the intimidating professor Charles Pirtle remarked, "aren't satisfied until they control their neighbor's territory." The joke, of course, is that once you conquer one neighbor, you suddenly find yourself with new neighbors; conquest knows no end. Once the Soviet Union collapsed in 1991, however, China suddenly neighbored multiple newly created Central Asian republics—bordering more of them than Russia itself—putting it in position to dominate Mackinder's fabled geopolitical "Heartland."

China had inadvertently been preparing for this moment since the conclusion of its civil war in 1949, when it immediately began "Develop the West" campaigns to pave highways, construct railways, and install electricity lines—and move millions of Han Chinese—gradually westward to subdue Tibet and Xinjiang, which border on these former Soviet republics. When the 1991 watershed arrived, China quickly settled trivial border disputes with all of them and launched a quarter century of checkbook diplomacy aimed at expanding its western infrastructure network even farther. Tibet and Xinjiang were once barriers to China even reaching Central Asia, but much as the Qin dynasty established sturdier roads to deploy force across the kingdom at the tail end of the Warring States Period in the third century B.C.E., infrastructure paves the way for dominance.

Empires have historically expanded only as far as manpower, technology, finances, and climate would allow. Napoleon's fateful Russian campaign in the winter of 1812 is only the most famous example of how foreboding realities have overwhelmed even the most confident military plans. From Genghis Khan through Tamerlane, the barren Central Asian steppe was easy to conquer but difficult to hold with mobile garrisons traveling far from Samarqand. The nineteenth-century railways that brought the Turkic khanates under Soviet control were poorly maintained outside wartime. Indeed, many say that when the Soviet Union collapsed, the Tajiks were the last to find out.

China represents the next phase for Central Asia after Mongol-Turkic empire and Soviet backwater: Eurasian resource corridor. China is taking advantage of the fractured mess on its western frontier to reorganize the region around supply chains rather than states, replacing its arbitrary Stalin-era maps with those of new oil-slicked iron Silk Roads.

The engineering marvels of today will reshape the geopolitics of tomorrow. The scaling power of modern industrial infrastructure makes Russia's or Kazakhstan's size and flat terrain an unimpressive obstacle in China's calculations—especially since the completion of its high-altitude rail line to Tibet. Landlocked Kazakhstan recently proposed a "Eurasian canal" that would allow its ships passage from the Caspian to the Black Sea and out to the Mediterranean through the Bosporus. No doubt neighboring China might find this an interesting project to sponsor.

There is no precedent for the current wave of highways, pipelines, and railways forming east-west axes of logistical efficiency. Unlike the nineteenth-century "Great Game" era when Britain and Russia sought to demarcate Central Asian territory, China merely wants to steer the direction of its energy flows. Instead of the majority of its oil and gas flowing north and west through Russia, new pipelines from Kazakhstan's and Turkmenistan's gas fields on the Caspian Sea direct resources east to China's Tarim basin. Xi Jinping's latest moniker, "Silk Road Economic Belt,"* portends the region's transformation into a collection of midsize urban nodes anchoring transport and energy corridors. Each road, bridge, tunnel, railway, and pipeline rewrites the functional code of the countries it crosses, while new energy grids and irrigation systems turn their resource mismatches into pragmatic swaps. China's strategy isn't to formally occupy these countries but to ease passage across them. It wins the new Great Game by building the new Silk Roads.

---

* This has also been widely referred to as "One Belt, One Road."

And yet powers from near and far have jumped on the Silk Road bandwagon. The United States calls its cross-border electricity initiatives between Tajikistan, Kyrgyzstan, and Afghanistan the New Silk Road, while Kazakhstan is spearheading a "Silk Wind" multimodal freight corridor through the Caucasus and Turkey, which Turkey is promoting in the other direction through its Modern Silk Road program that Europe is underwriting. For its part, Russia comes up with a new acronym every few years for what amounts to a Eurasian customs framework. Over time, as Chinese citizens spill over into sparsely populated Central Asian countries and merchants from across the region circulate in all directions, western Chinese cities such as Urumqi and Horgos become what Samarqand and Bukhara were in centuries past: melting pots of Chinese, Russians, Pakistanis, and Turkic peoples gathering in search of the best deals. The more Silk Roads, the better.

Eurasia represents two-thirds of the world population, economy, and trade, and that is before it genuinely fuses together into a connected mega-continent through voluminous durable infrastructures that will smooth and speed commerce. China's and Europe's construction of high-speed rail networks is compressing trans-Eurasian rail travel to a matter of days rather than months. Rail transport is faster than shipping and cheaper than flying, eating away at shipping's leadership in volume and airfreight's in value. In 2012, only 2,500 containers were transported by rail from China to Europe, but this is predicted to grow exponentially to up to 7.5 million containers by 2020 (still about one-tenth of Europe-Asia oceanic trade).[1] In addition to the $43 billion being spent between China and Russia on their direct rail connections such as an enhanced Trans-Siberian Railway, the frictionless, duty-free Trans-Eurasian Railway already traverses seamlessly from Chongqing through Kazakhstan, Russia, Belarus, and Poland to Duisburg in Germany. Multinationals are cleverly riding coattails on China's new Eurasian Silk Road axes. After concentrating 70 percent of its Chinese workforce in Chongqing, HP is the anchor customer of this new semiprivate and paramilitary-protected rail service, soon to be joined by China's own Asus. In 2013, the China-Europe Railway was also inaugurated linking Zhengzhou in Henan province (a large manufacturing hub for Foxconn) to Hamburg, delivering electronics in around half the time as shipping.

The more such rail corridors are developed, the more rail travel becomes like airline travel, with no stops or checkpoints at borders between origin and destination. Another branch will eventually fork southwest from Kazakhstan through Turkmenistan, Iran, and Turkey through Serbia's capital, Belgrade—where the first China-Balkans Summit was held in late 2014 and China has financed a new bridge over the Danube River—and finally to Budapest. In 1241–42, the Mongols managed to cross the frozen Danube during an exceptionally cold winter and continue their Hungarian rampage. If the Mongols could penetrate southeastern Europe using horse relays and signal flags, China can surely do it in the age of high-speed rail.

Western scholars wasted over a decade pretending that Chinese participation in the World Bank, IMF, WTO, and other institutions signaled its desire to play along with a Western-centric order rather than noticing how China joined these institutions mostly to water them down while at the same time creating separate frameworks such as the Asian Infrastructure Investment Bank (AIIB) to advance its own agenda. The AIIB is budgeted to spend about ten times as much in Asia as the Marshall Plan did in Europe, mostly to finance roads, railways, pipelines, electricity transmission, and other connectivity across Eurasia to smooth its own westward expansion. The timing is propitious: Just as the crumbling postcolonial and former Soviet republics on its periphery desperately need new infrastructure, China is converting its piles of cash into credit for distressed neighbors to rebuild themselves—by buying China's overproduction of steel and cement and with the assistance of swarms of Chinese labor.

The AIIB also represents a reform of the international system from the outside—because Western powers were unwilling to reform from within. Indeed, the AIIB's creation provoked Western countries to adapt to it rather than the reverse: Britain, Germany, Australia, and South Korea have joined the AIIB.[2] Even Japan's announcement of a separate $110 billion infrastructure fund for Asia to rival the AIIB will actually accelerate the smoothing of more Asian bottlenecks for China's benefit. Japan's investments enhance mainland Asia's connected destiny.

"MINE-GOLIA": WHERE (ALMOST) ALL ROADS LEAD TO CHINA

For a brief moment in 2009, I was the most hated man in Mongolia. In June of that year, I gave a TED talk titled "Invisible Maps" in which I referred to the landlocked and sparsely populated nomadic country as "Mine-Golia." I argued that its landlocked geography, rich natural resources, and export-dependent economy made it a sitting duck in a supply chain world. Perhaps I could have better sugarcoated the punch line: "China isn't conquering Mongolia; it's buying it."

By the time the video went viral on Mongolia's television stations and websites, citizens had plenty of time to huddle in their satellite-dish-topped yurts and ponder my animated map of China's borders subsuming their own. Maps are mere representations, but show people one they don't like, and you'll incur their wrath. Verbal warnings that the country was being gobbled up by Chinese mining companies merely pique interest, but a map showing their sovereignty being erased before their eyes is wicked sorcery. I was persona non grata.

Some months later, at the World Economic Forum's annual meeting at Davos, I had breakfast with Mongolia's president. I only needed to be introduced as "Mr. Mine-Golia" for a seat at the table to be cleared. After we established that I was simply *observing*—not *advocating*—

China's takeover of his ancient and glorious homeland, the air warmed just a bit. With vintage Asiatic hospitality, he kindly insisted I come visit Mongolia as soon as possible.

In July 2010, I set off from London in a three-ton, early 1990s model Land Rover truck that had served as a British army field ambulance in Bosnia. Loaded up with basic medical equipment and supplies, our team of three joined the Mongolia Charity Rally destined for Ulaanbaatar, where we planned to donate the vehicle—a beast we gently named Betsy—to the country's emergency medical services. If Betsy could make the thirteen thousand kilometers in one piece—driving across Europe and Russia with the steering wheel on the wrong side—she'd be enlisted as a mobile field hospital, essential for reaching the country's sparsely dispersed nomads.

After four weeks, five breakdowns, one sledgehammer, two tow trucks, six vodka bottles in bribes, and one truly near-death experience in remote Siberia, we made it to the hundred-meter-tall stainless steel statue of the mighty Genghis Khan in the vast Terelj National Park outside Ulaanbaatar. I felt at home: As the only person in my high school with the letters "Khan" in his last name, my nickname has been "Genghis" since the ninth grade.

Throughout my appearances in Mongolia, whether a public lecture in the nation's parliament house or on television shows, one question was the constant refrain: "What do we do now that we've become Mine-Golia?"

Mongolians know almost all their raw materials go to China and that Chinese influence in their politics and economy has grown excessive, but they hadn't yet undertaken serious steps to counter it. Chinese companies have bribed Mongolian officials and bought up large numbers of mining companies (called junior miners) to increase their share of prospecting licenses. After a mining export boom (mostly to China) during which Mongolia didn't sufficiently upgrade its infrastructure, the commodities slump (due to China) forced Mongolia to look for major foreign investment (from China) in building out its infrastructure (to China). Petro-China now leads Mongolia's oil exploration, and the Chinese coal giant Shenhua is investing in the rail lines, while the new north-south "Steppe Road" is planned to cut straight through the country connecting Russia and China. Mongolia has only three million people but needs about six thousand kilometers of railway for its mining sector. Though Mongolia had decided to continue using its Soviet-era wide-gauge rail lines, in 2014 it suddenly announced that new rail lines from Tavan Tolgoi (the world's largest coal mine) and other mines would be built on China's narrow gauge.* That's how you buy a country without conquering it.

China's neighbors are ground zero for this phenomenon. Landlocked countries are prisoners of geography, and infrastructure is the only way out. But their infrastructure depends on neighbors to connect through, thus it isn't fully sovereign. The question then is, who controls and profits from it?

Like Gazprom pipelines in Ukraine, when China builds infrastructure outside its own borders, it claims forms of *extended sovereignty*. By becoming an investor, asset owner, and supply chain operator in another country, China gets preferential market access and becomes part of the strategic decision-making process over how resources will be managed. China does not export ideology but binds countries to it through infrastructural tethers. The Mongolian army's joint exercises with U.S. Marines and hosting of NATO exercises are the wrong kind of preparation for supply chain tug-of-war with China.

---

* Oyu Tolgoi, one of the world's largest copper mines, is also conveniently located just eighty kilometers north of the Chinese border in the Gobi Desert.

KUBLAI KHAN'S REVENGE:
THE RETURN OF
SINO-SIBERIA

There is no avoiding friction when more than four billion people rub against each other in the arc from Northeast Asia through Southeast Asia to South Asia. The only way to dissipate the pent-up energy of large contained populations is to promote flows across them. China now has more neighbors than any other country in the world, and though in recent decades it has fought wars with Vietnam and India, today its strategy is to avoid conflict while maneuvering to control supply chains. The result will be a functional map that harks back seven centuries to Eurasia's mighty Mongol Empire.

The best place to view this dynamic is along the world's second-longest border between two great powers: Russia and China. A decade ago, when I first wrote about China's gradual demographic and resource colonization of Russia's vast, resource-rich, and depopulated Far East, it earned no shortage of hate mail from Moscow. But a topic that was once taboo is now a going concern. The three-thousand-kilometer Amur River separating the two is less a border than a porous natural feature of a much broader Sino-centric energy, food, and water ecology.

China and Russia have become a supply-demand partnership, not a geopolitical bloc. Russia has land and resources; China has people and money. Russia's infrastructure is in decay; China could rebuild it in five years. It is false to portray Sino-Russian relations as an anti-Western alliance, because Russia has no greater long-term threat to its territorial integrity than the absorption of its entire eastern flank by China. What their relationship in fact underscores is that there are no more reliable alliances, only complementarities—transactional axes of convenience obeying the dictum to keep one's friends close but one's enemies closer.

There are in fact two Russias: the Europe-facing population centers west of the Ural Mountains and the vast Siberian region east of the Urals—which is seven times larger than "European" Russia but with less than one-tenth of the population. What our maps don't reveal is the extent to which Chinese have settled in Russia's eastern regions both seasonally and permanently, as shuttle traders and to operate factories producing finished goods out of Russian timber and minerals. Their intermarriage with the less than five million remaining Russians—almost half of which are Turkic, Eskimo, and other ethnic minorities—is accelerating the region's mutation into a mongrel Sino-Siberian civilization. One day, perhaps, the opportunity for poetic justice will present itself: Seeking to ensure physical protection, civil rights, and quality services for its expatriates in Russia, China may begin to deploy private security guards and hand out passports to mixed-race and minority peoples across the Far East (as Russia has done in Abkhazia, Crimea, and elsewhere). But China has made no plans to alter the de jure map of its border with Russia, only the de facto one. After all, any forcible shift in the border would risk the only retaliation Russia is capable of to defend such a remote territory: nuclear weapons. Meanwhile, the de facto map is quickly coming to resemble that of the thirteenth-century Mongol emperor Kublai Khan, whose Golden Horde ruled modern-day Siberia and Korea, conquered all of China, and stretched as far as Ukraine and Iran. As the creative cartographer Frank Jacobs puts it, "Like love, a border is only real if both sides believe in it."[3]

As the first major rail bridge is completed across the Amur River into China's Heilongjiang province—whose population together with Manchuria's other two provinces totals over 100 million—Russia's rail terminus will soon be in China. The same is true for Russian gas. In 2014, Vladimir Putin signed a $400 billion agreement with Xi Jinping in which Gazprom develops new Siberian gas fields and a new East Siberian pipeline is built to carry thirty-eight billion cubic meters per year to China (about 20 percent of its annual demand). Previously, Russia had been reluctant to send energy supplies directly to China—lest it become a captive supplier. But as energy prices sank and Putin sought a public relations victory amid Western sanctions, Russia was compelled to sign a long-term contract favorable to China. Rosneft has even agreed to offer the China National Petroleum Company (CNPC) a stake in its giant Vankor field, acknowledging that such stranded resources would only ever have one customer. Not only do the Urals divide Russia in two, so do its supply chains.*

It is amusing to hear analysts describe Russia and China's dealings as making little financial sense, as if energy resilience can be boiled down to dollars and cents. This is why grand strategy should never be made by M.B.A.'s, who think in terms of quarterly returns rather than return on investment. For China, the payoffs are priceless, for it diversifies China's energy inflows and lessens its dependence on the Strait of Malacca.†

Russia's own "pivot" to Asia began years before America's and also includes designating its largest Pacific outpost, Vladivostok, as a "free port," with reduced customs and special zones for logistics, industry, ship maintenance, recreation—and agriculture. During my drive to Mongolia in July 2010, Russia was struck by the worst heat wave ever recorded in the country. Wildfires flared across the country, and thick smog blanketed cities, together killing fifty-six thousand Russians. Severe crop failures forced the Kremlin to ban all grain exports, sending global wheat prices soaring. What I didn't realize at the time was that we were witnessing one of the proximate causes of the Arab Spring—the culmination of frequent political unrest sparked by rising staple prices in bazaars from Port-au-Prince to Dhaka to Tunis and Cairo. (Should we be surprised? The crop failures of 1788 were a major cause of the subsequent year's Parisian bread riots and French Revolution.) It turns out this episode of agricultural volatility was not unique: Russia's 2012 drought was even worse than in 2010.

---

* The Asian powers China, Japan, South Korea, and India (as well as America's Exxon) also have stakes in Rosneft's developments on energy-rich Sakhalin Island. Within two decades, East Asia's energy grid could be as dense as in Europe.

† Also, the more China builds out its domestic energy network to utilize its own natural gas supplies, the less coal it will eventually need to burn—making this strategic deal an eco-friendly one as well.

IN THE COMING DECADES, climate change will accelerate Russia's supply chain integration into East Asia. Thanks to global warming, Russia will no longer have to choose between its domestic food market and its international exports. Russia is warming faster than any country in the world: As its permafrost thaws and retreats northward, vast expanses of fertile soil rich in natural phosphorus fertilizer will open for growing ever more food—mostly for China. Whereas currently Russia exports only wheat and plant oil, Russia will become a major exporter of poultry and fish, perhaps twice as much vodka as it already does, and fresh mineral water. But before Russia's freshwater supply is bottled and trucked to European grocery stores and cafés, it may first be diverted to quench China's insatiable thirst. Quite unlike Canadian leaders who hesitate to export water, in 2010 Putin's Natural Resources minister Yury Trutnev declared, "We must not buy Perrier. . . . We must sell our water abroad."[4]

Plans to divert Russia's northern rivers to the south such as the Northern River Reversal Project date back over fifty years to Khrushchev, who found it "useless" that they flow to the Arctic rather than powering agriculture and industry. In the 1970s, several fifteen-kiloton nuclear bombs were even used to level land for the Pechora-Kama Canal to link Siberian rivers with Volga basin tributaries closer to Europe.* (The result was a giant atomic crater now serving as a fishing lake.) All of this was planned decades ago—before China's 1.5 billion people began facing acute water shortages.†

China—long known as the hydraulic civilization—has for millennia used dams, canals, and irrigation to steer its rivers along

---

* The former Soviet republics in Central Asia would have massively benefited from more irrigation for their parched and desiccated lands such as the dried-up Aral Sea on the border of Kazakhstan and Uzbekistan.

† Overexploitation of rivers for agriculture and industry has dried up at least half of China's fifty thousand rivers while massively polluting the remaining rivers. Today China has only one-fifth the world's average water availability per capita.

population centers. The fifth-century B.C.E. Grand Canal, linking the Yellow and Yangtze Rivers and connecting Beijing to Hangzhou, remains the world's longest artificial river. Modern China possesses enormous renewable water resources, but they are not located where its people are. Because 60 percent of China's water supply resides in the country's south and west, while most of its industrial usage is in the north and eastern coast, it is now undertaking the ambitious South-North Water Transfer Project that will divert the abundant water of the Tibetan Himalayan plateau along three routes to northern China at a cost of over $40 billion. Controlling rivers means controlling the kingdom—uprooting millions and altering the flow patterns of the Ganges and Brahmaputra Rivers in the process, on which one billion people downstream in Pakistan, India, and Bangladesh depend.

The equivalent north-to-south hydro-engineering in Russia could provide potable water for hundreds of millions of urban Chinese, irrigate increasingly scarce arable land, and even be used for industry and water-intensive hydraulic shale gas fracking. Needless to say, China has already thought of all this, sending a delegation from the Yellow River Water Authority to Russia for preliminary discussions on such massive hydro-canals.* Though pumping water over long distances and around mountains requires huge electricity generation and power stations, Russian energy is not a resource in short supply. Russia's water will inevitably irrigate more agriculture both on Russian and on Chinese soil. The only question is how much of the food supply chain China will control.

Much of Russia's future is being mapped at this longitude, five thousand kilometers from Moscow and only half as far to Beijing. Russians have long viewed the mighty Lena River as a source of vitality and strength. The geopolitical oracle Halford Mackinder even coined the name "Lenaland" to describe this zone impermeable to

---

* China is also buying large stakes in Russian fertilizer companies such as Uralkali (the world's largest potash producer) to get them to drop prices. It has even begun partnerships with Singaporean companies to jointly expand food-processing operations in Russia.

coastal powers.[5] Lenin created his very nom de guerre as homage to the place of his Siberian exile. Yet today one can visit the region's crucial city, the seventeenth-century mining town of Yakutsk on the western bank of the Lena, to find a lonely but apt metaphor for Russia's tragedy. The Sakha Republic, of which Yakutsk is the capital, is as large as India and holds massive deposits of oil, coal, gold, silver, tin, and a quarter of all the world's diamonds. Yet the city is sinking into the soil faster than any place in the world, its buildings propped up by stilts that need to be dug deeper and deeper each year to find solid ice below. For Yakutis, climate change is quicksand. They will have to leave their land, their history, and their natural riches to be tugged south on barges toward Lake Baikal, where they can be loaded onto sturdy freight railcars on a refurbished Trans-Siberian railway to China.

The geography of Eurasian resources precedes Russia's contingent political borders: Political control above may ultimately be determined by who best connects to the commodities below. Russians are learning to sympathize with the Mongols and the Kazakhs. Kazakhstan, the only landlocked country in the world larger than Mongolia, lies just thirty kilometers from Mongolia's far western border. The Altai region, this truly remote four-corners zone between Russia, China, Mongolia, and Kazakhstan, is a spectacularly empty expanse—but not for long. Russia and India are moving forward—with Chinese approval—with plans to construct a $30 billion pipeline from the Altai region across western China to India.

This north-south energy axis will pass just east of China's Afghanistan border, a tiny sliver known as the Wakhan Corridor that also borders Tajikistan and Pakistan. Since the Soviet withdrawal from Afghanistan near the end of the Cold War and throughout America's post-9/11 occupation, China steadily rose to become Afghanistan's largest foreign investor due to its stake in the Aynak copper mine and its growing interest in lithium (essential for batteries). Afghanistan's technocratic president Ashraf Ghani made his first state visit to China to lure its newly rediscovered neighbor into more investments in roads, railways, and mining. After centuries of relations that amounted to little more than trading fruits, China has begun to pave across Afghanistan as well. For the first time, China is converting its proximity into connectivity. Soon, the U.S. occupation will seem a mere footnote in comparison.

Nothing tells us more about the future of geopolitics than tracing infrastructure plans on the ground. Competitive connectivity reminds us how limited a role militaries have in ultimate victory. Today, as the remnants of American military hardware such as $500 million worth of G222 planes are sold off as scrap metal, China is further ramping up infrastructure projects across the war-ravaged country to reach another ancient civilization seeking to regain its place on Eurasia's new Silk Roads: Iran.

IRAN: THE SILK ROAD RESTORED

While China already imports large quantities of oil and gas across the Indian Ocean from the Arab Gulf countries and Iraq, the grand prize along the Eurasian Silk Road is Iran. Iran's opening after decades of isolation is the latest phase in its promiscuous geopolitics. During World War II, the "Persian Corridor" was crucial for Allied supplies of arms to the Soviets to counter the Axis on the eastern front. Early in the Cold War, the United States backed Shah Reza Pahlavi, who took power after the U.S.- and U.K.-backed 1953 coup of Prime Minister Mossadegh. But after Iran's theocratic 1979 revolution and Iraq's invasion in 1980, the United States began selling weapons to Saddam Hussein, as did the Soviet Union, which resented the ayatollah's wiping out the country's communist Tudeh Party. Over the course of the decade-long war, however, the United States also covertly sold arms to Iran, as did communist countries from Yugoslavia to North Korea. The Soviet Union also became a major supplier to Iran by the end of the war, while China liberally sold small arms and heavy weapons to both sides. Containing both Iraq and Iran, preventing their war from spilling over into Saudi Arabia, deterring the Soviet Union from expanding its Afghanistan invasion into Iran, and keeping the flow of Middle East oil open clearly led to ironic and contradictory patterns of alignment.

The future will be even more complex as China seeks to access Persian energy supplies, Europe and America compete to sell into its market while containing its nuclear program, Western reliance on Gulf energy supplies diminishes, and Iraq and Syria crumble. In the bizarre labyrinth of Middle Eastern geopolitics, multiple opposing scenarios can simultaneously unfold: Great powers and even some Sunni Arab nations can open up to Iran, while a Saudi-Iranian proxy war rages in Iraq and Syria (something of a reprise of the 1980s Iran-Iraq War). Meanwhile, the United States can continue to base military forces in the Arab GCC countries (to counter the Iranian threat) while ironically being perceived as abandoning them in favor of Iran.

From the predicted certainty of conflict with Iran during the Bush administration (and even Obama's first term), Iran is now one of the liveliest cases of tug-of-war. Geopolitical competition for regional dominance goes hand in hand with competition to sell into its eighty million population of mostly urban youth. For both East and West, this means building as many Silk Roads to Iran as possible.

The world wants to do business with Iran. As with the Indo-Pak nuclear tests of 1998, geostrategic and economic shifts eventually overwhelm attempts to maintain universal sanctions. Russia made major oil agreements and plans to sell surface-to-air missiles, China signed huge gas and infrastructure deals (including boring a multi-lane tunnel through the Alborz Mountains to reduce travel time between Tehran and the northern cities by the Caspian Sea), India sold substantial refined petroleum, Turkey traded gold, and French and Chinese banks laundered billions. Even the removal of Iranian banks from the SWIFT interbank network didn't cut the country off from trading physical goods. Additionally, under the American-led sanctions regime, it was actually American companies that exported more to Iran than more sympathetic Europeans through lobby groups like USA*Engage that were granted blanket waivers on food and medical-related items.

The template of Myanmar demonstrates how if the United States constructively uses a mix of carrots and sticks, it can expand its leverage in the tug-of-war over Iran. Starting in 2012, the United States rapidly lifted sanctions on investment into Myanmar while maintaining a blacklist of shady companies and tycoons with which American companies were prohibited from doing business. Despite these frictions, American firms from Coca-Cola to GE have deepened their roots in the country, giving the Burmese government options to cancel Chinese projects knowing that a higher-quality Western partner is waiting in the wings.

Iran, too, wants the option to multi-align. Today Iranian middlemen in Dubai and London wave around dossiers announcing $70 billion of essential foreign investment deals. They remind audiences that Iran's 2014 cancellation of a $2.5 billion CNPC project for the joint development of the South Azadegan oil field is a sign that an open Iran might spend on Western quality goods and services over China's often underwhelming technology. Starting in 2014, both Boeing and GE were given licenses to sell spare parts and conduct aircraft maintenance in Iran. Even Iran's entrenched Revolutionary Guard is preparing for a post-sanctions world by privatizing its various companies to attract investment while attempting to slip under the radar of the U.S. Treasury.*

Iran's political and commercial tentacles already dominate across the southern confluence of the Tigris and Euphrates Rivers (the Shatt al-Arab) in Iraq's oil-rich and Shia-populated Basra province. Now it is Iran, rather than Iraq, that is taking a hard line against Kuwait, whose plans for a massive new port could block large ships from entering Iraq's only deepwater port at Umm Qasr and which is again conducting the same horizontal drilling under their border that sparked Saddam's invasion in 1990.

And yet, despite the deep suspicion between Shiite Iran and the

---

* One example is the blacklisted Khatam al-Anbiya (Sea of the Prophets), an Iranian Revolutionary Guard Corps–owned conglomerate that controls oil, highways, and ports and has over $50 billion of contracts with the Iranian government, including a refinery, petrochemical plants, and pipelines at the South Pars field.

Sunni Arab states, they too are seeking to commercially penetrate their far larger rival as Emirates airlines has done with its multiple daily flights. The U.A.E.'s agricultural ministry is exploring investments to boost Iran's farm output to shorten its own food supply chain, while Qatar and Iran will jointly develop a portion of the massive South Pars gas field.

Turkey, meanwhile, has no inhibitions about dealing with Iran and offers a conduit to Europe that avoids the Arab world's turbulence. In addition to the planned freight rail from China through Central Asia and Iran to Turkey and Europe, a "Persian pipeline" could add huge natural gas supplies along the same route. Europeans are coming rapidly from the other direction. Turkish Airlines currently holds (together with Emirates) 75 percent of Iran's international flight market. Lufthansa's share will take off as more Western passengers arrive.

Tehran today is a megacity left off the lists of enticing Asian destinations such as Istanbul and Cairo, but that too will change. The overland route is already restoring historical passages: The British-operated Jewels of Persia luxury train now travels from Budapest across Turkey to Tehran and around a circuit of historical sites. Eventually, a Caspian Rim railway circuit will carry on through Mashhad to Ashgabat in Turkmenistan and onward to Almaty and China.

When I visited Iran in mid-2015, diplomats spoke little about the nuclear negotiations. Instead, they pulled out large maps to point to pipeline routes that could link Turkmenistan to Pakistan and railways across northern Afghanistan to Tajikistan and China. In the coming years, we'll hear much more from the Economic Cooperation Organization, a 1960s body now redefined to focus on railways and trade linkages between Turkey, Iran, Pakistan, and all the former Soviet Central Asian republics. Not for centuries has Persian civilization leveraged its geography to be as connected as it will be in the decades to come.

Iran's society wants nothing more than this. With two-thirds of the population under the age of thirty, Iran is a postrevolutionary society trapped in a revolutionary state. Its reactionary theocratic regime thrives on isolation, while its bulging youth cohort craves connectivity. During the days I spent motorcycling around Tehran, I met dozens of Iranian "re-pats" who have flocked back to set up tech incubators and capitalize on the low cost of living and entrepreneurial scene. Iran already has nearly full mobile phone penetration and close to 60 percent Internet access, the highest in the Middle East. With Western e-commerce sites such as eBay and Amazon blocked, local champions such as Digikala and Esam are growing exponentially.

Low oil prices mean Iran must rapidly diversify its economy, investing in modern infrastructure and building viable export sectors such as automobile manufacturing. Especially after its transportation linkages decayed during the 1980s Iran-Iraq War, Iran is left with under a thousand kilometers of quality expressway and less than five thousand kilometers of railway. To truly attract large-scale foreign investment, it has set up half a dozen more FTZs that have no visa requirement and offer long-term tax exemptions and 100 percent foreign ownership.

Iran's opening will not resolve the Middle East's borders. In fact it will add a thick layer of economic linkages and political subterfuge to an already befuddling regional bazaar, one that will grow more complex even as it becomes less opaque. Then only one country will remain to represent the triumph of flow over friction: North Korea.

NORTH KOREA: AN IRON SILK ROAD THROUGH THE HERMIT KINGDOM

In addition to the landlocked giants Kazakhstan and Mongolia, one other vulnerable country borders both Russia and China: North Korea. But whereas Kazakhstan and Mongolia have undertaken various political and economic reforms since communism, North Korea has for decades remained hopelessly repressed, first in pursuit of its own antiquated ideology of self-reliance known as *juche* and then due to smothering international economic sanctions. Far from autarky, North Korea has instead found itself in a pernicious form of dependence that comes from near-total isolation: Almost all North Korean exports go to China, and almost all food, fuel, and other basic goods enter North Korea through China.

North Korea is an extreme country that evokes extreme emotions. It is run by a despotic dynasty with its own acronym among Asia watchers: KFR, for Kim family regime. It starves its citizens, tortures them in gulags, and operates an all-pervasive police state. Pointing out these facts placates conservatives (and even liberals) in Washington who seek to claim a moral high ground but achieves absolutely nothing. Yet for all the country's nuclear saber rattling, sinking of South Korean ships, and imprisonment of foreign missionaries, the new pattern that is emerging between North Korea and its neighbors is one of increasing connectivity: Flows are prevailing over frictions.

When I traveled to the "Hermit Kingdom" in 2012, I was obliged to visit grand revolutionary monuments and absorb videos of anti–South Korean and anti-American propaganda. But I also witnessed a country whose ideology and infrastructure are reaching the end of their shelf life. Pyongyang's concrete housing blocks have infrequent water supply at best, while its buses belch and sputter their final choking puffs. Since Soviet fuel subsidies collapsed in the early 1990s, China has increasingly been playing hardball, freezing delivery of oil, food, and other essential goods to keep the North Korean regime in check. Any ideological bonds the countries once shared—in the 1950s, it was said they were as close as "lips and teeth"—have fizzled as quickly as their economies have diverged: China is now the world's largest economy, while North Korea lacks a credit rating. In 2014, China acquiesced in American requests to cut off North Korea's Internet access as retaliation for the cyber attack against Sony Pictures allegedly orchestrated from Pyongyang. The capital's reigning conspiracy theory is that China will invade from the north, prompting the regime to move tanks to their border.

China, of course, has more constructive plans than merely occupying North Korea. It has invested in an industrial zone at North Korea's Rason, an ice-free port nestled near the corner where all three countries meet on the Sea of Japan. By building a railway to Rason's port, China gains an entirely new coastal access on the other side of North Korea, strengthening its hand in accessing Arctic shipping routes.

Russia too has plans for its almost forgotten neighbor. In 2014, Vladimir Putin dispatched Yuri Trutnev, his adviser on Northeast Asia, to Pyongyang to forgive North Korean debt, relaunch previously suspended investments, and explore a gas pipeline across their narrow border. Almost simultaneously, during a state visit to South Korea, Putin called for an "Iron Silk Road Express" from Russia to Seoul—with a stop in Pyongyang. Russia now also compensates for China in sending oil to North Korea and in exchange may get up to a million North Korean army reservists to serve as laborers in their barren border region. South Korea doesn't want to fall behind either in the race to engage in its estranged cousin's stuttering rehabilitation and is thus expanding investment in the Kaesong Industrial Complex and the railway line meant to connect Seoul to Pyongyang.* Competitive connectivity has come even to North Korea.

Cautiously and haltingly, North Korea is becoming another major example of a World War III scenario that won't be. Instead, the large-scale supply chain integration of the country is taking off. The most visible—and growing—signs of this shift are its special economic zones. Kaesong employs over fifty thousand North Koreans producing parts for the automaker Hyundai, as well as watches and shoes at wages far lower than in China. One foreign investor I met runs a factory there that makes DVD players, which North Koreans then take home to watch smuggled videos from the South. If sanctions were lifted on exports of computer parts and other electronics coming out of Kaesong, the zone's honest revenues could

---

* Proposals have even been put forward to turn portions of the heavily fortified demilitarized zone into a nature park given its unique ecosystem of flora that has blossomed during decades of minimal human trespassing.

surge from $500 million to billions of dollars annually. In 2014, Kim Jong Un announced that each North Korean province should develop its own special economic zone as well; they have no choice, because Pyongyang provides the outer cities and regions with almost nothing. Several delegations of North Korean urban planners have been traveling to Vietnam and Singapore studying how to set up areas such as the Wonsan reserve featuring Yellow Sea beaches and nearby skiing. Do we prefer that North Korea counterfeit currency and flood China and the West with opium poppies and crystal meth from its drug labs or join legitimate international manufacturing and tourism supply chains?[6]

Geology guarantees that North Korea will emerge as a supply chain node. The country is literally a gold mine of rare earth minerals essential for electronic gadgets. Mining operators from Australia to Mongolia are keen to tap its gold and magnesium deposits. The global supply of these precious metals is far too scarce for the world—particularly the electronics manufacturing leader China—to patiently wait for North Korean regime change. As one expert on the North Korean economy put it, "China wants the entire supply chain."[7] And indeed, global consumers are already complicit in China's extraction of the North's minerals: In 2014, corporate filings required by the Dodd-Frank legislation revealed that IBM and Hewlett-Packard hardware contains North Korean minerals integrated by Chinese suppliers—not that their corporate management or shareholders even knew it.

Seen in isolation, North Korea's baby steps toward becoming a more open and viable economy are insignificant: industrial joint ventures, importing foreign cars, limited Internet access, mobile phones with international dialing, and a new ski resort. But taken together, they begin to look like an early draft of the kind of national business plan China undertook in the late 1970s. Indeed, China is set to outsource thousands of menial manufacturing jobs to North Korea in the coming years.

There is much more in North Korea that is attracting sustained international interest. Its mighty rivers could be a key hydropower resource both to electrify the country and to sell power to China and South Korea. The North also produces agricultural staples like rice, corn, soybeans, and potatoes that private equity firms are buying to ride the next wave of international agribusiness. Choson Exchange, the most prominent international nongovernmental organization (NGO) operating in North Korea, is training thousands of young professionals—especially women—in entrepreneurship and workplace skills, even bringing delegations of Western venture capitalists to the country.

Even if all the planned ports, special economic zones, industrial parks, real estate developments, mining projects, worker-training programs, and mountain ecotourist parks currently on the drawing board were executed to perfection, fifteen years from now North Korea could at best resemble post-communist Romania, where low-grade industry, farming, and mining remain economic staples. It would still be climbing out from the ranks of the world's poorest countries, but it would be more open and free.

All North Koreans are oppressed, and at least a third of the population is destitute, but it is not a nation of depraved lunatics. Foreign appreciation of their cultural offerings reminds them that they are a rich civilization trapped in an anachronistic state. The more tourists, business travelers, cultural delegations, and other visitors that go to North Korea, the more the society comes to depend on—and seek—their presence for money and knowledge from the outside world. North Koreans are not automatons but citizens, loyal but misinformed. Like Iranians and Cubans, they are told one story but increasingly encounter other viewpoints through media and tourism. Just as Iranians mutter about the "Supreme Leader" more as someone who cramps their style, many North Koreans can barely disguise their desire for sweeping change.

Pyongyang's teenagers are clearly more interested in pizza than reciting ideological poetry. Whether in schools, billiard halls, or karaoke bars, ordinary people are surprisingly open about their concerns. I met parents who resented their children being conscripted to dance and sing in the spectacular Arirang Mass Games, the seasonal performance that features up to 100,000 acrobats, flag bearers, card flippers, and other astonishing acts of synchronization. They simply wanted their kids to learn piano, do their math homework, and learn English.

All dictators surely get a tingle down their spine when autocrats are chased from power in countries such as Libya and Egypt. The common response is to dig in one's heels and ruthlessly stifle all dissent at home. Ruthlessness can only carry the young Kim Jong Un so far, however. Pyongyang's enormous street murals revere his father, Kim Jong Il, and revolutionary hero grandfather Kim Il Sung, while the young Kim lacks any such cult of personality. Instead, he relies on the old clique that served his elders to continuously dole out anti-Japanese propaganda, nuclear threats, and intimidation of the South. His every appearance is a choreographed demonstration of authority.

Yet if the young Kim can oversee his country's steady rehabilitation without alienating the powerful vested interests in the military, he might spend the next decades not as an isolated pariah but as a transformational reformer. Rather than being restricted from most international travel, he could enjoy European basketball games as he did during high school in Switzerland. Kim is not the man to send missiles raining down on South Korea, and he hardly complained when its activists attached thousands of mini marshmallow-chocolate pies to helium balloons and sent them floating over the border.

As with Iran, waiting for the North Korean regime to collapse or be deposed is wishful thinking. The threat of regime change directly undermines the kind of steady engagement needed to change the diplomatic dynamic from hostility toward reconciliation. In 2014, South Korea's president, Park Geun-hye, gave a speech in Leipzig, Germany, explicitly touting reunification in which there would be a natural division of labor between the industrial South and the agricultural North. While that may be the destination, the pathway will be different from Germany in 1990, when East Germany formally ceased to exist through a carefully managed international process.

Instead, North Korea is already being gradually transformed from a nuclearized minefield buffer state into a passageway between China and Russia, on the one hand, and South Korea, on the other. It is far more likely to remain autocratic than to democratize. That is precisely why supply chain integration is a better strategy than political humiliation. While all sides benefit from North Korea's normalization, one long-term question that emerges, both on China's periphery and far beyond, is whether China can hold on to its supply chain empire.

THE SUPPLY CHAIN STRIKES BACK

Supply chain empires of the past have been undone by a combination of indebtedness and inflation at home and unrest and competition abroad. Falling silver imports from South America hastened the decline of the Spanish Empire, while four Anglo-Dutch wars spread over a century gradually weakened Dutch control of South Africa and Ceylon. Divergent priorities in imperial capitals have also been a major factor. British investors poured money into Indian railways assuming the Raj would last forever, but the growing independence movement—and the British prime minister Clement Attlee's acquiescence in it—effectively chased weary London investors out of India.

Supply chain wars are nothing new to China—except they have historically gone in the other direction. When the Qing dynasty emperor Daoguang seized and destroyed British opium stock in Guangzhou in 1839, Britain responded with overwhelming force, occupying Hong Kong and imposing extraterritorial rights across the country. For China, the Opium Wars marked the beginning of a century and a half of humiliation from which it feels it is only now recovering.

The principal geopolitical question for many countries today is not whether the United States and China will go to war in the Pacific but whether China will use its supply chain empire to inflict "unequal treaties" on them the way the British did to China two centuries ago. Since the 1990s, China's checkbook diplomacy has underwritten nearly frictionless commercial expansion, buying up raw materials in pricey long-term contracts from Argentina to Angola in exchange for building schools, hospitals, government offices, and highways. It pledged noninterference in local politics, which actually meant selling unlimited arms to governments to preserve the status quo. China managed to—and still does—maintain good relations with important pairs of regional rivals: Brazil and Venezuela, Saudi Arabia and Iran, Kazakhstan and Uzbekistan, and India and Pakistan.

But in a growing number of countries, the honeymoon is over; the blowback has begun. All superpowers eventually suffer blowback; it's just a matter of time. Ironically, the CIA itself coined the term to warn of the consequences of its role in the chain reaction that led to Iran's anti-American hostility following its 1979 revolution. That same year, in yet another spark of long-term blowback, the CIA began its largest clandestine operation—funding the anti-Soviet mujahedeen that eventually devoured the Red Army—which also spawned the Taliban that sheltered the 9/11-mastermind, Osama bin Laden.

China already knows blowback: Its heavy-handed pacification of its largest province, Uighur-Muslim-populated Xinjiang, led to a suicide car-bomb attack right on Tiananmen Square in Beijing in 2013 and dozens of other terrorist incidents. But the blowback against China abroad is different. China's global presence is defined not by its military but by its supply chains. Its key agents abroad are not intelligence agencies but state-owned companies. For China, supply chain blowback *is* geopolitical blowback. It is also a reminder that building infrastructure abroad doesn't guarantee China will ultimately control it. The winners in supply chain geopolitics are still far from certain.

Blowback reminds us that we live in a world of complexity rather than linearity and of the compressed timescales of today's feedback loops. European empires lasted up to six hundred years before anti-colonial independence movements combined with the stress of

World War II brought about their retreat.* China, however, has had barely a decade of truly global encroachment yet already faces counter-maneuvers. It must learn practically overnight what took Europe centuries. China cannot be a new colonial overlord, because the age of colonialism has passed, replaced by transparency and time-taught suspicion of foreign powers. The supply chain can strike back.

With alarm bells going off from Zambia to Mongolia whenever a corrupt deal is struck, Beijing has to be cautious rather than brutal. So far, Beijing has preferred to build cooperative relations across entire continents, not get dragged into using its muscle to enforce every contract that has been hijacked from Congo to Kazakhstan. Such restraint has helped China build a global supply chain empire without fighting a single skirmish. But there are growing frictions. Kidnappings and attacks against Chinese oil and gas workers are on the rise from the Niger delta to southern Sudan. Zambian miners have violently rebelled against their Chinese employers' slave wages and slave-driving tactics, on several occasions trampling, crushing, and killing them deep inside mine shafts. Chinese long-term purchases might turn out to be more like short-term rentals. Much as the British prime minister, Harold Macmillan, recognized in 1960 the inevitable "growth of national consciousness,"[8] the simultaneous and uncoordinated blowback against China is an abiding feature of a tug-of-war world.

Resource nationalism is also a clever legal tool countries use to ward off Chinese supply chain intrusion. Kazakhstan and Mongolia have designated their key mineral deposits as "strategic assets" off-limits to foreign purchase. China is invited only to co-develop them as service providers. The smartest governments demand that China employ more locals, spend more on skills training, transfer more technology, and manufacture more products locally. They want

---

* Portugal, the first truly global empire, took its first colony, the Muslim city of Ceuta in North Africa, in 1514 and gave up its last colony, Macau, to China in 1999.

more of the value added brought in, rather than just carted out. They want not just a horizontal role in the supply but a vertical one. They are doing to China what China has done to the West.

Because China still needs massive quantities of raw materials to fuel its decades-long urbanization drive, it has every incentive to play along—for now. Indeed, even though China does not have the luxury of colonial dominions, it does have an appetite to absorb risk, a budget to meet any price, and a demand for resources no other country can match. China's cash-rich and state-backed giants thus negotiate from a position of great leverage. Until Congo, Myanmar, Mongolia, and other commodities-dependent countries find more export markets, they are ultimately resource hostages to China.

When push comes to shove, China can also play financial hardball. China's Export-Import Bank has loaned more than $20 billion more to sub-Saharan countries since 2001 than the World Bank, fueling concerns about another cycle of massive indebtedness. Angola is the kind of country that keeps China happy: It benefits from essential Chinese road construction and other projects and enough money to pay off creditors. Zambia, meanwhile, is (once again) taking on unsustainable debt burdens to finance spending. And because it has seized some Chinese mining operations, it certainly can't raise revenue by taxing Chinese companies more. Countries under severe financial stress don't go bankrupt so much as sell off more and more assets and control of their industries. They become more supply chain republics than sovereign ones. What assets might China seize back if Zambia defaults?

Western governments and companies shouldn't just sit back and wait for China to overstep and inspire blowback. If they don't step up to compete with China along the supply chain, they will leave developing countries with little choice. It is ironic, then, that the U.S. Congress actually shut down for several months in mid-2015 America's own Export-Import Bank—nicknamed the Bank of Boeing, though it also benefits other major U.S. companies like GE and

Caterpillar—whose loans make it cheaper for foreigners to acquire American goods while actually generating an annual profit for the U.S. Treasury.

Around the world, China finds itself at different points on the imperial life cycle: seduction and expansion, exploitation and co-dependence, or self-assertion and blowback. But the common denominator is that a high degree of dependence on China—whether big countries like Russia or smaller ones like Zambia—creates both stability and certainty, on the one hand, and tension and resentment, on the other. While China has taken full advantage of Myanmar's geography by building new pipelines and roads connecting them, Myanmar seems to fear China much less than before: A viral SMS campaign in late 2012 warned, "Chinese get out. We're not afraid of you."

As EMPIRES RETREAT, INFRASTRUCTURE changes hands and purposes. The farther imperial Russia built the Trans-Siberian Railway east of Lake Baikal, the more it became part of Meiji Japan's motivation for attacking Russian-held Port Arthur in Manchuria in 1904. But after Japan's defeat in World War II, Russians took over the Japanese railways on the southern half of gas-rich Sakhalin Island. After America's withdrawal from Iraq, both the Iraqi army and ISIS have helped themselves to the hardware left behind.

Inevitably, China's sprawling supply chains will take on military dimensions. China now gathers constant on-the-ground intelligence about the deeply troubled places where it drills and scrapes for resources from Venezuela to South Sudan. It has also deployed thousands of peacekeepers to UN operations from Haiti to Lebanon, conducts joint military exercises with dozens of partner nations, and allegedly has undercover PLA soldiers protecting oil fields in Sudan. Eventually, it will extend its naval presence around the Indian Ocean rim (such as a planned base in Djibouti) to remain close to places where it might have to suddenly rescue workers or send in reinforcements—potentially from its growing ranks of private security contractors.

The supply chain war could become quite literal—potentially on China's own borders. The gold, gas, oil, and uranium deposits of Pakistan's Baluchistan province have meant the grinding suppression of Baluchi nationalism at the hands of the Pakistani army and Chinese state-owned mining companies. Pakistan's Baluchis thus view Gwadar port as a Chinese-backed Punjabi colonial project, and Pakistan's overt invitation in 2013 for China to use Gwadar as a naval base only heightened their suspicions. The Baluchistan Liberation Army has attacked pipelines, blown up crowded buses, and killed numerous Chinese engineers near Gwadar. In 2014, its attack on a major power station plunged most of Pakistan into darkness. The Baluchis might have been more content had their coastal hamlet not become a major shipping and energy hub, but now that it has, they will fight even more fiercely to control the supply chain.

China doesn't want to send troops to protect its investments in Central Asia, but it may have to. America's drawdown in Afghanistan means China must cut more of its own deals with Kabul (which it is now selling weapons to) but also with local governors, warlords, and even the Taliban to keep its mines, roads, and other infrastructures from being attacked. But there is a well-worn saying that "you can rent an Afghan, but you cannot buy one." While today it is hard to imagine China making the same tragic mistakes as both the Soviet Union and America in putting so many boots on the ground in hostile terrain, China could have its very own version of the Afghanistan quagmire . . . in Afghanistan.

No amount of "soft power" can substitute for cutting a fair deal. If building railways and spreading the English language were all it takes to maintain an empire, the British Raj would still be thriving. Colonialism is passé. It's a world where nobody wants to be a colony; everyone wants to be a hub.

CHAPTER 10

HOPSCOTCH ACROSS THE OCEANS

AN EMPIRE OF ENCLAVES

FOUR HUNDRED YEARS BEFORE HALFORD MACKINDER ISSUED his famous dictum declaring the Central Asian "Heartland" the geographic pivot of history, the Spanish conquistador Hernán Cortés made an equally extravagant claim in 1524: "He who controls the passage between the oceans may consider himself master of the world."[1] By the early sixteenth century, Manila was the thriving midway point for Seville's round-the-world trade as its merchants raised revenue for the Crown through heavy trade with Ming China and carried eastward through the East Indies across the Pacific Ocean to Acapulco in Mexico (then called New Spain) and back across the Atlantic to Spain. King Philip II's armada of two-thousand-ton oceangoing galleons maintained a monopoly over the "spice trade" that also included silk, porcelain, pearls, and other luxury goods.

Five centuries after the Spanish galleon trade, mankind is once again a coastal maritime civilization with dense connectivity among dozens of major ports enabling greater volumes of commodities and goods flows. But who controls the passages between the oceans?

Maps 16, 18, 23, 27, 31, and 32, corresponding to this chapter, appear in the map inserts.

On February 24, 2014, on the tiny Caribbean island nation of Trinidad and Tobago off the eastern coast of Venezuela, the vice president of China Harbour Engineering Company Yingtao Shi signed an agreement to construct a new special economic zone and transshipment port.* While Trinidad is best known for being the home of calypso music, what sets it apart from other Caribbean nations is an economy driven not by cocoa and sugarcane but by petroleum, which accounts for half its GDP and most of its exports. As the Panama Canal expands to accommodate ever more—and larger—ships while ports along the U.S. East Coast from New Jersey to Miami expand to berth them, Trinidad is ideally suited as a dry-dock location for Chinese goods to be divided up before sailing north to America or south to Brazil. No wonder, then, that the Chinese Export-Import Bank financed almost the entire deal.

Scholars have struggled to classify China's twenty-first-century rise. Within Asia, there are clear parallels to the tribute system that operated under the Ming dynasty, when smaller regional nations from Central and Southeast Asia paid obeisance by kowtowing to the emperor. Some thus cite Bismarck as a template, referring to the late nineteenth-century Prussian statesman who strengthened Germany's position without upending the Continent's overall stability. But Bismarck's order lasted less than thirty years before a Franco-German counter-coalition emerged. The rest is history.

A better analogy for understanding twenty-first-century China lies not in Europe's continental but in its maritime history— particularly the seventeenth-century Dutch Empire. While the Spanish and Portuguese Crowns were the first truly global empires (and were for half a century united until 1640), they physically subjugated (through violent conquest and even genocide) large swaths of Latin America, Africa, Asia, and Oceania. For Lisbon and Seville, these possessions were extensions of their Iberian homeland. The Dutch, by contrast, operated in a less brutal and more commercial

---

* The name of the capital city, Port of Spain, is a reminder of the country's colonial past, though it changed hands several times between Christopher Columbus's arrival in 1498 and independence from Britain in 1962.

fashion. The Dutch East India Company, chartered in 1602, is considered the world's first multinational corporation that issued stocks and bonds to finance expeditions. In its efforts to undermine Portuguese control of the lucrative spice trade and Spanish control over its Low Countries (modern-day Belgium), the Dutch deployed more merchant ships (five thousand) and traders (almost one million) over a two-hundred-year period than the rest of Europe combined. Indeed, the Iberian-Dutch and Anglo-Dutch rivalries were about controlling not the oceans but access to ports east of Suez. We owe the concept of "freedom of the seas" to the Dutch legal scholar Hugo Grotius, who in his 1609 work *Mare liberum* argued that the oceans should be international rather than sovereign territory.

There are remarkable similarities between Amsterdam's strategy four hundred years ago and Beijing's today. It is the Dutch model of infrastructure for resources that China follows, not British or French colonialism that sought to administer and socially engineer entire societies. Though the Dutch used force in alliance with local rulers to oust the Portuguese and establish administrative control— particularly in Sri Lanka and Indonesia—the objective was to secure trading posts and harness natural resource wealth, not to conquer the world for God or country.* Two hundred years earlier, the great Ming admiral Zheng He's fifteenth-century "Treasure Fleet" voyages had also established China's peaceful relations with kingdoms as far as East Africa. Like Ming China, the Dutch were about trade, not territory: They were an empire of enclaves.

China has had plenty of time to study how to set up and manage such overseas enclaves because that is what European powers did for centuries in China itself through their colonial concessions such as Hong Kong and Macau. In recent decades, China has built dozens of such special economic zones not only inside its own borders but also across Asia, Latin America, and Africa. SEZs are the commer-

---

* The Dutch also briefly held parts of Brazil, South Africa, and India. In Indonesia, the Dutch built up what are today Indonesia's major cities such as Jakarta and Bandung and over seventy-five thousand kilometers of roads to connect them and other ports and facilities.

cial garrisons of a supply chain world, enabling China to secure resources without the messy politics of colonial subjugation.

But how to secure access to them when only the United States
has a navy capable of global power projection and can block the
major "sea lines of communication"? China has only one aircraft
carrier (of dubious quality), but like the seventeenth-century Dutch
it operates the twenty-first century's largest merchant marine fleet
of over two thousand vessels—barges, bulk carriers, petroleum
tankers, and container ships—that sail all the oceans, including increasingly the Arctic. By contrast, there are currently fewer than one
hundred U.S.-flag-flying ships on the oceans. China has also been
closely studying the nineteenth-century American naval strategist
Alfred Thayer Mahan, who argued that the most valuable purpose
of maritime sea power projection was to expand commerce. Over a
century ago, he argued for annexing Hawaii and building the Panama Canal to take advantage of a faster-paced global economy
driven by steam power and telegraph cables, writing, "The world
has grown smaller. Positions formerly distant have become of vital
importance."[2] Today it is China that builds, operates, and in many
cases effectively owns critical ports and canals that underpin its
growing supply chain empire. (The Hong Kong–based Hutchison
Whampoa runs both ends of the Panama Canal.) As China's trade
tentacles span the oceans, will it too send armed galleons to escort
its oil tankers and freight-laden ships around the world?

"MOBILE SOVEREIGNTY"

On the morning of May 2, 2014, a deepwater oil-drilling rig took
position at 15°29'58" north latitude by 111°12'06" east longitude,
180 miles south of China's Hainan Island and 120 miles east of
Vietnam's Ly Son Island. Over two months, the Haiyang Shiyou 981
(HYSY 981) drilled two oil wells. By July 15, it was gone.

When we think of sovereignty, we think of (bordered) territory.
Most of the earth, however, is covered by oceans whose ownership
has always been ambiguous. Within two decades of the Dutch

scholar Hugo Grotius advocating freedom of the seas (*Mare liberum*), the English jurist John Selden formulated a response aimed at affirming control over offshore waters: *mare clausum* (closed sea). Today many coastal nations claim exclusive economic zones stretching two hundred nautical miles from their shores, with dozens of overlapping claims causing legal friction and naval skirmishes. In navigating global waters for commercial gain, China is a reminder of Grotius and the Dutch. But when it comes to the South China Sea, China uses an audacious term even Selden would have blushed at: "blue soil."

While China has come late to the South China Sea waters in search of energy resources, it has been clever to focus its attention on areas already identified—and auctioned—by PetroVietnam to Exxon as well as Indian, Russian, and other companies that have long been operating under Vietnamese licenses. It has also deployed new technologies such as the HYSY 981 mobile deepwater drilling rig that allow for the kind of kinetic maneuvering previously possible only on land. Wang Yilin, the chairman of the state-owned oil company CNOOC, has called these towable, deepwater rigs "strategic weapons," part of China's "mobile national sovereignty."[3]

"Mobile sovereignty" is not a term one could have conceived of with seventeenth-century technology, but sturdy and maneuverable platforms such as the HYSY 981 are the movable supply chain islands of today's geopolitics. Rather than occupy territory or claim waters, they stealthily enter disputed areas, explore and extract energy reserves deep undersea, and are then towed away to international waters. They don't require a permanent perimeter defense, only temporary coast guard and navy ships that protect them while they drill and extract the black gold beneath. When tensions ratchet toward the boiling point, they can be pulled back as a sign of goodwill. Now that China has acquired this latest technology, it is no longer dependent on foreign oil companies less willing to partner with it in disputed waters; it can just go it alone. China is building far more HYSY-like platforms than it is aircraft carriers.

China, Vietnam, and the Philippines are all signatories to the

UN Convention on the Law of the Sea, widely considered the "constitution for the seas," yet historical claims stemming from previous wars and bilateral agreements have trumped respect for its provisions. China's now infamous "9-dash line" map—most recently issued with ten dashed lines—depicts sovereign claims hanging downward like a tongue along the Vietnamese coast, along Borneo island, and past the Philippines to Taiwan. It would be like America claiming the entire Caribbean to Venezuela's coast as its own—which was indeed the gist of the early twentieth-century Roosevelt corollary to the Monroe Doctrine. But China's aggressive maps and aerial defense identification zones are meant not to deny others' usage of the South China Sea but rather to position itself to better harvest as much as possible of the estimated thirty trillion cubic meters of natural gas and ten billion barrels of oil deposited under disputed waters.

China's "use it or lose it" approach also involves installing brick-and-mortar airstrips, lighthouses, garrisons, signals stations, and administrative centers on neglected or abandoned islands in the Spratly and Paracel chains.* Fiery Cross Reef in the Spratly Islands has become the epicenter of what some call an "island factory" where large-scale sand dredging and land reclamation are used to build up and connect separate shoals into larger islands.

Sand has become a weapon. By its very nature, sand is shape-shifting, both irreducibly granular and yet a major ingredient in concrete. Though silica-based quartz is one of the most abundant minerals in Earth's crust, finding the right type of sand for the world's construction boom has meant dredging rivers and beaches, scraping the ocean floor, and shipping massive quantities across the world—even paradoxically from Australia to sand-rich Dubai—in a $70 billion annual market.[4] The use of sand in topographical engineering is a literal example of supply chains serving state building:

---

* The PLA has referred to this as a "cabbage strategy," building up infrastructure on contested islands while surrounding them with layers of fishing boats, coast guard vessels, and warships such that "the island is thus wrapped layer by layer like a cabbage." The United States calls these tactics "salami slicing."

Singapore's inexhaustible appetite for sand has led to tiny Indonesian islands completely disappearing through erosion, while Malaysia's sand exports have officially ceased, but other sand-rich countries such as Myanmar and the Philippines continue the lucrative sales.[5] With sand as its ammunition, China has established robust facts in the water such as Fiery Cross Reef, assuming de facto control while de jure sovereignty is arbitrated indefinitely.

There has been widespread backlash against China over its South China Sea maneuvers. As news broke of the HYSY 981's appearance near the Paracel Islands in mid-2014, Vietnamese protesters rioted across the country and torched manufacturing plants belonging to China—or so they thought, for they mistakenly attacked Taiwanese, South Korean, and Singaporean factories jointly operated with Vietnamese companies as well. (Note to supply chain allies: Hang your national flag outside your facilities.) As satellite imagery revealed China's accelerated island building on Fiery Cross Reef, the United States sent its P-8A Poseidon surveillance plane for a precariously up close look.

And yet China has probed deeply into others' domains without evoking genuinely strategic countermeasures. Confrontations have proliferated, but escalation has been controlled. While the United States can try mightily to deter military aggression, it has very little strategy toward supply chain expansionism. There is no doubt that China's unilateral assertion in the South China and East China Seas inspired America's hastily crafted "pivot" policy of rebalancing naval and air force assets toward Asia, but even with more U.S. battleships and bombers located in Asia, is it willing to use them?

All militaries prefer quick and decisive wars to long and protracted ones, but the further one looks into the future, the more indeterminate the scenarios become. The United States has gained expanded basing rights in countries such as Japan, the Philippines, and Australia, but the new B-1 bomber is described only as "rotating" through, never actually being "based" there. At the same time, the U.S. Navy is investing in mobile floating bases around Guam, currently out of reach of Chinese battle groups. But that will change quickly as China develops advanced attack submarines, missiles, and other armaments that could spell disaster for America's giant carriers while rapidly modernizing and expanding its navy to eventually assert itself in the Pacific. Invisibility cloaks for aircraft, swarming autonomous stealth drones, and of course ubiquitous cyber hacking all indicate a quantum future for the location and nature of conflict in the high-tech Asian theater.

Beyond the hardware, we cannot foresee how a U.S.-China conflict would play out without looking at supply chains. In 1917, German submarine attacks on Allied merchant ships directly brought the United States into World War I, and in World War II it was American subs that obliterated much of Japan's merchant fleet. Any incident involving China's commercial flotilla would surely be considered an act of war, inviting reprisals against American warships and bases—as would surely spell the immediate bankruptcy of America's Walmart, 70 percent of whose merchandise is imported from China (and which has been buying e-commerce companies such as Yihaodian.com to boost sales *in* China). Even the U.S. military currently relies on China for everything from computer chips to lightbulbs. Direct confrontation is thus not in anyone's interest so long as China needs peace for growth, America needs China for its hardware, and Southeast Asia is dependent on the South China Sea waters as the conduit for almost all its exports.

Supply chains provide a de facto solution to what look like de jure problems. There is no shortage of precedents for jointly exploiting energy reserves in strategic waters. Close to one hundred years ago, Norway and Russia settled tensions over Spitsbergen Island in the Svalbard archipelago in the far northern Arctic Ocean, agreeing that it would be governed by Norway but open to all for commercial extractive activity. In 1979, Thailand and Malaysia established a joint development authority over more than one dozen gas fields lying across both countries' continental shelf, creating a board of eminent political figures and energy company executives to manage and oversee profit sharing. As with the "Persian Gulf," the South China Sea should be Chinese only in name, while in practice countries jointly produce and profit from resource deposits much as Qatar and Iran do in the world's largest gas field. Thailand's and Malaysia's slogan from the 1970s nicely captures the sensible course forward for today: "Let's all drink from the same well."

There is no more important region to boost the diversity of oil and gas supplies to avert resource wars than Asia. Technology and trading have combined to turn very local natural resources such as natural gas into global ones through LNG tanker transport. Since the first LNG tanker sailed from Algeria to London in 1964, as many as six hundred LNG tankers will soon be crisscrossing the world connecting supply and demand. (And unlike oil, there is no gas cartel.) Chevron, which has been operating in Asia for a century, develops almost half the gas reserves of Indonesia, Thailand, and Bangladesh and leads production of Western Australian gas as well—all mostly offshore reserves that require LNG tankers to ship.* An LNG terminal network and Asian gas pipeline grid, along with a gas-trading hub to replace rigid contracts with flexible pricing, would together represent the triumph of supply-demand complementarity over geopolitical division.† For Asians, "Drill, baby, drill" is a rallying cry for both energy security and regional stability.

SOVEREIGNS OF THE SEA

China's state-owned oil companies and the American navy are not the only players in the maritime great game for undersea resources. Powerful and quasi-stateless global firms have also developed their own type of mobile sovereignty: very large floating structures. Shell's Prelude, for example, is a floating liquefied natural gas plat-

---

* Chevron and Total are also actively developing gas reserves in China's Sichuan basin and Myanmar's offshore blocks. Especially because European governments have been hesitant to exploit their own shale deposits, their energy companies have been actively seeking mandates in Asia.

† At the same time, America's surging LNG supply, combined with the Panama Canal expansion, will cut the distance to ship LNG from Louisiana to Asia by half.

form three times the size of Sydney's opera house and weighing five times more than America's largest aircraft carrier. It can extract, liquefy, store, transport, and off-load natural gas all in one facility. Unlike older rigs, the Prelude—and the more than two dozen new oil rigs doing ultra-deepwater drilling off the coast of Brazil and in the Arctic—no longer need to be moored to the ocean floor. Instead, they use GPS-driven dynamic positioning systems that direct hydraulic jets to constantly hold the rig in position. With no pipes ever touching a country's sovereign shore, they can evade enormous costs related to pipelines and refineries, the employment of host country nationals, environmental impact measures, and anything the company has been obligated to do under traditional contracts. The first Prelude is headed for the Browse Basin of Western Australia, while its siblings currently under construction by Samsung Heavy Industries in Korea's Geoje shipyard will operate off the shores of Malaysia, East Timor, and Mozambique, bringing them billions in revenues but without Shell getting dragged into the messy local politics that have bogged it down for decades in Nigeria.

Shell's Prelude is the largest but not the most maneuverable vessel under construction in South Korea's shipyards. That honor goes to the Danish shipping giant Maersk's Triple-E container ship,* the true mascot of the supply chain world. The Triple-E is to ships what the Airbus A380 is to planes: a supersize embodiment of hyperglobalization. Like the Prelude, the Triple-E is almost twice as long as America's biggest aircraft carrier but like the A380 is an object in perpetual motion. Too wide for the Panama Canal and too tall for the cargo cranes at any American port, it plies the Europe-Asia route from Rotterdam through the Suez Canal and across the Indian Ocean to Singapore, Hong Kong, and Shanghai—and back. The

---

* "Triple-E" stands for efficiency, economy, and environment. The Triple-E travels at slower speeds, uses waste-heat recovery to generate additional power, and emits 50 percent less carbon per container than other cargo vessels. The sixty-thousand-ton steel ship is 98 percent recyclable, and 95 percent of its parts have a "cradle-to-cradle passport" to track their life cycle.

total fleet of twenty Triple-E mega-ships outnumbers all the world's aircraft carriers and by 2020 could be crossing the Pacific, Atlantic, and Arctic Oceans as well.

Now imagine for a moment that a Maersk Triple-E sets sail from Shanghai bound for Rotterdam, carrying its full capacity of 36,000 Nissan cars, 180 million Apple iPads, 110 million pairs of Nike shoes—or some combination of these and other goods. As it crosses the South China Sea between the Paracel and the Spratly island clusters, it is hit—and sunk—by a long-range torpedo fired by a Chinese submarine aimed at a Vietnamese navy ship harassing CNOOC's HYSY 981 oil rig. Against whom would this be an act of war? Maersk, the ship's operator? Denmark, the ship's home government? South Korea, the shipbuilder? The companies whose aggregated goods amount to $4 billion in concentrated risk? The thick tangle of suppliers—including, ironically, companies in Vietnam and China—that will lose revenues for goods not delivered and sold? Whether or not such a scenario ever occurs, an attack on the Maersk Triple-E would be an attack on globalization—which is an attack on everyone.

Shipping companies are the original archetype of stateless corporations, loyal more to the flows of commerce than nationality. Largely controlled by German, Norwegian, Danish, Dutch, Greek, and Chinese tycoons, they can be owned by an offshore entity in the Cayman Islands, hoard profits in Switzerland, and operate trusts and accounts in Singapore. Each ship is actually something of a quantum asset, registered in Liberia, flying the tax-free "flag of convenience" of Panama, and owned by a special-purpose vehicle in Cyprus to limit liability from sinking cargo or environmental calamity. In 1990, only 23 percent of the world's merchant fleet of more than ten thousand ships was listed or domiciled offshore; now it is 72 percent.

The shipping industry has for millennia been the foundation of intercontinental commerce and still transports 90 percent of the world's goods trade. Indeed, the world's leading shipping lines don't need to be taught how to navigate complex global capitalism; they invented it. Shipping between Mesopotamia and India across the Arabian Gulf dates to 3000 B.C.E., while on the Mediterranean Sea ancient Greek merchants in Rhodes pooled premiums to reimburse themselves in the event of a lost ship or sunken goods. The medieval Hanseatic League of northern Europe and the maritime juggernaut of Venice issued legal codes for insurance contracts and even nurtured the reinsurance industry—insurance for insurers—without which the risks to finance the capital-intensive shipping industry might have become too large to absorb. In the 1680s, Edward Lloyd's coffee shop in London grew from a watering hole for sailors and shipowners into what is still today the world's largest marine insurance and information broker. This partnership between shipping and insurance is thus the very foundation of globalization.

Many economists are skeptical about adding so many new tankers to the market at a time of slowing economic growth. Indeed, the largest shipping companies are supporting each other through the current downturn: Maersk, CMA CGM, and Mediterranean have formed an informal alliance to reduce their collective operating costs. But global shipping volumes are projected to double between 2015 and 2030 to more than one billion containers, meaning whoever invests in connectivity today has the upper hand in the commercial traffic of tomorrow. Rolls-Royce is even planning trials of its prototype transoceanic pilotless cargo ships. The global maritime supply chain network may one day run on autopilot.

ESCAPING THE "MALACCA TRAP"

Supply chain infrastructures work in tandem across the planet, inadvertently synchronized to suddenly shift global flows. At the turn of the twentieth century, transcontinental American railways together with the Panama Canal undermined the Strait of Magellan (Cape Horn) route under South America. In the early twenty-first century, the most strategic waterway for energy and goods—the counterpart to the Strait of Hormuz on the other side of India—lies just outside my front door: the Strait of Malacca. At its narrowest point just off the southern tip of Singapore, Indonesia's largest island of Sumatra lies easily visible just 2.8 kilometers away. Throngs of joggers, cyclists, golfers, swimmers, tai chi practitioners, Jet Ski riders, and tourists absorb the daily vista of hundreds of ships and supertankers carefully navigating the strait, mostly taking for granted that it is the most heavily trafficked maritime passage connecting the Indian and Pacific Oceans. Until it isn't.

Singapore is literally an island within the strait, though the Phillip Channel to its south is the exclusive crossing for major vessels. Greeks and Romans, Arabs and Indians, all sailed through the strait prior to Portugal's frequent crossings in the early sixteenth century to establish its settlement of Macau in China. The Dutch and the British jostled for a century for control over the strait, agreeing to keep it open for each other and friendly nations. Lacking any significant natural resources of its own, Singapore has thrived on this geography, becoming a trading, transshipment, oil refinery, and services hub. When Singapore was founded in 1819, Sir Stamford Raffles said, "Our object is not territory but trade."[6]

While Western analysts focus on China's military maneuvering in the South China Sea, the purpose of its island-building activities is ultimately to access sufficient raw materials *east* of the Strait of Malacca to avoid dependence on this narrow choke point. It wants not to control the "throat" between the Indian and the Pacific Oceans but to *avoid* it as much as possible. Competitive connectivity is thus heating up to capture the spoils from facing both the Indian and the Pacific Oceans as Malaysia, Thailand, and Indonesia also do. As these countries learn to better connect their geography—with China's help—they threaten Singapore's centrality.

Like highways and railways, energy pipelines and canals embody how countries are remapped to enhance the efficiency of global connectivity. Oil- and gas-rich Malaysia is growing so quickly (while its supplies decrease) that it is already a natural gas importer. In 2013, near the old spice trade center of Malacca on the Andaman Sea

(Indian Ocean), Malaysia opened an LNG importing and regasifi-cation terminal to rival Singapore as a gas-trading hub. One year later, it announced construction of a petrochemical complex just east of Singapore in Johor (Pacific Ocean).

While Malaysia is trying to displace Singapore in energy mar-kets, an ambitious scheme for a canal across Thailand's narrow Isthmus of Kra could cut Singapore and the Strait of Malacca off entirely. The idea of carving a canal across the Isthmus of Kra dates to the seventeenth century. Ferdinand de Lesseps, the French devel-oper who constructed the Suez Canal, visited Kra in 1882, but Brit-ain was able to preserve Singapore's dominant port status. Today, however, modern technology combined with Asian energy demand and Chinese willpower makes the Thai Canal not just a plausible but even a logical and desirable alternative to the "Malacca trap." The Kra Canal could also become, along with South Sudan, an-other example of supply-chain-related secessionism. Thailand has for decades failed to constructively settle the ongoing dispute with its southern Muslim populations centered on Pattani province, cre-ating a window for China and (Muslim-majority) Malaysia to po-tentially conspire to support their secession if they promise to allow the canal's construction. As Thailand's economy stumbles along after its most recent military coup in 2013, the Thai Canal is its best hope of improving its strategic utility as well, even if it means losing some sovereignty over its restive southern provinces.

The Thai Canal is also one project both mega-engineering rivals China and Japan can agree on. Hours before Japan's attack on Pearl Harbor on December 7, 1941, the Japanese Imperial Army launched the war of the Pacific as it landed on the Isthmus of Kra, invading Thailand and British Malaya and eventually capturing Singapore in what Churchill considered the "largest capitulation" in British his-tory. Seven decades later, neither China nor Japan wants to conquer Thailand or Singapore. Japan is by far Thailand's largest foreign investor and could underwrite the $20 billion project together with China, which would also provide the thirty thousand workers needed. For both, it would be a small price to pay to shorten shipping times and achieve strategic resilience. Armies cannot do this as well as infrastructure can.

While Japan has also massively stepped up its investments in Myanmar, these fundamentally serve Chinese interests as well. With Japanese support, Yangon's refurbished port will capture some container traffic from the Bay of Bengal before it reaches the Strait of Malacca. A twelve-billion-cubic-meter natural gas pipeline from Myanmar's Maday Island to China's Yunnan province has been joined by a $2.5 billion oil pipeline from Myanmar's Kyaukphyu port (which is also being developed into a 350-square-kilometer SEZ) that can carry 500,000 barrels per day of Middle Eastern and African oil—both avoiding Strait of Malacca shipping.

In neighboring Bangladesh, a major Chinese-built bridge finally spans the Padma River (or Lower Ganges) that had cut off the country's entire southwestern territory, helping bind the sinking nation together. Near Bangladesh's Myanmar border, China is bidding to construct the Sonadia port to ease the export of goods from the many "garment villages" to which its own low-wage production has been off-shored. Both Bangladesh and Myanmar are thus becoming conduits for avoiding the Strait of Malacca and instead towing or trucking goods and resources up to southern China—perhaps on the refurbished Stilwell Road up from the Andaman Sea.*

China's overall strategy is classic Sun Tzu: a combination of deception and bait and switch. While its aggressive maneuvers in the South and East China Seas have brought the Pacific Ocean back onto the geopolitical radar, its longer-term strategy is to build Indo-Pacific infrastructures (including overland across Eurasia) that allow it to avoid the Strait of Malacca altogether. One generation from now, trans-Eurasian rail and new Southeast Asian canals could have the same impact on the Strait of Malacca that America's transcontinental highways and the Panama Canal had on the Strait of Ma-

---

* The competition to leverage Bangladesh's geographic access to Southeast Asia is one reason why in 2015 the Indian prime minister, Modi, settled decades-old border disputes with Bangladesh through land swaps, allowing India to focus on snatching the Sonadia port project away from China.

gellan a century ago. The most significant geopolitical interventions will prove to be not military but infrastructural.

THE MARITIME
SILK ROAD

Ports are to containers and goods what airports are to people and their luggage: the conduits for millions of daily crossings, transactions, and deliveries. Just as airport arrival and baggage services are increasingly automated, so too are ports. Shanghai is now connected via the thirty-two-kilometer Donghai Bridge to the Yangshan Island mega-port, which features state-of-the-art traffic control towers, management nerve centers tracking hundreds of ships, tens of thousands of containers, and hundreds of (soon driverless) trucks at the same time. From Yangshan to Melbourne to Long Beach, terminal operators are using electronic data interchange software to optimize berthing schedules, deploying autonomous vehicles and virtual reality to accelerate their loading and unloading speeds, and partnering with logistics companies such as Shipwire to coordinate warehouse inventories with freight rail to efficiently distribute goods like blood vessels through the planetary circulatory system.

Throughout history, competition among port cities has revealed who is winning the supply chain tug-of-war. Since ancient times, ports have fortified harbors to ward off invaders and levied import taxes to profit from their role as conduits to the hinterland. In the fifth century B.C.E., Greek city-states banded together to repulse the Persian armies of Xerxes. During the Middle Ages, the Hanseatic League assembled an alliance of 170 Baltic and North Sea trading ports and their navies to defend their commercial orbit.

Being a connectivity hub or passageway pays handsomely, making today's maritime competition more intense than ever. Global cargo volumes have doubled in the past twenty years, requiring all the world's major ports and canals to expand, upgrade, widen, and deepen. The Suez Canal, through which already 25 percent of world shipping transits, launched an expansion plan in 2014 that will eventually allow for the simultaneous northbound and southbound flows of ships, thus doubling its capacity. The Suez Canal expansion is by far Egypt's greatest contribution to the world today, and boosting its role in intercontinental connectivity will double its transit fee revenues to an estimated $13 billion by 2020.

But the fastest growth in trade volumes is taking place entirely east of Suez. In the 1970s, transatlantic shipping represented 80 percent of global trade; by 2013, it was only 40 percent. The trade nexus of China, the Middle East, and Africa now accounts for more than half of world trade, with massive new port projects, canal dredging, pipeline construction, and supertanker deployments magnifying the flows of goods and energy crossing the Indian Ocean. This "Maritime Silk Road" from the Middle East to the Far East, from Dubai via Singapore to Shanghai, is once again the world's main trade passageway.

As in Southeast Asia, the path around the Strait of Malacca goes over land. India has long considered itself the geographic hegemon of South Asia but done little to prove it, opening the window for China to displace India as the largest economic partner of all its neighbors (except Nepal). For fifty years, China has subsidized the construction of the high-altitude Karakoram Highway network that begins in Chinese Xinjiang and follows the Indus River traversing Pakistan to the Arabian Sea. Now this route is being upgraded into the multibillion-dollar China-Pakistan Economic Corridor including railways and power stations—which specialized units of the Pakistani military have been designated to guard more carefully than they do the country's borders. Infrastructure is making China a two-ocean power: Pacific and Indian. Once pipelines are constructed through Pakistan, China can pump Middle Eastern energy overland into its rapidly growing western provinces. The sleepy Arabian Sea port of Gwadar could become China's most reliable overseas naval base, where it could station the attack submarines being built in nearby Karachi. No wonder one Chinese general has even called Pakistan "China's Israel"[7]—the ally it would never abandon.

Lying less than a hundred kilometers west of Gwadar, the Iranian port of Chabahar also wants to be a gateway for goods from Central Asia (especially the former Soviet "Stans" and Afghanistan) to reach the Arabian Sea. India has taken the lead in developing Chabahar to gain a foothold on the other side of Pakistan and allow Afghan trade to bypass Pakistan as well. But Iran and Pakistan's ties are strengthening with China's funding of a crucial gas pipeline between the two. The Indian-funded Zaranj-Delaram highway in western Afghanistan may well just be smoothing another Chinese path to the Arabian Sea.

Iran and Pakistan also have a natural allegiance to Oman, a collection of oases that has for centuries gathered fishing and pearling populations from Zanzibar (which it ruled through the eighteenth and nineteenth centuries) to South Asia. Oman actually owned Gwadar at the time of the Indian subcontinent's partition and independence, selling it to Pakistan in 1958 after a geologic survey indicating its hammer shape jutting into the Arabian Sea made it an ideal location for a natural deepwater port. A sizable contingent of Baluchis hailing from the region that straddles Iran, Pakistan, and Afghanistan remains in Oman today, having served in regiments of the Oman army and as a loyal palace guard to the sultan.

Given its mixed demographics and seafaring heritage, Oman is unique in the Arab world for codifying freedom of worship for all faiths, and it attempts to be similarly neutral in its diplomacy. Oman has taken a very different approach to Iran from its Gulf Arab neighbors. In 2013, it signed a twenty-five-year agreement to begin Iranian gas imports. Furthermore, together with India—from which one-third of Oman's population hails, including many citizens whose merchant houses have built up fortunes—Oman has planned undersea pipelines to distribute Iranian natural gas.

CHINA IS NOT A STRANGER to the Indian Ocean either, having sent Admiral Zheng He's "Treasure Fleet" as far as East Africa a full century before Portugal rounded Africa's southern cape. But it was European colonial powers that competed over the lucrative Indian

Ocean spice trade as intensely as they did for Latin America's gold and silver. The Portuguese established forts among the coastal Indian kingdoms of Calicut, Goa, Kochi, and Kannur, and the island kingdom of Kotte, gradually displacing the Venetian and Ottoman traders who previously dominated Indian Ocean trade.

Kotte, which came to be known as Ceylon under Portuguese rule, was a crucial trading hub for cinnamon, cardamom, black pepper, and gems. After passing to Dutch and then British control, Ceylon became independent in 1948. With grand ambitions to strategically supervise the Indian Ocean, it could well have become as successful as Dubai or Singapore before either of them. Indeed, shortly before Singapore's own independence in 1965, Lee Kuan Yew traveled to Colombo in search of a role model of a postcolonial, multicultural, former British parliamentary democracy and decided Ceylon was it. But the government takeover by Sinhalese nationalists and alienation of the Tamil minority, including changing of the country's name to Sri Lanka, all contributed to ethnic strife, secessionism, and a brutal civil war that lasted forty years until 2010.

A full six hundred years since Zheng He's Indian Ocean journeys, China has returned to Sri Lanka, underwriting the modernization of its ports as transshipment hubs for its gargantuan export volumes. China's so-called string of pearls strategy has been to develop maritime access points on either side of India such as Myanmar's Maday Island, Sri Lanka's Hambantota port, and Pakistan's Gwadar. Chinese money rebuilt Hambantota after it was devastated by the Indonesian tsunami of 2004 and has upgraded most of the national highways and roads, cutting the travel time between any two major Sri Lankan cities by half.

Under the former strongman president Mahinda Rajapaksa, infrastructure and weapons made Sri Lanka China's best friend in the Indian Ocean, especially as they helped him brutally terminate the country's civil war. But just as Myanmar has capitalized on global investor interest to boost its leverage in the tug-of-war with China, so too has Sri Lanka, whose current president, Maithripala Sirisena, warned his countrymen that Rajapaksa had put their country on the path to becoming a "slave colony" to China, to which it owes more than $8 billion. Sri Lankans are mindful that even Zheng He's peaceful maritime expeditions carried thirty thousand troops. In 1411, the Kotte kingdom's ruler, Alakeshvara, refused to pay tribute and pledge obeisance to the visiting Chinese admiral, for which he and his family were shackled and sent off to bow before Yongle, the Ming dynasty emperor.

India is making the most of Sri Lanka's growing suspicion of China. With Chinese-built infrastructure, Sri Lanka has already made big gains in tourism and exports of textiles, garments, and tea. Now India can leverage China's infrastructure to more efficiently deliver its own projects for Sri Lanka, from railways to housing, and use the island as a reliable back office and outsourcing site for call centers and car part assembly for the huge south Indian market of 300 million people.

The Indian Ocean is once again the epicenter of competitive connectivity. In the fifteenth and sixteenth centuries, India's coastal kingdoms haggled with European colonial merchants to get the most favorable terms for carrying their goods to far-off markets. But whereas Sri Lanka became a European colony from the fifteenth century onward, this time it is prepared to resist any Chinese overextension beyond the projects that are mutually beneficial—armed with Chinese weapons.

ATLANTIC CITIES

The competition to shape maritime trade routes has become as intense in the Atlantic as in the Indian or Pacific Ocean. When the Panama Canal opened in 1914, it devastated Chile's lovely colonial port of Valparaíso, where ships no longer needed to dock on their way around the Strait of Magellan at the tip of South America. Panama City is now positioning itself as the Dubai of Central America—the longest flight in the world now connects the two cities—upping its game in sectors such as real estate, free trade zones, and aviation, even attracting Asian airlines to make stopovers in Panama en route to South American destinations. And with a major expansion of the canal under way (just missing the centennial completion goal) to allow for simultaneous two-directional flow of large post-Panamax tankers, Panama will once again dent Valparaíso's recent comeback as a pit stop for ships once too wide for the Panama Canal. Already Valparaíso's container traffic trade with the United States is falling by double digits every year. Eventually, cruise ships may outnumber tankers as the city refashions itself into a cultural tourism hub.

Efficiently reaching America's Eastern Seaboard is a strategic imperative for consumer and tech goods exporters such as Japan, South Korea, and China. Even with the Panama Canal expansion, it would still not be able to handle either the Maersk Triple-E or the Valemax, which is why it may have a rival next door as early as 2020. Nicaragua, one of the hemisphere's poorest countries, is moving ahead with plans for the 220-kilometer-long Grand Canal (longer and wider than the Panama Canal) just north of its border with Costa Rica. The Grand Canal and deepwater port project is backed by the Chinese telecommunications tycoon Wang Jing, who claims that the $50 billion (twice Nicaragua's GDP) project would create fifty thousand jobs. Importantly, the Nicaragua canal is targeting not just container ships but commodities freighters and fuel tankers that carry iron ore, coal, LNG, and protein-rich Brazilian beef and soy.*

America's East Coast ports such as Norfolk, Virginia, and Savannah, Georgia, are carefully watching Central America's canal competition, with some moving feverishly to deepen berths, add supersize cranes, and install 3-D scanners to accelerate cargo processing. In 2014, Miami took aim at these rivals' upgrades by dredging deeper shipping berths and opening a $1 billion tunnel that will allow the five thousand trucks that come in and out of the port daily to pass under the cruise ship terminal and drive straight up I-95—reaching Atlanta before cargo bypassing Miami for Savannah would.

---

* China's beef imports in 2006 were nearly zero; by 2018, they may reach 500,000 metric tons.

Miami in turn will soon face competition from its friendly Latino offshore cousin Puerto Rico. Leveraging the tax-free status and location inside America's security perimeter, Puerto Rico's massive new Port of the Americas will subsume the entire southern city of Ponce and allow for efficient transshipment of smaller cargoes up and down the entire East Coast as well. Puerto Rico has also become a favored American tax haven, changing its laws in 2013 to eliminate capital gains taxes to attract the investment of ultra-high-net-worth hedge fund managers such as John Paulson, who calls it the "Singapore of the Caribbean."[8] Just as Tennessee and Michigan compete for automotive assembly, America's onshore is now competing with America's offshore in ports, shipping, and finance as well.

Over the horizon, America's southern ports may also be welcoming goods from what just a few years ago seemed the most unlikely of origins: Cuba. Thirty miles west of Havana, in the same city of Mariel from which over 100,000 Cubans desperately fled for Florida as Soviet subsidies evaporated, the Brazilian firm Odebrecht has begun construction of a gigantic free trade zone and container port that will be managed by the Port of Singapore Authority. The Mariel port will allow foreign companies 100 percent ownership of their facilities and tax-free status in exchange for the jobs created in manufacturing and logistics facilities. Chinese commercial delegations have made multiple visits to Cuba recently, preplanning operations that will take advantage of America's reestablishment of diplomatic and commercial relations.

Not all new superports and maritime hubs will succeed in capturing major value from shifting global supply chain patterns. Some may never be finished, some will get displaced by ones better located or better run, some may be ruined by rising sea levels or natural disasters, and some may be knocked out by terrorist attacks or civil wars. But all of these mega-infrastructures and the canals and supertankers linking them are signs that we are increasingly a coastal urban civilization reengineering the planet to smooth intercontinental connectivity—for supply to meet demand. When it comes to maritime flows, there is one remaining frontier that might rival today's most transited corridors in its efficiency: the Arctic.

THE CAPITAL OF
THE ARCTIC

In 2013, Facebook opened its biggest data center outside the United States in Sweden's Arctic Circle to leverage naturally low temperatures to cool its thousands of servers. But the Arctic's chill is becoming less so every year. Stoked by human-accelerated climate change, Arctic temperatures have risen a full four degrees Celsius in just the past half century; the summer ice coverage is only half what it was in 1979. Almost two hundred Alaskan towns are at risk of sinking into the softer foundations beneath them or being sucked into the sea. The Eskimo village of Newtok, 480 miles west of Anchorage, is completely relocating its physical infrastructure before it is wiped away. At the same time, from Canada to Sweden, thriving cities are sprouting where once there was only frozen tundra, becoming vital nodes of the new Arctic economy. There is an irony to Greenland's ice sheet being a key driver of Indian and Pacific islands sinking while it gains its own sovereignty from Denmark.

The Arctic has become an entire swath of the planet we have barely accessed before and are beginning to use heavily—evolving our human and political geography along the way. Once impenetrable half the year, the Arctic Ocean is becoming traversable year-round. In 2010, Russia issued only four permits for Arctic sea passage; in 2013, it issued four hundred. That year, the nineteen-thousand-ton *Yong Sheng* sailed from Dalian to Rotterdam in thirty-five days. At present, more than fifty times more cargo traverses the Suez each year than the Arctic, but because temperatures rise faster at the earth's poles (while water levels rise faster at the equator), the Arctic could become a major reliable shipping route by 2020.

Ice-free Arctic shipping features two major corridors: The Northern Sea Route, taken by China's *Yong Sheng,* connects the two ends of Eurasia (the Far East and northern Europe) over Russia, through the Bering Strait and past Russia's Kamchatka Peninsula—a full two weeks faster than the Suez Canal route. Meanwhile, the Northwest Passage connects East Asia to North America's East Coast by passing over Alaska and Canada instead of Russia, shaving ten thousand kilometers off the Panama Canal route.

A third Transpolar Sea Route could cut even closer to the magnetic North Pole and upon reaching Iceland—or Scotland, which has plans for its own Arctic transshipment hub—fork off to either Europe or North America, where ships could also sail into Canada's majestic Hudson Bay all the way down through James Bay, where goods could be on- and off-loaded just under one thousand kilometers from Toronto, or to the Port of Churchill in Manitoba at the geographic center of Canada, where rail connections await to the rest of the country.

The Arctic is crucial to our global future not just for shipping but also for resources. As western Siberian gas fields run down, the Arctic is Russia's largest source of new gas production. Western energy majors such as America's Exxon, France's Total, and Norway's Statoil are joined at the hip in the Arctic with Russian Rosneft and Gazprom, deploying advanced drilling platforms and navigating massive icebergs across hundreds of thousands of square kilometers to exploit oil and gas deposits from the Barents Sea near Norway to the Chukchi Sea near Alaska. Sanctions have only briefly interfered in this cooperation: While it has violently changed borders in Ukraine, Russia has also carefully settled Arctic disputes with Norway in the Barents Sea and the United States in the Bering Sea to ensure its good standing with its fellow Arctic Council members.* In 2015, it submitted a claim to 1.2 million additional square kilometers of the Arctic seabed where approximately eight hundred oil and gas fields hold reserves estimated at 50 percent of Russia's current total. Rosneft's chief, Igor Sechin, has described Russia's efforts

---

* In 2015, however, Russia and China conducted their first joint naval exercises in the Arctic, with warships from both countries crossing the Bering Strait.

as creating a new "oil province"—a very natural feature to find on the functional map of a supply chain world.

So far, the Arctic has been a case of countries not fighting over resources but quickly resolving disputes in order to attract more investment *into* resources. The Canadian scholar Michael Byers argues that the Arctic is the closest thing to a blank slate in international relations because under international law no state has sovereignty over the North Pole. This is not to say that the Arctic isn't claimed, however. Russia and Canada have effectively undisputed sovereignty over most of the crucial shipping lanes near their northern shores, while the United States, Norway, and Denmark have designated exclusive economic zones stretching two hundred miles from their coasts. In 2007, Russia planted a one-meter-high titanium flag on the seabed near the North Pole and in 2014 conducted its largest military exercises since the collapse of the Soviet Union in the high Arctic. It now has an Arctic command with two permanent brigades. More nuclear-armed submarines have also been deployed to the Arctic, and a naval outpost has been established on Wrangel Island in the Chukchi Sea near the international date line. Canada too has put Arctic policy front and center—captured in former Prime Minister Stephen Harper's memorable phrase "Use it or lose it." As part of its "Northern Strategy," Canada has built up its coast guard, invested in new icebreakers, set up military logistics centers across the Northwest Territories, begun regular drone surveillance flights, and tested a fleet of stealth snowmobiles code-named Loki. In 2010, Canada hosted the G7 finance ministers in Nunavut, the Arctic province where thirty thousand Inuit live in a space as large as western Europe. Quebec's ambitious Plan Nord lays out energy grids far into its presently uninhabited but hydropower-rich northern expanse. Even the U.S. Navy in 2014 released the oddly titled "Arctic Roadmap" on how to manage long-range maritime operations in an environment with minimal infrastructure. Because President Obama authorized Arctic drilling in 2015, more intense naval patrols of the waters off Alaska will follow.

The Arctic now has many sovereigns, and mapping tools have

become crucial in establishing rights to territorial authority in pre-viously uncharted geographies. A recent survey of a two-thousand-kilometer-long undersea Arctic mountain range established that it is connected to Greenland's continental shelf, giving Denmark claims over the North Pole previously held only by Canada and Rus-sia. But how many nuclear submarines does Denmark have?

As the Arctic ice cap melts away, similar maneuvers are begin-ning to play out on the world's opposite pole, Antarctica. The only continent without a native human population, each summer Ant-arctica hosts almost four thousand scientists from over thirty coun-tries working at a hundred research stations and field camps. As many as forty thousand tourists now arrive each year as well, mostly on cruise ships from Argentina. Though about a dozen countries have various claims on Antarctica, making its political map appear like a pizza with overlapping slices of various sizes, the 1961 Antarc-tic Treaty bans any military activity or oil prospecting. That has not stopped China from sending ice-breaking ships to clear the way for geologic surveying to determine if hundreds of billions of barrels lie beneath the ice and rock. In 2015, China signed a ship refueling agreement with Australia to facilitate these long-distance voyages of commercial colonization.

Asia's economic giants gush at every new Arctic and Antarctic energy discovery, for it means that much less oil and gas they need to import from the volatile Middle East through the Strait of Ma-lacca. China, Japan, and South Korea are even happy to provide the transportation, having built a hundred new LNG tankers (and sev-eral icebreakers) since 2009 alone. China has been relentless in try-ing to get a piece—or many pieces—of the Arctic action. It has sought to buy large tracts of land in Iceland, a move rejected by the country's parliament, while the Chinese billionaire Huang Nubo has bought pristine mountainous land in Norway's far northern Lyngen, while bidding for a mineral-rich fjord up for sale on Spits-bergen Island. After years of lobbying, China has also been granted observer status in the Arctic Council, where it hopes to sway Den-mark toward allowing greater investment in Greenland's iron ore and uranium deposits. No wonder China tacitly supports Greenland's independence movement.

THE ARCTIC IS A VAST, transnational transit and resource zone, but it still needs a capital. Like Fort McMurray in Canada's Alberta, Norway's Kirkenes is becoming an Arctic boomtown with a population growing by several thousand every year and ever more weekly workers who still reside elsewhere. The core supply chain node for the region's logistical potential, Kirkenes will one day be known as the de facto capital of the Arctic. At 69° north latitude, it is the northernmost city in the world. Though it lies as far east as Istanbul, it shares a time zone with Oslo and Zurich. Perhaps this doesn't matter, because it's dark for three straight months a year and has round-the-clock sun for another three months. As temperatures rise, however, winters may not reach the current minus-forty degrees Celsius, while the growing population capitalizing on Arctic commerce will enjoy what one local businesswoman advertises as "sunset-free Bohemian summer nights."[9]

Two hundred years ago, the indigenous Sami people had free rein over this snowy world of reindeer herds and majestic fjords. During the Cold War, Finnmark, as the region is known, was the only place where NATO and Russia directly bordered each other. As the last part of Norway to enter the kingdom, Kirkenes is still referred to by Norwegians as "Norway's Russian city." Several thousand Russians live there; signs are in both languages. The E105 highway starts in Kirkenes and stretches 250 kilometers east to Murmansk, then southward to Moscow two thousand kilometers away—the same distance as Oslo. A special "border visa" exists here for any Russians or Norwegians living within thirty kilometers (soon to be extended to sixty kilometers) of the border so they can freely cross back and forth.

Russia has the most to gain from the new Barents Sea regional cooperation framework that funds oil exploration, fishing, shipping, tourism, and industrial upgrades. Nikel—named very much for the base metal it produces in nearby mines that coat the city in black dust—is the sister city of Kirkenes lying just seven kilometers on the other side of the border. Nickel is cheap and plentiful, and Kirkenes helps Russia get more of it to Asian markets faster.* The belt from Kirkenes to Kandalaksha on the White Sea is becoming Russia's most modernized industrial zone, with companies like Rusal importing top-tier Western equipment to meet global demand for high-quality aluminum.

Life in border regions ironically liberates people from the bordered thinking of their compatriots living far away. There is scarcely a business in Kirkenes that doesn't have partners across the border in Russia and vice versa. For them, connectivity across the border is an enduring reality, while sanctions are just an episode. Up here, business as usual is better than borders.

Kirkenes is becoming a multistate capital run more by chambers of commerce from surrounding countries than politicians. It is where one sees a regional economy of supply chains growing together and amplifying an entire region's connectivity to the world. Norwegian companies such as the Tschudi Group are constructing a sizable new harbor, oil terminals, and transportation facilities to bind the key regional hubs more seamlessly together and efficiently promote the inflow and outflow of goods. Iron ore mined across Sweden and Finland will also benefit from speedy shipment out of Kirkenes. In the northern Swedish city of Kiruna, eighteen thousand people have been relocated to accommodate the expansion of mines to meet Chinese demand. Finland is extending its national north-south highway trunk all the way through the Lapland capital city of Rovaniemi (which claims to be the "official" home of Santa Claus) to Kirkenes, as well as expanding rail lines used by mining companies to cart away minerals to the port—where hulking Chinese dry-bulk ships await.

The Barents region thus embodies how a seemingly empty space can be as cosmopolitan as a pulsing global city, as well as the deep

---

* Soviet infrastructure had so crumbled in the Arctic region that food from Africa was sometimes delivered on nuclear submarines, with sacks of potatoes instead of missiles in the tubes.

geopolitical textures that make such a seemingly stateless system work. It is also becoming a cultural community unto itself that transcends the region's nationalities. Andreas Hoffmann, a curator with a Ph.D. in "Nordism" (Northism), traces the Arctic identity to eighteenth-century artists and musicians and sponsors regular exhibitions that challenge the region's arbitrary political divisions: a hockey game played on a frozen lake between Russia and Norway where the midline is drawn on the ice along the "border," and a chessboard that resembles the four-country Nordic border zone on which all the pieces are white and each move further blends their identities. At the monthly Transborder Café event he hosts, over seventy nationalities gather in a cozy bar to spark regional initiatives and celebrate the local Sami culture. Visitors from near and far are enjoying exhilarating new tourism offerings such as the Barents Safari, a mix of Arctic tundra survival training and fishing with steel traps for giant Kamchatka crabs recently imported from Russia and breeding in the fjords. (Whale watching had also grown for a decade until rising water temperatures pushed the whales even farther north.)

The combination of viewing the globe from the top rather than the side, living in an extreme climate that defies borders, and forging a common Arctic culture leads to fresh relational thinking about geography. "China is our neighbor now," jokes Hoffmann. "It's just 20 days away by ship!"

BY 2100, THE BROADER Persian Gulf geography is projected to be too excruciatingly hot and humid for humans to safely spend more than a few hours outside.[10] The twentieth century witnessed the population of the global south eclipsing that of the north, but the twenty-first century may require mass migrations from south to north as equatorial and southern populations stricken by the triple whammy of increasing temperatures, drought, and rising sea levels flock toward more temperate and agriculturally productive regions. As Canada and Russia become massive agricultural breadbaskets that could produce most of the world's subsistence crops, their almost completely depopulated geographies will need workers to run the agribusiness industries. Over time, their maps will feature far sturdier roads, railways, and towns. The current population of the Arctic region is only 4 million people. It could rise to 400 million in our lifetime.

Managing a more populous and busy Arctic region will be a full-time job for Norway. "Oslo's diplomatic forays in the Middle East and Peace Prize are just the luxury of being rich. The less oil Norway has, the more it will redirect its focus to the Arctic, where it can craft a regional model that might actually work," snaps the Arctic's top strategic thinker, Rune Rafaelsen, once head of the Barents Secretariat and now mayor of Kirkenes. He makes a good point. A century ago, at the conclusion of World War I, Norway innovated a model for conflict resolution by opening access to its strategic and resource-rich Svalbard archipelago to all countries provided the island remained demilitarized. Spitsbergen, Svalbard's largest island, is getting a modern art museum and in 2008 inaugurated the Seed Vault, a high-tech facility holding 1.5 million seeds from thousands of plant species that serve as a DNA backup in the event of major global crop failure.

The seeds will likely need to be sprinkled across the Arctic region itself, for a world that is four degrees Celsius warmer than today could bring mass desertification and crop failure to almost the entire planet south of Canada and Russia.* Perversely, the thawing permafrost of Russia's Siberia and Canada's Northwest Territories has made the world's northern latitudes a giant bog that releases five or more million tons of methane (a greenhouse gas) per year, accelerating the demise of ecosystems lying to their south. The face of global warming will no longer be belching Chinese factories or the congested highways of Los Angeles but the endless tundra of Canada and Russia. The two largest countries in the world are thus

---

* The combination of Syria's perennial droughts and civil war prompted the very first withdrawal of seeds from the vault in 2015.

winners from global warming, even as their geography becomes a leading climate change culprit.

The precedent for what the Arctic region might look like as its population surges is South America, a continent first colonized by Iberian imperialists, then populated by African slaves, with waves of wanderers coming over the past two centuries due to the Irish famine of 1845–52, the German revolution of 1848, the Japanese World War I–era rice crisis, the Holocaust, and the Lebanese civil war. South America today is a continent of bounteous biodiversity, almost completely urbanized and ethnically intermingled.

A more proactive redistribution of the world's potential nine billion people in emerging fertile geographies might make the planet less claustrophobic, as well as more equitable, sustainable, and productive. Mid-twentieth-century concerns over world population growth and food shortages led some legal scholars to argue that a few million Australians could not justify possessing an entire continent while billions were deprived basic nourishment. As the earth's overpopulated equatorial latitudes experience drought, crop failure, and desertification while the depopulated far northern latitudes experience thaw, warming, and abundance, will mass migrations to Canada and Russia turn them into internationally governed agribusiness colonies?

Because neither country would suddenly accept the burden of massive numbers of new citizens, there are initial financial and administrative costs that would need to be managed by international agencies and investors. But both Russia and Canada would also benefit massively from doubling or tripling—or, in Canada's case, quintupling—their populations. Climate migrants wouldn't be moving into barren spaces: Russia has more than a dozen cities of under one million people whose death and emigration rates far exceed the birthrate. Even though new residents would not be national citizens, their presence would generate enormous economic activity for governments and businesses to service. One hundred years from now, Sino-Siberia could be populated both by the Chinese and by climate refugees from around the world.

PART FOUR

FROM NATIONS
TO NODES

CHAPTER 11

IF YOU BUILD IT, THEY WILL COME

DUBAI: HOME TO
THE WORLD

THE WORLD'S MOST VISITED CITY, THE MOST DIVERSE CITY, THE city that never sleeps . . . New York, of course. London, for sure. Paris, once upon a time. Soon, however—and for quite some time after—that city will be Dubai. Sitting at the crossroads of West and East, North and South, Dubai is brashly claiming the title of "center of the world."

By 2017, Dubai will welcome more visitors per year than London or Paris. The Dubai Mall, located at the base of the world's tallest building, the Burj Khalifa, was visited seventy-five million times in 2013, more than any other place on earth. Dubai, rather than New York, is already the world's leading "melting pot," with a far higher—over 90 percent—foreign-born resident population (versus 38 percent for New York). Dubai airport's Terminal 3 is the ultimate crossroads of civilizations; it transits more travelers per year than any other—particularly between midnight and 5:00 a.m. Dubai literally never sleeps. With its massive fleet of Airbus A380 planes, Emirates airlines makes Dubai the only place from which one can fly nonstop to every major city on earth, and construction is under way round the clock to build the even larger Dubai World

---

Map 17, corresponding to this chapter, appears in the first map insert.

Central airport able to accommodate up to 200 million passengers per year just in time for Dubai to host the World Expo in 2020. Physical connectivity is a service; Dubai is its leading provider.

As an experiment in catapulting from feudalism into postmodernity, Dubai has no equal. Great cities constantly evolve to stay relevant to the times, and Dubai has reinvented itself every generation, from pearl fishing to oil to transshipment and, more recently, infrastructure, real estate, tourism, and services—doubling in size with every step. According to the McKinsey Global Institute's Connectedness Index, only six cities in the world qualify as major hubs across all categories of flows they absorb and transmit—goods, services, finance, people, and data: New York, London, Hong Kong, Tokyo, Singapore, and the newest entrant on the list, Dubai.[1]

Dubai represents the vanguard of a new type of global city. Its vision is not to replicate great cities of the past—other than building life-size replicas of their main monuments in its amusement parks. Rather, it is becoming a new kind of city with a new kind of identity, a truly global node whose virtue is not its rich cultural heritage but its stateless cosmopolitanism and seamless global connectivity. For the increasing millions who call Dubai home, to be there is to be *everywhere,* which can be superior to traditional notions of great cities being deeply rooted *somewhere.*

Dubai's story is instructive in how a city can rise meteorically in a single generation and literally bend the world its way. Though Dubai was a notable pearling settlement over five hundred years ago, the sleepy maritime protectorates known as the Trucial States only earned a place on the global map with the discovery of modest quantities of oil in the early 1970s—just as they gained independence from Britain and hastily (and somewhat reluctantly) formed a federation called the United Arab Emirates. Shortly thereafter, one of the world's first—and still most successful—modern free zones was set up at Jebel Ali, allowing unrestricted capital and labor mobility to rapidly build a larger way station for oil tankers and container ships transiting from Europe to Asia. Jebel Ali became the region's biggest and most modern port, while newly independent

Yemen, whose crown colony of Aden was the most strategic refueling port for the British Raj, slid into civil war. Aden's location had earned it homilies as the "chief emporium of Arabian trade." Today that crown belongs to Dubai.

Through the 1970s, the U.A.E.'s population quadrupled as throngs of South Asians came to work in the thriving oil sector and service industries. The gold and textile trade surged as well. Today Dubai's population is 70 percent South Asian, and Asians label the Gulf region not "Middle East" but rather "West Asia." Remittances from the U.A.E. to India amount to $30 billion per year, far larger than from any other part of the twenty-five-million-strong diaspora. When private bankers need to service their high-net-worth Indian clients, they usually head to Dubai. For both Pakistan's Bhutto clan and its recently ousted military leader, Pervez Musharraf, Dubai is the exile of choice.

As the world's main interregional gateway, Dubai caters to all continents at the same time. As capital and demographic flows from south to south and south to north augment the traditional flows from north to south and west to east, Dubai is the conduit for entire new patterns of investment. At the Annual Investment Meeting, an everyman's Davos type of gathering for thousands of investment seekers from over one hundred developing countries, I met Moroccan property developers, Ethiopian dairy farm owners, the president of Russia's Tatarstan Republic, Indian construction magnates, and dozens of other entrepreneurs who would only have ever connected and figured out how to become part of each other's supply chains in a place convenient to all of them: Dubai.

In the traditional but affluent beachfront district of Jumeirah, the aesthetic matches the geography of being the halfway point of the world: patisseries next to sari shops. An even further concentric circle of cultures is represented: Burger King and Chinese massage parlors. Commerce and culture are deeply intertwined in Dubai. Its relations with Persian civilization have been guided by proximity across the Strait of Hormuz and its large Iranian population (up to a quarter of Dubai's indigenous population actually traces its origins to Iran) rather than the Sunni-Shia divide that poisons the region's geopolitics. Even with the toughest sanctions in place, Dubai's banks continued to find ways to finance trade with Iran, while bulging wooden dhow boats in Dubai's creek laden with computers and refrigerators sail daily and nightly to Bandar-e-Abbas. As Iran's diplomatic thaw unfolds and its commercial rehabilitation accelerates, no city is better placed than Dubai as a launchpad to access its eighty-million-strong market.

The U.A.E. has also opened its doors to China, now its largest trading partner, with over 250,000 Chinese now residing in Dubai (and more than 280,000 tourists per year) and using it as a reexport hub for two thousand businesses selling basic goods from construction materials to toys. More recently, senior Chinese figures from state-run banks have also arrived on the scene, not only managing pan-Arab portfolios but meeting with European and Arab investors to plot joint infrastructure finance projects in Africa—for which Dubai is the offshore staging ground as well.

Emirates airlines already flies to more cities in Africa than any other carrier. Dubai Ports World leads infrastructure projects from Senegal to Angola to Djibouti. In addition to the thirty thousand Somalis already in Dubai, another forty thousand Kenyans now reside there and work in industries from construction to hospitality. Africa's youngest billionaire, Ashish Thakkar, a Ugandan of Indian descent, got his start shuttling back and forth to Dubai's bazaars to purchase secondhand computer parts. Now he runs his IT, real estate, manufacturing, and social ventures out of Dubai.

TWO KINDS OF POSTCOLONIAL COUNTRIES were born in the mid-twentieth century: those that have built viable modern infrastructure, and those that are living on borrowed time as their colonial infrastructure decays. It was not foreordained that India and the U.A.E. would take such radically different developmental paths. During the British Raj, Gulf Arabs used to travel to India and send remittances home to Arabia. Today the demographic flow is completely reversed. India did not have oil, but it didn't have to choose agrarian socialism as an economic doctrine either.

The U.A.E.'s nascent energy sector and openness to immigrants attracted legions of South Asians, including my whole family, which left India in the 1970s. During my childhood there, we took long drives from Abu Dhabi through Dubai all the way to the beaches of Khorfakkan on the Arabian Sea, a seemingly endless journey alongside soft sand dunes, but without air-conditioning.

While the U.A.E. federation has been legally united for over forty years, it has taken decades of economic modernization and infrastructural spending to *physically* unite the seven emirates into an efficient coastal archipelago. Ever since Sheikh Rashid bin Saeed al Maktoum pushed to build Jebel Ali port, Dubai has had a one-track mind to build bigger, taller, better. Mohamed Alabbar, chairman of Emaar Properties and a crucial adviser to the current Dubai ruler, Sheikh Mohammed, was first sent to Singapore for five years in the late 1980s, an experience he compares to going to soccer training during Brazil's football heyday. He returned to Dubai believing that state building is every bit as much about physical modernization as institutional.

Dubai demonstrates how world-class infrastructure makes the difference between a convenient crossroads and a global hub. Indeed, "Dubai" no longer appears like a singular place anymore but rather is shorthand for an entire connected country for which it is the commercial and demographic center. Dubai, Sharjah, and Ajman are now effectively one expanding urban cluster, while Abu Dhabi's oil-fueled expansion has funded urban growth ever closer toward Jebel Ali, which has become a Dubai satellite city and the final stop on its elevated, driverless metro rail. With enormous financial support from Abu Dhabi, the northern emirates of Umm al-Quwain, Fujairah, and Ras al-Khaimah are also busy developing their ports and tourism sectors, while major highways now crisscross the desert to connect all seven oases to each other. Especially since Abu Dhabi bailed out Dubai's debt during the financial crisis, people increasingly refer to the country's core as Abu Dubai.

Though they compete for the prestige of their airlines, height of their skyscrapers, and number of stars attached to their glitzy hotels, they are becoming more harmonized with each passing year. As Switzerland has been for centuries, the U.A.E. has become something of a "cities-state," a devolved federation with an organic internal division of labor and deepening common identity.

Dubai also provides an opportunity to forge a new greater Arab identity beyond the combative secular nationalism of the postcolonial era. It has become the de facto capital of the Arab world, the meeting point for Arab movers and shakers as Cairo and Beirut were in past eras. From the Lebanese civil war to the U.S. invasion of Iraq to the Arab Spring, Dubai has consistently capitalized on regional misfortune: Hundreds of thousands of Lebanese, Egyptians, Syrians, Iraqis, and others have sought refuge there as their own countries' prospects have dimmed. The top Arab bankers, artists, entrepreneurs, and athletes have all taken up residency, and the U.A.E. is now cleverly offering some of them citizenship. As its passport rises in the ranks of global mobility, those from failed Arab states now compete to hold Emirati nationality, seeing it as a guarantee of stability and a ticket to the rest of the world.

The U.A.E.'s rise evokes enormous jealousy and contributes to significant brain drain. Its lack of a deep tradition of indigenous cultural creativity irks many of its newest residents: the intellectual and artistic refugees from Cairo, Beirut, Baghdad, and Damascus— the Arab world's historical knowledge and cultural centers. But this is precisely why Dubai should not be compared with its predecessors. It does not seek to replace them but is a platform for their survivors.

While elsewhere frustrated Arab youth turn to violence, those who can make it to Dubai channel their energies into productive ventures. As Chris Schroeder captures in his detailed and hopeful survey of the Arab tech scene, *Startup Rising,* Dubai-based investors and entrepreneurs have set up mobile education, e-commerce, artisanal pottery, solar cell manufacturing, and outsourcing operations across the Arab world, especially in their home countries.

From Morocco to Jordan, every Arab country hopes to have just one mini-Dubai to spark their long marches to modernization. In 2015, Egypt contracted Alabbar's firm Capital City Partners to build a new Singapore-size city between Cairo and the Red Sea as a solution to Cairo's incurable congestion.*

More broadly, Dubai is the role model for almost every city in the world suddenly stumbling into wealth. Azerbaijan's glitzy capital, Baku, is hailed as the "Dubai of the Caspian," while Angola's capital, Luanda, a perpetual construction site, aspires to be the Dubai of Africa. Resource-rich countries rank among the world's unhappiest, yet according to the 2013 *World Happiness Report* the U.A.E. now ranks above the United States and Luxembourg and at the top of the Middle East, which is otherwise the world's unhappiest region.

The success of Dubai provides yet another challenge to assumptions of Western democratic superiority. Even as Arab monarchies face growing calls for accountable and inclusive rule, they also demonstrate rapid leapfrogging from feudal (and feuding) clans to hybrid technocracy underpinned by monarchic stability. The "hybrid" is key: Dubai has become the world's epicenter of free-zone development. Its master planning is a strategic exercise in attracting supply chains and centers of excellence. For every category of global flows, there is a physical zone. Media City houses satellite television stations, Internet City for Web companies, Healthcare City for medical and pharmaceutical firms, and other self-explanatory names such as Textile Village, Auto Parts City, Carpet Free Zone, and DuBiotech. Taken together, Dubai in particular and the U.A.E. as a whole contains more than three-quarters of the more than two hundred SEZs found across the entire Arab world today. Eventually, the Dubai Logistics Corridor will link Jebel Ali with the Dubai World Central airport and multiple SEZs—a two-hundred-square-kilometer free zone within the ultimate free-zone city. When a city

* Similarly, Dubai-based Buroj Property Development has been contracted to build a $4 billion "tourist city" just outside Bosnia's capital of Sarajevo.

accrues such a dense layering of special economic, administrative, trade, logistics, financial, and other zones and authorities, it becomes a place where the royal family presides over a supply chain system all but disembodied from its actual soil.

Dubai's actual governance is so complex that it is often unclear which law governs the ground beneath one's own feet. The glittering Dubai International Financial Centre (DIFC), for example, obeys the commercial arbitration laws of the International Chamber of Commerce in Paris. In recent years, local U.A.E. courts have referred cases within their domestic jurisdiction to the DIFC courts, effectively pushing their own legal disputes laterally offshore for them to be more competently adjudicated. Similarly, in Media City, website access and censorship rules are entirely different from the rest of the country, because this SEZ is home to BBC, CNBC, Reuters, and other international media. Foreigners often set up companies in offshore "Creative Zones" located (onshore) in other emirates such as Fujairah, granting them residency permits that they then use to set up and fully own onshore companies.

The ruling class knows full well that were it not for upgrading to superior international standards for governing every sector, Dubai would have remained little more than a shipping entrepôt. Most important, opening the door to foreign-operated zones has paved the way for a post-oil future in which already 75 percent of Dubai's economy is construction, real estate, finance, manufacturing, retail, and other services. As Dubai's rapid rebound since the crisis has proved, governments and companies working hand in hand is crony capitalism only in theoretical orthodoxy.[2] In the real world, it is part of strategic economic survival.

DESERTS ARE LIMITLESS PLACES, but only with modern desalination and irrigation—and air-conditioning—has man been able to colonize the desert at large scale rather than merely, though with great fortitude, crossing it as Bedouin have done in the Sahara and the Gulf's fabled Empty Quarter. With the full benefit of modern

technologies, Dubai's expansion plans involve nothing less than rep-
licating itself endlessly southward toward the Empty Quarter
through concentric rings of real estate developments whose footprint will be larger than Beijing, London, Paris, New York, Barcelona, and several other major cities—combined. Rem Koolhaas, the
audacious and outspoken architectural theorist and practitioner,
has devised a master plan for the brand-new Waterfront City for 1.5
million inhabitants halfway between Dubai and Abu Dhabi, an example of the kind of "starter-kit metropolis" he believes can become a replicable urban template to rapidly create demographic
anchors for mega-urban regions across the Middle East and Asia.

Dubai itself still needs to get some of the basics done such as a
sensible street-numbering system and more public hospitals. As its
population swells, it has only two days' water supply in the event of
disruption to its desalination plants. (It has begun to drill for water
in deep desert basins as well.) There is therefore still much for Dubai
to build aboveground, underground, and by the sea. Western economists chronically underestimate emerging market demand, accusing
places such as Dubai of building fanciful castles in the desert. But
without infrastructure, there would be fewer jobs, less economic diversification, and little resilience.

Dubai today offers a quantum leap in quality of life even for
those coming from European welfare states because they shift from
paying high taxes to no taxes and from struggling on two incomes
to becoming single-income households living in luxury. Understanding Dubai's popularity does not therefore require a radical
new approach to deciphering "the good life." Western societies too
have been built on the back of imported labor dating from colonial-
era slavery to postcolonial migrants to a guest worker underclass.
Domestic workers in London and Los Angeles also live in parallel
economic and social universes. In all global cities, this segregation
is actually the result of the mutually beneficial co-location of first
and third world populations. Several million South Asian laborers
have toiled for months or years on end on the many construction
projects that have made Abu Dhabi, Dubai, and Doha glittering

icons. They come to build it but will never truly live in it. Everyone has a different view of these men. For most, they seem to blend into the background, others view them with great pity, very few with gratitude. In the West, people have evolved a false piety; they are uncomfortable acknowledging their comfort with this new medievalism. In Dubai (and Singapore), they are not.

Money has long replaced Arabic as the official language of Dubai. Its daily lingua franca has become English and among South Asians Hindi and Urdu, but the glue that binds everyone together is the desire for stability, prosperity, and connectedness. Dubai has become a safe zone from Islamist fundamentalism: Its security apparatus, surveillance technologies, and political tentacles keep it free from radical terrorists operating on its soil. Inevitably, Dubai has also become a thriving black market for electronics, a money-laundering haven, and a bridgehead for Chinese and Indian gangsters and their criminal networks. From five-star hotels on Sheikh Zayed Road itself to seedy motels in Deira, the law of supply and demand clearly outweighs Islamic edicts against adultery or prostitution. There is no doubt that many Arabs go to Dubai to forget that they live in Muslim countries.

IF EVER A CITY embodied the phrase "If you build it, they will come," it is Dubai, the fastest-growing city in the world. Its population tripled from 1968 to 1975, doubled from 1989 to 2009, and will double again to an estimated 4.5 million people by 2020. Americans who've run out of luck on Wall Street, Europeans seeking lower taxes, Africans fleeing poverty and tyranny, Indians, Russians, and Iranians with suitcases of money, Filipino hotel workers, and Chinese enterprise owners all coalesce in what has become the capital of the rest of the world. While western European nations are weary of immigrants, the U.A.E. is welcoming them in at an unprecedented rate.

Dubai is thus not only the Arab world's melting pot but the leading global one as well. Dubai is the *anti*-nation-state: It has almost no indigenous citizens left. Indeed, it is perhaps the most racially diluted city in the history of the world. The streams of immigrants arriving from around the world are creating a comfortably deferential microcosm of the world's diversity devoid of exclusive identities. Each residential compound is a global village.

Rem Koolhaas has anointed Dubai "the ultimate tabula rasa on which new identities can be inscribed."[3] Indeed, the city represents the foremost experiment in remapping identity and loyalty beyond traditional nationhood toward post-national urban hubs. Whereas the average expat tenure in Dubai or Singapore used to be two to three years, now it is indefinite. Expats have become permanent migrants. The more people plant roots in Dubai, the more their own sense of transience evolves into an immigrant mentality of making efforts to integrate and accrue rewards. Already much of Dubai's establishment has been run by foreigners for decades. Across the public and private sectors, every single position of responsibility held by an Emirati is backed up by a team of foreigners. As their personal and professional stakes in Dubai's success have grown, foreigners have set up schools, forged petitions to block beachfront real estate projects, lobbied for permanent residency rights tied to property ownership, and sought to be included in the all-important *majlis* gatherings in which leaders listen to and consult with the population at large to sound out issues and gather ideas. Over time, it has become their "home" as much as the countries they came from.

And yet the U.A.E. is a country where noncitizens have no inalienable rights. Strictly speaking, they are a constituency of investors. Even if families have lived there for decades and it is their only home in the world, they must renew their residency permits every two to three years. Even as more and more people imagine themselves working and eventually retiring in Dubai (it's a lot safer than Mexico), almost the entire population lives in this oxymoronic state of "permanent transit" in which they are legally second-class citizens. This gives Dubai's authorities the right to send anyone packing.

The rulers' top priority is, rightly, the Emirati nationals who have been loyal subjects for generations. They are given lavish subsidies to maintain their contentedness, forcibly promoted in foreign companies through an upscale affirmative action program known as Emiratization, and hold the upper hand in the all-important real estate market. But extreme wealth has meant the onset of serious lifestyle diseases such as obesity for men and plummeting fertility for women (now among the lowest in the world). As the relentless demographic dilution of Emiratis continues, the U.A.E.'s most noted intellectual dissident, Abdulkhaleq Abdulla, speaks of the "agony of being a minority in my own country."[4] He laments that Emiratis are too few in number and powerless over the forces reshaping the country to enjoy for much longer the global phenomenon Dubai has become. When we sat together for an audience discussion at the 2012 Art Dubai festival, he used a word perhaps only he is allowed to in public: "extinction." It is as if the Filipina or European boutique owner greeting a fellow foreigner with the Arabic "As-salamu alaykum" is doing so out of respect to a local population that no longer exists.

A decade from now, when Emiratis become ever more the figureheads and well-kept indigenous curiosities in their own country, the ruling class will have to fully accept the uniquely cosmopolitan project they have created. As mutually beneficial as the arrangement has been between the sheikhs and their soon-to-be entirely foreign population, there is an existential risk that also faces a place of such unique demographics and connectivity: Should catastrophe strike— either economic or geopolitical—would people leave as quickly as they came, abandoning their tax-free affair for the sober realities of their original homes?

To build longer-term loyalty as a global capital, Dubai will have to offer its residents rights beyond just the conveniences of 24/7 capitalism. For example, the authorities might begin to offer permanent residency to non-Arabs.* As the city transitions from being a

---

* At present, naturalization of non-Arab foreigners remains a limited and opportunistic occurrence. The few known cases have taken place after about thirty years of residence, and it has only been granted to Muslims with very strong domestic patrons.

place where residents are "always expats" to a place that is everyone's "global home," it can build a system where freedoms and obligations are better balanced. A Dubaian could proudly be anyone whose primary residence is Dubai.

Dubai is a laboratory for the extreme mixture of demographic and economic forces. The outcomes are uncertain, but the experiment continues. The results, though, are not Dubai's but all of ours. As the urban scholar Daniel Brook rightly states, "Apologizing for Dubai is apologizing for the world as it is."[5]

FIRST PORT OF CALL

In November 2013, I flew to Jeddah, Saudi Arabia, and then drove to a place not yet on the map, a new city under construction on the Red Sea coast that combines special economic zones targeting consumer goods, automotive assembly, and information technology with residential neighborhoods meant to house upwards of two million people. Launched through an IPO and listed on the Saudi stock exchange, King Abdullah Economic City (KAEC) is, according to its CEO, Fahd al-Rasheed, the "world's first fully integrated private city."[6]

Part of the "Dubai effect" on the Arab world has been that new ports are vigorously competing to *displace* the U.A.E.'s Jebel Ali as the region's gateway to the Arabian Peninsula's booming markets—particularly Saudi Arabia itself. Jebel Ali had first mover advantage on its side, not geography. Once KAEC's ultramodern new port is fully operational around 2020, Saudi Arabia can begin to capture the lion's share of the container cargo traffic passing from the Mediterranean through the Suez Canal into the Red Sea, cutting shipping time and efficiently funneling goods outward over high-speed rail lines and ten-lane highways—land bridges across the vast desert to Mecca, Medina, Riyadh, and beyond. KAEC is how Saudi Arabia can gain an enormous amount of logistical flow at the expense of Jebel Ali.

KAEC is not just a commercial venture but a strategic necessity.

For decades, Saudi's eastern military and oil compounds such as Dhahran and Dammam have dominated its geopolitical perspectives. For the ruling al-Saud dynasty in Riyadh and its American protectors, keeping oil flowing and containing both Iran and Iraq were the kingdom's strategic priorities. But with Saudi oil production waning, the country must take advantage not just of its geology but of its geography. A global logistics hub such as KAEC is how Saudi can insert itself into other supply chains beyond oil.

KAEC is a monumental investment not just to leverage the country's Red Sea geography but also to employ and educate future Saudi generations. Like other Arab countries, Saudi Arabia faces a demographic crisis: Its population has grown from three million in 1950 to thirty million today, with half the population below the age of twenty-five. The country needs to double its housing capacity from four million to eight million units by 2020. Thus far, more than fifty companies have bought into the land and begun to install factories and equipment at KAEC. Jaguar Land Rover has announced plans to construct a new assembly plant, making it the regional hub for exporting high-end cars both to other Arab countries and to the Mediterranean region. This is rather appropriate, because Jeddah is where the campaign for female drivers in Saudi Arabia began. Economic opening and investment always bring about change, however small, in the social fabric. Saudi Arabia will be no different. Jobs in education, health care, and administration will increase, and women will have to fill them, especially as the country seeks to displace a substantial share of its imported workforce to reduce Saudi unemployment, which is four times higher among women than men.*

John Macomber of Harvard Business School, an expert on start-up cities and urban economic competitiveness whom I met at KAEC,

---

* KAEC is also home to the country's first dedicated innovation lab, SiNova, and nearby is the King Abdullah University of Science and Technology, which was developed in collaboration with leading Western universities and focuses on environmental sciences and crop engineering, key areas for a post-oil and pro-employment Saudi economy.

sees its potential to flourish. He advises new cities to have a clear purpose before breaking ground, build competitive and clean infrastructure (meaning high setup but low operational costs), design proximate clustering of zones into a master plan, develop mixed-use commercial and residential spaces, offer a transparent regulatory environment, provide high-quality management and services, and have a viable economic strategy focused on growth rather than just real estate.

Jogging along the soccer fields and beachfront cafés sprouting up on KAEC's Red Sea corniche, I found it easy to imagine that the chance to live and work in a congestion-free new city would lure thousands of young Saudis away from more crowded cities. New cities can help dissipate dense and unproductive populations, liberating their energy into more gainful endeavors. New and dynamic centers will invigorate the kingdom, even as they devolve power gradually away from Riyadh.

As the hub for several of Saudi Arabia's new city developments, Jeddah is emerging as the country's Red Sea capital. From its humble origins as an ancient fishing village and entrepôt for trading tortoise shells, spices, and frankincense, Jeddah was anointed the gateway to the holy cities of Mecca and Medina in the seventh century. Over time, this mellow seaside oasis has become a bustling city of over five million residents and the hub for an archipelago of new urban developments stretching hundreds of kilometers. The city's modern and moderate commercial class, like the maritime city itself, is intrinsically open to the world.

The business of religion is also providing a major boost to the Jeddah region. Driving east, I witnessed a construction bonanza aimed at creating jobs, diversifying the economy, and managing the twelve million and growing annual visitors to Mecca and Medina each year, one-quarter of whom come for hajj. As I neared Mecca, I saw massive tractors and cranes busily carving out new highways and roundabouts from the rocky hillsides. Three small mountains surrounding the Grand Mosque itself are being leveled to make way for gargantuan hotels (including the world's largest, the Abraj

Kudai) and a clock tower that dwarfs Big Ben. Jackhammers pound away day and night to construct a giant granite addition to the mosque, as well as a multistory elevated walkway for the throngs of pilgrims walking in centripetal circles around the giant black Kaaba.

The fastest-growing source of new visitors to Saudi is not surprisingly the continent with the most rapidly growing number of converts to Islam: Africa. Sixty thousand years ago, there were two main passages for man's earliest migration out of Africa into Mesopotamia: the Sinai Peninsula and across the Red Sea over the Bab el-Mandeb Strait, which like the Bering Strait was as much as a hundred meters lower before the current cycle of climate change. A decade or two from now, that crossing will be much easier again with the planned construction of an ambitious fifty-four-kilometer bridge connecting Djibouti to Yemen. This new Afro-Arabian linkage will feature a strikingly quantum phenomenon: twin cities on either side of the strait—both called Al-Noor, referring to the light of Allah's guidance. On the Arabian side, Al-Noor would connect to Yemen's capital, Sana'a, from which a 750-kilometer road is under construction (with World Bank funding and Chinese execution) into Saudi Arabia's holy Hejaz—and by extension via Saudi's expanding infrastructure network all the way to Dubai. On the African side, a more robust road network would branch out from Djibouti's Al-Noor to East Africa's major economic centers of Addis Ababa, Khartoum, and Nairobi.

JEDDAH IS NOT THE ONLY major coastal hub that seeks to displace Jebel Ali as the Arabian Peninsula's first port of call for trade. Much as KAEC will capture European shipping volumes coming through the Suez Canal from Europe, the sleepy sultanate of Oman may do the same for the surging Maritime Silk Road trade across the Indian Ocean, with container ships of cars, electronics, medicines, chemicals, textiles, and many other products sailing west and mostly oil and LNG shipped east. More than 70 percent of the goods offloaded at Jebel Ali are actually bound for Saudi Arabia, but only after sailing through the narrow and perilous Strait of Hormuz into the Arabian/Persian Gulf. In 2012, customs delays at the U.A.E.-Saudi border crossing at Al Ghuwaifat led to a line of five thousand trucks stretching thirty kilometers and taking more than one week to process.*

While Oman already has a number of ports near its main cities such as Salalah, the new port at Duqm will be the country's first fully integrated port and supply chain hub. Partnered with the Dutch port of Antwerp and under the tutelage of Singaporean management, Duqm's free trade zone alone is three times the size of Singapore. With freight rail and highway corridors extending northward to the capital, Muscat, and the U.A.E., and eventually across the Empty Quarter into Saudi Arabia, Duqm will offer Asian exporters a chance to avoid Jebel Ali altogether—slashing the queue of trucks crossing into Saudi Arabia to a trickle. Once both KAEC and Duqm are up and running, Jebel Ali needs to have transitioned toward a more diversified economy of logistics and real estate along the "Abu-Dubai" corridor. Otherwise things will be rather lonely on Jebel Ali's artificial palm island project.

Supply chains are auto-programmed to follow the logic of flow, always seeking the most efficient route to reach their destination. The competition among ports around the Arabian Peninsula is equally intense in another arena of strategic infrastructures: oil terminals. Currently, eighteen million barrels of oil pass through the perilous Strait of Hormuz every day (one-third of all oil shipped by sea and 20 percent of oil traded worldwide). Saudi Arabia, Kuwait, and Iraq depend on the strait for the 85 percent of their exports that then cross the Indian Ocean and the Strait of Malacca to China, Japan, and South Korea, as do major gas exporters such as Qatar. In the event of a disruption of energy shipments through Hormuz, the U.A.E. offers its customers the ability to fill up their tankers at the port of Fujairah on the Gulf of Oman side of the strait. Meanwhile, Iran depends on shipping oil through Hormuz too—but only

---

* Over three million people and almost two million vehicles cross this border annually.

until it completes a massive export terminal at Bandar Jask on the Gulf of Oman. Like the Strait of Malacca, Hormuz is a major geopolitical choke point, which is why the U.A.E. and Iran are connecting their way *around* it.

LAGOS: AFRICA'S GLOBAL CITY

If the "Dubai effect" takes root in Africa, it will be in Lagos, Africa's largest city. When Lagos's governor Babatunde Fashola first visited Dubai, he found it "absolutely audacious. It put rockets in my shoes."

Lagos is not only Nigeria's economic capital but also the megalopolis for at least a dozen surrounding countries. As I drove along the expanding light-rail network on the city's western periphery, it was easy to imagine how this artery could eventually stretch through Benin and Togo through Accra in Ghana to Abidjan in the Ivory Coast—an urban corridor of some fifty-five million people crossing four international borders. Together, they have graduated from slave trade hub to supply chain hub. Along the way, resource-rich Nigeria and Ghana are Anglicizing the smaller former French and German colonies in between them. Benin feels more like a suburb of Lagos than a country, much as Bulgaria (the poorest EU member) is effectively a suburb of Istanbul (creating a corridor I call "Istanbulgaria"). Anyone interested in understanding West Africa's emerging dynamics—or merely in self-preservation—needs a detailed map of this urban archipelago.

As the economy of Lagos swells to the size of Kenya's, it is becoming ever more a quasi-independent city-state and regional capital. Devolution also drives the city's self-reliance as the federal government in Abuja cuts its budgetary contribution to the city while Fashola increases municipal tax rates and collection, spending 60 percent of the city's budget on roads, garbage trucks, a China-inspired bus rapid transit

system, and an enlarged civil service to administer them.[7]
Nigeria needs Lagos more than Lagos needs Nigeria.

Nigeria is at best a federation, and certainly not a nation.
Of the country's more than three hundred major ethnic
groups, the Yoruba dominate the southwest, the Hausa the
north, and the Igbo the southeast. While the 1960s witnessed the genocidal Biafran War in which the Igbo attempted to secede, today's violence is much more centered
on the Muslim insurgency in the country's north, led by the
ruthless terrorist group Boko Haram. Some believe the Nige-
rian military itself set up Boko Haram to justify a bloated
security budget that already amounts to one-quarter of
GDP—certainly an African case of blowback. Others accuse
Muslim parliamentarians of seeding Boko Haram to destabilize the state and stoke the secession of half the country's
population.

Even as investors hail Nigeria as a great engine of African prosperity, and architects praise Lagos as a template for
the continent's renaissance, the brutal civil war will likely
see the country further federalize in order to remain man-
ageable at all. This might be for the best, because the veneer
of unity is costly and untenable, and Nigeria should rather
focus on modernizing and curbing corruption in its oil sector and creating jobs for the more than 50 percent of youth
who are unemployed, especially in rural areas. (Male youth
unemployment holds one of the most statistically significant
correlations to social and political unrest.)

Lagos is a microcosm of Nigeria's juxtaposition of staggering wealth and poverty. On one manicured beach on the
central Victoria Island district, European, African, and Arab
soccer teams compete in the corporate-sponsored Copa
Lagos tournament, complete with overpriced drinks and
scantily clad cheerleaders. Nearby on the Lekki Peninsula,
an upscale "smart city" district called Eko Atlantic is under
construction, promising high-class living with ocean views.

In between, however, roving teenage gangs control access to the beach, demand fees to protect your car, and harass passersby on the boardwalk. A dozen kilometers away, I paid two fat wads of naira to armed gangsters for the privilege of paddling a rickety canoe through the feces-infested swamp known as Makoko, home to over 100,000 people. In 2012, Fashola sent in paramilitary police armed with chain saws to shred this driftwood slum, a move that earned praise and resentment in equal measure. Given that Lagos's population has grown from 1.4 million in 1970 to over 14 million today, he seemed to be taking a page out of the playbook of Mumbai, another creaking peninsula replete with extravagance and destitution, vibrancy and futility. But in a regional magnet such as Lagos, cleaning up the streets and underpasses must mean more than sweeping away the people, for countless millions more are coming.

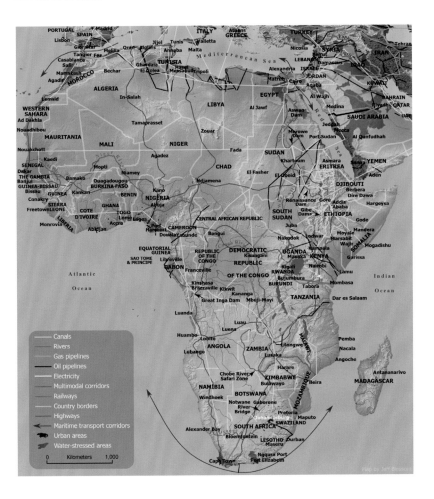

Africa is still more a collection of subregions than a united continent, but new transcontinental highways and railways, hydroelectric dams and electricity grids, and oil and gas pipelines are transforming its arbitrary postcolonial map into one where African societies are better connected to one another.

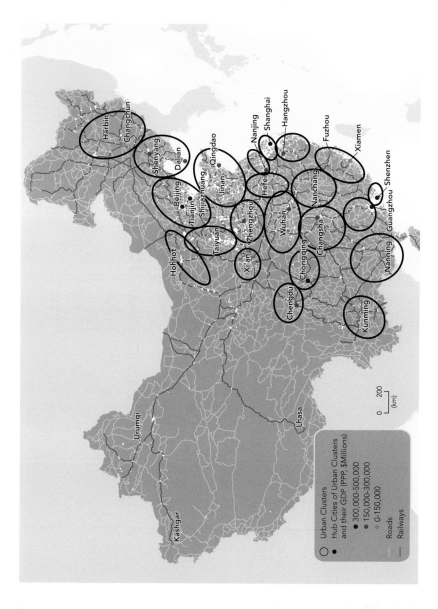

China is functionally reorganizing itself around approximately two dozen megacity clusters, each internally integrated through dense transportation networks, while high-speed rail connects the entire country.

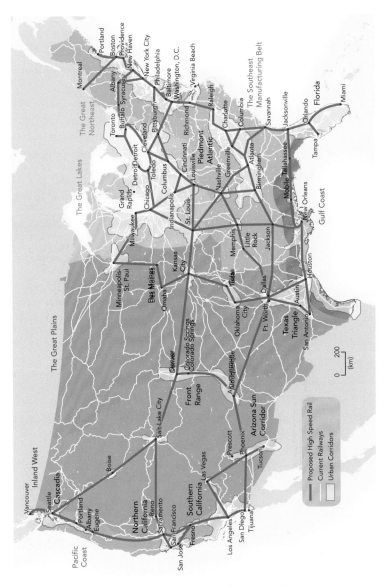

America's functional economic regions have broader geographies than the traditional map of fifty states but center around key city hubs. High-speed railways and Internet cables could efficiently connect American cities together, creating a "United City-States of America."

Canada, the United States, and Mexico are increasingly integrated through cross-border infrastructures, resource sharing, trade, and investment.

23. THE SOUTH AMERICAN UNION

South America is almost fully urbanized, with most people living along the Atlantic and Pacific Ocean coasts. New energy and transportation linkages are enabling the continent to trade more efficiently across both oceans, especially with Asia.

24. ASPIRING TO ECONOMIC COMPLEXITY

The Complexity Outlook Index (2013) ranks countries according to their potential to improve productive capabilities. Canada, Brazil, India, and China are among the countries that could gain the most from rising trade with partners whose technologies and other know-how could raise the complexity of their own products and exports.

25. FROM COMPLEXITY TO GROWTH

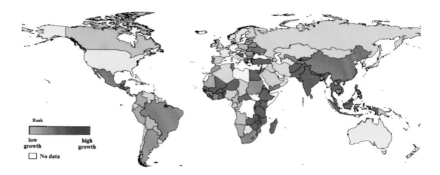

A projection of the countries most likely to achieve high growth rates to the year 2023 based on improvements in productive capabilities embedded in their exports. India, Southeast Asia, and Africa show the greatest improvement.

26. SUPPLY CHAINS ARE BECOMING MORE DISPERSED AND COMPLEX

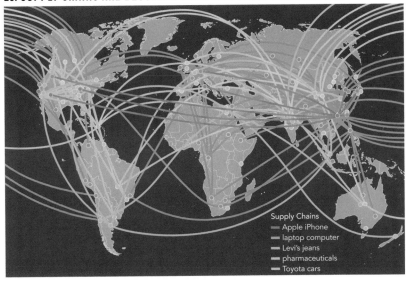

Supply Chains
— Apple iPhone
— laptop computer
— Levi's jeans
— pharmaceuticals
— Toyota cars

From electronics to textiles to pharmaceuticals, supply chains are becoming more distributed in response to local market pressures such as more demanding consumers.

27. WHICH ROLE MODEL FOR CHINA?

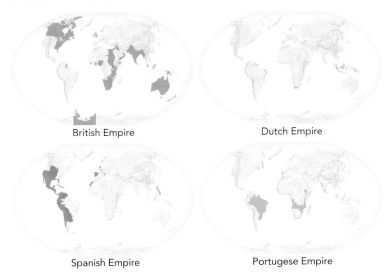

British Empire

Dutch Empire

Spanish Empire

Portugese Empire

Of Europe's globe-spanning empires of the past five hundred years, the Dutch were an empire of enclaves focused more on trade than territory.

28. A MAP OF MINERALS

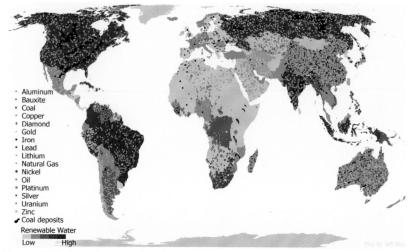

- Aluminum
- Bauxite
- Coal
- Copper
- Diamond
- Gold
- Iron
- Lead
- Lithium
- Natural Gas
- Nickel
- Oil
- Platinum
- Silver
- Uranium
- Zinc
- Coal deposits

Renewable Water
Low   High

The world's hydrocarbon and mineral resources predate and transcend our political borders. Infrastructure, supply chains, and markets move reserves from where they are to where they are consumed.

29. WORLD FOOD SUPPLIES

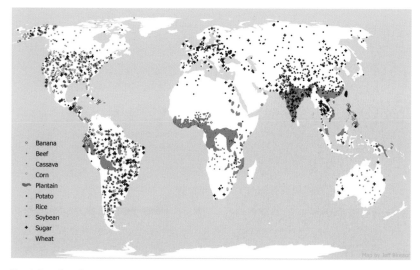

- Banana
- Beef
- Cassava
- Corn
- Plantain
- Potato
- Rice
- Soybean
- Sugar
- Wheat

North America, South America, Europe, India, China, and Australia have the largest agricultural resources. The United States, Australia, and several European nations are the world's biggest food exporters.

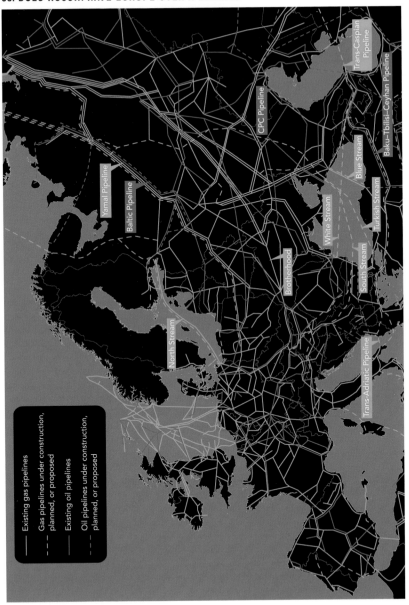

New oil and gas pipelines from the Caucasus, Central Asia, and the Mideast reduce
Europe's energy dependence on Russia, while new Russian pipelines avoiding Ukraine
diminish its role as a transit state.

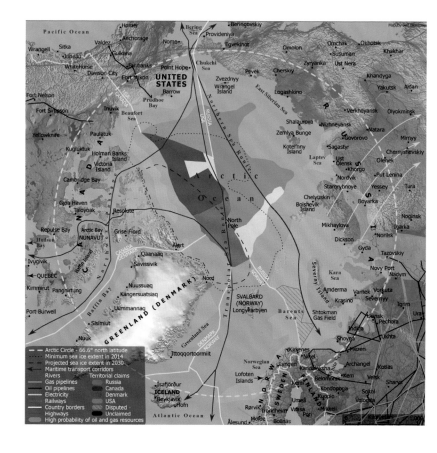

As the Arctic ice melts, the terrain and resources beneath are increasingly contested. At the same time, the combination of rising temperatures, new resource discoveries, and emerging transportation corridors means more population centers, infrastructure investment, and connectivity across the northernmost parts of the world.

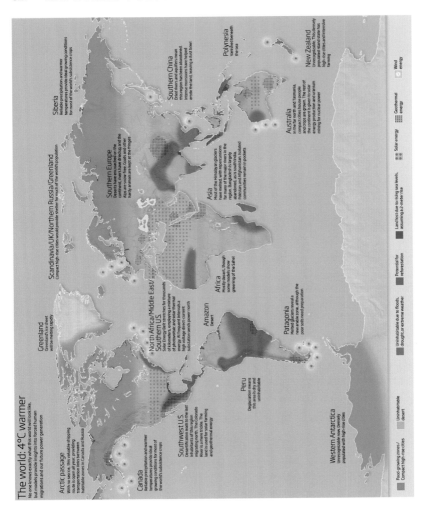

The world: 4°C warmer

No one knows exactly what this world will look like, but models provide insights into our future power generation and our future power generation

Arctic passage
With no sea ice, this valuable shipping route is open all year, providing transportation links between habitable zones in Canada and Russia

Canada
Reliable precipitation and warmer temperatures provide ideal growing conditions for most of the world's subsistence crops

Southwest US
Desertification leads to the last inhabitants of this region migrating north. The Colorado River is a mere trickle. The land is used for solar farming and geothermal energy

Peru
Deglaciation means this area is dry and uninhabitable

Western Antarctica
Unrecognizable now. Densely populated with high-rise cities

Greenland
Greenland's ice sheet will be melting rapidly

North Africa/Middle East/Southern US
Solar Energy Belt stretches for thousands of kilometers, employing a mixture of photovoltaic and solar thermal energy. At frequent intervals a high voltage direct current substation sends power north

Amazon
Desert

Patagonia
Melted glaciers reveal a new arable zone, although the poor soils need preparation

Scandinavia/UK/Northern Russia/Greenland
Compact high-rise cities would provide shelter for much of the world's population

Southern Europe
Deserts have encroached on the continent, rivers have dried up, and the Alps are snow-free. Goats and other hardy animals are kept at the fringe

Africa
Mostly desert, though some models show greening of the Sahel

Asia
Most of the Himalaya glaciers have melted, with repercussions for many of the major rivers in the region. Bangladesh is largely abandoned, as is south India. Pakistan and Afghanistan. Isolated communities remain in pockets

Siberia
Reliable precipitation and warmer temperatures provide ideal growing conditions for most of the world's subsistence crops

Southern China
Dried rivers and aquifers mean this region has been abandoned. Intense monsoons have helped erode the land, leaving a dust bowl

Australia
In the far north and Tasmania, compact cities house people and crops are grown. The rest of the continent is given to solar energy production and uranium mining for nuclear power

Polynesia
Vanished beneath the sea

New Zealand
Unrecognizable. This densely populated island state has high-rise cities and intensive farming

Legend:
- Food-growing zones / Compact high-rise cities
- Uninhabitable desert
- Uninhabitable due to floods, drought, or extreme weather
- Land lost due to rising sea levels, assuming a 2-meter rise
- Potential for reforestation
- Solar energy
- Geothermal energy
- Wind energy

The continued rise in global temperatures will have a seismic impact on life worldwide: The Amazon rainforest will become a desert, Himalayan glaciers will disappear, and much of the world's two largest countries (China and India) will have to be abandoned. The world's two largest and most depopulated countries, Russia and Canada, will become the only reliable food-producing geographies, and potentially home to billions of climate refugees.

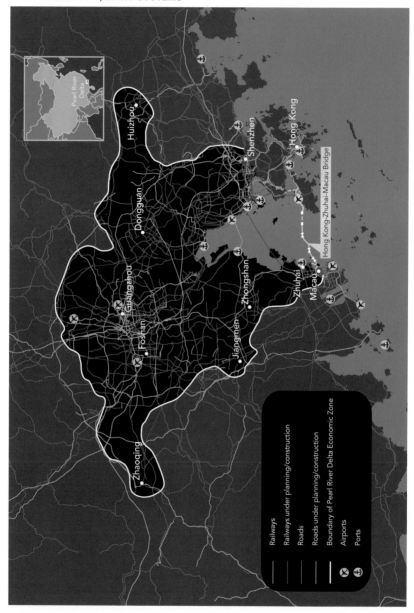

From Guangzhou to Hong Kong, the Pearl River Delta megacity is becoming one integrated economic corridor covering a dozen cities. By 2030 its population could reach 80 million with an economic output of $2 trillion.

34. GLOBAL DATA FLOWS EXPANDING AND ACCELERATING

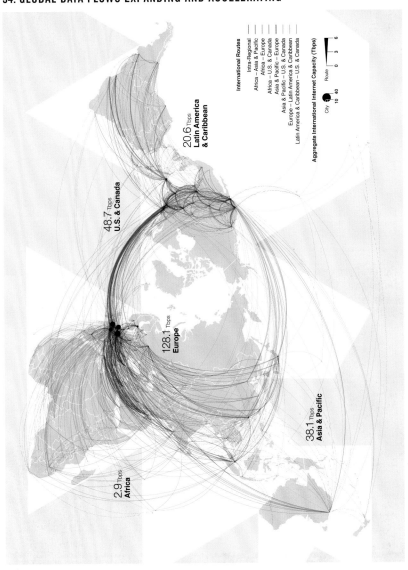

International Routes

Intra-Regional
Africa – Asia & Pacific
Africa – Europe
Africa – U.S. & Canada
Asia & Pacific – Europe
Asia & Pacific – U.S. & Canada
Europe – Latin America & Caribbean
Latin America & Caribbean – U.S. & Canada

Aggregate International Internet Capacity (Tbps)

City   Route

10 40   0   3   6

20.6 Tbps
Latin America & Caribbean

48.7 Tbps
U.S. & Canada

128.1 Tbps
Europe

38.1 Tbps
Asia & Pacific

2.9 Tbps
Africa

Interregional data transfer routes are growing among major cities on all continents.
Terabytes per second (Tbps) capacity is a proxy for the volume of data transferred across
borders within each region. Europe ranks far ahead of the rest of the world.

35. GLOBAL MIGRATION: ORIGINS AND DESTINATIONS

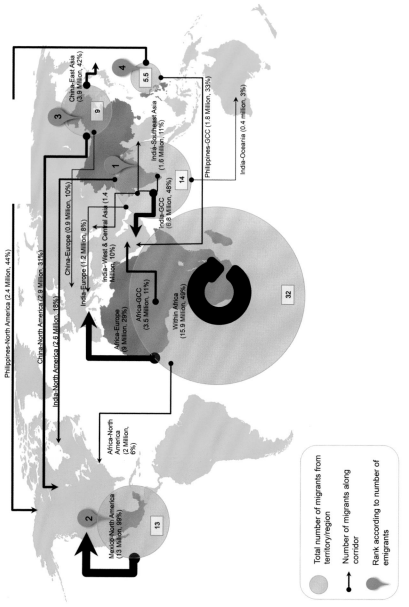

China-East Asia (3.9 Million, 42%)

China-Europe (0.9 Million, 10%)

China-North America (2.9 Million, 31%)

Philippines-North America (2.4 Million, 44%)

India-North America (2.6 Million, 18%)

India-Europe (1.2 Million, 8%)

India-West & Central Asia (1.4 Million, 10%)

India-Southeast Asia (1.6 Million, 11%)

India-GCC (6.8 Million, 48%)

Philippines-GCC (1.8 Million, 33%)

India-Oceania (0.4 million, 3%)

Africa-Europe (9 Million, 29%)

Africa-GCC (3.5 Million, 11%)

Within Africa (15.9 Million, 49%)

Africa-North America (2 Million, 6%)

Mexico-North America (13 Million, 99%)

Total number of migrants from territory/region

Number of migrants along corridor

Rank according to number of emigrants

Africa, India, Mexico, the Philippines, and China are the largest sources of migrants crossing borders and continents. Lines connect origin and destination, indicating the number of migrants along each corridor and the percentage of the origin country's total number of migrants.

36. A WORLD ON THE MOVE: MIGRANTS SURGE AS THE WORLD POPULATION EXPANDS

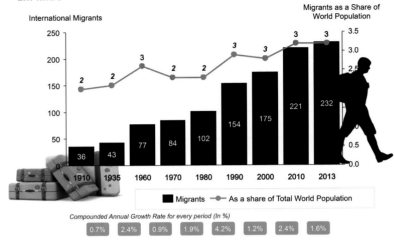

International Migrants

Migrants as a Share of World Population

Compounded Annual Growth Rate for every period (In %)

| 0.7% | 2.4% | 0.9% | 1.9% | 4.2% | 1.2% | 2.4% | 1.6% |

The total number of people living outside their country of birth continues to rise, even as it holds steady as a small percentage of the total world population.

37. GLOBAL HUBS BECOME DEMOGRAPHIC MELTING POTS

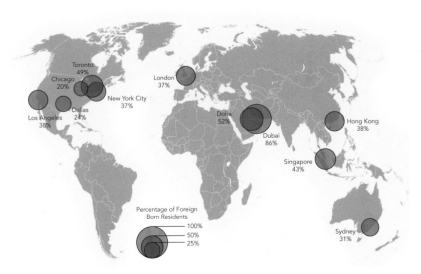

As the number of global migrants surges, connected and open cities feature ever-higher percentages of foreign-born residents. With South Asian nationals making up the majority of its population, Dubai's indigenous population is the smallest of any major city.

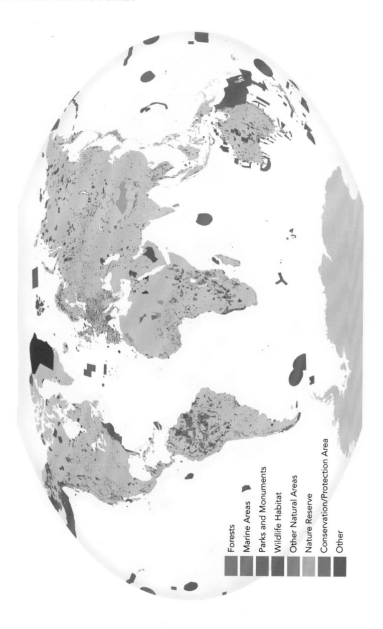

Forests
Marine Areas
Parks and Monuments
Wildlife Habitat
Other Natural Areas
Nature Reserve
Conservation/Protection Area
Other

Governments are designating fragile ecosystems as protected areas and partnering with companies and civil society groups to monitor and restore them.

CHAPTER 12

GETTING ON THE MAP

POP-UP CITIES

THE RECENTLY PUBLISHED *GLOBAL TRENDS 2030* REPORT OF THE
National Intelligence Council includes a very plausible scenario
called "Non-state World" in which urbanization, technology, and
capital accumulation together accelerate the rise of special economic zones effectively run by capitalist forces: "It is as if the central government acknowledges its own inability to forge reforms
and then subcontract out responsibility to a second party. In these
enclaves, the very laws, including taxation, are set by somebody
from the outside. Many believe that outside parties have a better
chance of getting the economies in these designated areas up and
going, eventually setting an example for the rest of the country."[1]

My only quibble with this fine analysis is that it describes the
world of 2013, not 2030. Dozens of governments have long since
given up pretending they can live up to their responsibility to provide "public goods." Instead, the market provides them in the form
of these "enclaves" that are very much run "by somebody from the
outside": the supply chain.

Throughout history, the pattern has been the same: Cities carve
out their own commercial authorities in order to serve as preferred
gateways to their hinterlands and to efficiently connect to allied cit-

Maps 1, 20, and 33, corresponding to this chapter,
appear in the map inserts.

ies and forces across oceans and borders. Over two millennia ago, Greek port cities such as Delos (the mythological birthplace of Apollo) formed the oldest free-port system, a trading network that spanned across Phoenician and other Mediterranean civilizations. Over one thousand years later, the medieval free ports of Europe's Hanseatic League, including Bremen, Lübeck, Hamburg, and Danzig, successfully maneuvered around European monarchies to maintain their autonomy. The Renaissance Italian city-states of Venice and Genoa also served as leading trade entrepôts for centuries, followed by colonial British ports like Hong Kong and Singapore that were designed such that the entire city serves as a free trade zone.

The post–World War II competition to boost manufacturing and exports led to many economic nodes from Shannon, Ireland, to Puerto Rico and Mexican maquiladoras on the U.S. border being reconfigured as foreign trade zones or export processing zones (EPZs) to attract cheap labor and investment and gain market share.[2] In the 1960s, the United Nations Industrial Development Organization began promoting SEZs as an infrastructure and growth template. But whereas it felt SEZs were a temporary phenomenon, an administrative anomaly needed only to jump-start economies, they have in fact become the world's most rapidly spreading urban form: There are more than four thousand SEZs around the world, the pop-up cities of a functional supply chain world.

Cities can be thought of as ancient social technology, infrastructures that aggregate people into a dense and productive division of labor. But humanity's rapid urbanization only means that people are moving into cities, *not* that the cities are prepared for their arrival. Successful economic strategy today must therefore include strategic city-level investments to absorb the masses and catapult societies into modernity.

SEZs have proven to be enormous catalysts for connectivity and growth across underdeveloped countries. In 1979, Deng Xiaoping designated Shenzhen, then a fishing village north of Hong Kong, as China's first special economic zone. Since that time, Shenzhen has grown into a thriving international hub of fifteen million people with a per capita GDP a hundred times larger than three decades ago.[3] That same year, Mauritius opened its first textile SEZ and launched itself on a 6 percent growth path and all but eliminated unemployment. The Dominican Republic's first SEZ in garment manufacturing created 100,000 jobs while diminishing the country's reliance on agriculture. In the late Cold War, the third world demanded a new international economic order, a global redistribution scheme including the relocation of industries from north to south, price supports for developing-country exports, lower tariffs, and a robust international food program. What followed was excessive borrowing, bad debts, uncontrolled inflation, and messy defaults. Urbanization and connecting to global supply chains have proven to be a much better path to progress.

SEZs and the supply chains they serve represent the unbundling of territoriality. Investors are willing to go into SEZs for low-cost labor and protection from regulatory hassles, while governments need foreign investment to create jobs and train workers, import technology and skills, and provide a demonstration effect for the rest of the economy. So far, it has proven to be a win-win combination: Sacrifice some sovereignty in order to become a productive member of the supply chain world.

In the 1980s and 1990s, a new wave of industrial parks and technology clusters that focused on higher-value areas such as call centers, software programming, and logistics management emerged in both developed and developing countries. Their role models were America's already established Stanford Research Park in Palo Alto and Research Triangle Park in North Carolina (which also became a foreign trade zone in the 1980s). Bangalore and Hyderabad, today India's IT jewels, benefited from diaspora talent, investment from multinationals such as Texas Instruments, and support from a new agency called Software Technology Parks of India.

India's population has quadrupled to 1.2 billion in the past sixty-five years since independence, but only in the past few years has India even begun to modernize its infrastructure. In such underdeveloped countries, SEZs are therefore just a new name for the

century-old establishment of corporate cities such as Jamshedpur
in eastern India, the country's first planned industrial city founded
by the family patriarch Jamsetji Tata. Hence it also goes by a more
common name: Tatanagar. India has never been a place where
the government leads and the private sector "fills the gaps," but
rather the opposite: Companies represent half of national infrastructure investment and provide most services, especially private
health clinics and schools. The situation is no different—if only less
organized—in other overpopulated countries from Nigeria to Indonesia. Coca-Cola bottling plants, Chevron gas production facilities,
and Firestone rubber plantations are just some of the thousands of
supply chain nodes run by companies where all services, and even
security, are largely provided by the employer rather than the state.

Like manufacturing in China or oil exploration in the Middle
East, welcoming in foreign supply chains is the only way the world's
periphery has any hope of ever joining the core. The main channels
through which technology is diffused in emerging economies are
foreign trade (buying equipment and new ideas directly) and foreign
investment (having foreign firms bring them to you). SEZs are where
both happen at the same time.

While China has already joined the global economic center of
gravity, much of the world still has a long way to go. SEZs represent
a strategic option to escape histories of failure and, as China did,
achieve in twenty years what took two hundred in the West. Mauritius, for example, used EPZs to graduate from agriculture to textiles
and then investment zones and tax treaties to shift to financial services, which now make up more than 70 percent of its economy
versus less than 5 percent for agriculture. By making itself Africa's
offshore financial hub, it is both a gateway for sizable pools of Asian
investment into the continent and the source of 40 percent of the
FDI that enters India. Not bad for a country whose sugar-driven
economy of the 1960s generated a per capita income of $200.*

---

* On average across developing countries, participating in the intermediate stages of
product creation represents 30 percent of GDP and far more if SEZs are used not just
for specialization but also to diversify into more complex industries.

FROM EXCLAVE
TO ENCLAVE

The NIC 2030 report actually used the wrong term for SEZs, referring to them as "enclaves." In fact, the perception of foreign-run zones on national soil implies that they are *exclaves,* restricted and walled off—"spatially fortified" in urban planning parlance—both segmented from the economy (requiring specially imported skills) and segregated from the society (isolated from local communities). The test of whether a country leverages SEZs—as China and Mauritius have done—thus lies in translating the presence of exclave bubbles into national economic development. Unless countries raise their standards to contribute to global value chains, free trade alone won't actually benefit them other than ensure they are flooded with cheap Chinese goods. As Hubert Escaith of the WTO has pointed out, it is by leveraging foreign investment to improve infrastructure, education, and social systems that free trade becomes a two-way street. That way SEZs are no longer autonomous islands but engines of local economic dynamism.

There is always spillover from SEZs to the host country; the only question is whether governments seize the opportunity brought by multinationals to create jobs, raise wages, and transfer skills. For example, because Vietnamese footwear and garment workers get paid 50 percent more by foreign firms than local ones, they rank in the top 20 percent of households nationally. The focus of the Vietnamese government has thus become broadening the tax base to build out infrastructure across the country, expand housing, emulate foreign-run schools, and create more joint ventures—steps that lift even more families out of poverty. Even though Vietnam remains politically opaque, the growing scale and range of SEZs in the country demonstrate how serious it still is about its economic future. With its young and hardworking population earning it a reputation as a "little China," Vietnam has more than sixteen thousand active FDI projects from the ports of Da Nang to IT parks now housing Intel's largest Asian chip foundries.

Whereas previously SEZs were exempt from local regulations and even civil laws, today developing countries are becoming smarter and more confident, establishing parastatal agencies to represent national interests such as higher wages and standards and promoting local industry within the zones. There is no doubt that many of today's new SEZs are negotiated in secret, with fees paid in exchange for not paying taxes later. But smart governments also use their leverage to end tax holidays early and ensure technology and skills training that benefits society.

SEZs are also crucial sites of experimentation for reforms that can eventually become national policy. For example, Malaysia's Multimedia Super Corridor hosts hundreds of animation, gaming, and other tech companies that compete for government grants and venture capital funding. By serving as a home for independent websites, it has created a space for press freedom to emerge. Malaysia is also evidence of how SEZs located far from capitals can avoid the excessive meddling and real estate boondoggles governments are so often tempted by. Whereas Kuala Lumpur has stifled two of its nearby signature projects called Cyberjaya and Putrajaya, the southern province of Johor's autonomy in negotiating FDI and hosting myriad Singaporean SEZs has propelled it to be the country's fastest-growing province. The strongly Chinese-populated northern city of Penang facing the Strait of Malacca has launched the Penang Paradigm movement to rekindle the dynamism that made it the first overseas location for an Intel microchip plant in the 1970s. Taking advantage of Western tariffs on the Chinese solar industry, Penang has attracted the U.S.-based First Solar and other investors to catapult Malaysia into third position worldwide in solar panel manufacturing. As one young Malaysian parliamentarian told me while driving around his district, "No amount of money can solve our political problems." But devolution and SEZs can. Bureaucrats in Kuala Lumpur would never come up with the ideas of designating bicycle lanes and establishing corporate partnerships to promote creative preschool learning the way Penang's own officials have.

Ultimately, countries should aim not to set up lots of SEZs but to *be* such singular zones of nondiscriminatory investment and one-stop efficiency. Slovenia, for example, has phased out its foreign trade zones; the country is a transparently run EU member with an educated workforce and competitive tax regime, so it no longer needs them. Hong Kong and Singapore have evolved from trade entrepôts to global cities with thriving societies and loyal residents from all over the world. What began as SEZs can become multidimensional cities with life beyond the supply chain. The Suzhou Industrial Park in China now has modern arts and cultural centers, a Liverpool University campus, and its own Singapore-style pension scheme. It has become a full-service community of belonging. Urban purists have nostalgic visions of all cities resembling Jane Jacobs's Washington Square Park. But while there is much to be adapted from neighborhoods that promote pedestrian civic life, many cities must urgently catch up to the present (and future) before they can become reflections of the past.

CHINA'S SUPERSIZE SEZS

No country has as many SEZs, new cities, and megacities as China. While SEZs have powered China's export sector and growth, many were designed as single-industry clusters that proved vulnerable to global economic fluctuations—remember Dongguan, China's Detroit. Just two coastal clusters of provinces centered on Shanghai in the east and Guangdong in the south have less than a quarter of China's population but have been responsible for 80 percent of its exports. Over the next two decades, however, as China moves an estimated 300 million more people (especially non-*hukou** registered migrants) into new districts of megacities (and entirely new cities) in interior areas, it wants to make sure that none are either too congested or too sprawling and all are large enough to be self-sustaining. On balance, the strategy is working: Second-tier cities

---

* *Hukou* refers to the system of permits that regulates Chinese citizens' residency rights in the countryside.

such as Zhengzhou, Zhuzhou, Hengyang, Xiangyang, and Guiyang all now have higher growth rates than their more famous coastal role models.

Because urbanization in China is both voluntary and directed, both a necessity and a land development boondoggle, it has built far ahead of demand, resulting in numerous "ghost cities" such as the infamous Kangbashi in Inner Mongolia, which is built for one million people but currently houses only thirty thousand. Regulations have since been modified to allow new construction only when city centers get overcrowded, resulting in slower urban growth but with higher utility—and hopefully quality: Because Chinese buildings tend to last only half as long as those in developed countries (fifteen years versus about thirty-five years), less construction now still means more later. The wrenching side effects of rapid urbanization—a mass of marginalized migrant workers, high local government debt, and an oversupply of housing in many cities—are all germane to becoming a collection of 350 million urban consuming households.

Many believe the future of the Chinese economy hinges on whether it can escape the "middle-income trap." As it transforms from a command to a market economy, it must move sufficiently up the value chain, raise productivity, and rebalance toward consumption so that most of its citizens can command higher wages. Can China's economic master planning and urbanization strategy come together to elevate its vast civilization toward the "Chinese Dream" of national prosperity?

In the summer of 2014, while traveling around the Pearl River delta region of southern China—a loop from Guangzhou via Zhongshan to Zhuhai and Macau and up the eastern side via Hong Kong, Shenzhen, and Dongguan—I witnessed firsthand how a country's economic master plan is as important as its military grand strategy. In 1990, a decade after China's opening to the world economy, primary industries such as agriculture, mining, and fishing represented 27 percent of its economy, while secondary sectors such as manufacturing and construction were 40 percent, and the tertiary sector of services (retail, transportation, health care, tourism, and others) was only 30 percent. By 2010, agriculture had fallen to 10 percent, and manufacturing had risen to 46 percent and services to 44 percent. A tour around the Pearl River delta reveals some of the most novel strategies in combining urbanization, SEZs, and innovation to breed megacities that become pillars of innovation and growth.

As capital of Guangdong province, Guangzhou has been the administrative nerve center presiding over the delta's manufacturing miracle, perhaps the greatest seismic shift in supply chains that has ever taken place. Guangzhou has many historical associations, from the thirteenth-century visit of Marco Polo (who admired its giant shipbuilding industry) to its role as a hub for the East India Companies of Holland, Denmark, France, and Britain. During the Chinese Civil War, Nationalist forces led by Chiang Kai-shek briefly retreated to Guangzhou. Ever since 1957, Guangzhou has utilized its key geography just 120 kilometers north of Hong Kong to host the annual Canton Fair, China's largest import-export convention, which attracts 200,000 buyers from over two hundred countries and territories.

Guangzhou's first lesson is the importance of administrative harmony. In addition to the Guangzhou Free Trade Zone, which was founded in 1992 to facilitate trade and logistical services for industrial products, the Guangzhou Nansha Export Processing Zone, focused on automotive assembly, biotech products, and heavy machinery, was strategically placed near the international airport and Shenzhen's modern new port. Then, between 2005 and 2009, several districts of Guangzhou were merged into more streamlined units, while Guangzhou and Foshan themselves merged to pave the way for a master plan for the entire delta region. While China strictly controls its borders to the outside world, its internal ones are coming down.

The second lesson from the delta region's evolution is leveraging openness. Being located near Hong Kong had its perks even before the 1997 handover from Great Britain. Not only has the colonial entrepôt remained the largest source of inward investment into mainland China, but the delta's export-oriented districts have used that investment to build modern facilities competitive with Hong Kong's. Shenzhen's container port terminal now ranks as one of the world's busiest, and with duty-free import and export and special five-day business visas more investors and traders can now circumvent Hong Kong and do business directly on the mainland. Even as Shenzhen seeks to surpass Hong Kong, its authorities have announced a plan to effectively merge with it to create the "Hong Kong–Shenzhen metropolis."

The Pearl River delta is also a case study in the clustering of capital, technology, and knowledge industries. Thanks to Foxconn and other manufacturing giants, by 2013, 40 percent of the world's electronic devices had some portion of their assembly done in Shenzhen, including products from Apple, HP, Microsoft, Nintendo, Samsung, and Sony. Equally important, it is home to two of China's most valuable companies, Huawei and Tencent. The Shenzhen stock exchange has also become one of the world's largest—growing at nearly 50 percent per year—with heavy trading of state-owned companies as well as its local heroes such as the alternative energy leader Suntech Power, the electric car manufacturer BYD, and many tech start-ups.

A city's architectural identity can adapt to suit the supply chains of a new century. As Guangzhou has graduated from factory town to financial center, its glittering central business district features the aerodynamic 103-story-tall IFC tower, modern art museums one would expect to find in Zurich, and an opera house designed by Zaha Hadid. Just outside the city, the Singapore-run Knowledge City and Guangzhou Science City were built to resemble a low-rise version of Silicon Valley, with leafy boulevards that feature bronze statues of Albert Einstein and the mathematician John von Neumann. Singapore has opened a branch of its elite Chinese-language Hwa Chong Institution while also partnering with the local government to develop new curricula for the South China University of

Technology, which already graduates some of the country's top entrepreneurs establishing companies in digital industries such as cloud computing and GPS navigation, materials engineering, renewable energy, biotechnology, and pharmaceuticals.

High-quality infrastructural unity gives the entire delta region a sense of seamlessness even though Hong Kong and Macau have unique legal arrangements with the mainland and movement for Chinese around this mega-zone is governed by a sort of postmodern *hukou* system. High-speed rail lines make the journey from Guangzhou to Hong Kong in under two hours. Broad highways, hovercraft and ferries, extra-long rapid transit buses, and a combined bridge and tunnel connection between Macau and Hong Kong all make the delta's cities feel like nodes of a much larger megacity corridor expected to grow to 80 million people with a $2 trillion GDP by 2030.

Another Chinese megacity cluster in the making is the Bohai Economic Rim, which links Beijing, Hebei, Liaoning, Shandong, and Tianjin with efficient high-speed rail connections. Sitting at the mouth of the Hai River with access to the Yellow and Yangtze Rivers via the Grand Canal, Tianjin has been a naval gateway into China for centuries and became a crucial treaty port controlled by Europeans after the Opium Wars. While it has always been a shipping center, the reinvestment of its annual double-digit growth rates has created high-end jobs in airline manufacturing and other sectors. Today Tianjin boasts China's highest income per capita ($13,500, which is $1,000 higher than Shanghai). Its downtown business district is now home to the most industrial investment funds in China, making it the headquarters for financial innovation and even commercial courts for intellectual property dispute resolution with foreign companies. Like Shanghai, it plans a free trade zone. Tianjin also hosts China's National Supercomputing Center, where the world-leading Tianhe-1A is located. Tianjin Eco-city, another project of Singapore's Singbridge agency, has been built from scratch as a low-emissions headquarters for high-end research and commercialization in areas such as LED lighting, digital animation, and alternative energy. Tianjin Eco-city may come to represent the inversion of what China stood for in the twentieth century: quantity over quality.

While Guangzhou is the capital of southern China and Tianjin a high-tech ecosystem, Chengdu is the unofficial capital of the rest of China. Better known for its spicy food and panda sanctuaries, Chengdu, because of its geography, has been designated by the State Council as the country's central logistics, commercial, science, and communications hub. It is connected by high-speed rail to nearby Chongqing, now China's largest city, and is the midway point for the high-altitude rail that climbs into Tibet. Chengdu has also lured ever more direct flights from Europe for the global firms that have established R&D and logistics campuses there. But their goal is no longer only to *export* from China but also to sell *into* China, specifically the 25 percent of China's population concentrated in six provinces located between Chengdu and the coast: Shanxi, Henan, Hubei, Hunan, Jiangxi, and Anhui.

Taken together, the stories of Guangzhou, Tianjin, and Chengdu demonstrate how the largest and until recently one of the poorest countries in the world has rapidly moved up the value chain and achieved broad socioeconomic transformation. The way these cities have strategically assumed roles in the global division of labor embodies the kind of economic master planning that every major city in the world must undertake to remain relevant in the twenty-first century. Focusing on the right cities and right supply chains lies at the heart of why China is the world's largest economy and newest superpower.

China is not yet so confident that it doesn't need more free zones to boost its international credibility—which is why it has so many that they practically blanket the whole country. Alibaba has even taken charge of an entire pilot zone on Hainan Island where it will provide its cloud computing and e-government platforms, as well as a branch of its e-commerce-focused Taobao University. If China ultimately succeeds in overcoming the middle-income trap, strategic urbanization will have been a big reason why.

MASTER PLANNING
FOR MEGACITIES

The more advanced SEZs China builds, the more even rich countries are picking up on what was once considered a poor state's model—both to stay ahead of and to connect to China's key new hubs. South Korea's Songdo International Business District is the most advanced such "smart city" effort. With zero-emissions buildings, homes outfitted with telepresence monitors, and large R&D centers for Cisco, Microsoft, and other major IT companies, Songdo is a high-tech hub serving the two billion people within a three-hour flight radius of Incheon Airport outside Seoul. South Korea is already one of the world's most advanced and competitive economies, and yet, as John Kasarda and Greg Lindsay write in *Aerotropolis,* Songdo is a city built "to fight trade wars"[4]—in other words, as a new Korean weapon in tug-of-war.

Other modern societies also see free-zone infrastructures as strategic levers. Japan's "Abenomics" includes deregulated SEZs in Tokyo, Fukuoka, and other cities where the government hopes to attract entrepreneurial private capital to lend credibility to its reforms. The London-based property developer Stanhope recently contracted with China's Minsheng Investment and Advanced Business Park to overhaul East London's Royal Albert Dock near the City Airport as a tax-free bridgehead for Chinese and Asian businesses.

Beyond wealthy countries, far more countries have megacities that need Chinese-style thinking. Population growth and urbanization have taken cities to a scale never imagined. The largest cities of the West—New York, London, Moscow—have less than half the population of the developing world's megacities such as Mumbai and Jakarta. And with the exception of Mexico City and São Paulo in Latin America and Lagos and Cairo in Africa, all of the world's most populous metropolises are in Asia.

Megacities are metabolic ecosystems constantly circulating demographic flows; daytime populations can be millions more than in the evenings. They are so large that major new infrastructures—even cities *within* the "city"—are needed so they can become less congested polycentric clusters. Those who can afford to move out of the downtown cores of Beijing and Shanghai are living not in "suburbs" but in satellite towns of gated compounds within the metropolitan orbit.* By contrast, the lack of adequate infrastructure (as well as the presence of militant politics) in cities like Caracas and Karachi has made them ungoverned black holes: expanding masses with immense gravity that suck in surrounding areas. Here urbanization is not high-rises, public housing, business districts, and sewage treatment plants but slums, black markets, and lawlessness. The arrival of each new peasant into the peri-urban concentrations surrounding cities like Manila and Jakarta, Lagos and Cairo, only magnifies the challenge of building sufficient housing or delivering basic public services at scale.

For countries to get on the global economic map as productive hubs rather than failed states, no investment is more important than basic infrastructure. Infrastructure is not just a road; it's a trampoline. As the former World Bank chief economist Justin Yifu Lin has pointed out, one unit of infrastructure spending unlocks more consumption than one unit of income. Ninety percent of the economic growth in the developing world comes from jobs in labor-intensive, low-skilled areas such as construction, textiles, agriculture, and tourism. The construction sector alone generates the most jobs of any sector. This should be the era of the urban planner and master builder.

There is nothing accidental about the need for up-front capacity in housing, transportation, health care, energy, education, and other basic areas. Building campuses for knowledge industries is so im-

---

* China's urban sprawl has hastened due to cheap Japanese and Korean scooters, followed by even cheaper Chinese-made ones, which muscled over bicyclists while expanding the effective range of commuting. While China is now trying to encourage bicycling again, other cities have learned the lesson and are banning scooters, taxing automobiles, building more public transport, and designating more pedestrian zones.

portant for the Philippines that it has set up a parastatal Bases Conversion Development Authority to turn military facilities such as Clark Base near Manila into zones for small and medium-sized enterprises (SMEs), start-ups, and joint domestic-foreign R&D centers. If it can train tech workers at a higher standard on its own soil, it is less likely to lose them to brain drain.

If the government cannot make basic infrastructure investments or harness its natural resources and human capital, it can at least become a facilitator for the private sector to maximize the country's comparative advantages. That is why heavily indebted governments—and thousands of their cities—are turning to the markets for finance and public-private investment support (such as the G20 is promoting) to jump-start their infrastructure needs. Even as the cost of hardware is falling, companies such as GE, Philips, and Cisco have stepped up to install solar panels to LED streetlights at their own expense in order to capitalize on the revenue from such utilities as urban populations swell. The willful construction of new cities from scratch or upgraded districts of megacities to accommodate burgeoning populations can make the difference between sustainable and inclusive societies and total social disorder.

CITY BUILDING AS
STATE BUILDING

There is no worse corruption than the oppressive inefficiency of societies where basic mobility is hampered by nonexistent infrastructure. It's like life without the wheel. Yet three-quarters of the world population—whether urban or rural—lacks basic infrastructure and utilities. In 2013, a rupture along a 250-kilometer water pipeline supplying half of Dakar's water forced many of its three million people to spend their days lining up at wells and water trucks. More than half of all Africans lack electricity, and 60 percent of South Asians lack sanitation. One-third of the global population still lives in deep poverty—including half the world's children—with the next two billion people coming from developing countries with inadequate health and education services. McKinsey estimates an $11 trillion shortfall in investments in basic housing.

So desperate is their lack of physical and institutional foundations that we should seriously consider whether the biggest problem with state building is the state itself.[5] It is not foreordained that all states eventually achieve territorial sovereignty and political stability. In many postcolonial regions, the supply chain world is taking root far more quickly than competent governance. Instead of taking today's political geography as sacred, therefore, we should get the functional geography right first, stabilizing and connecting urban areas inside and beyond their national boundaries to better align people, resources, and markets. This means *city building* should be seen as the path to state building—not a by-product of it.

There is no greater imperative than to build and maintain basic infrastructure assets. Dozens of weak states perpetually exist in a form of semipermanent trusteeship of international aid donors who use conditionality as leverage to co-determine countries' laws and policies. While such neocolonial arrangements keep states from failing completely and numerous populations from starving, they don't provide a long-term strategy for elevating the state altogether. State-building interventions in recent decades have been far too focused on ushering in democratic politics rather than rebuilding societies from the bottom up. It is as if the liberal intelligentsia has forgotten that the post–World War II Marshall Plan (officially known as the European Recovery Program) was first and foremost a $13 billion stimulus package to invest in rebuilding infrastructure across western Europe. The hardware came first.

It is hard to see how lofty goals of nation building mean anything without basic connectivity. From Libya to Iraq to Afghanistan, America's nominal efforts to support weak governments have focused on counterinsurgency. But to hold a territory, you must hold its cities. The mantra of "Clear, hold, and build" should be far more literally applied to building infrastructure and local popular sentiment; the latter is much more likely to come with the former. Building—and protecting—connectivity is the critical mission.

America's aid and stabilization agendas are competing conversations and bureaucracies, and where they have agreed on what needs to be done, they have been pitifully uncoordinated in doing it.* After more than $100 billion spent on half-baked projects across Afghanistan (such as industrial parks without electricity), the north-south Salang Tunnel, on which most internal Afghan trade depends, remains a crumbling disaster, forcing trucks to travel an extra three hundred kilometers and sixty hours through the Hindu Kush Mountains to get to and from Kabul. Similarly, the Kajaki Dam on the Helmand River is southwestern Afghanistan's most vital source of electricity and irrigation, but the United States may never complete its rehabilitation after more than a decade.

There will be plenty more opportunities to get it right: Other perennial rock-bottom countries on the Fragile States Index such as Somalia, Chad, Sudan, Zimbabwe, Congo, and Central African Republic are all resource-rich states in need of decent infrastructure first and foremost. The Arab Spring further revealed underlying symptoms of overpopulation, corruption, and inadequate infrastructure that are present in at least fifty more states.

There cannot be a successful country without a stable city. Do not believe for a moment that education and other "soft" priorities should take precedence over hard infrastructure in driving large-scale national development. As the economist Charles Kenny of the Center for Global Development argues, having concrete instead of mud floors in village homes could cut the incidence of parasitic disease by 80 percent, while paving roads boosts home values and stim-

---

* The United States has woken up to the need for an infrastructure focus by setting up an interagency working group that links the National Security Council and the Millennium Challenge Corporation to set up special-purpose vehicles that give grants for infrastructure but monitor them like private equity investors through board seats and milestones before disbursing more funds. Such structures have been used to bring new renewable power projects online in Mongolia and Indonesia and road networks in the Philippines better able to withstand natural disasters such as Typhoon Haiyan.

ulates economic activity. Prosperity isn't sustainable without connectedness. Even in New York City, the urbanist Mitchell Moss has argued, "it's far more important to have a MetroCard than a college degree."[6] Transportation and communication are the true pathways to social mobility.

As the world's urban masses become the overwhelming majority of the global population, the so-called youth bulge is not an impending challenge but an actual one. If it is not put to work today, then it will not earn enough income to stabilize socially and settle professionally. An estimated 30–40 percent of the world population works in the informal economy, a supply-demand universe if ever there was one. Hernando de Soto, the pioneering advocate of property rights for the poor, has pointed out that most of the self-immolating Arabs during early 2011 were extralegal entrepreneurs cut off from the capital they needed to start businesses capable of surviving food price shocks and petty local corruption. They represent the industrious yet dispossessed youth I've seen loitering around Morocco, Libya, Egypt, Jordan, Pakistan, and elsewhere—those who would choose jobs over jihad if the former were offered but take the path that provides them shelter and respect. Financial inclusion strategies for the poor won't stop Islamist fanatics, educated engineers, or thrill-seeking Arabs and Pakistanis in Europe from swarming to battle, but it would diminish their recruitment base, both in the region and internationally. "Draining the swamp" is done not through dropping leaflets but by investing in jobs. The way to hearts and minds is through the stomach.

Supply chains offer a remedy to the disorderly reality of failing states. They empower anchor cities of once destitute nations such as Rwanda and Myanmar to get a foothold in the world economy. "Being broken is a competitive advantage," says the post-conflict reconstruction expert Keith Fitzgerald.[7] Building up supply chain nodes such as SEZs can also be a solution to the problem of permanent refugees in unstable borderlands. Since the early 1980s, more than fifty thousand mostly ethnic Karen refugees driven out of Myanmar have lived in the Mae La refugee camp on the Thai-

Burmese border. But now the Mae Sot district has become a major gateway for the thriving trade in gems and teak (and black market in drugs and people trafficking) between the two countries as Southeast Asia's economies integrate. This has made it a hub for Chinese trading companies, Thai businessmen, and other investors who are working with the locally elected mayor—who is pushing hard for SEZ status—to make the creaking city an efficient business transit center.

SEZs are also attractive to countries that want to preserve what functionality they have left and avoid becoming failed states. The NYU economist Paul Romer, a champion of adapting the Hong Kong or Singapore model to the third world, has promoted "Charter Cities" in Latin America and Africa in an attempt to leapfrog their governance and economic planning. Honduras, the most violent country in the Western Hemisphere, has recruited foreign engineers, lawyers, urban planners, and investors to run numerous politically autonomous Zones for Economic Development and Employment, each with an industry-specific master plan. They are designed to get the legal, economic, administrative, and political structure right on the first try.

Nation builders tend to fail at political engineering. They should instead focus more on infrastructure and job creation and less on elections and political parties. One consequence of a world of smaller and less aggressive units, however, might be less pressure on these statelets or city-states to democratize. A global agenda more dominated by supply chain building than democracy building will simply want newly formed or post-conflict entities to be stable and economically viable so that they don't become humanitarian burdens (again). And yet it may deliver better governance in the end than what we see in the world's nascent democracies.

LEAPFROGGING TO
HYBRID GOVERNANCE

The supply-demand world reveals everyone's strengths and weaknesses. Talented labor, competitive wages, abundant raw materials, robust physical security, advantageous regulations, and other positive variables all attract sticky investment, while political volatility, unpredictable regulations, excessive taxation, poor infrastructure, lacking public safety, and other negative factors drive it away. SEZs are how most countries can shift their ledger from the negative to the positive side in the shortest span of time.

SEZs have become a de facto part of most national economic plans today, opening a window to modernize their institutions in a manner appropriate to the supply chain world. Some argue that SEZs are an easy way for governments to induce growth without fundamentally reforming—as if they would have reformed anyway without the incentives SEZs provide. But governments don't start to act the way they should simply because World Bank consultants suggest it. When land is given to political cronies, resources are siphoned and no social benefit ensues. When land is given to SEZs, by contrast, regulations are transformed, jobs are created, supply chains expand, productive assets are maximized, workers are trained, and local communities benefit. SEZs are catalytic, not parasitic.

SEZs are evolving into a new kind of polity, located within the sovereign geography of the state but globalized in their governance and functionality. They belong as much to the global supply chain as to the host country. The new hybrid governance of pop-up cities features one seat for the federal government, one for the host municipality or province, one for domestic construction or other infrastructure player, one for a foreign investor, one for a global technology service provider, and so on.[8] This way, all parties work to align their interests, and the encroachment of central governments can be kept in check.

And yet a supply chain world can bring severe whiplash as investors move assets to cheaper production sites and competing high-tech centers. Better infrastructure and regulations make capital more fungible. The bonds of loyalty that fixed investment used to symbolize are evaporating, replaced by the transactional calculus of supply chain masters. A decade ago, shifting production out of China seemed an onerous burden. Today Western, Japanese, and even Chinese companies have joined the tide of off shoring out of China to lower-wage countries such as Bangladesh, whose large-scale textile SEZs have overtaken China in garment exports. But as its textile workers' wages double, India, Myanmar, and Cambodia are waiting to capture business into their own SEZs. Supply chains put places on the map and also leave them to wither.

The competition among SEZs is now relentless. They can quickly be eclipsed unless they become economically diversified and locally inclusive, generating jobs in services and other areas that improve their organic city-ness. Governments thus make tough demands on companies to transfer technology and train locals such that even when foreign capital moves on, the supply chain does not necessarily leave with it.

CHAPTER 13

SUPPLY CHAINS AS SALVATION

*There is only one thing worse than being overrun
by multinationals, and that is not being overrun
by multinationals.*

—Ulrich Beck

WHO RUNS THE
SUPPLY CHAIN?

In January 2013, DNA tests revealed that the frozen beef hamburgers and lasagna sold in British grocery stores contained substantial traces of horse meat and pork. The search into the food supply chain led regulators from IKEA stores in the Czech Republic (so much for *Swedish* meatballs) to Romanian abattoirs. A French investigation of a Romanian company exporting clearly labeled horse meat led to a Cyprus-based meat trader owned by a British Virgin Islands–owned holding company that had relabeled the meat before circulating it around the EU.

In April 2013, London shoppers went about their busy weekday mornings. Parents stopped into Tesco and Sainsbury's to pick up Aptamil, a reliable baby formula favorite made by the French food company Danone, only to find it out of stock. For months prior, Chinese businessmen had been buying up as much Aptamil as they could from wholesale distributors and selling each carton for double the price on Taobao (the Chinese eBay) to mainland mothers

Maps 1, 24 and 25, corresponding to this chapter,
appear in the map inserts.

concerned about the poor quality of Chinese baby formula (from which at least a dozen Chinese babies had died of poisoning). British pharmacies and grocery stores suddenly had to ration the popular baby formula.

On April 24, 2013, the upper floors of the Rana Plaza garment factory and apartment block in the Savar district of Dhaka, Bangladesh, collapsed and pulled down the whole building. When the search for survivors was called off one month later, 1,127 people were declared dead, making it the deadliest structural failure in history. While shoddy construction, corrupt management, poor regulation, and chaotic response are typical of the Bangladeshi manufacturing sector, the unprecedented scale of the tragedy and the factory's customers—Primark, H&M, and Zara, among others—brought weeks of intense media scrutiny.

In August 2014, it was revealed that Western fast-food chains in China such as McDonald's and KFC had served beef and chicken that had been expired for several years. The meat was sold to them by Shanghai Husi Food, a subsidiary of their largest supplier, the U.S.-based OSI Group, and certified by local Chinese authorities. Who was responsible for the oversight: foreign restaurants, local meat vendors, or Chinese regulators?

Each of these four episodes from 2013 and 2014 was a major news story with dramatic implications for food safety, child health, textile workers' rights, and the image of corporate brands. All were examples of complex, opaque, and poorly governed supply chains spanning continents, revealing how they have evolved from transactions that need to be approved at borders into preapproved connections that invisibly penetrate borders. If the supply chain runs the world, who runs the supply chain?

Infrastructure is by and large like the Internet, open for use to all. Supply chains, by contrast, are like intranets, networks of collaborators. Standards are easier to enforce within intranets than on the Internet as a whole.

The phrase "interconnected global economy" has become a cliché. We take for granted that our fruits and vegetables arrive on ships from Latin America, our iPhones are assembled in China, and our IT help desk is located in India or the Philippines. Even when e-commerce cuts out the traditional retailer or middleman, the sheer complexity of production and distribution of many high-tech products has required a near doubling of the number of transactions needed to create a finished product in the first place. Thus even as our concerns about supply chains increase, our dependence on them grows.

It takes great care to trace and manage supply chains. The Rana Plaza garment factory in Dhaka was the epicenter of six layers of suppliers—clearly more than anyone realized or was actively managing. To ensure the thousands of uniforms they purchase every year are made sustainably, administrators and student delegations from United World Colleges (K–12) in Singapore travel to factories in interior Malaysia to monitor facilities' compliance with World Responsible Accredited Production codes of conduct. As of 2014, all school clothing is made from 100 percent recycled polyethylene terephthalate bottles and woven by workers in ethically responsible garment factories.

We cannot influence what we're not connected to. As Paul Midler documented in his supply chain tell-all, *Poorly Made in China*, China's state-owned enterprises face no market accountability to maintain high standards; their only aim is to cut costs. Witness the contaminated baby milk and Mattel's recall of stuffed bear toys whose eyes could fall out and choke children. The trust networks of factory managers rarely extend past the next link in the supply chain, let alone to the broader Chinese or global consumer population. It was six thousand *Chinese* babies poisoned by the melamine formula, not foreigners. No wonder many Chinese find American fast food safer and healthier than that of their local vendors who have used sewer oil for cooking—and why the Virginia-based Mars corporation has opened its largest food safety center in China.[1] The more supply chains internationalize, the more standards improve.

Firms not connected to international supply chains aren't connected to the growing ethics of supply chain governance either.

Only international supply chains—particularly of companies based in wealthy, liberal, Western countries—face consumer pressure points that can have impact where government regulation falls short. The Bangladesh garment factory and the jobs it creates might not have existed were it not for Western retailers, and its collapse would barely have been noticed by Western consumers were it not for their connection to those brands. Bangladesh's new building code is being designed not by lax local authorities but by a consortium including seventy European companies whose reputations depend on avoiding a repeat of the Rana Plaza disaster. Similarly, a franchise business can be more accountable due to strict rules set forth by a powerful parent company. McDonald's has more capacity to inspect itself, and more incentive to protect its brand, than any government can devote to monitoring it. Similarly, the West African societies where children work in cocoa fields don't raise wages or build schools the way Nestlé can.*

SUPPLY CHAINS WERE ONCE thought of as spurring a race to the bottom; now it is clear they are how countries race to the top. Even China and India needed to open to foreign investment to attract supply chains, stimulate reforms, and generate the capital necessary to spread development. As the Nobel laureates Robert Solow and Edmund Phelps have pointed out, foreign firms pay higher wages, bring in new technology, and boost worker skills and productivity. They inject dynamism and capitalize on people's resourcefulness. They help countries turn their Scrabble pieces into words.

The fact that so much infrastructure (such as utilities and afford-

---

* Supply chains can thus advance what Harvard's Michael Porter calls "shared value." John Gattorna, author of *Dynamic Supply Chains,* believes the very concept of supply chains should be renamed "value networks" for the widespread benefits they bring, such as adapting essential products to the price points of local markets, building infrastructure that benefits small businesses, and training and educating local workers. Stanford Business School's Value Chain Innovation Initiative manages a growing library around the social, environmental, and other positive impacts of modifying supply chain management.

able housing) and access to markets come from the private sector has engendered a new dynamic between capital and labor, governments and markets. This should not mean that we are heading toward a privatized world where those who have purchased welfare care nothing for public goods. Rather, it is an opportunity for governments to leverage these new models to deliver welfare to those they have left behind. The Edelman Trust Barometer reveals a steady decline of trust in government in the West and a steady rise of trust in business worldwide. Respondents desire a new mode of governance in which public and private leaders are more accountable to the people—mainly by being more efficient at delivering jobs and welfare. As states come to depend more on corporations, the distinction between public and private, customer and citizen, melts away.[2] When national citizenship provides little benefit, supply chain citizenship can matter much more.

Luring supply chains *in* is the fastest way *out* of stagnation. Indeed, hitching countries to the globalization train is no longer a strategy any serious activist or watchdog NGO group opposes. Codes of conduct and certification schemes help to monitor factories, timber harvesting, or diamond mining, but they are not a substitute for the foreign investment that harnesses resources and employs the workforce in the first place. Even in markets rife with labor abuses, Business for Social Responsibility and Human Rights Watch don't advocate boycotts but rather roll up their sleeves and work directly with companies to improve standards through training programs and safer technologies. Supply chains were not designed as a system of justice but have become a crucial vehicle for the delivery of rights.

The supply chain has thus become a circuit of belonging. Many multinationals have also come to view their suppliers as extensions of themselves, their mindset expanding from singular loyalty to shareholders toward responsibility to local stakeholders as well. At the same time, employees feel bonds to corporate headquarters and investors across the world who often contribute more to their livelihoods than their governments do. Where such progressive evolution has not occurred, labor strikes have forced huge write-downs onto the balance sheets of mining and manufacturing companies, teaching them that caring for the supply chain and everyone along it is a sound long-term investment. The more supply chain interdependencies expand, the more true corporate citizenship emerges.*

The paradox of the growing power of corporations is that even as their autonomy grows, their role as service providers does as well. Supply chain management has thus become a board-level issue, but expanding supply chain reach is viewed as a paradigm-shifting opportunity. Logistics operators such as Li & Fung and the largest retail conglomerates such as Unilever have modified their business models and delivery mechanisms to target the billions of people at the "bottom of the pyramid." They represent a dramatic scaling of social enterprises that use innovative packaging, distribution, and sales models that get sanitation, cement, mosquito bed nets, and nutraceuticals the last mile. If mobile phones can find their way into more people's hands than toothbrushes have, then clearly it is possible for supply chains to deliver the basic essentials to everyone as well.†

BEYOND THE LAW?

Energy and commodities extractive companies are perhaps the most permanent embodiment of the supply chain empire. When countries are desperate for foreign investment, they may sign away entire towns to foreign companies. In the late 1990s, Romania's government offered the Canadian firm Gabriel Resources the rights to Europe's largest gold and silver mine called Roşia Montană. But public

---

* As the reputation-building guru Simon Anholt explains, companies initially sign up for corporate social responsibility projects for cynical reasons—buttressing their image—but eventually they realize that doing good *is* how to improve their image. Anholt calls this the "loophole in human nature."

† Ashoka, the pioneering social enterprise organization, has launched the Hybrid Value Chain initiative to support businesses that deliver health care and housing to disenfranchised people and offer them "full economic citizenship."

backlash against the terms—75 percent ownership for Gabriel Resources—and the use of cyanide for gold separation forced the Romanian parliament to mothball the project. It is now reconsidering what it should get in return for giving Gabriel the "license to operate." Even though Gabriel is seeking $4 billion in damages from the Romanian government for breaching contracts, Romanians are emboldened to stonewall until they get a more dignified deal with more environmental safeguards. In a similar case in 2014, Chile's Supreme Court fined Barrick Gold and froze its operations at the massive Pascua-Lama gold and silver mine over concerns that its operations would pollute a nearby glacier. Against the enormous financial and lobbying power of the extractive industry, sovereignty is sometimes the best—and only—bargaining chip.

Latin American countries such as Bolivia and Venezuela have made a sport out of expropriating foreign-owned energy and utilities assets, with Spain being a particularly abused target. When Argentina capped water prices to ensure affordable water access (citing the emerging "right to water" norm), it was effectively a declaration of war on the water conglomerate Suez. But Latin governments have also learned that scaring away investors is a Pyrrhic victory—especially when energy prices fall. While Rafael Correa of Ecuador once declared Chevron an "enemy of the state" for polluting Amazonian territory during operations from 1964 to 1990, Argentina is now desperately wooing Chevron to extract gas from its giant Vaca Muerta shale formation—even promising to clean up its erratic investment laws as part of the deal. Peru has made itself the new darling of the resource investment community by making its laws predictable around income taxes, royalty fees, and concession rights.

Some of the largest Western multinationals are deeply dependent on unstable geographies—and vice versa. Since 1926, Firestone has operated the world's largest rubber plantation in Liberia that has driven the country's main export. While Firestone has been implicated in child labor violations and payments to Charles Taylor's murderous rebel regime during the country's recent civil war, it has also employed generations of families and effectively governs an entire town. In 2014, it rapidly stood up its own medical facilities to protect more than 100,000 people at risk of contracting Ebola.

Since 1937, Shell has contributed to most of Nigeria's oil and gas field production projects while generating more than a quarter of its global reserves. Nigeria, the most populous country in Africa, depends existentially on Shell's oil extraction for its budget, yet its population expects public services to come from Shell as much as from the government. Given the absurd levels of corruption, it is never clear who is in charge or who is exploiting whom. Nonetheless, the stability of all of West Africa, and the plans of countless investment funds hoping Nigeria becomes an African economic powerhouse, hang in the balance.

Make no mistake that Liberia and Nigeria would *not* be better off outside global supply chains—though they would be better served by stronger supply chain governance through policy innovations such as the Extractive Industries Transparency Initiative (EITI) that create revenue management frameworks as far upstream as possible, working directly with governments, multinationals, international lenders, and civil society to track production and profits while steering spending toward infrastructure and social goods. With an estimated $100 billion of offshore natural gas, one of the world's newest and poorest countries, East Timor, needs EITI if it ever hopes to catapult to the status of the next Brunei.*

Whereas EITI remains optional, new European corporate transparency laws and recent American legislation mandate that compa-

---

* New technologies in the extractive industry will force more countries to appreciate and harness its presence before it's too late. Rio Tinto, for example, employs sixty thousand people across six continents. Especially in the poorest parts of Indonesia and Papua New Guinea, as well as even Aboriginal regions of Australia itself, Tinto's services are what pass for governance: Minerals are the source of wealth; Tinto is the agent of development. But technology upgrades are reducing the need for human labor in its projects. The company now operates a giant fleet of autonomous trains and trucks at mines in Western Australia, has automated drills that deliver greater precision, and is using alternative power sources in some machinery to cut back on imported fuel on project sites. As with Shell's floating Prelude, mining companies may have less need to work with local communities even when they operate completely onshore.

nies clean conflict minerals out of their supply chains. But while this has forced companies to deeply assess and modify their sourcing practices for gold, tin, cobalt, tungsten, and other minerals, it has also left thousands of Congolese miners without even the meager incomes they earned before. Abandoned by one supply chain, they have no choice but to turn to another: militant groups smuggling minerals across borders to fuel insurgencies.

Rather than walking away from natural resources due to blanket regulations at home, Dutch companies such as Philips are at the forefront of setting up local companies to mine conflict-free minerals in Congo, with efforts backed up by social enterprises such as the Amsterdam-based Fairphone, which is working with Africans to manufacture their own mobile phones, offer servicing plans, and ultimately recycle them as well—holding on to the full supply chain. The supply chain is most useful when it is cleaned up on-site rather than scared away.

TO MOVE OR NOT TO MOVE?

The supply-demand world exposes some painful realities about what governments value most between natural and human resources. Many communities in China and India have been uprooted and resettled while their ancestral lands flooded to make way for dams and reservoirs. Botswana's Kalahari Bushmen had been left to their pastoral ways—until rich diamond mines were discovered beneath their traditional grazing habitat. Despite these shameful expulsions, far more people move voluntarily *to* supply chains than are moved forcibly *for* them. In Mongolia alone, at least 100,000 so-called ninja miners drift across unregulated mines panning for gold day and night, earning slave wages in the hopes of satiating Chinese demand. Even if all the world's climate refugees are added to the ledger of those wronged by the excesses of the supply chain world, the number is still a small fraction of the masses of humanity that are on the move to cities, factory towns, SEZs, and other nodes in search of jobs in the service of global supply chains.

And yet the great irony of the supply chain world is that even as people increasingly cling to the global webs that represent work and welfare, these too can disappear as global markets and corporate priorities shift. In just the past few years, mining towns from Australia to Brazil that boomed while exports surged have just as quickly gone bust, leaving residents effectively on their own with no alternative livelihood.

People in search of work often have no choice but to fulfill some demand somewhere, even if it is deemed immoral or illegal. Sex traffickers prey on low-earning or unemployed women making garments and handicrafts, funneling them from eastern Europe or Asia to Japan or Saudi Arabia. They are sleazy, profiteering middlemen, but they are just the chain, not the market. The actual solution lies in providing women with the alternative means to resist exploitation. In Vietnam, for example, women making bamboo roofs who have been put out of business by hyperefficient Chinese manufacturers have now found jobs making bamboo decorations for Gucci. New supply chains rescue them from the consequences of redundancy.

Of the estimated forty million people enslaved as bonded laborers around the world today, more than half are in four large countries: India, Pakistan, Russia, and China. When traffickers lure or kidnap young Africans, South Asians, or Filipinos and smuggle them to faraway countries (including an estimated fifty thousand in the United States), only directly managing the supply chain can stem the flow or legitimize the work. The state of California, for example, requires employers to provide documents certifying the origin of their workers. "Safe migration" programs engage with recruiters and employers each step of the way to ensure respect for workers' rights. This way they are neither stuck penniless at home nor indentured abroad. Such frictions against the illicit global market for slave labor combat the base temptations of market efficiency.

Sometimes the middlemen can be converted too. Soaring Asian demand for ivory has wiped out African elephants in the Congo. Chinese will pay up to $24,000 for a sturdy white tusk, even if it is only used to make fancy chopsticks. The Lord's Resistance Army has poached dozens of elephants in eastern Congo to fund its guerrilla campaign against the Ugandan government. Where the government barely protects humans, let alone animals, only outside-funded programs such as Poachers to Protectors in Odzala National Park can compel hunters into training programs within the more sustainable tourism industry. In Somalia, armadas of warships and private flotillas won't stop piracy attacks on oil and cargo tankers, while basic fishing boats would help Somali fishermen return to a more legitimate economy.

Bringing better supply chains to people is the only way to prevent them from being exploited by worse ones.

GETTING BEYOND CORRUPTION?

The world is awash not only in cheap capital but also in crony capital as trillions of dollars of wealth seeking safe havens from government crackdowns are laundered into real estate and other assets from New York and London to Dubai and Singapore.

The world's economic pie is growing larger, and everyone wants a slice. The same trends free-market advocates celebrate such as privatization and foreign investment liberalization also enable surging volumes of corruption worldwide. As Indian scholar Nayan Chanda elaborates, "Globalization does not cause corruption, but the opening up of a country to trade and investment by foreigners has created opportunities for bribery and malfeasance on a scale greater than at any other time in the past."[3]

Though we will never live in a corruption-free world, the question is how costly it is for economic and social progress. China's public expenditure is higher than any country in the world, and so too is the estimate of its misallocated capital, but then overall there is progress because the former's virtues outweigh the latter's vices. In India and Russia, however, corruption is crippling. India loses an estimated $100 billion per year in illicit capital outflows, whether through fraudulent invoicing or black money, an amount three times larger than the amount of FDI it receives. Africa loses twice as much each year in corruption and tax evasion as it receives in aid.

Generally speaking, more competitive economies are less corrupt, but today many of the fastest-growing economies rank very poorly on corruption.[4] Clearly there is a level of corruption investors can tolerate if it means guaranteed stability for their projects. Most corruption discourse fails to distinguish between the transactional or micro-level realities of getting things done (such as paying bribes to get permits) and structural corruption that is baked into the essence of countries in potentially irredeemable ways. Countries in the former category are much better off than those in the latter.[5] Malaysia, for example, ranks fiftieth in corruption but sixth in ease of doing business. In other words, investing there isn't cheap, but it's worth it.

While bringing in investment and supply chains may lead to a higher volume of bribery and corruption, they are also the main catalyst for reforming the structural corruption of dirigiste economies such as Egypt where the state makes all the decisions—usually bad ones. Most companies desperately want governments to reduce the bureaucratic inefficiencies that delay business and hurt their own people. And because they can move their capital to less corrupt countries with growing ease, there are greater incentives than ever for reform. A supply-demand world could therefore be more competitive but less corrupt at the same time.

THE GLOBAL
UNDERCLASS REVOLT

On a recent trip to Johannesburg, I didn't really get to see Johannesburg. For two days, I was confined mostly to Sandton, the neighborhood home to white elites, five-star hotels, multinational headquarters, and upscale car dealerships. You could be mistaken for thinking you were in San Jose, California, with classy residential compounds and cutting-edge corporate parks. The difference is that Sandton lies right in the middle of Gauteng, the fast-growing province that encompasses the capital, Pretoria, and is home to fourteen million people, mostly poor blacks living in townships and inner-city areas.

We live in a world of Gautengs. Whether the tech hub of Gurgaon in the National Capital Region of India or the chic malls of Makati in central Manila, the more populous and globally connected cities become, the more their countries feature a *double stratification*—not only between urban and rural but also between these wealthy, globalized cores and the expanding peripheries of underclass neighborhoods and slums. Urbanization has accelerated the domestic inequality that globalization has enabled.

Economic segregation has made our cities as stratified as those of the Middle Ages. As societies degenerate into haves versus have-nots, privileged versus disenfranchised, national unity becomes a myth. Maps that reveal the very bumpy landscape of well-being *within* cities are thus far more revealing than data comparing national averages of income, life expectancy, education levels, and other indicators.

Cities can be either humanity's most civilizing force, uniting people in the peaceful pursuit of opportunity, or cauldrons of marginalization. Urbanization and inequality are a combustible mix. Ferguson in 2014 and Baltimore in 2015 are reminders of the consequences of evaporated social trust in America. Across rich and poor countries, many cities have become more fortified than elastic, with police and paramilitary private security patrolling key public and private institutions. As Joseph Stiglitz argues, we are entering "a world divided not just between the haves and the have-nots, but also between those countries that do nothing about it, and those that do."[6] Far more countries fall into the former category than the latter.

Urban guerrilla warfare has a new face: In Turkey, the Revolutionary People's Liberation Party-Front, a Marxist-leaning youth collective that bombed the American embassy in Ankara in 2013 and hurled grenades inside Istanbul's resplendent Ottoman-era Dolmabahçe Palace, has taken its battle to the streets to combat corporate gentrification schemes that raise land prices while squeezing citizens to the margins. Simply creating more soccer clubs to pacify the masses won't work anymore. Even though urbanization tends to undermine authoritarian regimes by easing collective action, regimes can resort to heavy-handed policing in the name of maintaining stability in their all-important cities.[7] Governing dense, diverse, and unequal populations will differentiate successful global nodes from failing states.

The Occupy Wall Street movement that began in New York City was an early response to the marginalization of the masses—the so-called 99 percent—and a sign of what is to come. Financial markets have enriched the upper class, while outsourcing and automation have ravaged the working class. Economic inequality results in both political inequality—oligarchic rule by wealthy elites—and a weaker economy overly dependent on a narrow base of consumption. The painfully high long-term jobless rate in the United States reflects the plight of its mostly young under-skilled workers who have become invisible in the overall economy. The simultaneous yet uncoordinated mass protests from New Delhi to Istanbul to São Paulo (and the violence that rocks Johannesburg and Nairobi) are a reminder that the same dozens of countries considered hot "growth markets" also exhibit the revolutionary symptoms of ancien régime France.

This new global resistance—combining upstart political parties, networked labor groups, hacker collectives, and antitechnology activists—has caught the establishment worldwide off guard with its tactics and stamina, and its rumblings will destabilize more and more governments in the years ahead. While some have labeled such movements antipolitics, they are anything but apathetic. They have shifted the contours of economic debates and the metrics used to measure value creation away from only capital generation toward social benefit. The coming decades will witness many novel combinations of their network power. Marx is laughing from the grave: The global underclass revolt has begun.

Marx argued that borderless capitalist exploitation required an equally borderless proletarian response; otherwise the state could not be abolished in favor of a truly egalitarian society.[8] Today's globally connected supply chains give workers leverage because a disruption in just one link of the chain ripples globally. In 2015, labor strikes at California's ports led to delays in delivering millions of dollars' worth of Chinese New Year gifts sent from China to relatives on the West Coast. The bottom rungs of the supply chain have become a political force: In South Africa, the National Union of Metalworkers has splintered from the ruling African National Congress and formed a new socialist-leaning party.

In the tug-of-war between capital and labor, the latter is also starting to network as multinationals have. Manufacturing companies have long been able to threaten workers with moving operations to lower-wage countries, but unions are learning to build a more coordinated front. For example, Germany's IG Metall has been backing America's United Auto Workers efforts to promote unionization in the southern United States. Interestingly, it does so in its own interest: Mercedes has built a plant in Alabama that is taking jobs away from Germans; if Alabamans negotiate for higher wages, Mercedes could bring the jobs back to Europe.

Unions are also having a decisive impact on international commercial negotiations. In 2014, China's government-backed Chengshan Group's tire factory workers went on strike and scuttled the Indian company Apollo's takeover of the American Cooper Tire & Rubber because they did not want to work for a debt-saddled Indian company. Chengshan actually bought out Cooper's majority stake in their joint venture. Rather than expanding into Asia through its planned merger, Cooper has gotten smaller.

The spread of multinationals emboldens foreign workers precisely because they would not otherwise be able to protest so strongly against state-run employers. Chinese workers have staged major walkouts on Walmart as they seek greater leeway to unionize. This is emblematic of the arc of confidence communities go through as their initial gratitude over the presence of foreign investment gradually turns to resentment of perceived exploitation.

If history is a succession of aristocratic orders and class struggles, then only a new configuration of class will alter the cycle. As the world population nears its peak, we cannot pretend that demographics are a growth engine if only the same two billion people at the top are genuine contributors to productivity and consumption. The global economic pyramid—with the 1 percent at the top controlling about half the total wealth—has a thin "middle class" earning $4 per day and a fat base of about half the world's people earning about $2.50 per day or less.* The vast majority of humanity spends much of its disposable income on the basics of food and water, health and education—services weak governments scarcely provide. The world economy will continuously struggle to sustain long-term growth until this pyramid becomes a diamond—with the billions at the base elevated into a large middle class at the center.

When growth no longer comes from adding more people, it can only come from increasing connectivity *among* people, unlocking their potential to interact with one another. This is why the divide between the 1 percent and the 99 percent is a false one: While their incomes have diverged, capturing the benefits of wealth requires creating incentives for the 1 percent to invest its capital in more job-creating enterprises. Indeed, it is private companies such as family-owned German SMEs that tend to be more willing to absorb the

* According to a Pew Research Center report published in July 2015, although poverty is falling worldwide, only 13 percent of the world population can be considered "middle class," defined as living on $10–$20 per day.

additional costs of remaining rooted, while public companies are more likely to outsource jobs to cut costs and please shareholders. Private companies are also the forefront of holistic accounting that takes into account social capital. The Mars corporation, for example, together with Oxford's Saïd Business School, is studying the candy company's support for small-scale entrepreneurs in the slums of Nairobi, Jakarta, and Manila to measure their value creation to the community and using the results to rate the performance of Mars's sales managers. The solution to inequality is neither higher taxes nor tax amnesties but more inclusive supply chains.

Capitalist societies—that is, all societies—have defaulted to tacitly ranking people, both citizens and otherwise, by their economic value. China unofficially subdivides its massive population according to urban businesspeople, farmers, rural migrants, wealthy expatriates, and so on. Prime real estate in America caters to the top 20 percent, while retailers write off the lower 80 percent. Many governments clearly place greater value on foreign investors than their own citizens. The silver lining in what seems an otherwise crass and mechanically unequal treatment is that the numbers show—as they clearly do in America—just how many millions of people could be far more productively engaged nation builders. It is precisely in this large-scale urban and rural underclass that investment should be directed.

SPEND NOW, GAIN LATER

In recent decades, the combination of rapid Asian growth and high commodities prices spurred a super-cycle of wealth creation and modernization. The next growth wave will come from cost savings from low commodities prices and low interest rates enabling investment from continents of legacy infrastructure such as North America to regions seeking to harness their human masses such as Southeast Asia. Now is the time both to build markets and to connect them. Connectivity is the most important asset class of the twenty-first century.

For investors looking to capitalize on cheap credit and to commit assets to the real economy rather than phony financial derivatives, there is nothing more concrete than infrastructure. Infrastructure is an asset class capable of generating higher returns than fixed income and less volatility than equities. Though it requires debt in the short term, there is no long-term growth without it. The benefits of investing in infrastructure are immeasurable, creating flow opportunities that enhance mobility, boost productivity, and spur social transformation. As the former World Bank chief economist Justin Lin argues, capital markets, multilateral institutions, and other structural funds should focus on strengthening regional banks so they can finance large-scale infrastructure that creates jobs and connects societies.*

There is no better example than America's own Interstate Highway System, ushered in by President Dwight Eisenhower in the 1950s. Having participated in an exhausting cross-country convoy from Washington to San Francisco in 1919 along the degraded, muddy, and potholed Lincoln Highway (America's first transcontinental road) and then witnessed the advantages of Germany's sturdy *Autobahn* highway network during World War II, Eisenhower lobbied the nation to enact a "grand plan" of over sixty-five thousand kilometers of highways at a cost of $25 billion. To this day, it is impossible to imagine America's modern prosperity without it.†

The same is true of China. Since the financial crisis, China's economic stimulus has focused on infrastructure such as highways, housing, metros, and railways. According to Deutsche Bank, such

---

* Among the major international organizations devoting significant resources to global infrastructure investment are the World Bank, G20, Organisation for Economic Co-operation and Development (OECD), New Development Bank, and Asian Infrastructure Investment Bank.

† Studies by the Federal Highway Administration have argued that over its first forty years, the Interstate Highway System delivered peak economic gains of $38 billion annually to the U.S. economy by reducing costs of transportation and increasing productivity and generated more than $1 trillion in cost reductions. At present, however, two-thirds of the U.S. transportation budget is spent on operations and maintenance rather than new investments.

fiscal stimulus has delivered twice the multiplier effect on GDP growth as has America's monetary stimulus. While Western economists have criticized China for "over-investing," the World Bank has found that high-speed rail connections to over a hundred Chinese cities have hugely benefited productivity by putting companies and workers much closer to their markets and customers. Even as China's fixed asset growth decreases, the gains from efficient mobility are evident for everyday workers, Alibaba shoppers, and millions of internal tourists and migrants taking advantage of affordable transportation all across the country.

The lesson from America's postwar period and China today is that infrastructure is not a one-off investment but a set of connective arteries to be constantly nurtured. Prominent American economists such as Robert Gordon of Northwestern and Tyler Cowen of George Mason argue that the U.S. economy is plagued by falling productivity gains, poor infrastructure, a technological innovation plateau, declining education standards, and rising inequality; its transportation system remains too slow and inefficient to meet its export targets. And yet, deeper capital investment is the largest source of productivity growth in the U.S. economy. After decades of neglect, crucial infrastructures are now being upgraded and expanded. The investors Warren Buffett and Carl Icahn are reviving the commercial freight rail industry, and Google is rolling out fiber with speeds of a thousand megabits per second in dozens of cities nationwide. With Congress unwilling to spend on infrastructure as it did in the 1950s, only opening up the floodgates to more foreign investment can provide the capital infusion needed to put Americans to work on this project of generational renewal.

Countries that sustain high investment rates of 25 percent or more—in infrastructure, innovation, and institutions—have steady and lasting growth. Infrastructure investment is much stickier than factories, for roads and railways cannot be uprooted and sent somewhere cheaper. Governments searching for how to employ masses of people need to focus on both hard and soft infrastructure—nontradable sectors that are less likely to be automated in the near term such as commodities, construction, hospitality, education, and health care. These are among the highest-employing sectors in the world, and while they cannot be shipped out, they benefit from investment flows in while creating enormous second-order economic gains for overall welfare.*

Capital expenditure pays itself back in operational revenues. Today the IMF no longer preaches austerity but promotes debt-fueled infrastructure investment that creates jobs and boosts productivity through higher-quality transportation, telecoms, and other services. Smart governments are unlocking more investment for infrastructure by cutting subsidies, offering equity and loan guarantees, and setting up financial vehicles such as partnerships with the International Finance Corporation (IFC) and risk insurers such as the Multilateral Investment Guarantee Agency (MIGA). Colombia, Mexico, the Philippines, and now India have created special funds to protect investors, guarantee decent returns, and guard against political interference. The more countries open themselves to inflows from the multiplying pools of global capital, the more the financial supply chain can support real ones.

THE FINANCIAL
SUPPLY CHAIN

Balloons grow much larger than bubbles. Despite the tech, real estate, and energy bubbles that have popped over the past two decades, the global economic balloon continues to inflate and expand. Central banks have set ultralow interest rates and massively expanded credit, providing lifelines to treasuries and corporations while stoking a global carry trade whereby cheap money remains consistently available. Though global debt rose $56 trillion (equiva-

---

* For every airport, highway, rail connection, and electricity grid, jobs are created in repairs and maintenance, vehicle sales and leasing, retail and food outlets, energy sales and utilities monitoring, and medical and educational facilities. See "Strategic Infrastructure: Steps to Prepare and Accelerate Public-Private Partnerships" (World Economic Forum, May 2013).

lent to almost one full year of global GDP) from 2007 to 2014 alone, the world's major currency powers—the United States, the euro-zone, China, and Japan—continue to print money such that they have become their own largest creditors (meaning most of their debt is held domestically), insulating themselves against foreign sell-offs of their currency. Even as the next bubbles pop—whether Chinese real estate or American equities—the larger balloon continues to inflate: Bain & Company estimates that the world's total financial capital could reach $900 trillion by 2020.

Within the global financial system, enormous asset pools collect in and flow out of leading financial centers. Like the sturdy iron Silk Roads stretching across Eurasia, these vectors form a new "permanent capital" with longer time horizons, greater ability to withstand volatility, and stronger appetite to invest globally. The world's billionaires, whose total number has doubled since the financial crisis to more than two thousand, are emblematic of this trend. Billionaires are both individuals and *instividuals*—institutional individuals—that can operate on the scale of companies through their own family offices. Their financial orbits represent the world's single largest pool of capital at $46 trillion. They are joined by pension funds whose investable capital is over $40 trillion. While European pension portfolios lead the way in infrastructure investments abroad, Asian funds (which represent half of the top twenty) are aggressively joining them in scouring ever more globally for returns to meet their rising domestic obligations, along the way lobbying aggressively for China, India, Nigeria, Turkey, Mexico, and others to raise their quotas for foreign investment in specific sectors such as real estate, telecoms, financial services, and infrastructure.[9] Insurance funds represent another $30 trillion in assets that have been historically rooted in national portfolios but today have also become more like capital networks looking for greater exposure to local markets. Additionally, the most vanilla of financial products, mutual and bond funds, which collectively represent another $30 trillion, are increasing exposure to foreign equities as well, putting money into mid-cap and large-cap companies abroad while leveraging their growth to generate returns for mom-and-pop retail investors at home.

Official capital holdings have also expanded steadily in recent years. Central bank reserves have climbed to over $8 trillion, mostly concentrated in Asia, where governments are channeling ever more of this cash into government investment vehicles known as sovereign wealth funds (SWFs), collectively valued at $6 trillion, which are starting to deploy their capital in more adventurous ways across real estate, banks, and other companies (especially to compensate for falling revenues as oil prices decline). SWFs often invest with private equity funds, estimated to hold slightly more than $2 trillion in assets, or hedge funds that represent another $2 trillion in capital. As banks have become more regulated, hedge funds have moved far beyond just trading in public markets to offer credit services (like banks) while also acquiring companies (like private equity).

The more all these players invest in each other and co-invest with each other, the harder it becomes to disentangle them. A new terminology is emerging to describe massive yet diffuse entities such as BlackRock, whose $4.5 trillion in assets come from a globally diversified base: They are now called "alternative asset management conglomerates" or "diversified financial institutions" that manage pools of permanent capital they can invest across any asset class such as government debt in emerging markets. They constantly scan markets for trophy real estate assets, underpriced equities, fee-generating infrastructure such as airports and toll roads, or technology start-ups. By making direct investments in foreign countries and establishing joint ventures, global asset managers become one with local partners, getting around investment restrictions to receive better treatment. From sub-Saharan Africa to Indonesia, one in every four mergers and acquisitions deals is in an emerging market, but most are backed by savvy first-world financiers who provide crucial business insight and technology upgrades to bring local companies to the next level.

There are many kinds of "banks." Misinformed anticapitalist commentators seem unaware of how significant the linkage between the financial and the real economies already is. Both banks and non-bank financial institutions (from asset managers to credit unions) have in fact contributed enormously to project finance, retail bank formation and lending, business founding and cash flow, technology acquisition, and international expansion of hundreds of thousands of companies across the developing world. In America, these non-bank institutions have taken over the lion's share of the lending, whether to bail out millions of underwater mortgages or to fund mid-market businesses.[10]

The financial-real economy linkage is equally important in emerging markets. From 2009 to 2014, foreign holding of local government debt doubled, allowing governments to invest more and local banks to lend more (in their own currencies) to small businesses such as gas stations and grocery stores and to individuals for mortgages. Especially as growth slows and they are forced to draw down reserves, such countries will have to allow unrestricted foreign investment into their stock exchanges to ensure their companies have the capital they need to employ people and build businesses. Without the risk-taking appetite of private investors, credit markets across the developing world would be in as sorry a state as their infrastructure, undercapitalized and institutionally rudimentary.

Trade finance is a perfect example of markets doing their best to help people build connectivity. According to the WTO, 80 percent of global trade is supported by financial institutions, but postcrisis regulations (such as Basel III, which requires banks to hold more capital onshore) inadvertently choked this crucial conduit between the financial sector and the real economy that helps companies produce exportable goods and has proven to be a reliable investment given its low default rate. Funds such as the European Investment Bank and the Abraaj Group have stepped in to back region-wide funding exchanges for the Middle East and Africa so that SMEs can more easily raise capital. Germany has five times more such *Mittelstand* companies than the entire United States (which has four times as many people), indicating a much greater emphasis on rooted entrepreneurs such as toolmakers who can benefit from trade finance to expand to growth markets in Asia. The spread of European SMEs into Asia and ASEAN SMEs into the rest of Asia, Africa, and back to Europe is a testament to how channeling global capital to local companies creates real and productive new flows.

The financial crisis taught that too much capital concentrated in too few hands generates enormous risks. But unwinding global finance would be the worst form of throwing the baby out with the bathwater. Capitalism does not have to be corporatism. If financial markets are how capital is multiplied, then financial supply chains are how that wealth is spread. We should take advantage of the balloon of global liquidity to unleash more financial supply chains that link capital to value-creating assets such as companies and infrastructures. A world of greater capital distribution would be a more stable one.

PART FIVE

TOWARD A
GLOBAL SOCIETY

CHAPTER 14

CYBER CIVILIZATION AND ITS DISCONTENTS

The Internet is the first thing that humanity has built that humanity doesn't understand. It is the largest experiment in anarchy that we have ever had.

—ERIC SCHMIDT, CHAIRMAN, GOOGLE

INVISIBLE INFRASTRUCTURE

HE INTERNET WAS BORN TO OVERCOME DISTANCE: SCIENTISTS based at research stations around the world sought efficient tools to process and share enormous volumes of data. CERN, the laboratory where the World Wide Web was created, also symbolizes the border-neutral preferences of the scientific community in that it occupies a thirty-kilometer circumference spanning Switzerland and France. Today the Internet stands out as an embodiment of this quantum world. It is everywhere yet difficult to "see." It enables connections that can also disappear instantaneously. Data can be filtered and blocked; it also fragments into locked and coded packets that reassemble only for the intended recipient. Everything that is digitized can simultaneously appear in multiple places, whether a book, music, or even a "live" event. In the quest to compute more data faster than ever, scientists are applying the principles of quan-

---

Map 34, corresponding to this chapter, appears in the second map insert.

tum entanglement and super-positioning to multiply the capacity of photons to transmit data.

Yet while the increasingly borderless supply chain world was born out of the state system, the Internet seems to have been born borderless but is acquiring the trappings of interstate divisions. Which force will win the cyber tug-of-war?

What we call "tech" companies are very much technology *infrastructure* companies. Telecommunications has leapfrogged all other forms of connectivity. Whether through copper phone lines, signal relay towers, undersea Internet cables, or low-orbit satellites, handheld mobile hardware can now connect to any other communications device from just about anywhere in the world. Telecom companies spent $2 trillion on mobile infrastructure between 2009 and 2014 and will deploy another $4 trillion by 2020 to expand access and raise connectivity speeds worldwide.[1]

Connective infrastructure companies are expanding into digital empires. Google began as a Web browser but has become a global data utility. In the race to provide pervasive and low-cost connectivity, Internet service providers are effectively becoming telecoms themselves, with Google launching Wi-Fi Zeppelin blimps to connect off-grid populations to its services; meanwhile, Internet-based telephony such as Skype or WhatsApp has all but eliminated calling charges; there is no "roaming" on the Internet. No matter how much they compete for eyeballs and data, Google and Facebook agree that there is no higher virtue than expanding connectivity, hence their partnership to launch more satellites to serve the "Other Three Billion."* In the most remote corners of the world where there are neither hospitals nor electricity people have solar or motion-powered mobile phones. Without looking too far into the future, one can easily foresee a world where almost everyone has a

---

* Web user data, long stored in digital silos, is now being harvested for sale through increasingly sophisticated services such as Facebook's Atlas that allow advertisers to track users' digital footprint across mobile, tablet, and other channels to target ads according to device.

smartphone with 4G (and eventually 5G) broadband Internet access.*

Today at least three hundred undersea Internet cables crisscross the earth like yarn wrapped around a ball, carrying 99 percent of intercontinental data traffic.† When faraway places enjoy enhanced connectivity, the meaning attached to their location begins to change. Just one fiber cable has propelled Kenya onto the digital map, with Google, IBM, MasterCard, and other companies setting up research labs in the budding "Silicon Savannah." The landlocked countries Uganda and Zambia both got their first fiber-optic cables connected from the Indian Ocean in 2014. They are still physically landlocked but digitally connected.

Telegeography maps of Internet cable routes thus reveal the growing density of ties across vast geographies. The North Atlantic Ocean has the largest number of cables, followed by the Pacific, where a new seventy-five-hundred-kilometer Google data-link cable (simply named Faster) connects California to Japan and onward to other Asian shores to carry the projected tripling of Asia-Pacific Internet data flows between 2013 and 2018 to forty-seven exabytes per month.‡ As with intercontinental airline routes, direct Internet cable connections will gradually expand between South America, Africa, and Asia, reflecting their growing ties as well. The melting of the Arctic ice sheet has even made it possible to lay a new Polar-net cable over the North Pole directly connecting London and Tokyo. As the science fiction writer Neal Stephenson has written,

* There are already more mobile phone subscriptions in the world than people alive because many people in cities such as Dubai and Hong Kong have several accounts each.

† Many submarine Internet cables have been laid along the same strategic sea lines of communication where the British navy installed telegraph cables in the late nineteenth century. The telegraph was the first communications system decoupled from transportation. *The Economist*'s technology editor Tom Standage cleverly termed the telegraph the "Victorian Internet."

‡ Cross-border Internet traffic grew twenty-fold from 2002 to 2012 and accelerates each year.

"The cyberspace-warping power of wires changes the geometry of the world of commerce and politics and ideas that we live in. The financial districts of New York, London, and Tokyo are much closer to each other than the Bronx is to Manhattan."[2]

More than thirty million people are employed in the software industry, either as professional developers or in ICT operations. Interestingly, they are almost equally divided into thirds according to the Americas, EMEA, and Asia-Pacific geographies. By 2017, India is expected to catch up to the United States with approximately five million software developers. But software is one of the most globally connected industries. IBM, Cognizant, and many other "American" tech firms have more workers in India than in the United States, and more than one-third of "Indian" software production is for American companies or exported to the United States.

Many people take the Internet for granted as an invisible infrastructure, but in fact the junctions between the physical and the virtual worlds are growing with complex ripple effects. Just powering the ICT industry consumes 10 percent of the world's electricity, indicating what a drain on natural resources cyber civilization can be.[3] Data centers have now become lucrative real estate. The physical footprint of digital empires has certainly jacked up the cost of living in San Francisco. Amazon's demand for programmers, salespeople, warehouses, and data servers is redrawing Seattle's skyline. Hundreds of towns from California to Missouri have blocked Walmart from opening stores that threaten their retail outlets, but they can't stop Amazon from doing the same by delivering straight to one's door. At the same time, Bitcoin began as a niche cryptocurrency, but people increasingly live off it in the "real" world; if it acquires a banking license to issue credit, it could outmaneuver banks in reaching the bottom billions. Mobile transmission technologies are eclipsing the need for giant towers, and more digital payment and e-commerce mean fewer physical coins: Sweden is going cashless and Canada has stopped minting pennies, something the United States might do as well, meaning less consumption of nickel and other metals. So the Internet is powered by coal but saves us copper and steel. Even as borders between the real and the virtual worlds have come down, are they going up within the Internet itself?

WALLED GARDENS OR BUMPS ON THE INFORMATION SUPERHIGHWAY?

The Internet is a universe of flows and frictions with no governance outside the participants within it. Most of the Internet has been in private control since its creation. Today approximately thirty corporations control 90 percent of world Internet traffic; Google alone manages an estimated 20 percent of the Internet's content through websites, storage, and enterprise apps. ISPs, the current backbone of the Internet, prefer self-management and self-regulation to heavy state involvement. Furthermore, the publicly accessible Web is but a small fraction of the total Internet. The Dark Web of anonymous Tor-encrypted networks and Bitcoin transactions, the Deep Web of unindexed pages, corporate intranets, and other publicly unsearchable databases make up the vast majority of the Internet's content.

Though the Internet has no central authority, it is moving from its halcyon days as an ungoverned stateless commons with only technical supervision into a geopolitical arena of intense complexity. The Web's founding father, Sir Tim Berners-Lee, has warned against strategic manipulation and advocated a cyber Magna Carta that guarantees the Internet remain a neutral utility. But it is too late: The Internet already shows signs of both digital sovereignty and feudalism, with rivalries not mapping neatly onto political geography. As the U.S. Commerce Department steps down as the de facto Webmaster, the Internet's governance is evolving beyond the bottom-up, multi-stakeholder framework managed by the Internet Corporation for Assigned Names and Numbers (ICANN) for the past two decades toward a system with greater unilateral government interventions as well as international oversight through the International Telecommunication Union (ITU). But the U.S. government doesn't need to be the Internet's regulator to penetrate into its furthest corners and swallow infinite quantities of data: The PRISM program of the National Security Agency (NSA) enabled it to access almost everything one could want to know.

Perversely, however, it is the reaction to the NSA's surveillance programs that has "Balkanized" the Internet. Countries of all stripes have asserted their digital sovereignty, either to protect their citizens from invasions of privacy (Germany) or to gain access to more of their citizens' data (Russia). China is launching an allegedly unhackable quantum communications network between Beijing and Shanghai, with plans for a corresponding global satellite network. Whether these governments seek to monitor, filter, or protect digital flows, the geographic (and legal) location of servers, cables, routers, and data centers now matters as much as the geography of oil pipelines. The differences are crucial, however. Internet data can be replicated infinitely and exist in multiple places at the same time. Additionally, it can be rerouted or smuggled "in" to its destination, while the receiver has the ability to come "out" as well to access it. If data is the new oil, it is certainly much more slippery.

It is true that the Internet is no longer a truly borderless, parallel universe. Even Twitter, the world's most free and unfiltered medium of one-to-many expression, preemptively restricts content banned in various countries, while Google Maps loads tailored maps approved by national authorities based on the user's server location. Yet even if software or data services have to be customized to national restrictions such as after the EU's 2015 decision invalidating the "Safe Harbor" agreement with the United States, these represent only partial frictions, not blockages. Just because India, Pakistan, and Turkey demand that thousands of webpages deemed offensive to the government be removed from Facebook, it doesn't mean that the whole world has fallen prey to digital censorship—especially because copycat pages appear on Facebook itself as quickly as anything taken down.

Even China cannot succeed in its pursuit of the oxymoronic-sounding "network sovereignty." Governments deploy expensive systems to block certain websites, while far cheaper tools such as Tor, virtual private networks (VPNs), and uProxy enable individuals to circumvent such restrictions. Malaysian and Chinese startups have integrated VPNs into their apps directly to enable more users to access blocked content. Some filtering is thus not the same as totally blocking, which as Arab dictators have learned guarantees their citizens will come onto the streets to protest.

Setting the locations for the physical servers and routers is the geopolitics *of* the Internet, while cyber war is geopolitics *in* the Internet. Cyber war is a quantum type of conflict: Weapons are intangible, their power can be observed but not measured, and there are no fixed stockpiles or arsenals. There are also no laws of war for cyber war, nor is deterrence simply a matter of correlating forces. It is a perpetual war of hack attacks to damage military hardware (as the Stuxnet virus did to the Iranian nuclear program), steal corporate data (as Russian hackers have done to Western banks), or access government data and advanced technological intellectual property (as China's PLA cyber unit 61398 has successfully done against prominent American companies). The alleged Chinese hack of the U.S. government's Office of Personnel Management, in which data on up to four million federal employees was lifted from federal servers, shows that data is as susceptible to invasion as borders.

The more connected the Internet becomes to the real world, the more lethal cyber attacks can be, such as electromagnetic pulses that manipulate or shut down critical infrastructure. The "Internet of Things" has thus also become the "Internet of Threats." Hence today's spy agencies seek to recruit IT staff, not just defense officials. Cyber alliances have formed such as the Digital Five of the U.K., South Korea, Estonia, Israel, and New Zealand—disparate but advanced countries agreeing to securely host each other's servers. Palestine and Kurdistan act like virtual states through their Internet servers hosted in friendly territories, illustrating how the Internet enables even stateless communities to conduct elections and manage international diplomatic and economic relations. But alliances can also be illusory in cyberspace. Indeed, cloud communities take on not just governments but also each other, such as when Anonymous declared war on ISIS in 2014 or when a hacker group stole $5 million worth of Bitcoin from Europe's leading exchange Bitstamp in 2015.

The supply chain world's blending of geopolitical and commercial agendas very much applies to cyberspace as well. The NSA revelations legitimized a surge of techno-nationalism. Particularly in China, where PLA officers were directly named in an American industrial espionage investigation, Microsoft and Cisco were suddenly delisted from government and corporate procurement mandates, replaced by indigenous products such as a Chinese operating system. China also demanded that software sales within the country include backdoor access to source codes. China has taken some of the best foreign know-how and protected its companies behind the Great Firewall while they scale up for global competition. The UnionPay network to rival Visa, the BeiDou satellite network to rival GPS, and a new class of digital giants such as Alibaba and Baidu are all examples of Chinese products and services now competing internationally after (by default) securing the massive home market.

Rising frictions between Western and Chinese firms, however, still take place in the context of technological interdependence as represented by the vastly expanding flows of Chinese capital and data moving outside the country's borders. Chinese software developers, for example, greatly depend on coding platforms such as GitHub. The China International Payment System, launched in 2015 to accelerate RMB-denominated trade, will also have to communicate and exchange with international partners *more,* not less, to become a useful agent of extending Chinese influence. Digital tug-of-war, much like that over finance and supply chains, is about steering flows, not stopping them.

India, Japan, and South Korea have also achieved a degree of digital independence in that they have the requisite supply of engineers and domestic companies, market depth and payment systems, cyber-security tools, and other ingredients for a self-sustaining domestic technology sector that provides the full spectrum of Internet services. This cyber autarky is crucial in an age of denial of service cyber attacks and other disruptions. But very few countries can offer quality alternatives. For emerging markets such as Vietnam and Malaysia, attempting to build indigenous systems means wasting billions of dollars when instead they can take advantage of low-cost Infrastructure as a Service cloud-based software, data storage, and enterprise applications. In such countries, citizens also suffer the double whammy of having their data no longer secure "offshore" but vulnerable "onshore." Subjected to restrictions on online speech and data security violations, citizens mobilize not just on the Internet but *for* their right to unfettered use of it, shifting their data to new Google, Amazon, or other services safeguarded from government intrusion just as Chinese and Russian citizens move their cash abroad. (Amazon revenues from Web services now equal those from e-commerce.) Alongside the Web and the Deep Web, there will also be a "Safe Web." The cloud may indeed prove to be safer than the ground.

The more diversified a society's connections to the Internet are, the more its people can evade government censorship. But more ISPs and Internet cables also mean more redundancy for the government. Over sixty countries have only one or two ISPs, placing them at severe risk of Internet cutoff such as when China blacked out North Korea's Internet in late 2014. The Internet is often analogized to utilities such as banks or power companies, industries where small, local failures have cascaded into giant meltdowns such as the 1920s collapse of the banking system or the 1970s oil embargo that threw the world economy into recession. Preventing a similar type of cyber catastrophe requires building more distributed capacity for data storage and access: greater resilience through connectedness, not isolation. More connections—even those one cannot control—are better than fewer that one can.

The Internet was designed as a network structure; its purpose is to connect nodes, not represent nations. Even as some governments have installed roadblocks, detours, potholes, and other blockages within their geography, they have failed to compel the companies steering data to do their bidding.[4] Tech companies seek cover from the government when they need it, such as in negotiations with China or Russia, but also freedom from it, especially the IRS and the FBI. That Google, Facebook, and Amazon have dealings with the U.S. State and Defense Departments doesn't make them government surrogates. Indeed, the American intelligence community complains that tech companies are selling out their national security needs by working separately with European governments to conform to the privacy protection demands of their citizens while selling sensitive technologies to rival powers. Google and Amazon do not take any government funding for research so as to protect their intellectual property; in 2015, Google refused to participate in DARPA's robotics challenge. Tech companies' funding of R&D at universities to benefit their commercial priorities is rising, while government support is falling. Ultimately, it is the technology edge that determines who has leverage, not sovereignty.

Similarly, law enforcement agencies have used the Cyber Intelligence Sharing and Protection Act to justify more federal and police snooping and gathering of warrantless information, while the NSA used ISPs such as AT&T to boost surveillance of emails. But this does not make them government servants. To the contrary, the Internet Society continuously engineers Internet architecture to better protect against surveillance, while tech firms have actively invested in evading the excessive scope of NSA programs for their users' and customers' data. Lavabit, a secure email provider used by Edward Snowden, shut itself down in 2013 rather than hand over its SSL keys to the FBI. Microsoft has resisted U.S. government efforts to demand access to some of its users' data that is held outside the United States. Apple's iOS 8 and the latest Android both feature encryption protocols that no longer allow any access to user data—preventing not only the U.S. government but also hackers (particularly from China) who have exploited previous versions' back doors from accessing it.*

The Internet's earliest origins lie in efforts to create redundant communications in the event of enemy attack. Today it is becoming a network that can withstand any rupture, whether physically uprooted submarine cables or digitally disrupted services. The Internet now exists independently of the governments that created it; they function within cyberspace, not the reverse. The militarization of cyberspace thus does not prevent the Internet from remaining a universe of voluntary association, online commerce, and competition for mind share. Even as frictions emerge that block or ground certain data in national jurisdictions, still it continues to grow more diverse and complex. As with globalization, the system tends toward greater interaction capacity.

THE DIGITAL
IDENTITY BUFFET

Science fiction writers who extrapolate from current technology to pre-imagine scientific breakthroughs paint a large arc of human-technology co-evolution in which our present phase of multiplying identities through digital personae graduates to virtual avatars autonomously acting on our behalf in a parallel but integrated cyber universe and eventually a fusion of four-dimensional capabilities with full-sensory haptic experiences allowing us to teleport our minds to distant physical spaces without changing location. Then we arrive at the Matrix.

---

* The anti-NSA backlash has given rise to new devices and services to provide encrypted intranet-like communications. For example, large Silicon Valley IT companies are collaborating on OpenStack networking data centers that provide secure cloud-based services. Swiss companies are offering secure data storage in underground bunkers, and private data cables are being laid between San Francisco and Los Angeles. Silent Circle offers an array of secure software services such as operating systems and apps, as well as an encrypted handset called the Blackphone. The rise of quantum computing also promises unbreakable encryption and even cyber-security keys that will be able to detect eavesdropping through sensors that detect subatomic gravitational signatures.

While the "death of distance" has been proclaimed for decades, today's combination of urbanization and transportation, communication and digitization, capital markets and supply chains, together make a powerful case against geographic determinism. Each infrastructure investment and technological innovation advances our connected destiny. Indeed, the Internet is not merely a conduit for simple signals but the repository of complex data. It is becoming, as many scientists have analogized, something of a "global brain." The virtual reality pioneer Jaron Lanier argues that digital globalization "repatterns" the world, shifting our collective organizing protocols toward a new kind of network efficiency. The question is not whether this shift is happening but rather the degree to which everyone participates.

In the beginning, the Internet was a place to which we went; now it is a space where we are, a universal norm as pervasive as having a medium of exchange (money), system of belief (religion), or political regime (government).* Yet the Internet has more netizens than any country has citizens and more participants than any religion has believers.

Cyber civilization expands along digital rivers and tributaries much as human civilization has grown along natural ones. The map of the Internet is constantly changing, enabling new communities while remapping existing ones. Rather than national digital clusters connecting the way governments do, virtual communities assemble dispersed individuals and transcend physical geography. With the rise of digital e-residency schemes such as Estonia's, borders are no longer synonymous with formal membership in "national" services.

Geodesic maps that cluster cyber communities based on the density of ties within and across them show us this topology of digital networks and sentiments. Identity becomes an amalgamation of social preferences expressed through traditional categories such as re-

---

* As *The Economist* claimed in late 2014, "Hyperconnectivity is a new cultural environment for all human behaviour." *The Hyperconnected Economy*, October 2014.

ligion and ethnicity as well as newer communities built around professions, experiences, and causes. Danah Boyd of Microsoft Research, a pioneer in geo-social demographics, has tracked how digital natives naturally view the Internet as a portal of empowerment through which they discover and develop this broader set of identities and hold them to be as significant as those into which they are born.*

In 2014, the online community BitNation began piloting a blockchain-based ID system: Anonymous, decentralized, and secure, it provides a hybrid of a cyber passport and a Bitcoin ATM card. Virtual currencies have accelerated the rise of a borderless digital marketplace, within which multiplying cloud communities form what the political economist Michel Bauwens calls a "P2P civilization."[5] The MIT Media Lab co-founder Sandy Pentland calls these relational modes of identity building the new "social physics."[6] As the balance shifts between the importance of the physical and the virtual *where,* the government monopoly on media, narrative, and identity is disappearing forever.

Connectivity brings individuals the choice to belong to other places than those they do or to have loyalty to multiple places at the same time. We now incorporate some measure of our own sense of self-worth by our connectivity, not just our cultural and national identities.† The phrase "your network is your net worth" applies very much to individuals and nations both.

---

* Inspired by the work of Durkheim, social network analysis investigates relationships of all kinds—commercial, political, transactional, personal—to form a picture of the new kinds of nodes, clusters, links, and communities that emerge from connectivity.

† MIT's Immersion software allows individuals to depict their positions within networks of people rather than from a geographic standpoint, while companies such as Relationship Science assess a person's real-world network value based on virtual connections.

SPREADING THE
CONNECTIVE WEALTH

The Internet enables forms of social and economic capital that were unimaginable just two decades ago. We are each a unit of know-how—what Ricardo Hausmann calls a "person-byte"[7]—capable of adding value to global supply chains. Billions of people lack the respect they deserve as human beings but stand to gain a modicum more dignity as they become person-bytes in a connected global society.

Indeed, in modern societies one cannot get a mobile phone without formal proof of identity, but for the bottom billions connectivity is the gateway *to* identity. Getting a phone number is often a person's first legal transaction, yet most of the world's mobile accounts are prepaid numbers that require no deposit, bank account, credit card, or fixed address. And in dozens of countries where there are more mobile phone numbers than bank accounts, the former will simply replace the latter as a portal to both communications and banking.

We should not underestimate the intrinsic value of digital connections in a hybrid reality. Critics such as Harvard's Robert Putnam and MIT's Sherry Turkle who point to digital life as eroding family bonds ignore the importance of these new and more diverse relationships, as well as how digital communications reduce transaction costs and free up time for new kinds of engagement, learning, consumption, or investment. For example, Skype calling minutes increased by 500 percent from 2008 to 2013, no doubt bringing many families closer together while also enabling individuals to more easily afford to learn everything from the piano to Mandarin.* We should also remember that in low-trust societies such as

---

* In just three years from 2011 to 2014, the number of international "friends" people have on Facebook has doubled. Furthermore, as the number of connected people increases, the value of services such as real-time inter-language communication (via Google Translate or Microsoft/Skype) will grow in accordance with Metcalfe's law.

Latin America, social media are essential to circulate accurate information to circumvent elite lies.

Connectivity is the platform for fuller societal development. IT is the fastest-growing and most dynamic sector of the global economy. New technologies have always given rise to entire new industries as their infrastructures are installed and then deployed widely. Since the Industrial Revolution, canals, railways, electricity, highways, telecoms, and the Internet have all followed this pattern, each enabling what the London School of Economics economist Carlota Perez calls a "quantum leap in productivity and quality across all industries."[8] Through bubbles and recessions, societies learn to guide these new technological forces to reduce inequalities arising in the installation phase by investing in education and inclusion during the deployment phase to build a new base of skilled workers. Fiber cables gave an edge to high-frequency traders, but Google Fiber is already being deployed for the masses. City governments are routing fiber cables through sewer systems, turning phone booths into Wi-Fi hot spots, and adding Wi-Fi service to subway trains.

By 2030, everyone in the world will likely have his or her own mobile phone and access to the Internet via smartphone, Wi-Fi hot spot, or mesh network. The more high-speed bandwidth is deployed across the world, the more citizens and consumers benefit from greater access to information, lower-cost products, and enhanced opportunities for employment. In the meantime, where physical connectivity is slow to catch up, digital infrastructure can compensate. "Bits to compromise for lack of atoms," muses Tom Standage.[9] Lacking libraries, people can access an infinitely larger empire of information on the Internet. The technology philosophers Manuel Castells and Pekka Himanen argue that such "informational development"—the capacity to advance one's own dignity through access to information—has become a fundamental right both for personal empowerment and for economic productivity.

Connecting to global flows creates jobs and brings wealth. It is not the Indian economy that unleashed the talents of its population but the digital supply chains that enabled its astounding rise up the ladder from services importer to exporter. Furthermore, countries that export lucrative services such as computer programming, back-office research, and medical X-ray consultation get the double bonus of attracting far more foreign investment into these sectors: more investment in, more exports out. The cost of financing technology companies has also plummeted. Venture capitalists and Wall Street banks now coexist in a much larger funding ecosystem alongside family offices, angel investors, and crowd-funding platforms such as Kickstarter, collectively delivering more capital more effectively than cumbersome public markets did in the past.

But the new economy needs the old economy: Digital services advance through modernized infrastructure. It is the combination of improved physical infrastructure and e-commerce that makes the supply chain world an increasingly seamless physical-virtual hybrid marketplace of goods, services, payments, and delivery. This can go global: Alibaba's fusion of e-commerce, logistics, and lending has made it a supply chain giant that has invested in partner firms from Israel to Singapore, with huge scope for growth in the United States. Its novel Alipay lending service also makes it a bank that recirculates capital among members—a credit union with a negligible default rate. If basic e-commerce regulations were standardized, the hundreds of thousands of SMEs around the world that trade internationally could better connect to and sell in growth markets. Ninety percent of eBay's commercial vendors have some cross-border sales. In a world where customs frictions remain a major bureaucratic headache, e-commerce "green lanes" can smooth the flow of legitimate goods across borders that are often still managed by corrupt agencies that siphon cash by slapping on phony border taxes. The more digital flows overcome physical borders, the more connectivity can benefit everyone.

THE GLOBAL
DIGITAL WORKFORCE

At any given time, my wife and I might be employing a Filipino during a typhoon, an Indian during a power outage, a Ukrainian during a war, a Tunisian during an upheaval—and even once a Malaysian unfortunately named Saddam Hussein—to manage our schedules or do Internet searches. They all work on short-term, delivery-based tasks via Upwork, the largest of the mushrooming number of virtual work portals (alongside Amazon's Mechanical Turk and Freelancer.com) that collectively provide at least 100 million people with more income than they would otherwise have. While Silicon Valley technology companies employ fewer workers than their industrial-age counterparts such as General Motors, their global services platforms facilitate portable and digital work for the connected masses whether posting advertisements, verifying addresses, photographing for registries, comparing prices for companies, or performing other basic tasks. A digital middle class is emerging whose prerequisite is not a broad consumer base or even a market economy but online connectivity.

Economists such as Ronald Coase sought to determine the optimal size of firms to reduce transaction costs in carrying out certain functions efficiently. Today's network structures that leverage growing frictionless connectivity shatter previous assumptions by expanding in scale without commensurate growth in size. Even as traditional productivity metrics still fail to capture all the benefits created by such connectivity, innovation itself very much depends on it. Digital supply chains are now dispersed by design, with companies (both those fixed in one place and those operating distributed workforces) seeking to engineer serendipity among colleagues through shared work spaces and online tools that allow for constant crowdsourcing among people who have never met. Data forensics reveals how coders from diffuse geographies swarm to collaborate on projects and build partnerships that last across diverse gigs.

The rapid emergence of a competitive global digital labor market is, however, a double-edged sword for the average Western consumer-worker. While many Asians on Upwork work three to four jobs simultaneously from public squares or coffee shops, under-skilled Americans face cyber-structural unemployment—especially with half of all jobs in advanced economies in tradable services sectors. If they are lucky, they just face a role reversal: Much as thousands of Indian call center workers have lived nocturnally to meet the needs of American customers, many American programmers and designers now work all night to service their Asian clients. Even then, they often work alone: Fifty-three million Americans were identified as freelancers in 2014, more than one-third of the entire workforce, and the number will only grow.* As many large companies either downsize or shift toward part-time models to assemble their teams on an as-needed basis, postindustrial society becomes a collection of digital temps not employed directly by their client but mediated through portals such as Wonolo, which acts as a task-brokering agency for Coca-Cola and other firms but provides employment for only hours at a time at short notice. The fastest-growth category of jobs in America is "perma-temps" who live off assignments garnered from sites such as TaskRabbit or Fiverr (where each gig earns $5).

When we speak about countries moving up the value chain, we have to specify whether we are referring to their companies or their people. While America's tech companies are the world's most innovative, the most common job in thirty out of the fifty U.S. states is truck driver: non-tradable, but perhaps soon automatable. Technological automation is making millions of even white-collar workers redundant through the growing analytic capacity of algorithms. Unless employees are re-skilled or up-skilled, they may drag society down even as the economy grows more productive and efficient with a smaller workforce.

Progressive governments are finding ways to harness the new reality of masses of part-time workers. The U.K.'s Slivers of Time

---

* This means self-employed, independent, part-time, or contingent workers.

program, which is funded by the government but privately run, creates micro-work scaled to one's availability, adding income to families while generating upwards of $500 million in annual tax revenue. In the aftermath of the financial crisis, Germany introduced a *Kurzarbeit* scheme to keep workers in their jobs part-time while using their remaining time to up-skill in programs jointly funded by industry, unions, and government.

Is the sharing economy another path to economic salvation? Platforms that enable the rental of assets owned by others such as automobiles or housing have created economic activity that is expected to reach over $300 billion by 2020. Uber and Airbnb enjoy skyrocketing valuations because they provide the marketplace for billions of connected individuals to transact among themselves. Sharing economy is in fact a misnomer: It is rather the full flourishing of self-regulated peer-to-peer capitalism, one in which people get paid for work in micro-increments, but as they do, connectivity becomes the foundation of whatever stability they have.

The nineteenth-century sociologist Émile Durkheim would celebrate today's shift from vertical dependencies toward horizontal interdependencies. Durkheim is as much the oracle for the cyber revolution as he was for the early Industrial Revolution, during which he witnessed rising worker specialization and argued that the "growth in the volume and dynamic density of societies modifies profoundly the fundamental conditions of collective existence."[10] By "dynamic density," he meant the quantity, velocity, and diversity of transactions that take place in an ever-expanding division of labor. The workforce that thrives on distributed tasks and sharing services is forming its own unions to gain a greater voice in cyber capitalism. Cross-industry groups such as Freelancers Union have grown in membership and influence as they advocate for higher minimum wages and offer flexible health insurance packages. The more robots and algorithms automate human labor, the more we will rely on our connectivity to each other for our economic well-being.

CHAPTER 15

THE GREAT DILUTION

A MONGREL CIVILIZATION

As a teenager, I used to be confused for Pete Sampras. It turns out it wasn't because of my serve-volley game and running forehand. In mid-2014, several months after mailing in a cheek swab of saliva to *National Geographic*'s Genographic Project (as nearly one million people in 140 countries have done), I logged in to read the results. To my dismay, it turns out my genetic ancestry is a blur of 22 percent Mediterranean (Sampras's family emigrated from Greece), 17 percent Southeast Asian, 10 percent northern European, and only about 50 percent Southwest Asian. And I thought I was just an un-exotic Punjabi.

National Geographic's data suggests that mankind's ancestry is mixed in ways few anthropologists even realized. Since man wandered out of Africa over sixty thousand years ago—the first wave of globalization—large-scale genetic mixing has occurred at regular junctures. Native Americans, for example, are descended as much from European and Middle Eastern genes as from the Altai region of Siberia.

Maps 35, 36, and 37, corresponding to this chapter, appear in the second map insert.

———

OUR GLOBAL GENETIC DILUTION is not a new phenomenon but a continuous process—accelerating through global connectivity. More than 300 million people are classified as expatriates living outside their country of origin, more than ever in history, their perpetual circulation leading to ever more demographic blending. Chinese and Asian migrants are intermarrying from America to Africa. Like climate change, interracial dilution is a gradual process advancing mostly without our noticing until suddenly it makes a quantum leap.

Today's mass, permanent migrations are remapping entire continents: North America is becoming a mestizo (European and Native American), Latin, and Asian mélange, Europe is blending with North African, Turkish, and Arab peoples, Afro-Arabian cultures continue their blending across the Red Sea, and Sino-Siberia is emerging in the Far East. If "demography is destiny"—as is also claimed—then our destiny is a global mongrel civilization.

Some also say, "Culture is destiny." Which culture are they talking about? Migration and racial mixing have made creating pure nation-states increasingly difficult despite centuries of wars fought precisely to create them. In fifteenth-century post-Reconquista Spain, the Crown sought to measure the purity of Spanish blood out of suspicion that many recent Christian converts (whether Muslim Moors or Sephardic Jews) retained secret loyalties to their original faiths. The *Limpieza de Sangre* policy forced individuals to kneel before a council at the Church of Córdoba and recount the names and birthplaces of several preceding generations to determine down to one thirty-second one's racial purity. It was, of course, in vain.

Today there are just over one dozen actual nation-states left in the world (defined as states that are exclusively home to one ethnic group): Albania, Armenia, Bangladesh, Egypt, Hungary, Iceland, Japan, Lebanon, Maldives, Malta, Mongolia, Poland, and

Portugal—with Bangladesh more populous than all the rest put together. Even the most recent two centuries of violent ethno-nationalist movements across Europe achieved political devolution but ultimately not ethnic purity. Instead, paradoxically, they also created the need for greater migration and thus dilution. The nation-state is quite literally becoming passé.

The xenophobic tone of European populists may lead us to believe that the retrenchment of national identity is the dominant sociopolitical theme of our time. It is not. Quite the opposite: The world's structural imbalances between rich and poor, young and old, and the ceaseless demographic dilution and cultural adjustments they necessitate are the greatest sociological phenomena of our era (alongside the impact of the Internet).

It is in Europe, where the modern nation-state was born, that its disappearance is occurring most rapidly. Despite attempts to curb immigration—especially after the November 2015 terrorist attacks in Paris—the steady flow of migrants continues. As with Latinos in the United States, African and Arab migrants in Europe tend to stay longer than expected and have higher birthrates than indigenous populations. The descendants of Turkish *Gastarbeiter* in Germany make up close to 5 percent of its population. The European cities with the highest Muslim populations—Brussels, Birmingham, Antwerp, Amsterdam, Marseilles, and Malmö—have entire neighborhoods consisting only of migrants. Marseilles is either the most African city in Europe or an African city in Europe. In London, more than 10 percent of children are now born to couples mixing African or South Asian with Anglo-European; Muhammad is the most popular name for newborn boys.

The number of refugees and asylum seekers—from both the Middle East and Africa—has also reached record levels. One million such migrants entered Europe in 2015 alone. The same upgraded rail networks and open borders that have promoted eastern Europe's modernization have also become pathways for hundreds of thousands fleeing the turbulent Middle East—even sneaking into the Chunnel at Calais in France to reach Britain. Many have taken even greater risks. Arabs from Syria and Africans from Eritrea pay extortionate fees to people smugglers who overcrowd them on rickety ferries that have sunk in the Mediterranean Sea, which European ministers have likened to a "graveyard." The EU's Frontex agency has been equipped with speedboats, patrol ships, and aircraft to interdict migrant vessels and set up processing centers on tiny Malta in the hopes of repatriating migrants to Africa rather than allowing them onto the mainland.* Without a pan-European migration policy, the free mobility Europeans have enjoyed since the 1980s Schengen Agreement is giving way to fences and filters.

And yet even as greater frictions are imposed on migration, the trend is clearly toward more flows. Recognizing the inevitable humanitarian burden, Germany is considering housing as many as one million migrants in the growing number of abandoned towns of the former East Germany as the national population ages and shrinks. One Egyptian billionaire has offered to buy a depopulated Greek or Italian island to repurpose for housing Arab refugees. Should the island's sovereignty matter more than its utility?

The United States expelled at least two million Mexican migrants during Obama's presidency, while Spain passed a law in 2014 allowing it to expel illegal North Africans en masse. By and large, however, countries that have capped immigration such as the U.K. or ejected foreign workers such as Saudi Arabia and Malaysia—in the hopes of both cutting unemployment and encouraging citizens to join the labor force—have observed that domestic and foreign labor often don't compete, because they largely belong to different— and highly complementary—circuits.† Not enough Americans will pick fruit and cotton to replace Latinos nor become a sufficient number of nurses and nannies to replace Filipinos. The older Amer-

---

* Australia has established entire artificial towns of detention centers in Papua New Guinea to deter migrants from trying to enter Australia at all. In 2015, Malaysia, Indonesia, and Thailand let boatloads of Bengali migrants simply float helplessly in the Andaman Sea.

† In 2011, Kuwait barred nationals of six countries—Pakistan, Iran, Syria, Yemen, Iraq, and Afghanistan—from entering the country.

icans get, the *more* immigrants the country needs to fulfill essential social functions rather than fewer. At the same time, the United States has learned that expelling Mexicans doesn't expel Mexican problems, which flow back in the form of the drug trade and gang violence. If migrants are sent back, they should be armed with skills and money to stabilize their own countries to eventually diminish the urge to migrate. Spain has learned the same lesson with Morocco: As soon as it cut aid across the Mediterranean, even more Moroccans sought to illegally enter the Spanish enclaves of Ceuta and Melilla. One way or the other, they eventually make it, changing Europe's social fabric in the process.

Over time, immigration has changed the complexion of European elites as well. Germany's 1954 World Cup championship team was made up entirely of ethnic Germans; its 2014 team was half foreign players who have become German citizens. The head of Germany's Green Party is Turkish, and a recent health minister was Vietnamese. Five hundred years since the Dutch humanist after which it was named, one-third of university students participating in the Erasmus educational exchange program have married a foreigner, producing over one million mixed-nationality "Eurobabies"—the first generation of post-national Europeans.[1] European genes are mixing globally as well: Danish and British sperm dominate the donor fertilization market, giving birth to two thousand half-European children across seventy countries each year. European genes are spreading even as populations decline at home.

By 2100, Japan's indigenous population is expected to plummet to about fifty million people, less than half its present size. Given their sub-replacement fertility rates, the choice for Europe, Japan, and other aging societies is immigration or demographic demise. Neither tax revenue nor infrastructure upgrades nor social services can be maintained without inflows of young workers from wherever they can be recruited. The fact that anti-immigrant agitation is prevalent in some European countries today therefore says little about the decisions they will be forced to make as their demographic imbalances become even more acute and they realize that greater migration is win-win, providing labor to care for natives and consumers who pay taxes that support social spending.

The tribal definition of the national "self" is being overtaken by reality, evolving toward norms more inclusive of diverse groups that legitimately call the tribalists' nation home. Remember that France's ban on head scarves and Dutch language requirements are *assimilation* policies. With public debts soaring, there is a pragmatic need to leverage migrants rather than continuing to view them as a burden. Farsighted countries create incentives for migrants to contribute in services what they cannot in wealth such as working in sanitation and infrastructure upkeep, while higher-skilled migrants work in health care and foreigner integration programs.* The blending will continue; the only question is whether cultural assimilation will succeed.

For close to three centuries, America has been the most attractive destination for talented migrants and the greatest assimilation society. Immigrants have founded almost half of Silicon Valley startups, and immigrant children have been high achievers in the classroom and now fill the professional class. They are a reminder that an America of only Americans would be nothing like the America with non-Americans who have become Americans.

But it is Australia that now leads the Organisation for Economic Co-operation and Development (OECD) by percentage of foreign-born residents at 27 percent, followed by Canada at 20 percent. The United States has the world's largest migrant stock of over forty million people, but this falls near the OECD average of 12 percent. Also, in light of America's enormous geographic size and history of immigration, a large foreign population in America feels much less like culture shock than it does in smaller European countries. Part of the reason Australia and Canada have such high immigration

---

* Migrant remittances also keep families afloat in their home countries, discouraging even larger numbers of migrants from fleeing in economic desperation.

rates is that they compete with America for global talent. The best and brightest from around the world no longer go only to America by default.

Western immigration patterns are showing signs of veering away from melting pot virtues toward more salad bowl effects as ethnic Hispanic and Asian enclaves seek sociocultural stability. Chinese, Indian, Pakistani, and other Asian migrants have become the largest share of new immigrants in the United States, the U.K., Canada, and Australia, with Arabic and Urdu the fastest-growing languages spoken at home in America. This has gradually reshaped electoral politics and parliamentary composition. One candidate for a seat representing a district of Toronto described the landscape as "the endless micro-geopolitics of wooing Armenians, Greeks—and don't forget the 'Macedonians'—Ismailis, Sikhs, and Filipinos, not to mention Koreans and Persians—both regime types and Shah loyalists. Then there are the Jews and mainland Chinese. Alliances are forming and shifting."[2] This is what postmodern democratic politics looks like in mongrelized communities.

The combination of urbanization and immigration has made Toronto—alongside London, New York, Dubai, and Singapore—one of the world's most diluted cities with as many or more foreign-born residents as native populations. Because cities must be open to trade (and traders) to survive, they are what the political theorist Benjamin Barber calls "naturally networked,"[3] evolving from the ancient homogeneous polis to the connected and diverse cosmopolis of today. A world that looks less like Iceland and more like Toronto, less Tokyo and more Dubai, needs a new political frame. Countries will have to hold themselves together through common laws and post-racial identities. When David Cameron was pressured by church groups in 2014 to declare that Britain should be a proud "Christian country," he faced a backlash from many who cling to Britain as a multi-faith or nonreligious society—something Londoners take for granted. A better articulation came from Tony Blair a decade earlier after the July 2005 Islamist terrorist attack in London, when he declared that there is a "British way of life" that would not bend to cultural enclaves seeking to impose their practices on others or create parallel systems of justice. The former sought an unrealistic exclusivity, while the latter suggested a progressive and inclusive civic pluralism.

Societies built on immigrant assimilation strive toward common identity despite racial differences. Singapore became a cosmopolitan hub through historical migrations from China and Indians circulating across the British Empire and then by design as Lee Kuan Yew insisted on multiethnic public housing to prevent any ghettos from forming. Today Singapore ranks as one of the world's most religiously diverse cities, with a surfeit of monuments for each religion. Only half of Singapore's population is citizens, and more than 20 percent of marriages are mixed race, mostly Chinese-Indian—creating a growing number of "Chindians" each generation. As Indian and Filipino migrant workers mingle in Singapore and Dubai, an "Indipino" race is emerging as well. The more mixed-race families become the social norm, the weaker pleas for ethnically based politics become. One of Lee Kuan Yew's longest-serving ministers, S. Rajaratnam, rightly said that to be Singaporean "is not a condition but a conviction."[4]

Such city-states are the incubators of the new mongrel global civilization because they can succeed only through inclusive rather than exclusive policies. For most cities, it is too late to prevent ethnic ghettos, but it is not too late for pragmatic mayors to promote place-based rights rather than identity politics. We have to think less in terms of ideal-type multiethnic states governed through mostly liberal parliamentary factions and more in terms of technocratic tool kits for dense cities, some highly ethnically mixed and others with Balkanized neighborhoods. Either way, the notion of "citizenship" seems a quaint anachronism as foreigners become permanent stakeholders. Jaime Lerner, the Brazilian architect who became a pioneering mayor of the southern city of Curitiba, calls cities "the last refuge of solidarity,"[5] places where many people must build and provide for themselves and thus cannot afford to tear themselves apart. Building common identity requires strategies to promote cohesion amid economic inequality. It is in this context that global cities have become crucibles for experiments such as Toronto's noncitizens voting in municipal referenda and New York's ID cards for half a million undocumented immigrants. The rapid feedback loops possible at small scale compensate for any deficit in cultural trust; indeed, they are the agents of building trust amid diversity.

Even as global cities embody centrifugal cultural forces, they are also the incubators of multiple identities. Their density and diversity allow individuals to explore and adopt multiple identities based on neighborhood and community, ethnicity and race, professional class or other association. In this way, cities do not trap but liberate. It is in geographies that lack choice where the only option is national identity, whereas in cities identity can be cumulative.

Nationalism is viewed as either a powerful human impulse to be celebrated or a dangerous force to be defeated. The former makes it seem immutable to change, and the latter creates a false antagonism between identity and accommodation. The spectrum of nationalist phenomena today spans European-style ethnic nativism against immigrant influxes as well as Asian geopolitical patriotism against historical rivals. That these forces continue to exist does not mean they will prevail.

Indeed, taken together, the surging trends of migration, urbanization, and proliferating identities present global cities as a major alternative to nations and nationalism as the foundations of global social order. The more cities make all residents meaningful participants by virtue of their contributions and obligations rather than differentiating by citizenship or ethnicity, the more loyalty to the city supersedes that to the nation. The Canadian scholar Daniel Bell calls this rising urban pride "civicism," a twenty-first-century rival to nationalism.[6] Civicism harks back to the ancient world of Athens and other Mediterranean societies where politics was open to all residents.

For today's mobile and itinerant youth, civicism seems a more fitting ethos than nationalism. Nobody would have believed in the early 1990s that Berlin would emerge as the world's coolest city, with ultramodern architecture, a buzzing tech scene, and productive cultural collisions unseen elsewhere on the Continent. I've been traveling and living in Germany off and on since the Berlin Wall fell. In the 1990s, integration was difficult: Only by learning to speak German like a German did I differentiate myself from the large Turkish population whom I resembled to the native German eye. Today it seems everyone is a foreigner fumbling his way through German—or just defaulting to English. In the 1990s, I had to commute an hour on various trains, trams, and buses to find a good Indian restaurant; today there are several in every neighborhood. In addition to the Turks, Russians, and Poles, Berlin has close to 100,000 Chinese, Vietnamese, and other East Asians.

Berlin thus emerges as Europe's most future-ready city, not just technologically, but demographically. Situated on the vast northern European plain with ample space to expand in all directions, Berlin has become an urban geography so vast that with only 3.5 million people it would feel vacant with double the population. This accounts for why its property prices have barely nudged in a decade and why it is in such deep debt. Its flamboyant former mayor Klaus Wowereit rightly boasted that his city is "poor but sexy,"[7] but it is not financially sustainable without more people. Officially, most European countries are cynical about the benefits of immigration, but in reality Africans, Arabs, and Asians are streaming in to study, work, and settle in livable cities like Berlin. Berlin's magic formula has been affordable rent, openness to immigrants, and lots of babies: It has the highest birthrate in Germany, especially the trendy areas of East Berlin, where students came in the 1990s and have stayed to raise families. The rest of Europe must learn from Berlin: Exclusive thinking is a recipe for suicide.

CHINA: IMPERIAL NATION-STATE

China is far more diverse than most realize. In addition to the dominant Han, China has many ethnic groups such as the Zhuang, Hui, Manchu, Uighur, Tibetan, Miao, and Mongol, whose higher birthrates make them a growing percentage of the population (though still barely 10 percent). Still, China will never become a racially inclusive melting pot like other great empires of the past. Instead, the Han use their numerical advantage as a weapon to dilute China's minorities. The ten million Muslim Uighurs of China's largest and most restive province of Xinjiang have been the main target. Uighurs are being encouraged or forced to scatter around the country to dissipate them, while within Xinjiang the Great Assimilation campaign offers $1,500 cash rewards for Uighurs who intermarry with Han (while banning Uighur women from wearing head scarves).

China has also become a magnet for hundreds of thousands of Western expats, African students, and Arab traders, but they are just a drop in the Chinese ocean amounting to less than 1 percent of the population. As in Japan, foreigners aren't considered locals even if they adopt the customs. Much as both the Ming and the Qing dynasties accepted Jesuits in the sixteenth and seventeenth centuries for their scientific acumen, today's foreigners are viewed as sources of talent and technology, recruited to serve the state's ambitions of building the "Chinese Dream."

China's demography far outstrips its political geography. Its Han core is secure, its minority-populated periphery is in a process of pacification, and its many depopulated neighbors are becoming supply chain appendages increasingly home to Chinese workers. With its low fertility rate and shrinking labor force, China may bring back some overseas workers, but with so many surplus single males, the so-called bare branches who have been a major factor in social instability throughout history, it is more likely to continue to push many abroad to toil on the frontiers of the empire. Indeed, while the vast majority of China's more than fifty million diaspora lives in Asia, more than two million have followed China's sprawling supply chains as far as South America and Africa. China is thus becoming more homogeneous at home while blending with societies beyond its borders.

GLOBAL PASSPORTS

For millennia, most people never wandered far from where they were born. Until just the past few decades, voluntary international travel for business or leisure was limited to the 1 percent elite of any society. Today, by contrast, over one billion people cross borders each year. The number of international tourists is soaring to new heights on the back of outbound Asians. Investment firm CLSA predicts that 200 million Chinese will travel abroad annually by 2020. The number of cruise ship passengers has more than doubled every decade, up to seventeen million in 2010. Royal Caribbean's largest ship, *Quantum of the Seas,* is in perpetual motion ferrying tourists across the oceans.

Even this short-term human mobility is bedrock to the world economy. The tourism and hospitality sectors represent more than 10 percent of global GDP and employ more than 250 million people. Connectivity is their lifeblood. In Africa, tourism has grown faster than other sectors and particularly benefits women. Travel warnings that cut off tourist flows are thus something of an inadvertent sanction. For example, U.S. advisories against visiting Kenya have led to a collapse of the coastal economy and increased rates of drug addiction and crime that can blow back as terrorism in Nairobi.[8]

The competition to attract flows of tourists, businessmen, and conventions has become a major force for dismantling consular frictions. At almost any Chinese consulate in the world, visas can be obtained within twenty-four hours: Provide some standard documents, and swipe a credit card. India, which for decades has received fewer annual tourists than tiny Singapore, has finally implemented an online visa-on-arrival authorization for most nationalities. The United States has spent $2.8 billion on new border-smoothing technologies such as EntryPass, knowing that easier visa procedures mean more tourists and revenues spent inside its borders. None of this would be possible without the data-sharing networks that allow airport immigration stations to replace the expensive consular functions in embassies worldwide. Already the fastest lane at many Asian airports is not for that country's citizens but for holders of the APEC Business Travel Card, who can be from any of more than twenty different countries. At JFK International Airport, citizens of nearly forty countries precleared through the Electronic System for Travel Authorization enter the same queue as Americans. In the coming decade, even more automated check-in, security, and border control systems are planned such that passengers around the world are cleared for exit on arrival before they even take off.*

Could digital technology and economic necessity bring us back to the bygone era of free mobility? For centuries before World War I, people traveled the world without passports. The fluidity of imperial zones such as the British Empire nurtured generations of cultural intelligibility among millions of people moving across colonies from East Africa to Southeast Asia. At the same time, European settlers arrived in North America as pilgrims fleeing monarchy or migrants fleeing famine. Passports were actually seen as feudal relics meant to tie people to the land they tilled. In 1871, the Italian merchant Giovanni Bolis wrote that eliminating passports would greatly improve commercial relations by liberating travelers from "harassment and hindrances." One century of world wars later, however, we have stumbled into a world where bureaucratization

---

* At present, U.S. Customs and Border Protection has preclearance facilities at the airports of cities such as Toronto and Abu Dhabi, sparing passengers traveling from those cities the tedium of American immigration processing at U.S. airports.

and fear have heavily restricted free migration despite overwhelming demographic imbalances and economic incentives. Capital is welcome everywhere, labor not as much.

And yet the benefits of immigration are always palpable both in the short and in the long terms. Immigrants have been crucial to America's housing sector rebound since the financial crisis. Illinois's Cook County, for example, has seen about 1 million native-born Americans leave the area since the 1970s, while 600,000 immigrants have moved in, many of whom have worked their way up to the status of first-time homeowners. Meanwhile in Europe, narrow-minded immigration policy has led to a shortage of more than one million IT sector workers, hampering its already anemic economic recovery.

On a global basis, opening borders to more migration would alleviate labor shortages, increase usage of public and private facilities, jump-start economic growth, and boost remittances. According to the OECD, even a 3 percent increase in labor mobility would add $300 billion per year to families at the end of the remittance chain, and a 10 percent increase in per capita remittance value would reduce the incidence of poverty by 3 percent across seventy-one countries. Michael Clemens of the Center for Global Development argues that opening the world's borders to even temporary worker flows could literally double world GDP.[9] The total benefits of more migration are actually incalculable.

There is also a moral case for returning migration to its origins as a supply-demand system rather than one oppressively and inefficiently managed by nations and borders. Migration restrictions are among the powerful factors perpetuating the punitive effects of the accident of birth. The global division of labor that can bring human civilization to a higher stage depends on freer movement of people. People should have the right to define their identity as freely and widely as possible, constrained only by the willingness of communities to accept them. Mobility thus ought to be one of the paramount human rights of the twenty-first century.

In generations past, people moved. Now they circulate. Migration today is more than permanent, one-directional relocation; it is a constant flux of multidirectional flows. Taken together, there are more migrant workers, overseas expatriates, political and environmental refugees, and trafficked people than ever in history. The supply-demand world is one where people circulate as much as goods and services.

Most poor country nationalities bring few meaningful benefits, neither inalienable rights at home nor access abroad. Their passports are not essential symbols of identity but bureaucratic prisons. Even as emerging markets gain more clout in the global economy, their citizens are often still subject to enormous delays and additional travel costs. If given the choice between mobility and national identity, many would choose the former.

The latest biometric and data-sharing technologies can liberate individuals from their country's poor reputations or policies. An independently administered "global visa" linked to Interpol and other databases could allow qualified individuals from Brazil, Saudi Arabia, Russia, India, China, Indonesia, and dozens of other countries visa-free access to all participating countries. A global visa would not replace national passports as an identification tool or the benefits of citizenship (such as voting and landownership), but it would provide a supplemental verification for international access. Providing one's personal data to the network of participating countries and border agencies may seem onerous to some, but for many it is a chance at liberation.

Indeed, a global visa could also be invaluable for the 150 million semipermanent migrant guest workers at the lower end of the value chain who crisscross the world's farmlands, construction sites, and other infrastructure projects, recruited, transported, tracked, housed, and paid by human resource agencies and contracting firms. The State Department's mid-2015 visa-processing glitch delayed tens of thousands of Mexican seasonal farmworkers from entering the United States, ruining their livelihoods and damaging time-sensitive American agricultural businesses. Wouldn't it be easier for these recurrent border crossers to have a visa to match their movement patterns?

The explosion in the number of such mobile workers who may never return "home" constitutes an entire demographic that depends more on the Independent Republic of the Supply Chain than any one nation. This global mobile workforce has limited rights; they cannot use public medical facilities and in places such as the U.A.E. and Singapore are required to live in barracks that prevent mingling with the host population. While they are precariously rather than steadily employed, they also represent a growing opportunity for portable insurance offerings to access basic services where they may need them rather than having to negotiate new packages—or having none at all—in each new place they arrive.

National security is another major reason why mobility will inevitably be divorced from nationality—both for the privileged and for the poor. Passports alone confer little if any certainty over a person's intentions, as evidenced by British citizens of Pakistani origin joining al-Qaeda in Afghanistan or Australian Arabs joining ISIS in Syria. Western passports have provided a cloak of credibility, but even they clearly no longer guarantee liberal values. Soon all individuals will have to be treated as such, providing biometric data and submitting to more rigorous checks against databases such as Interpol in order to be cleared for entry—no matter what passport they carry.

Who gets to live somewhere or travel someplace no longer has a clear answer. Countries compete to attract essential investment and talent while warding off those viewed as unessential or dangerous. The U.K. is becoming a testing ground for merit-based or wealth-based immigration, residency, and citizenship. While British citizens suspected of traveling to Yemen, Syria, or Pakistan for jihad adventurism may have their passports revoked, Russian billionaires fleeing Putin's policies and full-tuition-paying Chinese students are given red-carpet welcomes. Meanwhile, in 2013 the U.K. nearly implemented a policy requiring Nigerians, Indians, and Pakistanis to pay a £3,000 bond that would be forfeited if they overstayed their visas. So much for Commonwealth solidarity.

GLOBAL CITIZENS

A new global expatriate identity is emerging among permanent migrants who belong nominally to their country of origin, the country of their nationality, and their country of residence, no two of which need be the same. Such people belong to multiple circuits, fusing various identities rather than forcing themselves into national prisms. Investment bankers, management consultants, professors, athletes, and military mercenaries are all examples of mobile individuals for whom professional ascent often matters more than nationality or geography. Law, medicine, and even politics have become global circuits despite national restrictions. The very phrase "knowledge society" better describes this transnational milieu than it does any single country.

The ranks of this permanent expatriate elite caste represent a sizable new interest group. As one recruiter of Western business school graduates for consulting positions in India told me, "The number of international migrants and students used to be a rounding error; now it is a class."[10] Timm Runnion, CEO of Mobility Services International, one of the largest relocation agencies for Americans heading overseas, meets thousands of professionals who over the course of their careers identify more with their circuit than their place of birth. He sees loyalty becoming purpose-driven rather than location-driven. Consultants such as those from Accenture or McKinsey who are from one country, based in another regional office, and spend Monday to Friday in a third country are often given open tickets for weekends to go anyplace they want, including wherever they consider "home." Is a Google employee from Malaysia, educated in the United States, living in London, but assigned to the company's thriving campus in Nairobi a Malaysian, American, Londoner, or Googler?

The rise of a global circuit of professionals who think of themselves as "global citizens" transcending national identity has been noted since the 1990s. Derided as "Davos man" or "Cosmocrats," such elites have been criticized as being out of touch with local concerns and nationalist impulses. This logic has proven to be wrong on every count. It is not just Western elites who are susceptible to the notion of a greater transnational identity but particularly people from developing countries that most appreciate the opportunities Westerners take for granted. Indeed, the global expatriate class is not dominated by Westerners; it is a balanced demographic of Americans, Europeans, and Asians, as well as Latin Americans, Africans, and Arabs. Non-Western expats are not untethered, soulless aesthetes: They know very well the tough realities of life where they came from and continuously support families, charities, and scholarships in their native countries. They are also very local activists fully committed to global causes such as Kailash Satyarthi, the Indian child rights activist awarded the 2014 Nobel Peace Prize, who describe themselves as "global citizens" because their own governments have been so derelict in living up to humanitarian pursuits.

After a lecture at Barcelona's prestigious IESE business school, a Russian student once told me, "Thank God I work for a Wall Street investment bank; otherwise I would never get to travel and do interesting things." Her citizenship is a drag; her loyalty lies with whichever firm secures her work permits, whether a bank, clothing retailer, or oil company. The fact that she is still Russian doesn't mean that her talents should be wasted in Russia.

Talent development is another reason for the rise of supply chain identity. Some companies spend more on upgrading the skills of their employees than entire countries do on public education. Media conglomerate WPP, whose annual profits hover around $16 billion, invests over $100 million per year on the training of its staff of 170,000, whose numbers are greater in emerging markets than in the United States and the U.K. combined. Global services companies are only as good as their people, thus they consciously build a transnational community more aligned to the firm's mission than to any one nation. DHL and Unilever frequently relocate employees across markets, sponsoring their relocation to learn from counterparts within their value web. PwC conducts constant "re-skilling" of workers to transition to higher-growth client sectors as well. By building such "specific capital"—knowledge best used within the firm and its network or narrow industry—banks, consultancies, and other firms make themselves anchors of personal fulfillment and enjoy greater employee retention.

Multinationals want employees to represent the firm, not their nation. They actively do their part to dilute restrictive national business cultures. Consulting or software companies that run regional headquarters out of Budapest, for example, recirculate recruits from the Balkans to each other's countries. They do the same with Arabs around the Middle East. As a result, Serbs who have never been to Croatia, or Kuwaitis to Egypt, develop regional identities via the supply chain despite their nationalities and national animosities.

Russian students in Europe joining American banks, a Malaysian Googler in Africa, and Serbian consultants around the Balkans are all examples of a new generation that finds its calling beyond national boundaries and pledges allegiance to the Independent Republic of the Supply Chain.

CITIZENSHIP ARBITRAGE

Individuals, much like nations, can multi-align their loyalties in the marketplace of identities. Tycoons hedge against turbulence in their own economies by holding foreign passports even if it is against the law. This global tribe for whom mobility supersedes nationality is growing with the rise of what Credit Suisse calls the "mass affluent" (those with investible assets of up to $500,000). As a result, the citizenship market is booming, with loyalty as much a matter of where one puts one's money as what passport one carries.

It is difficult to think of citizenship as the basis of identity when it is up for sale worldwide, with countries engaged in a tug-of-war to recruit wealthy and talented individuals. European "golden visa" programs from Portugal to Cyprus offer citizenship in exchange for real estate investments that can be sold after five years of guaranteed

5 percent or higher returns: Foreigners are effectively getting paid to trade up to European nationalities. St. Kitts sells passports to Russians, Iranians, and Chinese for $400,000 each, using the revenue to finance resorts and in return enabling its new citizens to travel visa-free to more than a hundred countries. (Often just an "investor visa" will do for Russians seeking to shift their wealth out of the Kremlin's reach.) Taxes, of course, are zero (or near it). Eric Major, CEO of Henley & Partners, a company that advises wealthy clients on such fast-track citizenship programs, says, "There is a growing breed of individuals who don't have time to be in one country for more than four months."[11]

An entire class of oxymoronic "rootless citizens" is emerging: They have given up the citizenship of the country where they have roots and have no roots in the country where they are now citizens. For these people, nationality commands loyalty in inverse proportion to the tax rate. The competition to attract private investment by the globally mobile affluent class has reduced passports to what they really are: a travel document with varying degrees of convenience.

This is clearly true even of Americans. While Americans historically rank at the top of surveys of national pride, only Americans are taxed on their global income. This burdensome financial and bureaucratic friction has prompted approximately four thousand Americans annually to renounce their U.S. citizenship in exchange for that of Canada, Britain, Switzerland, Singapore, or a dozen other countries. Rather than join the rest of the world in limiting taxation to territorial activity, the IRS has doubled down on its efforts to capture revenues from Americans' global incomes. The result has been even more Americans expatriating, meaning ultimately fewer wealthy Americans paying taxes.

China appears to have its own version of this problem: Thousands of wealthy Chinese politicians and industrialists have fled with their often ill-gotten gains to Canada, the United States, and Australia, among other countries. Rather than sending the IRS,

China dispatches covert agents of the Ministry of Public Security to intimidate these rogue citizens into returning home—before they seek asylum and U.S. citizenship.

Inhabiting nations no longer means belonging to them exclusively. The great liberal philosopher Isaiah Berlin cautioned against understanding history as the progression of vast, impersonal forces and favored a humanistic appreciation of complex individual identities shaped by family, business, national, ethnic, property, or other bonds. Each is operationalized in different ways; none have full sway over one's decision making. A supply-demand world will feature ever more citizenship arbitrage, with loyalties not so much changing as dividing and multiplying.

CHAPTER 16

WHEN NATURE HAS ITS SAY,
GET OUT OF THE WAY

RETREAT FROM
THE WATER'S EDGE?

IN 1815, THE ERUPTION OF THE TAMBORA VOLCANO ON INDO-nesian Java killed seventy thousand people, unleashed a tsunami, spewed thick ash that caused drought and ruined crops across Asia (giving rise to the "Golden Triangle" opium trade), spread cholera across South Asia (inspiring the advent of modern medicine), brought summer snow to the East Coast of the United States and the "great panic of 1819" that caused America's first depression, and caused the breaking of Arctic and Greenland glaciers that sparked Arctic sea exploration. That was some eruption.

From meteor strikes to the ice ages, geophysical phenomena have profoundly shaped mankind. The fundamental geology of plate tectonics is always in motion, with earthquakes and tsunamis constantly shifting coastlines. But mankind is fighting back with technologies such as land reclamation, sea barriers, and earthquake resistant architecture. Geo-engineering techniques such as carbon dioxide removal and solar radiation management may even allow us to slow climate change.

Map 38, corresponding to this chapter, appears in the second map insert.

But technological prowess and resource abundance should not lead to hubris. Anthropologists such as Jared Diamond have asserted that the Rapa Nui people of Easter Island committed ecological suicide through rapid deforestation (using trees to transport their massive stone statues known as *moai*) and the resulting soil erosion that made the island agriculturally unsustainable. The fate of Easter Island now serves as the classic warning of the consequences of disrespect for nature's complexity.

Are Asia's skyscrapers the *moai* of the twenty-first century? While their towering architecture similarly exudes power over terrestrial dynamics, their geography betrays existential vulnerability. Today more than 1.5 billion of Asia's 4 billion people live within a hundred kilometers of the Indian or Pacific Ocean, where rising sea levels could overwhelm existing coastal barriers.* Based on projected sea level rise, 316 American cities and towns will be submerged before the end of this century as well. Mankind's voluntary concentration into a dense, coastal civilization is certainly efficient, but it may not be very wise.

As rising sea levels invite oceanic surges that can drown our urban habitats, will we be forced to de-urbanize just as quickly as we have concentrated on the oceans' shores? We can debate about geography, but we cannot debate with nature. A leaked Intergovernmental Panel on Climate Change study from 2013 warned that shifting oceanic currents and the increased frequency of extreme weather events will result in flooding, crop failure, heat waves, and escalating poverty in countries without the robust infrastructure and safety nets to ride out such ecosystem imbalances. A subsequent 2014 report formally recommended that countries invest in "relocation" strategies such as evacuation routes for the populations of cities like New Orleans and Dhaka, new inland settlements in higher-elevation areas, and

---

* Among the countries termed Low Elevation Coastal Zones with the most exposed territory and population centers are Egypt, Nigeria, Thailand, Bangladesh, Vietnam, the Netherlands, India, China, and the United States.

urban cooling centers for a generally hotter world. The old climate diplomacy focused on mitigating emissions; the new climate action is about resettlement and adaptive infrastructure.[1]

The Dutch dikes stand out as an example of man standing up to nature for more than eight hundred years, with sophisticated flood control systems allowing the Netherlands to survive as one of the most dense, low-lying countries in the world. In the 1950s, the Dutch began replacing medieval dikes with a network of over thirty-five hundred kilometers of levees built to withstand once-in-ten-thousand-year-strength storms. They have also reclaimed land, dammed rivers, installed drainage canals, and built hulking sea barriers against storm surges. But rising sea levels could ultimately get the better of Holland, which is why they periodically flood areas on purpose based on oceanic models and preemptively relocate affected villages. Smart infrastructure investment means that the Dutch people will likely survive the encroaching waves.

RIVERS OVER BORDERS

Since ancient times, rivers have been the lifeblood of civilizational survival. Rivers are often thought of as "natural" borders, but they are first and foremost natural shared resources. For the Romans, the Rhine River was the boundary to threatening Germanic tribes to its north and east, but for the Holy Roman Empire it was a crucial interior waterway. France under Louis XIV and Napoleon sought to control all lands west of the Rhine despite the linguistic boundary lying far farther west, while today again it is a common artery for Switzerland, southeastern France, Germany, and the Netherlands within the broader European commonwealth. Flowing from Germany's Black Forest to Romania's Black Sea delta, the Danube was similarly a key lifeline used by medieval merchants to reach deep into Europe's interior and today is still a vital conduit for trade and tourism for its landlocked countries. Ultimately, rivers connect rather than divide.*

Natural geography can help us leapfrog political barriers toward more functional logic. The fertile Indo-Gangetic Plain, for example, unites over one billion people across Pakistan, India, Nepal, and Bangladesh. The Fertile Crescent along the Tigris and Euphrates Rivers is the lifeblood for people across southeastern Turkey, Iraq, Syria, Jordan, Israel, Lebanon, and western Iran. The Nile River, the world's longest, is the primary water source for Egypt and Sudan, and its White and Blue tributaries serve nine other East African countries as well. Until colonization and independence, overpopulation and resource depletion, all of these were regions with cultural boundaries but far less formal borders. If they want to make it through the next fifty years, they will have to return to that model again.

HOW TO NEGOTIATE WITH NATURE

We can steer nature but never fully control it. Over thirty years ago, China began planting the world's largest man-made forest—the "Green Wall of China" stretching for over forty-five hundred kilometers—to combat the rapid expansion of the Gobi Desert, whose dust storms affect agriculture as far away as Japan and South Korea. The similar "Great Green Wall" has been launched by the African Union to combat the Sahara's southward encroachment on the semiarid Sahel belt.

But nature's complexity can't be so finely calibrated. Flooding

---

* Rivers also regularly demonstrate how meaningless political borders can be, such as when the Danube and the Mekong overwhelm their banks and levees and flood across multiple countries. The 2014 Balkan flood damage reminded many Bosnians of the genocidal Yugoslavian civil war of two decades earlier, but this time forcing neighbors to rebuild together.

from melting glaciers and coastal inundation from sea level rise are problems of too much water, while droughts and desertification are signs of too little. Rising sea levels threaten coastal settlements, while desertification overpowers once fertile terrain, together squeezing populations somewhere in the middle. Drying rivers and urban pollution threaten the drinking water of more than two billion people. Droughts in Somalia and Kenya's northern Rift Valley have created what some call a "permanent emergency" of migrant agrarian refugees wandering in search of arable patches for planting crops or grazing cattle, turning entire swaths on either side of the border into nomadic zones cared for by UN relief agencies. Collectively, they belong to the growing ranks of climate refugees—who already outnumber the world's political refugees—some of whom, such as in Darfur, are double victims of climate change and civil war.

Natural disasters and food crises have led the militaries of the U.K., the Philippines, India, Pakistan, and Mexico to reorient their operational training around domestic humanitarian contingencies as well as foreign military ones. Sometimes these are one and the same. In 2014, Brazil launched its largest military exercises: defending the Amazon rain forest from invasion. Militaries are increasingly following America's example of having substantial disaster response capabilities to support populations in the event of tsunamis, typhoons, earthquakes, and other catastrophes.

Large countries, like large animals, have greater survivability amid such sudden extreme scenarios because populations can move inward. Coastal cities, however, have to think much more carefully about their metabolism, the sources of intake of food, water, and energy, and the outflow of waste. They have to build resource lifelines both deep into the hinterland (if they have one) and with farther-off locations to ensure supplies in times of crisis. Venice, for example, may enjoy the economic fruits of devolution, but as its fabled architecture gradually sinks into the Adriatic Sea, it must be careful not to alienate Rome too much because its residents may one day need to abandon ship and retreat into the interior.

Sea level rise is just one side of the urban climate disaster coin;

the other is subsidence: cities sinking. The more cities sap and guzzle the groundwater beneath them, the more their limestone foundations compress, feeling more like quicksand. Giant sinkholes have suddenly appeared at busy urban intersections across China and Central America, as well as central and southern Florida, where entire homes have been sucked into the ground. Bangkok has sunk about one meter since the 1970s, which makes its almost annual flooding that much more devastating. Without replenishing underground aquifers as Tokyo has done, we could one day witness skyscrapers toppling.

China has therefore begun to drill deeper—not for oil, but for water. Lidar satellites have discovered large offshore freshwater aquifers under the seabed off the coast of northern Europe, America's East Coast, and China's Zhejiang province, which is now the center of a ten-year, $200 billion campaign to build out China's water infrastructure, including undersea tunneling and a subway-like network of water pipes to replenish onshore aquifers to alleviate subsidence.

In some cases, global warming actually creates opportunities to harness water supplies. Melting Russian permafrost has meant huge increases in the flows of the Volga and Ural Rivers into the Caspian Sea, raising its levels and washing away roads and beaches. And yet given its low saline level, the expansion of the world's largest inland sea will allow for the construction of irrigation canals deeper into parched countries on the southern Caspian such as Turkmenistan and Iran.

Building such complex water desalination, transportation, and recycling networks will be every bit as crucial to our future as oil and gas pipelines have been to date. Whereas enormous quantities of water have been used in energy production and mineral extraction, soon nuclear power will generate clean water for billions across Asia, the Middle East, and Africa. Israel has pioneered nuclear-powered water recycling, TerraPower (backed by Bill Gates) is developing reactors that use depleted rather than enriched uranium, and India is developing thorium reactors, all of which means cleaner and safer power. The very same regions most deprived of freshwater—the western United States, the Sahara Desert, the Arabian Peninsula, and Australia—are also rated the highest for leveraging concentrated solar power for electricity generation and water desalination.* Instead of watching its crops dry out with growing frequency, Australia could harness rainwater for irrigation and sustain more than double its current population.

One thing almost all cities could do better is maximize their local resources through more robust conservation and sensible pricing. In Switzerland, water pricing takes into account the full life cycle from collection, treatment, delivery, sanitation, and recycling. Singapore captures rainwater and has installed a nationwide supply of "New Water" clean enough that the island could easily ban bottled water imports altogether. If it did, it could spark a campaign that might dent the (ironically) massive carbon-emitting bottled water industry. Evian, beware.

Devolutionary pressures also play an important role in preventing urbanization from leading to the endless plunder of resource-rich hinterlands. There is growing resistance from indigenous populations from Brazil to India to China to their forced resettlement and the ecological damage caused by dams and mining projects. In Central American countries such as Honduras, Guatemala, and El Salvador, hundreds of activists have given their lives to expose the corrupt nexus of paramilitary security agencies and extractive companies that repossess farmers' land only to poison it for the people. Both the Mapuche tribe of central and southern Chile and the First Nation tribes of western Canada have gained formal self-governance rights and managed to block dam and pipeline projects on their lands.†

---

* Desertec, a consortium of utilities companies seeking to harness North Africa's solar energy for both the Arab world and Europe, represents an early effort to transmit solar power across large distances such as under the Mediterranean Sea.

† Canada's First Nation tribes oppose Enbridge's Northern Gateway pipeline to the Pacific Ocean that would disrupt their traditional north-south migration and communication patterns.

Many indigenous tribes may not survive this century, but their message puts them on the right side of history. The food, water, and other resources of depopulated areas are more crucial than ever, while the excess of cities undercuts their own lifelines. São Paulo, South America's largest city, has reached the crisis point. Cutting down the forests that steer major rivers into its reservoirs has undermined its own water supply: The pipes are still there, but there's little water left to feed them. Meanwhile, drought has diminished irrigation and hydropower, meaning the city is groaning both for water and for power—a particular irony for the world's most ecologically endowed country.

If we better map depleting resources such as glaciers and rain forests, we may better manage them. We should view our ecosystem as a *natural* infrastructure—directly linked to the physical counterpart we have built to harvest it. Almost half of China's GDP is generated from eleven provinces whose intense urbanization to meet growth targets has led to water stress as severe as that in Middle Eastern countries. Only if we stop paving over arable land and instead treat it like a strategic resource will we achieve a better balance between man and nature.

Mismanaged urbanization in one country creates ecological challenges that matter globally. China, where soybeans were domesticated thousands of years ago, now barely produces one-sixth of its own demand, instead importing almost seventy million tons of soybeans from the United States and South America, whose logistical bottlenecks have pushed up global prices. China and India together provide half the world's raw cotton and rice and nearly a third of its wheat and potatoes, but their water stress could also become a supply shock to the system. According to the World Resources Institute, nearly forty countries already suffer severe water stress, but global demand for water is projected to rise 50 percent by 2050 as the world population climbs to nine billion.

Water is essential for every industry such as agriculture, electricity, manufacturing, textiles, electronics, and mining; thus changes we make in any of these sectors can dramatically improve the prospects for water conservation or redirection. For example, because producing coal requires five times more water than natural gas, China's shift toward a gas-powered economy would liberate significant quantities of water for agriculture in water-stressed provinces such as Hunan and bring down food prices and reduce China's greenhouse gas emissions in the process.

Still, rapid urbanization and improved nutrition in developing countries—to say nothing of the increasing frequency of droughts and crop failures—together mean that the percentage of global food that crosses borders will at least triple from 16 percent today to about 50 percent within two to three decades. Fixing food supply chains is thus a matter of life and death on a civilizational scale.

Food security is achieved through a mix of boosting domestic production and robust connectedness. The United States is the most food secure nation due to its huge production at affordable cost. And for any crop that fails in a certain season, Americans can import from the world market. Even though Singapore is almost entirely dependent on food imports, it still ranks as one of the world's most food secure nations as well because it has diversified the sources from which it imports vegetables, fish, and other staples. China has begun trace quantity irrigation programs that drastically reduce the water intensity of farming while rehabilitating farmland, precisely the technologies and practices that must be emulated elsewhere to improve food security.*

More sustainable urbanization could also kick off the process of "giving back" to nature. From the Chesapeake Bay to villages in

---

* The Rockefeller Foundation has launched a consortium called the Global Resilience Partnership that uses satellite monitoring and big data to identify the capacity gaps of vulnerable geographies—whether teeming megacities or isolated rural communities—and design conservation policies for the former and micro-finance to boost output for the latter. When seed technology and big data around meteorological trends are applied to agriculture such as through the FieldScripts program devised by the Climate Corporation (recently bought by Monsanto), yields have massively risen and allowed for farmland to be more efficiently allocated to crop diversification.

Namibia and Finland, when societies abandon habitats they have polluted, resilient Mother Nature claims them back, gradually revitalizing their ecosystems. While the world rural population is in absolute decline, some Western countries are witnessing a mild amount of de-urbanization. In America, several thousand eco-conscious youth (including many college graduates) have returned to farming (not just marijuana), injecting life into otherwise defunct towns. Indeed, agriculture is one of the best performing asset classes in terms of both operational cash yields and asset appreciation. Japan's elderly farmers have been joined by some urban youth as well, who bring essential new mechanization technologies to keep agricultural output strong as the world's oldest country drifts into the sunset. A noble organic food movement has also demonstrated how natural planting of diverse crops at smaller scale can produce high-quality yields. In England, fifty-eight thousand people moved out of big cities between 2009 and 2010 to cope with the rising cost of living. Even in rapidly urbanizing China, some Beijingers fed up with the air quality have retreated to the foothills near southern Kunming. Where rising urban costs come together with the desire for more natural living, while broadband Internet reaches farms and forests, people could potentially choose to live closer to nature while working digitally. But so far, these are trivial anomalies compared with the pace of urbanization and the impact it has on skewing economies and societies toward cities.

It is a worthy objective to balance rapid urbanization with an appreciation for rural life. Though the wealth gap between urban and rural populations may continue to widen, the divide is very much a false one. Cities existentially depend on their hinterlands for food and water while providing technology and logistics to enable agricultural exports. Nature will not let us take any precious geography for granted.

MEASURING THE SUPPLY CHAIN'S FOOTPRINT

Attributing water consumption and greenhouse gas emissions to countries rather than industrial sectors is a leading example of how the supply chain world warps geography. Water footprint maps reveal that 75 percent of Britain's water consumption is actually embedded in products it imports from other places; simply flushing the toilet less is therefore not going to make the U.K. more eco-friendly. Given its massive population and rapid industrialization, China is both the world's largest water consumer and its largest greenhouse gas emitter, though the United States is a far larger emitter on a per capita basis. At the same time, at least 20 percent of China's water consumption for agriculture—and an even greater share of its emissions from manufacturing—are actually for *foreign* consumption. The task of greening China, then, is one not just for China but also for global supply chains.

Though a supply chain is not a single entity or place, it does have a footprint. The world's major airline fleets together would rank in the top five largest greenhouse gas emitters if organized as a single country. Just ninety companies—only one-third of them state owned—account for two-thirds of annual greenhouse gas emissions from industrial activity, ranging from Chevron, Exxon, Shell, and BP in the energy sector to Walmart and IKEA in retail. No less than 40 percent of "Chinese" emissions are attributable to Western companies that have outsourced manufacturing to China. Climate negotiations are premised on national emissions rather than on distributing energy-efficient technologies through supply chains—which is why they fail.

International organizations and liberal governments are instead switching their focus to using their role and leverage in supply chains to promote sustainability. The IFC's Equator Principles, for example, won't invest in projects dependent on coal-generated power unless there is absolutely no alternative. Norway's sovereign wealth fund, the world's largest, has divested from all coal-related investments. Investors, insurers, and asset managers have moved in a similar direction. Socially responsible investment funds actively screen a combined $4 trillion portfolio, looking beyond parent companies deep into their tens of thousands of suppliers to measure compliance with environmental standards. The Dutch fund manager RobecoSAM has co-developed a suite of Dow Jones Sustainability Indices covering two dozen industry clusters and issuing detailed reports on the practices of corporate leaders and their exposure to energy supply disruptions. Global reinsurance giants such as Swiss Re and Zurich Insurance insist that clients build sustainability into their supply chains or risk having their policies canceled. These are the pillars of an emergent "regulatory capitalism" that mixes government sanction and financial pressure to raise supply chain standards.

LOCATION, LOCATION, LOCATION

The world may soon be divided into livable and unlivable places. Even energy executives such as the former BP CEO John Browne argue that fossil fuels are as bad for the earth as smoking is for the human body. The renegade scientist-activist James Lovelock, who coined the term "Gaia" in the 1970s to describe the earth as a unified ecosystem, believes we have given the planet a fever. He predicts London will be underwater in twenty-five years, southern Europe will resemble the Sahara Desert, the Alps will have no snow, almost all coral reefs will be dead, and the world population could drop up to 80 percent by 2100. Those left alive could enjoy the Florida-like climate of Alaska and the Pacific Northwest or settle in balmy Toronto and Detroit, which in addition to being safely inland from rising sea levels also have ample supplies of freshwater.

We may have no choice but to actively accelerate our collective shift from political to functional geography. Entire swaths of the planet may have to be repurposed for large-scale resettlement of climate refugees. But this requires re-coding national domains into resource protectorates sustainably harvesting and distributing their agriculture, forestry, and marine assets for the rest of the world whose supplies have been wiped out.

This is not something we can plan for at the last minute. Today's supply chain world leaves no resource untouched, but we should not let it mine the planet until nature is plundered past the point of no return. Today we can witness almost everywhere the malign neglect or overexploitation of resources through government mismanagement, unsupervised corporations, or competitive geopolitical hoarding. But there are also early signs of a fourth option: sustainable supply chain administration through transparent, technocratic coordination.

When spaces are so important that everyone needs them but no one should control them, we can design mechanisms that maximize sustainability while enabling fair access to it. The International Union for Conservation of Nature (IUCN), the world's oldest and largest multi-stakeholder environmental organization, has devised the Protected Areas Categories System, which helps countries designate nature reserves, wilderness areas, national parks, natural monuments, species habitat management areas, seascapes, and sustainable resource development areas and finds the right partners, whether foreign government agencies, NGOs, or companies, to train and assist them to protect, regenerate, or attract tourists to these eco-zones. IUCN manages marine reserves for sharks in Belize, grizzly bear habitats in Canada, bird sanctuaries in Colombia, and six million hectares of the central Amazon near Manaus to stabilize the fishing industry. Even Russia is not averse to consulting with bodies like IUCN, which advised Moscow on how to protect the habitat around its $20 billion Sakhalin-2 gas project.

Since the 1970s, the European Union has also set up dozens of Special Areas of Conservation and Special Protection Areas that protect vulnerable habitats and species while still enabling socioeconomic activity. And since 2002, the Brazilian government has worked with the World Wildlife Fund, World Bank, German government, and others to build up Amazon Region Protected Areas that monitor a Switzerland-size area of the rain-forest basin through satellite and Web-based tracking and new timber procurement protocols; the Amazon's deforestation rate has since decreased by 37 percent. All of these areas are now effectively governed functionally rather than politically. The sovereign governments of the soil or shores in which they are located have transplanted their management to independent bodies for the benefit of the place itself, the state, and mankind. Similar principles are being applied to protecting biodiversity in the Arctic and preventing illegal fishing in the Pacific Ocean.*

Taking nature seriously means fully labeling resources on our maps the way we label states. Most maps only give the names of the oceans and seas, but should the rest of precious nature only have colors (green for forests, tan for deserts, brown for mountains, white for ice) rather than names? The biodiversity of South American and African rain forests, the mineral-rich oceanic seabed, the Arctic habitats, and other natural resource tracts are more than just inert background features. They are sacred geographies with crucial roles in our complex global system. If we clearly depict and label all the geologic features we know, we might work as hard to protect nature's boundaries as we do to defend political ones.

---

* The Circumpolar Biodiversity Monitoring Program is an alliance of scientists, governments, indigenous councils, and conservation groups that has designated areas for biodiversity protection and to serve as control sites for the measurement of the human impact on the entire Arctic region. In 2014, President Obama established the Pacific Remote Islands Marine National Monument, an area twice the size of Greenland rich in deep-sea coral reefs that the United States will monitor and protect from illegal fishing, and in 2015 the U.K. declared a zone twice the size of Britain around Pitcairn Island in the Pacific Ocean as a marine protected area.

FROM CONNECTIVITY TO RESILIENCE

The great project of the twenty-first century—
understanding how the whole of humanity comes to
be greater than the sum of its parts—is just beginning.

—NICHOLAS CHRISTAKIS AND
JAMES FOWLER, CONNECTED

A NEW MORAL COMPASS

IN THE EARLY YEARS OF THE TWENTY-FIRST CENTURY, ANTIGLO-balization activists descended by the thousands on major international summits and negotiations from the World Bank and the IMF to the World Economic Forum. Protesters representing interests ranging from Western labor unions to African farmers decried the unfairness of globalization, claiming it exacerbated north-south divides. Today we know they were wrong, and so do they. That's why the protests stopped.

The "anti" movements—anticapitalism, antitechnology, antiglobalization—always lose. They represent not universalistic humanism but parochial shortsightedness. Too little trade is a much bigger problem than unfair trade, too little Internet access is a much bigger problem than the digital divide, too little wealth creation is a much bigger problem than high inequality, and too few genetically modified crops is a much bigger problem than corporate farming. Decades of UN declarations calling for global economic redistribution would never have achieved what globalization has in a few short decades. When Bill Gates said in 2014 that the "world is better than it's ever been,"[1] we have globalization to thank.

The future always comes faster than we expect. Our ancestors awoke not knowing the world is round. Today we wake up knowing we are connected to a global grid with only a few degrees of separation between any two people. There is no doubt that connectivity brings greater complexity and uncertainty, yet the places where one can be sure that tomorrow will be the same as today are often the places one would rather not be.

If the world population has a common goal, it is the quest for modernization and connectivity—the latter a principal path to the former. Connectivity is unquestionably a greater force than all the political ideologies in the world combined. Deng Xiaoping, who managed to dismantle the Soviet-style communes of Mao's Great Leap Forward and even opposed the Cultural Revolution, subsequently launched the reforms of the 1970s that connected China to the world economy and catapulted it from backwater to superpower. The same is true of religions. In most places, religion and the marketplace peacefully coexist. The religious revival among the newly minted middle-class Indians and Chinese has much to do with showing gratitude and praying for continued success in the global economy. Both societies know that without connectivity they would have much less to be grateful for.

Connectivity has become the foundation for global society. After all, individuals connect with the rest of the world not through politics but through markets and media. Supply chains literally embody how we (indirectly) *feel* each other: Low-wage Asian workers keep the price of mobile phones down for consumers worldwide, al-Qaeda militants attacking a Saudi oil refinery spike gas prices for urban commuters, and Indian and Filipino call center workers solve everyone's tech conundrums. Whatever the degrees of separation, supply chains connect the Bangladeshi garment worker to the Saks Fifth Avenue shopper, and the Congolese miner to the diamond-crusted Vertu phone customer in Hong Kong airport. Nothing connects rich and poor, East and West, North and South, like supply chains. Tenuous as these links may be, we are more likely to *care* about things we are connected to than those we are not. Pollution floating over the Pacific from China to California makes Americans think about climate change more than sinking Pacific Ocean islands. The collapse of a garment factory in Bangladesh making clothing for Western brands garners much more attention—and action— than a blaze at a Chinese fireworks plant with few sales outside China. Connectivity enables the empathy that guides our ethical evolution.

A supply chain order is thus not a libertarian fantasy in which markets rule the world. Nor is it universal socialist paradise. It is an evolutionary reality that we should construct pragmatic strategies to harness rather than retreating into populist mythologies and antiquated vocabularies. For nearly a century, the writings of Max Weber have inspired the belief that modern states will ultimately provide the best economic, social, and political foundations of order. But today more than five billion people are chronically underserved and neglected by their national governments.

Even in the West, where the geography of birth has conferred advantages over the rest of the world, a relatively privileged fate is no longer guaranteed. As European governments cut payrolls, millions of citizens have been left to fend for themselves, while America's millennial generation may well fall below the income levels their parents achieved decades earlier. The future will be one of self-sufficiency rather than entitlement: There is no more right to be rich.

There is a false dichotomy between national societies as an organic ethical community versus what Harvard's Michael Sandel calls a "market society" that neglects community bonds. Rather than waiting for governments to provide justice, dignity, and opportunity, people are forming new associations—professional, commercial, virtual—not as a substitute for local social capital, but as an essential new kind of *global* social capital.

Global connectedness is thus an opportunity to evolve both our cartography and our morality. We should make the most of supply chains rather than just letting them make the most of us. A world remapped according to connections rather than divisions holds the potential to advance a shift from "us-them" mentalities toward a broader human "we" identity. There is no good reason to turn back.

The touchstone of morality in a global society is leveraging connectedness for utilitarian ends: achieving the greatest good for the greatest number of people. We must apply John Rawls's test of societal morality on a global scale, judging ourselves by how we treat those at the bottom and justifying inequality to the extent that it improves the lives of the poorest. There is still potential to turn what the economist Branko Milanovic calls "bad" inequality into "good" inequality, which motivates and enables efforts for achievement. We are, in fact, on the right track: Globalization and connectivity have improved the quality of life for billions of people even if they have also made high inequality inevitable.

The time has come for even bolder thinking about how to leverage near-total connectivity to advance large-scale human development. Infrastructures, markets, technologies, and supply chains are not only logistically uniting the world but also propelling us toward a more fair and sustainable future. But there is still a long way to go. Billions are still without roads and electricity; food is scarce; money is a luxury. Bad infrastructure and bad institutions stand in the way of bridging supply and demand. It is a moral imperative to overcome them.

There is no higher morality than allowing people to move to wherever they need to, whether to avert natural disasters, escape conflict, or search for work, and moving the world's abundant resources of freshwater, food, and energy to the people who need them. National sovereignty and territorial integrity are no longer sacrosanct principles; in fact, they can be highly immoral when populations are besieged in Sudan and Syria, when drought-stricken climate refugees aren't relocated to fertile territories, or when migrant workers are trapped in political purgatories rather than empowered to contribute and earn. The shift from political to functional maps helps us overcome rigid moralities that deliver neither justice nor efficiency and adopt a more utilitarian mentality by which governments don't so much *own* the world as manage parts of it within a global network civilization.

The cost of building this new planetary order runs into the hundreds of trillions, and so do its benefits, at least those that can only be measured financially. This, then, is the emergent global social contract: If we can manage to socialize (or even relieve) the costs accumulated in order to unlock the productive potential of billions of underserved and underemployed people, we will also collectively share in the wealth of a much richer global society. There is no formal consensus about what kind of global society we want, even as we are accelerating the construction of it. We should embrace and shape the journey.

Connectivity has also sparked a cognitive revolution by which we come to appreciate *globality* as a new baseline condition: There is a global dimension to everything. Neither Western nor Eastern ideas dominate, but wisdom flows in both directions, between Western tunnel vision and Eastern holism, between humanism and scientific materialism, between democracy and technocracy. Daniel Bell, a Canadian political theorist at Tsinghua University, argues that *harmony* is a viable bridge concept between East and West because in Confucian thought harmony seeks peaceful order but also respect for diversity in social relationships. It is not premised on uniformity as commonly portrayed. Choosing a seemingly "Eastern" concept such as harmony to drive new metrics would hardly privilege Asia: It is small Western countries such as Norway, Sweden, Switzerland, and New Zealand that rank highest on the Harmony Index. This emergent global culture deepens as the two global languages— English and code—further connect the world through software and real-time communications.

NETWORKS THAT RUN
THEMSELVES

We are building this global society without a global leader. Global order is no longer something that can be dictated or controlled from the top down. Globalization *is* itself the order. Power has made one full rotation around the world in the past millennium, from the late Song dynasty through the Turkic Mongols and Arab caliphates to European colonial empires to the American colossus. But whereas *Pax Americana* replaced *Pax Britannica*—with America becoming the world's policeman and lender of last resort over two generations—a *Pax Sinica* is not likely to replace U.S. dominance in the same linear fashion. Instead, the past decade's hype of the East surpassing the West, China replacing America, and the Pacific displacing the Atlantic is giving way to a multi-civilizational and multipolar world in which continents and regions deepen their internal integration while expanding their global linkages. Latin Americans, Africans, Arabs, Indians, and Asians all want a world in which they can multi-align and trade in all directions, not be subject to either American or Chinese diktats. They will play the great powers off each other more than they will accept unilateral impositions. They all believe—correctly—that connectivity rather than hegemony is the path to global stability. Supply and demand will shape how regions and powers interact. If America offers military support and technology, China provides infrastructure and export markets, Europe sends aid and governance advisers, and corporate supply chains smooth the flow of connections, this is the closest geopolitics comes to stars aligning.

Historical models of order have been built on spheres of influence, but a stable global society today must be based on co-creation across civilizations. Such a balanced system is what the Chinese scholar Zhang Weiwei describes as symmetrical rather than hierarchical. It is one in which maintaining stability requires self-restraint and mutual trust among diverse powers. These were the virtues that enabled the success of the nineteenth-century Concert of Europe after the Napoleonic Wars. As was the case two centuries ago, now is a time of great power peace during which a legitimate order must be designed. The United States and China will, in Henry Kissinger's words, "co-evolve," but they will do so in a global context far deeper than themselves. There are limits, then, to the lessons of the past. Neither the 1814 Congress System nor the 1919 Treaty of Versailles and League of Nations are the best guide to the future; if they were, neither World War I nor World War II would have happened.

For history not to repeat itself, we cannot wait for events to force a new paradigm of global strategic thought. Rather, we need strategies to avoid undesirable events. If the "Thucydides trap"—war between dominant and rising powers—is driven by the dangerous brew of fear and pride, then taking emotion out of the equation is crucial to transmuting great power rivalry. Regionalism and reciprocity become the most important barriers to escalation of tensions. Globalization's advance is the only antidote to the logic of superpower-centric rivalries—replacing war with tug-of-war. Making the world safe for supply chains eventually makes the world a safer place.

We also need a world of mutual connectivity rather than geopolitical hierarchy precisely because we cannot be sure of any power's or region's fate ten years hence. America could become less interventionist as it leverages its energy wealth to upgrade and invest in its own hemisphere. Europe could suffer political stasis and insularity as a result of its economic malaise. Asia could be beset by strategic rivalries that derail its spectacular growth.

America will remain a superpower for decades to come under almost any plausible scenario by virtue of its geographic scale, demographic and economic size, and blessedly abundant geology. A glorious trajectory would entail energy abundance and an industrial resurgence spurring an export surge, financial rehabilitation through greater Main Street lending, infrastructural overhaul with large-scale investments in transportation and digital connectivity, and a new social contract focused on strengthening education and health services. In this future, social mobility increases, innovation continues, and your cell phone calls don't drop every five minutes.

But there is also a decay scenario in which excellence continues only in pockets such as Silicon Valley, the energy boom benefits only limited industries but not rank-and-file workers who are automated into irrelevance, Washington fails to invest in national infrastructure and redistribute corporate tax gains, and low-wage immigrants add to the lower-class masses competing to cater to the aging population and the 1 percent. The United States becomes more a collection of peoples than a united civilization.

An accurate view of the future must combine elements of both scenarios: Washington politics will remain broken, and fiscal strain will persist due to growing entitlement spending; immigration will surge as Americans age and require care; technology innovation will rise to new heights; but inequality will persist, and devolution will steadily advance.

The same trends are playing out everywhere. With the tide of devolution sweeping the planet and states focused on self-preservation, global solidarity is more likely to emerge from connective supply chains than from vague treaties among divided nations. Societies will never feel the mutual empathy essential for global peace unless our maps and narratives emphasize their connectivity over political and territorial divisions. Even Immanuel Kant's oft-cited ideal of the comity of nations is logically inconsistent in today's world. Kant saw a legal federation of republics as the path toward perpetual peace, but today's complex world features many forms of self-representing communities. Kant's moral writings, which saw individuals as ends in themselves, thus clashed somewhat with his political views. Émile Durkheim, though influenced by Kant, better captures the view that global society has an essence greater than the sum of its components. Durkheim believed that an increasingly complex division of labor leads to functional interdependence and thus an organic societal solidarity in which individual uniqueness should be celebrated and cherished. Durkheim's dynamic density is growing as globalization creates more interactions based on comparative advantage. The global division of labor thus makes everyone better off by creating jobs in poor countries, reducing prices in rich ones, and expanding choice for all. This new era of pluralistic connectivity has arrived.

If, as Einstein famously stated, we cannot solve a problem with the same mind that created it, then the problems of a state-centric world require thinking beyond it. The yardstick of commitment to global connectivity is thus not loyalty to post–World War II institutions but the commitment to meeting the needs of the world's population. Global governance must therefore have a generative structure like the Internet: distributed coordination without central control, and mutuality among a growing number of participants in the network. Some view a world of entropy and reconfiguration as a greater risk to global stability than multipolar competition. They fail to see that connectivity is the cohesion beneath the chaos; it is what prevents the world from "falling apart" precisely when commentators lament that it is.

BUILDING A
BORDERLESS WORLD

Even competitive grand strategy advances a self-stabilizing world. As America, Europe, and China invest in infrastructure with their neighbors, promoting regional integration and advancing global connectivity, they ultimately—if inadvertently—contribute to greater collective resilience. Whereas the quest for oil drove the Nazis into the Near East and the Japanese to Malaya, today we have energy abundance rather than scarcity—not "peak oil," but "gas glut." For more than a decade, Westerners have feared that China was locking up raw materials with an imperialist impulse reminiscent of nineteenth- and twentieth-century European empires. But it turns out that China's huge investments in ramping up Latin American and African resource extraction have generated massive global supplies for the *world* market (even oversupply that has led to price collapses for certain commodities as China's own demand has fallen). And as a new class of refineries emerges that can handle the full range of heavy to light crudes, oil supplies will also become more fungible because the disruption of one supply source can be quickly replaced by another. Thanks to discovery and technology, supply and demand, rather than cartels, set energy prices.

In the long run, the competition over connectivity *reduces* our collective risk. When resources are widely distributed, governments are less likely to fear being cut off from access to precious raw materials, and thus to fight over them. There is no more need for "resource wars."

There are other ways in which the quest for strategic connectivity enables our abundant global resources to meet demands around the world. Consider the race to establish new trade routes and transit ports. While tactically it appears to be zero-sum, in fact the opening of the Arctic for year-round shipping and the construction of trans-Eurasian freight rail networks together ensure that a sudden closure of the Suez Canal from a terrorist attack or regional conflict would have minimal system-wide impact. The same is true for Internet cables: There are at least twenty submarine cable breaks per year due to targeted attacks or accidental ship anchor ruptures, but constantly laying more of them ensures redundancy for our exponentially growing data traffic flows. Distributed connectivity helps us avoid any single point of failure.

With the right investments today, the nine billion people on earth in 2050 could be more evenly distributed across the hemispheres while also being more mobile and adaptable to the unpredictable forces of nature. Indeed, in the coming decades many countries may need to build new inland cities to resettle populations affected by coastal flooding as sea levels rise. Volcanic eruptions and electromagnetic pulses may ground aircraft and necessitate high-speed hovercraft services across the Atlantic and Indian Oceans. Such investments may not be immediately lucrative commercially but will be essential when the time comes. Economists might call this "excess capacity," but in an unpredictable world it seems more like common sense.

A planetary civilization of coastal megacities should be more interested in supply chain continuity than imperial hegemony. Trading cities want coast guards and counterterrorism more than foreign occupations and nuclear weapons. They prefer constellations of relationships rather than a single overpowering Leviathan. A world of open mélange cultures such as Zanzibar and Oman, Venice and Singapore, would be a more peaceful world than one of Orwellian mega-empires. We should strive toward such a *Pax Urbanica*.

Each successive map of the future will feature more connections and fewer divisions. This is the appropriate response to the realities of our times: There has been no major global conflict in more than two generations, and the escalation of tensions is being carefully managed, tempered by rising trade and investment volumes worldwide. We expend huge effort to measure the value of activity within borders; it is time to devote equal effort to the benefits of connectivity across them.

There are no greater stakes than in the question of moving from a nations-borders world to a flow-friction world. We need a more borderless world because we can't afford destructive territorial conflict, because correcting the mismatch of people and resources can unlock incredible human and economic potential, because so few states provide sufficient welfare for their citizens, and because so many billions have yet to fully benefit from globalization. Borders are not the antidote to risk and uncertainty; more connections are. But if we want to enjoy the benefits of a borderless world, we have to build it first. Our fate hangs in the balance.

RECOMMENDED SITES
AND TOOLS FOR MAPPING

AJD GEOSPATIAL CONCEPTS

http://gisconsultingservices.com/

AJD Geospatial Concepts specializes in the organization, analysis, and mapping of geographic data for urban and regional planning; utility, environmental, infrastructure, and transportation management; business and political analysis; and 3-D topographic and flood analysis.

ARCGIS

https://www.arcgis.com/features/

ArcGIS is a mapping platform that integrates both public and self-collected data to tailor maps and dashboards for organizations to analyze sites and routes and optimize or predict traffic and other patterns.

ATLAS OF ECONOMIC COMPLEXITY

https://atlas.media.mit.edu/atlas/

The Atlas of Economic Complexity measures the amount of productive knowledge countries hold based on the products they create and exchange. It allows users to create a visual narrative of national progress in increasing economic complexity, which is a key indicator of economic growth potential, quality of governance, level of education, and other factors.

CAGE COMPARATOR

http://www.ghemawat.com/cage/

The CAGE Distance framework is used to evaluate international and interregional patterns of trade, capital, information, and people flows. It helps users to understand the role of differences in terms of geography, economics, administration, and culture.

CARBON MAP

http://www.carbonmap.org/

Carbon Map applies thematic data sets to geographic base layers to interactively animate, distort, and shade regions based on their contribution or vulnerability to climate change.

CENTER FOR GEOGRAPHIC ANALYSIS, HARVARD UNIVERSITY

http://worldmap.harvard.edu

WorldMap software, created and hosted by the Center for Geographic Analysis at Harvard University, allows for the creation of custom Web maps and easy selection and downloading options of diverse open source geospatial data sets to construct tailored maps.

CHRONOATLAS

http://www.chronoatlas.com/MapViewer.aspx

ChronoAtlas is a free interactive historical program that allows users to view political boundaries and cities at any point in history around the entire globe.

COASTAL SEA LEVEL RISE CALCULATOR

http://ngm.nationalgeographic.com/2013/09/rising-seas/if-ice
-melted-map

National Geographic's interactive map adjusts coastlines for all continents based on variable scenarios for sea level rise up to more than fifty meters (if both polar ice caps fully melt), depicting new shorelines and submerged coastal regions.

ESRI

http://storymaps.arcgis.com/en/

Esri's Story Map apps can be customized to produce thematic visual stories such as how rapid urban migration has given rise to a world of megacities.

ESRI MAPPING CENTER

http://mappingcenter.esri.com/index.cfm?fa=resources
.cartoFavorites

Esri's Mapping Center provides access to various resources that are used regularly by professional mapmakers and cartographers, enabling its users to create maps using ArcGIS.

FIRST MILE GEO

https://www.firstmilegeo.com/

First Mile Geo is a business intelligence software that enables users to collect, visualize, and monitor data collected online or off-line through mobile, SMS, surveys, or manual sources. Maps, dashboards, indices, and alerts can be generated in multiple languages.

FLEETMON

http://www.fleetmon.com/live_tracking/fleetmon_explorer

FleetMon is an open database of ships and ports worldwide that uses real-time AIS positioning data to visualize the location and movement of nearly 500,000 vessels, allowing for the analysis of shipping and trade patterns.

FLIGHT RADAR

http://www.flightradar24.com

Flight Radar 24 is a flight-tracking service that provides real-time information about positions of thousands of aircraft around the world.

GAPMINDER

http://www.gapminder.org/

Gapminder is a nonprofit venture promoting sustainable global development and achievement of the United Nations Millennium Development Goals by increased use and understanding of statistics and other information about social, economic, and environmental development at local, national, and global levels.

GATEWAY HOUSE

http://www.gatewayhouse.in/corridor_maps/corridorMaps/index .html

Gateway House's project on Asia's Strategic Corridors provides dynamic maps of infrastructure, energy, trade, and other linkages across Indian Ocean subregions such as South Asia, Central Asia, West Asia, East Africa, Southeast Asia, and East Asia.

GDELT

http://www.gdeltproject.org/

The GDELT project is a global database of the world's broadcast, print, and Web news from nearly every country in over a hundred languages starting in the year 1979. It identifies and codes people, locations, themes, sources, and emotions surrounding events and provides daily analysis updates.

GEOFUSION

http://www.geofusion.com/index.html

GeoFusion integrates virtual reality and 3-D visualization techniques into its GeoMatrix and GeoPlayer engines to produce near real-time visualizations used in industries such as aviation, defense, space exploration, education, and entertainment.

GLOBAÏA

http://globaia.org

Globaïa designs and promotes visualizations and animations at the intersection of art and science to raise awareness about social and environmental challenges.

GLOBAL SPATIAL DATA INFRASTRUCTURE ASSOCIATION

http://www.gsdi.org/SDILinks

The Global Spatial Data Infrastructure Association provides global, regional, and national links to spatial data infrastructures.

GOOGLE EARTH PLUG-IN

https://www.google.com/earth/explore/products/plugin.html

The Google Earth Plug-In is a free JavaScript API that lets users embed Google Earth in their webpages in order to navigate geographic data on a 3-D globe as well as build sophisticated 3-D map applications.

IMF DIRECTION OF TRADE STATISTICS

http://data.imf.org

The IMF's Direction of Trade Statistics presents current figures on the value of merchandise exports and imports disaggregated according to a country's primary trading partners.

IMMERSION

https://immersion.media.mit.edu/

MIT's Immersion software uses email meta-data to construct an individual-centric network map that represents one's personal and professional connections.

INSTAAR DATA SETS, UNIVERSITY OF COLORADO BOULDER

http://instaar.colorado.edu/~jenkinsc/dbseabed/

dbSEABED creates unified, detailed mappings of the materials that make the seafloor by efficiently integrating thousands of individual data sets.

MAP PROJECTIONS

http://bl.ocks.org/mbostock/raw/3711652/

The drop-down menu of this site allows you to scroll through many variations of global map projections.

MAPS-OF-WAR

http://www.mapsofwar.com/

Maps-of-War was established to help people understand the big picture of history, measured not in years but in centuries. It features animated videos of the historical progression of religion, democracy, and Middle Eastern empires.

MAPSTORY

www.MapStory.org

MapStory is a very user-friendly platform that allows anyone to create visual narratives through the construction of StoryLayers that can stretch across space and time and can be edited and expanded by members of the community.

MCKINSEY GLOBAL CITIES OF THE FUTURE

http://www.mckinsey.com/insights/economic_studies/global_cities_of_the_future_an_interactive_map

McKinsey's Global Cities of the Future is an interactive map that allows users to explore the cities and emerging urban clusters that will drive dramatic growth and demographic changes over the next generation.

NASA GLOBAL CHANGE MASTER DIRECTORY

http://gcmd.nasa.gov/

NASA's Global Change Master Directory maintains a complete catalog of all NASA's earth science data sets and services.

NATIONAL GEOSPATIAL-INTELLIGENCE AGENCY

https://nga.maps.arcgis.com/home/

The National Geospatial-Intelligence Agency provides public access to large volumes of satellite and other geo-data and imagery in support of scientific research, natural disaster recovery operations, and crisis management.

NORSE ATTACK MAP

http://map.norsecorp.com/

Norse, a cyber-threat analysis firm, provides real-time visualizations of global cyber war based on data collected every second from Internet and Dark Web sources, plotting origins of attackers and target attacks.

OPENSTREETMAP

https://www.openstreetmap.org/

OpenStreetMap is a crowdsourced mapping platform maintained by a user community that constantly updates data on transportation networks, store locations, and myriad other content generated and verified through aerial imagery, GPS devices, and other tools.

PLANET LABS

https://www.planet.com/

Planet Labs uses a network of low-orbit satellites to capture the most current images of the entire earth and form composite digital renderings that can be used for commercial or humanitarian applications.

SOURCEMAP

http://www.sourcemap.com/

Sourcemap provides end-to-end visibility into supply chain data from raw materials to end consumers, allowing for visualization of risks, calculation of costs, and planning for resilience.

VISUAL LITERACY

http://www.visual-literacy.org/periodic_table/periodic_table.html

Visual Literacy's Periodic Table of Visualization Methods provides instructive pop-up infographics summarizing dozens of key data and mapping techniques.

WELCOME TO THE ANTHROPOCENE

http://www.anthropocene.info

Welcome to the Anthropocene is a collection of short video journeys covering the past 250 years since the Industrial Revolution that depicts humanity's impact on the planet.

WORLD BANK PUMA SPATIAL DATA SETS

http://puma.worldbank.org/downloads/

The World Bank's PUMA, or Platform for Urban Management and Analysis, is the repository for urban spatial data and a geospatial tool that allows users to download data sets for direct visualization and analysis.

WORLDMAPPER

http://www.worldmapper.org

Worldmapper filters quantitative data through algorithms to produce unique cartograms that rescale geographies to depict their significance according to themes such as wealth, emissions, and Internet access.

WORLD MIGRATION

http://www.pewglobal.org/2014/09/02/global-migrant-stocks/

Pew Research Center's interactive map shows migration figures based on origin and destination countries for the years 1990, 2000, 2010, and 2013.

ACKNOWLEDGMENTS

WHEN ONE IS WRITING A BOOK ABOUT EVERYTHING, IT NEVER hurts to have the world's most knowledgeable individuals in one's corner. As always, I'm deeply honored for the time and resources the following people and institutions have provided in support of my research. With such a cast of collaborators, it goes without saying that any residual errors are my own.

Lectures and discussions at the Lee Kuan Yew School of Public Policy at the National University of Singapore have been a crucial sounding board, especially with deans, faculty, and fellows such as Kishore Mahbubani, Kanti Bajpai, Jing Huang, Kenneth Paul Tan, Will Bain, Heng Yee Kuang, Donald Low, Ora-Orn Poocharoen, Rahul Sagar, Jeffrey Straussman, Reuben Wong, and Irvin Studin.

The Singapore Institute of International Affairs has also been the site of energetic and informed conversations. I want to thank its chairman, Simon Tay, and its executive director, Nicholas Fang, for their leadership and cultivated insights and for involving me in timely events and the flagship Future 50 project.

The New America Foundation was a home away from home since the beginning of this trilogy in 2005. I'm proud to have been associated with Washington's leading group of strategic thinkers and grateful for the insights from friends and colleagues such as Anne-Marie Slaughter, Patrick Doherty, Barry Lynn, and Pete Singer.

The London School of Economics (LSE) continues to be a beacon for innovative geopolitical scholarship. I've enjoyed my affiliation with LSE IDEAS, now part of the expanded Institute of Global Affairs, and the free-flowing conversations with the prominent scholars and friends Mick Cox, George Lawson, Iver Neumann, Danny Quah, and Arne Westad.

Of the numerous researchers involved in this book, I am especially grateful to the outstanding work of two Lee Kuan Yew School Ph.D. students: Caini Hong, who, in the manner of some of China's best scholars, was shy but incomparably meticulous in data collection and analysis; and Kris Hartley, whose earnest ambition and creativity shone through in his background memos and in his numerous published works in urban economic strategy. I also deeply appreciate the research work conducted, often at strange hours across time zones, by Omar al Baraki, Peadar Coyle, Ahmed El Hady, Farzin Mirshahi, Soren Nieminen, Vanessa Quiroz, Damini Roy, Malini Sen, Yulia Taranova, Andrew Trabulsi, Mariam Wissam, Shira Wollner, Yinan Wang Liao, and Soenke Ziesche.

Some of the most towering intellects alive today have been steady intellectual mentors both for this book and generally over the past decade or more. It seems almost offensive to list them in one paragraph, but my appreciation for their brilliance and friendship goes beyond anything I can write: Graham Allison, Benjamin Barber, Eric Beinhocker, Daniel Bell, Ian Bremmer, Ann Florini, Tom Friedman, Robert Kaplan, Pratap Mehta, Pankaj Mishra, Charles Pirtle, Carne Ross, John Ruggie, Saskia Sassen, Richard Sennett, Nassim Taleb, and Scott Malcomson, who has edited my essays for close to a decade and kindly reviewed several chapters of this book as well.

Friends have witnessed many times the fine line crossed from casual banter to intense debate, usually marked by the unsheathing of my Moleskine notepad. Beyond the innocent bystanders caught in the cross fire, I want to single out those who have been consistent partners in productive discourse: Ozi Amanat, David Anderson, Scott Anthony, Matt Armstrong, Alex Bernard, Neel Chowdhury, Laura Deal, Jon Fasman, Howard French, Jared Genser, Jan-Philipp

Goertz, Jeremy Grant, Nisid Hajari, Niels Hartog, Seb Kaempf, Gaurang Khemka, Karan Khemka, Bernd Kolb, Mark Leonard, Greg Lindsay, Shaun Martin, Ann Mettler, Chandran Nair, Madhu Narasimhan, Pradeep Ramamurthy, Abhijnan Rej, Tom Sanderson, Rana Sarkar, Lutfey Siddiqi, David Skilling, Nick Snyder, Robert Steele, Dorjee Sun, Vijay Vaitheeswaran, Kirk Wagar, Chris Wilson, Art Winter, Jan Zielonka, and Teddy Zmrhal. Special thanks to my multi-country mountain biking companions Andres Sevtsuk of the Singapore University of Technology and Design (SUTD) (now at Harvard's Graduate School of Design) and Brian McAdoo of Yale-NUS for ideas that kept me stopping and scribbling on the trails.

Scenarios and complexity research have been crucial to the formulation of this book, and I want to thank leading experts in the field who have lent their foresight: Mat Burrows, Jeffrey Cooper, Jake Dunigan, Banning Garrett, Lee Howell, Ong Ye Kung, Holger Mey, Paul Saffo, Peter Schwartz, Dave Snowden, and Chris Tucker, who solicited my contribution to the U.S. Geospatial Intelligence Foundation's monograph on human geography, for which I am also grateful to other editors and contributors such as Lee Schwartz and Robert Tomes. At Zurich Insurance, I've benefited from the insights of experts on the globalization of risk such as Francis Bouchard, Linda Conrad, Tom de Swaan, Tine Thorsen, and Kai Truempler.

At the Q Symposium at the University of Sydney, my friend James Der Derian once again upended the foundations of the international relations field by curating a unique gathering on the relevance of quantum physics to world politics. I am very thankful to him and the symposium's participants, especially Alison Bashford, Tom Biersteker, Jairus Grove, Duncan Ivison, and David Reilly.

There are many people to thank for their unique expertise on various facets of our urban century and the devolutionary wave empowering it: Michele Acuto, David Adelman, Chris Arkenberg, Sam Asher, Daniel Brook, Mayraj Fahim, Kamran Khan, Barbara Kux, Jaime Lerner, Eddie Malesky, Richey Piiparinen, Francis Pisani, Lakshmi Pratury, Aaron Renn, Paul Romer, Sanjeev Sanyal, Arturo Sarukhan, Thomas Sevcik, Steven Sim, Shanker Singham, Anthony

Townsend, and Milan Vaishnav. Warm thanks to Avner de-Shalit and participants in the Hebrew University of Jerusalem workshop on the "spirit of cities": Jeremy Adelman, Gilles Campagnolo, Kateri Carmola, and Susan Clarke.

From Tianjin Eco-city to Guangzhou Knowledge City, thank you to the many dozens of officials who have hosted me at "smart cities" and special economic zones in China. I am similarly grateful to the managers of many other new urban developments on all continents for sharing their ambitious plans with me. Your projects are not yet on the map but surely will be thanks to your tireless efforts. Thanks also to Tony Reynard and Lincoln Ng of the Singapore Freeport for an insightful tour and conversation. At the Barcelona Smart City Expo 2014, I'd like to thank Ugo Valenti, Álvaro Nicolás, and Folc Lecha Mora. I appreciate learning about the inner workings of the City of London and its global strategy from Mark Boleat, Giles French, Anita Nandi, and Andrew Naylor. And thanks to Vicky Tsaklanou and Maria Dessipri at the Piraeus Container Terminal in Athens for sharing your vision.

My involvement on the board of trustees of the New Cities Foundation (NCF) has been a constant source of stimulating ideas about the future of cities. I'm grateful to John Rossant, Mathieu Lefevre, and the entire management team, as well as my fellow board members Anil Menon, Daniel Libeskind, and Fahd Al-Rasheed and the many insightful speakers and participants at NCF summits in Paris, São Paulo, Dallas, Jakarta, and Cityquest in Jeddah.

I've relied on many experts and practitioners from the leading institutions in global markets and finance to validate ideas and analyze economic complexity. Here I would like to especially thank Richard Baldwin, Carson Block, Bunty Bohra, Doug Carmichael, Ravi Chidambaram, Steve Drobny, Gerry Elias, Brooks Entwistle, Chris Eoyang, Pankaj Ghemawat, Mike Green, Victor Halberstadt, Charles Haswell, Simon Hopkins, Barry Johnson, Erik Jones, Mike Klowden, Pascal Lamy, Robert Z. Lawrence, Adam Levinson, Dave Lincoln, Antonio de Lorenzo, Thierry Malleret, Sarah Merette, Ilian Mihov, Brent Morgans, Tony Nash, Chris Oberoi, Adam Posen, Hari Rajan, Mykolas Rambus, Dilip Ratha, Razeen Sally, Sameer Shamsi, Kotaro Tamura, Arnaud Ventura, Richard Waddington, and Andrew Wong. Extra special thanks are due to Peter Marber for his profoundly constructive intellectual guidance over the years and his pinpoint observations and corrections and to Neeraj Seth, whose immense knowledge of global financial challenges doesn't inhibit him from thinking of creative solutions nor fortunately from sharing them with me.

Many expert thinkers on technology and its wide-ranging impact have provided forward-thinking ideas such as Scott Borg, Tyler Cowen, Marc Goodman, James Law, Daniel Rasmus, Tom Standage, Peter Thiel, and Vivek Wadhwa. Numerous innovators and doers in the information technology industry have also provided wideranging insights such as Jeff Jonas, Deepankar Sengupta, and Donald Hanson of IBM; Ann Lavin, Jared Cohen, and Will Fitzgerald of Google; Shailesh Rao, Aliza Knox, and Peter Greenberger of Twitter; Yinglan Tan of Sequoia Capital; John Kim of Amasia; Tom Crampton of Ogilvy; and James Chan of Silicon Straits.

Singapore is small in size, but big in ideas and action. There are too many individuals to thank for the daily interactions that have formed the limited portraits and references in this book. Nonetheless, I would like to specifically recognize the insights of senior figures from the National Research Foundation in the Prime Minister's Office, Jacqueline Poh and her team at the Infocomm Development Authority, Andrew Tan of the Maritime and Port Authority, Khoo Teng Chye and his team at the Centre for Liveable Cities, Philip Yeo and his colleagues at Singbridge, Manohar Khiatani and Aylwin Tan of Ascendas, Lim Siong Guan, Loh Wai Keong, and other executives from GIC (formerly the Government of Singapore Investment Corporation), Peter Ho, Chan Heng Chee, George Yeo, Beh Swan Gin, Vignes Sellakannu, Aaron Maniam, Lee Chor Pharn, Tan Li-San, and the organizers of events and discussions at the World Cities Summit, Civil Service College, and Human Capital Leadership Institute. I am ever grateful for the extensive time and thoughtfulness of leading Singaporeans such as Manu Bhaskaran, Ho Seng Chee, Vikram Khanna, Adam Rahman, Manraj Sekhon, Tan Su Shan, and Sudhir Vadaketh.

In Switzerland, various high-level gatherings have been very useful in comprehensively understanding what makes a leading nation tick. I'm grateful to Andreas Kirchschläger and Thomas Schmidheiny, as well as Mark Dittli, Pascale Ineichen, Urs Schoettli, and Toni Schönenberger from the Stars Foundation.

In addition to the dozens of countries I've traveled to in researching previous books, the past several years have allowed me to visit a number of countries for the first time such as Nigeria, Myanmar, North Korea, Mongolia, Estonia, Finland, and several others where connectivity has been playing out in intriguing ways. From Estonia, I'd especially like to thank Mark Erlich, Taavi Kotka, Tarvi Martens, Jaan Priisalu, Siim Sikkut, and Linnar Viik for making my visit so interesting, and in Finland special thanks to the great scholar-diplomat Alpo Rusi, Petri Hakkarainen, Antti Kaski, and Timo Rautajoki. For their warm hospitality during my unforgettable trip to Kirkenes in Norway, I'm very grateful to Andreas Hoffmann and his team at Pikene på Broen who host the Transborder Café. Special thanks in Oslo to His Royal Highness Haakon Magnus and the investment oracle Knut Kjaer.

For our conversations on the order and disorder across the Middle East and Africa, I'd like to thank Lauren Arnold, Neal Chandaria, Vimal Chandaria, Nick Danforth, Martyn Davies, Rajat Desai, Katayoon Eghtedar, Ziad Fares, Hassan Fattah, Lawrence Groo, Kevan Harris, Yasar Jarrar, Riad Kahwaji, Ted Karasik, Pardis Mahdavi, Peter Middlebrook, Afshin Molavi, Alex Perry, Sultan al Qassemi, Noah Raford, Masood Razak, Karim Sadjadpour, Nasser Saidi, Ismail Serageldin, Tarek Shayya, and Tark Yousef. For their immense hospitality and admirable stamina during my first trip to Iran, I'm deeply indebted to Roozbeh Aliabadi, Daniel Khazeni-Rad, Rouzbeh Pirouz, Ramin Rabii, Rouhollah Rahmani, and Cyrus Razzaghi.

The minds behind McKinsey & Company's research are worthy of praise for their incisive thinking on critical issues. I'd especially like to thank Chinta Bhagat, Penny Burtt, Diana Farrell, Andrew Grant, Rik Kirkland, Raja Pillai, Fraser Thompson, and Oliver Tonby for conversations over meals, over Skype, on the tennis court, and while wearing chemical suits on Jurong Island.

The world's geopolitical volatility requires shrewd focus and fresh analysis on border conflicts, energy markets, and the role of economics and the environment, all topics I appreciate having discussed with Saleem Ali, Aluf Benn, Linda Butler, Ranveer Chauhan, Bill Durch, Peter Eggleston, Espen Barth Eide, Adam Ellick, Keith Fitzgerald, Carl Ganter, Ben Judah, Srgjan Kerim, Kuntala Lahiri-Dutt, Bernice Lee, Jun Lin, J. J. Ong, Carter Page, Marko Papic, Ashwin Pavan, Rick Ponzio, Chin Thean Quek, Abhijnan Rej, Kevin Rudd, Ravi Sajwan, Enric Sala, Adam Sieminski, Laurence Smith, Paul Smyke, Mona Sutphen, Hans Vriens, Sergei Yatsenko, and Mikhail Zeldovich.

China also requires constant refreshing of analysis, and I am grateful for conversations with expert voices such as Braz Baracuhy, He Fan, Wang Gungwu, Mark Harper, Jun He, Bert Hofman, Benjamin Joffe, Eric Li, Leonard Liu, Peggy Liu, Kevin Lu, Rob McCormack, Dawn McGregor, Xiaoli Pan, Francesco Sisci, and Debra Tan.

The nexus of infrastructure, supply chains, and logistics has been integral to my research, and the thinking of the following individuals is visible throughout this book: Sara Agarwal, Vidar Andersen, Norm Anderson, Suman Bery, Karan Bhatia, Sergio Bitar, Jaime de Bourbon de Parme, Juan Chediack, Jan Chipchase, Mieke De Schepper, Elaine Dezenski, Thierry Drieens, Casper Ellerbaek, John Gattorna, Alison Kennedy, Thomas Knudsen, Mary Kuntz, George Kypraios, Peter Lacy, Åsa Larsson, Chris Logan, Nicolas de Loisy, Patrick Low, Pamela Mar, Bill Marin, Kathleen Matthews, Jennifer Newton, Oliver Niedermaier, Andrés Peña, Tony Prophet, Jordan Schwartz, Clara Shen, Ben Skinner, Jim Snabe, Abel van Staveren, Gee Boon Tan, and Alex Wong.

The creation of this book has deepened my connection to the cartographic community's many passionate and creative voices. Collaborations and conversations over the years with Frank Jacobs have as ever stimulated my thinking and plotting of the possible. Rey Dizon of MapStory provided helpful early maps to depict global infrastructure patterns, and Manjeet Kripalani and Akshay Mathur of Gateway House in Mumbai provided admirably detailed samples. Thanks to Mathias Holzmann of Mapbox, those early guides grew into the Connectivity Atlas developed by Development Seed. Joe Flasher, Ian Schuler, Robin Tolochko, and the many hardworking members of the Development Seed team deserve enormous credit for leading the gargantuan geo-data collection and visualization exercise now freely available to anyone, anywhere to explore. I am deeply indebted to them all for creating something far too dynamic to be grasped within the covers of a book.

My cartographic brain trust has been led by Jeff Blossom of Harvard's Center for Geographic Analysis as well as Tanya Buckingham and her team, especially the exceptionally talented Clare Trainor and Dylan Moriarty, at the University of Wisconsin's Cartography Lab, and Mona Hammami of the Crown Prince's Court in Abu Dhabi. They are all modern mapping magicians.

Thanks to those who have given anonymous inputs in the course of my research and interviews, and anyone inadvertently omitted. Your generous time and ideas have been invaluable in synthesizing this book. I apologize for any oversights but thank you all the same.

Now to thank those who have been with me on these journeys since the beginning. Will Murphy, my editor at Penguin Random House, was the first to consider my first book proposal more than a decade ago and has once again masterfully uncorked my dense drafts. I am also grateful to the executive team at PRH for their professional commitment to this book: publisher Gina Centrello, editor in chief Susan Kamil, senior vice president and deputy publisher Tom Perry, director of subsidiary rights Denise Cronin, and director of international sales Cyrus Kheradi, as well as all of their superb colleagues. I would also like to thank assistant editor Mika Kasuga for her even temperament and clever ideas on all aspects of this book; Barbara Bachman and her design team for handling so many complex visuals; Ted Allen and his copyediting team for their careful management of the manuscript; and my no-nonsense publicist, Greg Kubie, who always has his finger on the zeitgeist. I can't thank my agent, Jennifer Joel at ICM, enough for the many years of coaching and friendship.

No matter how ambitious the book, it always helps when one's own family is a virtual think tank unto itself. Both my parents, Sushil and Manjula Khanna, and my in-laws, Javed and Zarene Malik, have again lent their real-world expertise and comments on many issues discussed herein, as has my brother Gaurav, whose physics Ph.D. was invaluable in shaping material on complexity. My wife Ayesha's focus on urban technologies seeped in throughout the writing process, and our own next-generation offspring, Zara and Zubin, have rounded out the "Little Khannas" team that made this book a delightful undertaking from start to finish. They are already following their own maps.

NOTES

A NOTE ABOUT MAPS

1. In *The Clash of Civilizations and the Remaking of World Order,* Samuel Huntington left open the fate of whether Latin America belonged to the West or constituted a civilization unto itself.
2. Jerry Brotton, *History,* Introduction.
3. Some have called this nascent meta-discipline sociography.

CHAPTER 1: FROM BORDERS TO BRIDGES

1. These rates were enough to lift the industrializing West to levels of growth around 2 percent through the nineteenth century.
2. See Isabelle Cohen et al., *The Economic Impact and Financing of Infrastructure Spending* (Thomas Jefferson Program in Public Policy, College of William & Mary, 2012). In the early 1980s, the Oklahoma economist Pat Choate, best known as Ross Perot's 1996 vice presidential running mate on the Reform Party ticket, wrote *America in Ruins,* which warned of the country's infrastructural decay.
3. The World Bank provides a rough typology of basic infrastructures essential for development: http://data.worldbank.org/about/world-development-indicators -data/infrastructure.
4. The Stockholm International Peace Research Institute reports that worldwide military expenditures constitute 2.4 percent of world GDP. Military spending in the United States has fallen by almost 8 percent, while China's and Russia's spending has risen by 7.4 percent and 4.8 percent, respectively; Gulf Cooperation Council countries such as Saudi Arabia have also moderately increased military expenditures. See http://www.sipri.org/research/armaments/milex/milex_database/milex _database.
5. PricewaterhouseCoopers and Oxford Economics projection of capital project and infrastructure spending. See http://www.pwc.com/gx/en/capital-projects -infrastructure/publications/cpi-outlook/assets/cpi-outlook-to-2025.pdf. Estimates of current annual infrastructure spending already range from $2 trillion to $3 trillion. According to McKinsey, just to keep the current pace of GDP growth will

require $3.5 trillion per year in infrastructure spending; Bain & Company predicts $4 trillion per year by 2017.

6. The Dutch-Belgian border passes through people's living rooms and public cafés in the town of Baarle-Nassau—or Baarle-Hertog depending on which side of the invisible line you happen to be standing on. Either way, you are in the Schengen area of the EU. Due to an anomaly stemming from the 1783 Treaty of Paris, the 120 residents of Angle Township in Minnesota actually live within Canadian territory and use a phone booth jointly run by U.S. and Canadian customs to report their comings and goings.

7. See "More Neighbours Make More Fences," *The Economist,* Sept. 15, 2015.

8. "Why Walls Don't Work," *Project Syndicate,* Nov. 13, 2014.

9. Vaclav Smil, *Making the Modern World: Materials and Dematerialization* (MIT Press, 2007), p. 157.

10. Ron Boschma and Ron Martin, "The Aims and Scope of Evolutionary Economic Geography" (Utrecht University, Jan. 2010).

11. Michio Kaku, *Physics of the Future: How Science Will Shape Human Destiny and Our Daily Lives by the Year 2100* (Anchor, 2012).

12. In the dense but influential treatise *Empire* (Harvard University Press, 2000), the American scholar Michael Hardt and the Italian dissident Antonio Negri posit globalization as an unregulated and all-consuming force that has no fixed locus.

13. Today's complex global supply chains—hybrids of public and corporate actors—embody what the pioneering scholar James Rosenau called a "sphere of authority": a trans-territorial, cross-jurisdiction entity that has low institutionalization, low visibility, multiple public and private operators and rule makers, and immense public relevance.

14. From the original Six Sigma manufacturing optimization process has grown a suite of tools such as electronic data interchange that leverage supplier and buyer data and market conditions to forecast volume and demand shifts, and sensor networks to track inventories, improve efficiency, and reduce waste.

15. Accenture's Supply Chain Academy has managers from hundreds of Fortune 1000 companies enrolled in its thousands of online case study courses dedicated to achieving such business optimization.

16. "Geography: Use It or Lose It," remarks at the U.S. Department of State, May 25, 2010.

CHAPTER 2: NEW MAPS FOR A NEW WORLD

1. John Maynard Keynes, *The Economic Consequences of the Peace.* (Harcourt, Brace and Howe, 1920), Chapter II.4.

2. Peter Nolan, *Is China Buying the World?* (Polity, 2013).

3. "Flow Dynamics," *The Economist,* Sept. 19, 2015.

4. Financial flows (such as global banking, foreign investment, and portfolio capital) surged from $470 billion (4 percent of GDP) in 1980 to $12 trillion (21 percent of a much larger GDP) in 2007. After the financial crisis, the eurozone banking crisis and higher reserve requirements pushed capital flows back below 10 percent of GDP.

5. Turkey's Ayka Tekstil and Sweden's H&M are other major apparel manufacturers and brands that have expanded operations in Ethiopia.

6. See DHL's *Global Connectedness Index 2014,* http://www.dhl.com/en/.

7. Tiny Belgium's banks serve as custodial financial institutions holding $400 billion in U.S. Treasuries (almost 70 percent of its GDP) for major foreign purchasers such as China.

8. In 2013, this amounted to about $18 trillion in goods, $5 trillion in services, and $4 trillion in finance.

9. National Intelligence Council, *Global Trends 2030: Alternative Worlds* (National Intelligence Council, 2012).

10. Manuel Castells, *The Informational City: Economic Restructuring and Urban Development* (Blackwell Publishers, 1990).

11. Michele Acuto and Steve Rayner, "City Networks: Breaking Gridlocks or Forging (New) Lock-ins?," unpublished paper, 2015.

CHAPTER 3: THE GREAT DEVOLUTION

1. Additionally, according to one catalog, there are at least four hundred so-called micro-nations of eccentrics trying to launch their own countries whether in the wilds of America and Australia or on abandoned oil rigs like Sealand in the North Sea.

2. Alberto Alesina and Bryony Reich, "Nation-Building" (National Bureau of Economic Research working paper 18839, Feb. 2013).

3. Alberto Alesina and Enrico Spolaore, "Conflict, Defense Spending, and the Number of Nations," *European Economic Review* 50, no. 1 (2006).

4. In 1992, almost one-third of all the world's countries were experiencing significant political violence. Even worse, ethnic wars tend to last twice or thrice as long as interstate or intrastate conflicts.

5. Edward Luttwak, "Give War a Chance," *Foreign Affairs,* July/Aug. 1999.

6. These groups are collectively members of the Unrepresented Nations and Peoples Organization.

7. Sardinia is one of five autonomous Italian regions, along with Valle d'Aosta, Venezia, Sicily, and Trentino.

CHAPTER 4: FROM DEVOLUTION TO AGGREGATION

1. Antoni Estevadeordal, Juan Blyde, and Kati Suominen, "Are Global Value Chains Really Global? Policies to Accelerate Countries' Access to International Production Networks" (Inter-American Development Bank, 2012).

2. Stelios Michalopoulos and Elias Papaioannou, "The Long-Run Effects of the Scramble for Africa" (NBER working paper 17620, Nov. 2011). Just one of the many examples of European treatment of African territories as family heirlooms is Queen Victoria's gifting of Mount Kilimanjaro (on the border between Kenya and Tanzania) to her nephew Kaiser Wilhelm II of Prussia.

3. Philip Mansel, *Constantinople* (Penguin, 1997).

4. Antonia Guterres, quoted in "Global Refugee Figure Passes 50m for First Time Since Second World War," *The Guardian,* June 20, 2014.

5. Norimitsu Onishi, "As Syrian Refugees Develop Roots, Jordan Grows Wary," *New York Times,* Oct. 5, 2013.

6. A comprehensive study of seven potential scenarios advises that a two-state solution remains the most cost-effective for both Israel and Palestinians. See *The Costs of the Israeli-Palestinian Conflict* (Rand, 2015).

7. Jodi Rudoren, "In West Bank Settlements, Israeli Jobs Are Double-Edged Sword," *New York Times,* Feb. 10, 2014.

8. Stanley Reed and Clifford Krauss, "Israel's Gas Offers Lifeline for Peace," *New York Times,* Dec. 14, 2014.

CHAPTER 5: THE NEW MANIFEST DESTINY

1. Richey Piiparinen and Jim Russell, *From Balkanized Cleveland to Global Cleveland: A Theory of Change for Legacy Cities* (White Paper funded by Ohio City Inc., 2013).

2. Nearby Zhongshan is also an example of a tightly subdivided industry town: Dachong for mahogany furniture, Dongfeng for household appliances, Guzhen for lighting, Huangpu for food products, Shaxi for casual clothing, Xiaolan for door locks and acoustic products, and so on.

3. The Chinese academic Zheng Yongnian refers to the current status as "behavioral federalism."

4. Through the local government financing vehicles, Chinese municipalities are raising $1 billion per month through investment bonds—from home *and* abroad—to fund their growth projects.

5. Lydia DePillis, "This Is What a Job in the U.S.'s New Manufacturing Industry Looks Like," *Washington Post,* Mar. 9, 2014.

6. https://www.facebook.com/photo.php?fbid=506922386075591.

7. Richard C. Longworth, *Caught in the Middle: America's Heartland in the Age of Globalism* (Bloomsbury, 2009).

8. At the same time, Washington uses federal highway grants as a lever to impose on them unrelated regulations such as the drinking age and Medicare contributions. See Richard A. Epstein and Mario Loyola, "The United State of America," *Atlantic,* July 31, 2014.

9. Chris Benner and Manuel Pastor, "Buddy, Can You Spare Some Time? Social Inclusion and Sustained Prosperity in America's Metropolitan Regions/Working Paper," MacArthur Foundation Network on Building Resilient Regions, May 31, 2013.

10. Henry Zhang, "China to Build Cities and Economic Zones in Michigan and Idaho," *Policy Mic,* May 20, 2012.

11. Ben Tracy, "Lake Mead is Shrinking—and with it Las Vegas' water supply," *CBS News,* Jan. 30, 2014.

CHAPTER 6: WORLD WAR III—OR TUG-OF-WAR?

1. In early 2015, the trading house Itochu made the largest Japanese foreign investment ever in China, buying (together with Thailand's CP Group) a 10 percent stake in CITIC, one of China's oldest and most respected conglomerates.

CHAPTER 7: THE GREAT SUPPLY CHAIN WAR

1. Interview with author, July 18, 2015.

2. Enrico Moretti, *The New Geography of Jobs* (Houghton Mifflin Harcourt, 2012).

3. Josh Tyrangiel, "Tim Cook's Freshman Year: The Apple CEO Speaks," *Bloomberg Businessweek,* Dec. 6, 2012.
4. However, additive manufacturing and the sharing economy together do cause tremendous domestic dislocation. The construction sector is not tradable, but it can increasingly be automated as entire homes are designed, printed, and assembled out of 3-D printing kits, displacing contractors and builders across America and Europe.
5. "Bits, Bytes, and Diplomacy," *Foreign Affairs,* Sept./Oct. 1997.
6. Allison Schrager, "The US Needs to Retire Daylight Savings and Just Have Two Time Zones—One Hour Apart," *Quartz,* Nov. 1, 2013.
7. Adams Nager, "Why Is America's Manufacturing Job Loss Greater Than Other Industrialized Countries?," *Industry Week,* Aug. 21, 2014.
8. "How Big Companies Can Beat the Patent Chaos of India," *Fortune,* June 17, 2013.
9. Artem Golev et al., "Rare Earths Supply Chains: Current Status, Constraints, and Opportunities," *Resources Policy* 41 (Sept. 2014): 52–59.
10. Yogesh Malik, Alex Niemeyer, and Brian Ruwadi, "Building the Supply Chain of the Future," *McKinsey Quarterly* (Jan. 2011).
11. John Authers, "US Revival Warrants EM Strategy Rethink," *Financial Times,* May 16, 2014.
12. Barry C. Lynn, *End of the Line* (Doubleday, 2005).

CHAPTER 8: INFRASTRUCTURE ALLIANCES

1. Arnold Toynbee, *A Study of History: Abridgment of Volumes VII–X.* (Oxford University Press, 1957), p. 124.
2. Samuel P. Huntington, *The Clash of Civilizations and the Remaking of World Order* (Simon & Schuster, 1996), p. 239.
3. Mariano Turzi, "The Soybean Republic," *Yale Journal of International Affairs* (Spring/Summer 2011).

CHAPTER 9: THE NEW IRON AGE

1. Keith Bradsher, "Hauling New Treasure Along the Silk Road," *New York Times,* July 20, 2013.
2. As of 2015, the AIIB has fifty-eight members and two dozen on the waiting list.
3. "Why China Will Reclaim Siberia," *The New York Times,* Jan. 13, 2015.
4. "We must not buy Perrier . . . We must sell our water abroad," *Water Politics,* Oct. 28, 2010.
5. "The Round World and the Winning of the Peace," *Foreign Affairs,* July 1943.
6. See Gi-Wook Shin, David Straub, and Joyce Lee, "Tailored Engagement: Toward an Effective Inter-Korean Relations Policy" (Shorenstein Asia-Pacific Research Center, Stanford University, Sept. 2014).
7. Kristopher Rawls, quoted in, "Why China Wants North Korea's Rare Earth Minerals," CNBC.com, Feb. 21, 2014.
8. Speech delivered at the Parliament of South Africa, Feb. 3, 1960.

CHAPTER 10: HOPSCOTCH ACROSS THE OCEANS

1. Letter to King Carlos V, quoted in Frank Jacobs, "The First Google Maps War," *The New York Times,* Feb. 28, 2012.
2. A. M. Mahan, *The Interest of America in Sea Power, Present and Future* (Tredition Classics, 2011).
3. Brian Spegele and Wayne Ma, "For China Boss, Deep-Water Rigs Are a 'Strategic Weapon,'" *Wall Street Journal,* Aug. 29, 2012.
4. Vince Beiser, "The Deadly Global War for Sand," *Wired,* Apr. 2015.
5. Joshua Comaroff, "Built on Sand: Singapore and the New State of Risk," *Harvard Design Magazine,* no. 39 (2014).
6. Quoted in C.M. Turnbull, *A History of Modern Singapore, 1819–2005* (National University Press, 2009), p. 38.
7. Thalif Deen, "China: 'Pakistan is our Israel,'" Al Jazeera, October 28, 2010.
8. Katherine Burton, "John Paulson calls Puerto Rico Singapore of Caribbean," *Bloomberg,* Apr. 25, 2014.
9. Interview with author in Kirkenes, Norway, on Oct. 24, 2014.
10. Jeremy S. Pal and Elfatih A.B. Eitahir, "Future Temperature in Southwest Asia Projected to Exceed a Threshold for Human Adaptability," *Nature Climate Change,* Oct. 26, 2015.

CHAPTER 11: IF YOU BUILD IT, THEY WILL COME

1. McKinsey Global Institute, *Global Flows in a Digital Age,* 2014.
2. The financial dealings of Dubai's ruling family have opened it to accusations of opacity. Property developers in particular have had government investment vehicles and national banks as major shareholders and creditors, thus foreign investors before the financial crisis treated them like state-owned enterprises with an ironclad commitment from the oil-rich capital emirate of Abu Dhabi. But when the Dubai World conglomerate asked for a reprieve on interest payments in 2009, suddenly foreigners found themselves negotiating with private companies but ones whose directors were either royal family members or surrogates with close ties to the legal system—leading to a significant softening of the terms.
3. R. Koolhaas, O. Bouman, and M. Wigley, eds., "Last Chance," in *Al Manakh* (Columbia University Press, 2007), pp. 194–203.
4. Conversation at the Global Art Forum, Dubai Art Festival, Mar. 22, 2012.
5. Daniel Brook, *A History of Future Cities* (W. W. Norton, 2014).
6. Speech at Cityquest KAEC Forum, Nov. 25, 2013.
7. Gabriel Kuris, "Remaking a Neglected Megacity: A Civic Transformation in Lagos State, 1999–2012" (Princeton Project on Innovations for Successful Societies, July 2014).

CHAPTER 12: GETTING ON THE MAP

1. National Intelligence Council, *Global Trends 2030 Alternative Worlds,* National Intelligence Council, 2012, p. 135.

2. The World Bank identifies nineteen different terms for such zones such as "free trade zone," "foreign trade zone," "industrial free zone," "free zone," "maquiladora," "export free zone," "duty free export processing zone," "special economic zone," "tax free zone," "tax free trade zone," "investment promotion zone," "free economic zone," "free export zone," "free export processing zone," "privileged export zone," and "industrial export processing zone." Other studies have found up to sixty-six terms.

3. World Bank, "Special Economic Zones: Progress, Emerging Challenges, and Future Directions" (World Bank, 2011).

4. John D. Kasarda and Greg Lindsay, *Aerotropolis: The Way We'll Live Next* (Farrar, Straus and Giroux, 2011).

5. Rosa Brooks, "Failed States, or the State as Failure?," *University of Chicago Law Review* (Fall 2005).

6. Andrew Tangel, "Report Connects Jobs, Transportation Web," *Wall Street Journal*, Jan. 2, 2015.

7. Interview with author, July 11, 2013.

8. These hybrid regimes are not like the internationalized governance of countries under post–World War II occupation such as Japan and Germany, or the "informal empire" that characterized Soviet influence on the foreign and domestic policies of Warsaw Pact members, or the more recent post-conflict administrative authorities imposed on Bosnia, East Timor, and Iraq. Instead, hybrid regimes are more interested in supervising production than controlling geography. They focus on commercial levers such as investor protection treaties and operational control over SEZs. According to Oisín Tansey, hybrid regimes emerge due to the persistent international pressure exerted by outside powers to set their policy agendas, veto their laws, draft their legislation, bypass domestic enforcement, and influence leadership selection. See Oisin Tansey, "Internationalized Regimes: A Second Dimension of Regime Hybridity," *Democratization* 20, no. 7 (2013).

CHAPTER 13: SUPPLY CHAINS AS SALVATION

1. Foreign pharmaceutical companies are also crucial in cleaning up China's drug supply chain. The American medical distribution leader Cardinal Health, for example, has bought many small Chinese pharmacies and drug distribution companies to ensure reliable end-to-end, tamper-free delivery of sensitive cancer treatments and other essential drugs.

2. The United Nations has been ahead of the curve in terms of its intellectual agendas such as "human security," which sought to put individuals rather than states at the center of conflict discourse, and "sustainable urbanization," which remains the most cogent response to rapid industrialization and resource consumption. But it has little power to implement these visions absent public-private partnerships (PPPs) along the supply chain. There are many PPPs, but no definitive model that results in self-sustaining programs. However, a comprehensive Dutch government survey of the past decade of PPPs in the development arena concludes that while they are growing in number, PPPs are unlikely to succeed without the permanent involvement of public agencies, a sound regulatory framework around the recovery of costs and distribution of services, and appropriate partner selection based on com-

patibility and commitment. "Public-Private Partnerships in Developing Countries: A Systematic Literature Review" (Ministry of Foreign Affairs of the Netherlands, Apr. 2013).

3. "The Omnipresent Craft: Graft," *Straits Times,* Feb. 12, 2014.

4. Corruption, political volatility, and border frictions are considered the factors that most weaken competitiveness. See James E. Anderson and Douglas Marcouiller, "Insecurity and the Pattern of Trade: An Empirical Investigation" (NBER working paper 7000, Aug. 2000).

5. Vivek Sharma, "Give Corruption a Chance," *National Interest,* Nov. 2013.

6. Joseph E. Stiglitz, "Inequality Is a Choice," *The New York Times,* Oct. 13, 2013.

7. Jeremy Wallace, "Cities, Redistribution, and Authoritarian Regime Survival," *The Journal of Politics 75,* no. 3 (2013): 632–45. The Australian counterinsurgency expert David Kilcullen points out that as the world becomes crowded and coastal, militaries need high-resolution three-dimensional terrain maps of informal settlements.

8. The subsequent volumes of Hardt and Negri's trilogy, *Multitude* and *Commonwealth,* continue this intellectual struggle against capitalism's appropriation of property, advocating instead greater unity among dispersed communities of peoples.

9. One estimate suggests $2 trillion in emerging market pension assets allocated to other emerging markets by 2020. See Jay Pelosky, "Emerging Market Portfolio Globalization: The Next Big Thing" (New America Foundation, World Economic Roundtable policy paper, July 17, 2014).

10. Martin Neil Baily and Douglas J. Elliott, "The Role of Finance in the Economy: Implications for Structural Reform of the Financial Sector" (Brookings Institution, July 11, 2013).

CHAPTER 14: CYBER CIVILIZATION AND ITS DISCONTENTS

1. Julio Bezerra et al., *The Mobile Revolution: How Mobile Technologies Drive a Trillion-Dollar Impact* (Boston Consulting Group, Jan. 2015).

2. Neal Stephenson, "Mother Earth, Mother Board," *Wired,* Apr. 2012.

3. Mark P. Mills, "The Cloud Begins with Coal: Big Data, Big Networks, Big Infrastructure, and Big Power" (Digital Power Group, 2013).

4. Forrest Hare, "Borders in Cyberspace: Can Sovereignty Adapt to the Challenges of Cyber-Security?" (George Mason University, 2011).

5. "The Peer to Peer Manifesto: The Emergence of P2P Civilization and Political Economy," *Reality Sandwich,* 2008.

6. Alex Pentland, *Social Physics: How Good Ideas Spread* (Penguin, 2014).

7. Ricardo Hausmann, Cesar A. Hidalgo, and Sebastian Bustos, *The Atlas of Economic Complexity: Mapping Paths to Prosperity* (MIT Press, 2014).

8. Carlota Perez, "A New Age of Technological Progress," Policy Network, Aug. 22, 2014, p. 20.

9. Interview with author, Oct. 10, 2014.

10. Émile Durkheim, *The Rules of the Sociological Method,* trans. by W. D. Halls, Free Press, 1982 [1895], Chapter 5.

CHAPTER 15: THE GREAT DILUTION

1. European Union, *Erasmus Impact Study* (European Union, Sept. 2014).
2. Interview with the author, Jan. 13, 2014.
3. Benjamin R. Barber, *If Mayors Ruled the World: Dysfunctional Nations, Rising Cities* (Yale University Press, 2013).
4. Tommy Koh, "Seven Habits of a Singaporean," *Straits Times,* Sept. 11, 2013.
5. Interview with *Planeta Sustevenal,* Oct. 2007.
6. Daniel A. Bell and Avner de-Shalit, *The Spirit of Cities: Why the Identity of a City Matters in a Global Age* (Princeton University Press, 2013).
7. "Poor but Sexy," *The Economist,* Sept. 21, 2006.
8. Jeffrey Gettleman, "A Catch-22 in Kenya: Western Terrorism Alerts May Fuel Terrorism," *The New York Times,* Feb. 23, 2015.
9. Clemens, "Economics and Emigration."
10. Interview with author, Oct. 31, 2014.
11. Stephanie Ott, "EU Citizenship for Sale," CNN.com, Dec. 21, 2013.

CHAPTER 16: WHEN NATURE HAS ITS SAY, GET OUT OF THE WAY

1. Scenarios of enhancing the resilience to coastal flooding for New York City have been developed and are under consideration. See Jeroen C. J. H. Aerts et al., "Evaluating Flood Resilience Strategies for Coastal Megacities," *Science,* May 2, 2014, 473–75.

CONCLUSION: FROM CONNECTIVITY TO RESILIENCE

1. "Our Big Bet for the Future," 2015 Gates Annual Letter, available at: http://www.gatesnotes.com/2015-annual-letter

BIBLIOGRAPHY

Acemoglu, Daron, and James Robinson. *Why Nations Fail: The Origins of Power, Prosperity, and Poverty.* Crown Business, 2013.

Acuto, Michele. *Building Global Cities.* Oxford Programme for the Future of Cities, 2013.

Adler-Nissen, Rebecca. *Opting out of the European Union.* Cambridge University Press, 2015.

Aerts, C.J.H., et al. "Evaluating Flood Resilience Strategies for Coastal Megacities." *Science,* May 22, 2014, 473–75.

Alesina, Alberto, and Byrony Reich. "Nation-Building." National Bureau of Economic Research working paper 18839, Feb. 2013.

Alesina, Alberto, and Enrico Spolaore. *The Size of Nations.* MIT Press, 2003.

Anderson, Benedict. *Imagined Communities: Reflections on the Origin and Spread of Nationalism.* Rev. ed. Verso, 2006.

Anderson, David M. *Leveraging: A Political, Economic, and Societal Framework.* Springer, 2014.

Anderson, James E., and Douglas Marcouiller. "Insecurity and the Pattern of Trade: An Empirical Investigation." NBER working paper 7000, Aug, 2000.

Angel, Schlomo. *Planet of Cities.* Lincoln Institute of Land Policy, 2012.

Angel, Schlomo, Jason Parent, Daniel L. Civico, and Alejandro M. Blei. *Atlas of Urban Expansion.* Lincoln Institute of Land Policy, 2012.

Antholis, William. *Inside Out, India and China: Local Politics Go Global.* Brookings Institution Press, 2013.

Anthony, David W. *The Horse, the Wheel, and Language: How Bronze-Age Riders from the Eurasian Steppes Shaped the Modern World.* Princeton University Press, 2007.

Antweiler, Werner, Brian R. Copeland, and M. Scott Taylor. "Is Free Trade Good for the Environment?" *American Economic Review* 91, no. 4 (2001): 877–908.

Araya, Daniel, and Peter Marber. *Higher Education in the Global Age: Policy, Practice, and Promise in Emerging Societies.* Routledge, 2013.

Arrighi, Giovanni. *The Long Twentieth Century: Money, Power, and the Origins of Our Times.* Verso, 1994.

Arthur, W. Brian. *Complexity Economics: A Different Framework for Economic Thought.* Santa Fe Institute Working Paper, 2013-04-012.

Atkinson, Robert. *Understanding and Maximizing America's Evolutionary Economy.* ITIF, 2014.

Axelrod, Robert, and Michael D. Cohen. *Harnessing Complexity: Organizational Implications of a Scientific Frontier.* Basic Books, 2001.

Backaler, Joel. *China Goes West: The Coming Rise of Chinese Brands.* Palgrave Macmillan, 2014.

Bader, Christine. *The Evolution of a Corporate Idealist: When Girl Meets Oil.* Bibliomotion, 2014.

Baily, Martin Neil, and Douglas J. Elliott. "The Role of Finance in the Economy: Implications for Structural Reform of the Financial Sector." Brookings Institution, July 11, 2013.

Ball, Philip. *Why Society Is a Complex Matter: Meeting Twenty-First Century Challenges with a New Kind of Science.* Springer, 2012.

Banerjee, Abhijit, and Esther Dufflo. *Poor Economics: A Radical Rethinking of the Way to Fight Global Poverty.* PublicAffairs, 2012.

Barber, Benjamin R. *If Mayors Ruled the World: Dysfunctional Nations, Rising Cities.* Yale University Press, 2013.

Barford, Anna, Daniel Dorling, and Mark Newman, eds. *The Atlas of the Real World: Mapping the Way We Live.* Rev. ed. Thames & Hudson, 2010.

Barnett, Thomas P. M. *The Pentagon's New Map: War and Peace in the Twenty-First Century.* Berkley Trade, 2005.

Bar-Yam, Y. "Complexity Rising: From Human Beings to Human Civilization." In *Encyclopedia of Life Support Systems.* UNESCO, 2002.

Batchelor, Robert K. *London: The Selden Map and the Making of a Global City, 1549–1689.* University of Chicago Press, 2014.

Bauwens, Michel. *Political Economy of Peer Production.* Ctheory, 2005. http://www.ctheory.net/articles.aspx?id=499.

Beiser, Vince. "The Deadly Global War for Sand." *Wired,* Apr. 2015.

Bell, Daniel A., and Avner de-Shalit. *The Spirit of Cities: Why the Identity of a City Matters in a Global Age.* Princeton University Press, 2013.

Bell, Daniel A., and Yingchuan Mo. "Harmony in the World 2013: The Ideal and the Reality." *Social Indicators Research,* Sept. 2013.

Ben-Atar, Doron S. *Trade Secrets: Intellectual Piracy and the Origins of American Industrial Power.* Yale University Press, 2004.

Benkler, Yochai. *The Wealth of Networks: How Social Production Transforms Markets and Freedom.* Yale University Press, 2007.

Benner, Chris, and Manuel Pastor. "Buddy, Can You Spare Some Time? Social Inclusion and Sustained Prosperity in America's Metropolitan Regions." Working Paper, MacArthur Foundation Network on Building Resilient Regions, May 31, 2013.

Bennett, Lance "Logic of Connective Action." *Information, Communication, and Society* 15, no. 5 (2012).

Berggruen, Nicolas, and Nathan Gardels. *Intelligent Governance for the 21st Century: A Middle Way Between West and East*. Polity, 2012.

Berman, Ilan. *Implosion: The End of Russia and What It Means for America*. Regnery, 2013.

Bezerra, Julio, et al. *The Mobile Revolution: How Mobile Technologies Drive a Trillion-Dollar Impact*. Boston Consulting Group, Jan. 2015.

Bhide, Amar. *The Venturesome Economy: How Innovation Sustains Prosperity in a More Connected World*. Princeton University Press, 2010.

Bilakovics, Steven. *Democracy Without Politics*. Harvard University Press, 2012.

Bilmes, Linda, and Joseph E. Stiglitz. *The Three Trillion Dollar War: The True Cost of the Iraq Conflict*. W. W. Norton, 2008.

Blum, Andrew. *Tubes: A Journey to the Center of the Internet*. Ecco, 2013.

Blyth, Mark. *Austerity: History of a Dangerous Idea*. Oxford University Press, 2013.

Bobbitt, Philip. *The Shield of Achilles: War, Peace, and the Course of History*. Anchor, 2003.

Bodie, Zvi, Alex Kane, and Alan J. Marcus. *Investments and Portfolio Management*. McGraw-Hill/Irwin, 2011.

Bousquet, Antoine, and Simon Curtis. "Beyond Models and Metaphors: Complexity Theory, Systems Thinking, and International Relations." *Cambridge Review of International Affairs* 24, no. 1 (2011): 43–62.

Boschma, Ron, and Ron Martin. "The Aims and Scope of Evolutionary Economic Geography. Utrecht University (Jan. 2010).

Boyd, Danah. *It's Complicated: The Social Lives of Networked Teens*. Yale University Press, 2014.

Braithwaite, John. *Regulatory Capitalism: How It Works, Ideas for Making It Work Better*. Edward Elgar, 2008.

Brands, Hal. *What Good Is Grand Strategy? Power and Purpose in American Statecraft from Harry S. Truman to George W. Bush*. Cornell University Press, 2014.

Bratton, Benjamin. *The Stack: On Software and Sovereignty*. MIT Press, 2013.

Brautigam, Deborah. *The Dragon's Gift*. Oxford University Press, 2011.

Breiding, R. James. *Swiss Made: The Untold Story Behind Switzerland's Success*. Profile Books, 2013.

Bremmer, Ian. *Superpower: Three Choices for America*. Portfolio, 2015.

Brenner, Neil, ed. *Implosions/Explosions: Towards a Study of Planetary Urbanization*. Jovis, 2014.

Brenton, Paul, and Gözde Isik, eds. *De-fragmenting Africa: Deepening Regional Trade Integration in Goods and Services*. World Bank, 2012.

Brook, Daniel. *A History of Future Cities*. W. W. Norton, 2014.

Brooks, Rosa. "Failed States, or State as Failure." University of Chicago Law Review (Fall 2005).

Brotton, Jerry. *A History of the World in 12 Maps*. Viking, 2013.

Brown, Donald. *Human Universals*. McGraw-Hill Humanities, 1991.

Brynjolfsson, Erik, and Andrew McAfee. *The Second Machine Age: Work, Progress, and Prosperity in a Time of Brilliant Technologies*. W. W. Norton, 2014.

Buckley, F. H. *The Once and Future King: The Rise of Crown Government in America*. Encounter Books, 2014.

Burrows, Matthew. *The Future Declassified: Megatrends That Will Undo the World Unless We Take Action*. Palgrave Macmillan Trade, 2014.

Busch, Gary K. *Free for All: The Post-Soviet Transition of Russia*. Virtualbookworm.com, 2010.

Buzan, Barry. *From International to World Society?* Cambridge University Press, 2004.

Buzan, Barry, and Little, Richard. *International Systems in World History: Remaking the Study of International Relations*. Oxford University Press, 2000.

Callahan, William A. *Contingent States: Greater China and Transnational Relations*. Minnesota University Press, 2004.

Castells, Manuel. *The Informational City: Economic Restructuring and Urban Development*. Wiley-Blackwell, 1992.

———. *The Internet Galaxy: Reflections on the Internet, Business, and Society*. Oxford University Press, 2001.

———. *The Rise of the Network Society*. Blackwell, 1996.

Castells, Manuel, and Peter Hall. *Technopoles of the World: The Making of 21st Century Industrial Complexes*. Routledge, 1994.

Castells, Manuel, and Pekka Himanen, eds. *Reconceptualizing Development in the Global Information Age*. Oxford University Press, 2014.

Cha, Victor. *The Impossible State: North Korea, Past and Future*. Ecco, 2013.

Chandra, Kanchan. *Elections as Auctions*. www.india-seminar.com.

Chang, Ha-Joon. *Kicking Away the Ladder: Development Strategy in Historical Perspective*. Anthem Press, 2002.

Chase-Dunn, Christopher K., and Thomas D. Hall. *Rise and Demise*. Westview Press, 1997.

Chayes, Sarah. *Thieves of State: Why Corruption Threatens Global Security*. W. W. Norton, 2015.

Cheah, Pheng, and Bruce Robbins, eds. *Cosmopolitics: Thinking and Feeling Beyond the Nation*. Minnesota University Press, 1998.

Chellaney, Brahma. *Water, Peace, and War: Confronting the Global Water Crisis*. Rowman & Littlefield, 2013.

Chetty, Raj, Nathaniel Hendren, Patrick Kline, and Emmanuel Saez. "Where Is the Land of Opportunity? The Geography of Intergenerational Mobility in the United States." NBER Working Paper 19843, Jan. 2014.

Chief of Staff of the Army's Strategic Studies Group. "A Proposed Framework for Appreciating Megacities: A US Army Perspective." *Small Wars Journal* (April 2014).

Chinese Military Science Academy. *History of the War to Resist America and Aid Korea*. Military Science Academy, 2000.

Choate, Pat, and Susan Walter. *America in Ruins: The Decaying Infrastructure*. Duke University Press, 1983.

Choudhry, Sujit, and Nathan Hume. "Federalism, Secession, and Devolution: From Classical to Post-conflict Federalism." In *Research Handbook on Comparative Constitutional Law*. Edward Elgar, 2013.

Christian, David. *Maps of Time: An Introduction to Big History*. University of California Press, 2011.

Chung, J. H. *Changing Central-Local Relations in China: Reform and State Capacity*. Cambridge University Press, 1995.

Clad, James, Sean M. McDonald, and Bruce Vaughn, eds. *The Borderlands of Southeast Asia: Geopolitics, Terrorism, and Globalization*. National Defense University, 2011.

Clark, Christopher. *The Sleepwalkers: How Europe Went to War in 1914*. Harper Perennial, 2014.

Clemens, Michael. "Economics and Emigration: Trillion-Dollar Bills on the Sidewalk?" *Journal of Economic Perspectives* 25, no. 3 (2011): 83–106.

Clunan, Anne, and Harold Trinkunas. *Ungoverned Spaces: Alternatives to State Authority in an Era of Softened Sovereignty*. Stanford Security Studies, 2010.

Cohen, Isabelle, et al. *The Economic Impact and Financing of Infrastructure Spending*. Thomas Jefferson Program in Public Policy, College of William and Mary, 2012.

Coker, Christopher. *Can War Be Eliminated?* Polity, 2014.

———. *The Improbable War: China, the United States, and the Logic of Great Power Conflict*. Oxford University Press, 2015.

Coleman, Isobel, and Terra Lawson-Remer. *Pathways to Freedom: Political and Economic Lessons from Democratic Transitions*. Council on Foreign Relations Press, 2013.

Coll, Steve. *Private Empire: ExxonMobil and American Power*. Penguin Books, 2013.

Collier, Paul. *Exodus: How Migration Is Changing Our World*. Oxford University Press, 2013.

Comaroff, Joshua. "Built on Sand: Singapore and the New State of Risk." *Harvard Design Magazine,* no. 39 (2014).

Cooley, Alexander, and Hendrik Spruyt. *Contracting States: Sovereign Transfers in International Relations*. Princeton University Press, 2009.

Copeland, Dale C. *Economic Interdependence and War*. Princeton University Press, 2014.

———. "Economic Interdependence and War: A Theory of Trade Expectations." *International Security* 20, no. 4 (Spring 1996).

Copetas, A. Craig. *Metal Men*. HarperCollins, 1986.

The Costs of the Israeli-Palestinian Conflict. Rand, 2015.

Cottrill, Ken. "Transforming the Future of Supply Chains Through Disruptive Innovation." MIT Center for Transportation and Logistics, Working Paper, Spring 2011.

Craven, Paul, and Barry Wellman. "The Network City." *Sociological Inquiry* 43, no. 3–4 (July 1973).

Crowston, Kevin, and Myers, Michael D. "Information Technology and the Transformation of Industries: Three Research Perspectives." *Journal of Strategic Information Systems* 13, no. 1 (2004): 5–28.

Cunliffe, Barry. *Europe Between the Oceans.* Yale University Press, 2008.

Curtis, Simon. "Global Cities and the Transformation of the International System." *Review of International Studies* 37, no. 4 (2011): 1923–47.

Dalby, Simon. "Rethinking Geopolitics: Climate Security in the Anthropocene." *Global Policy* 5, no. 1 (Feb. 2014).

Davies, James, Rodrigo Lluberas, and Anthony Shorrocks. *Global Wealth Report 2012.* Credit Suisse, 2012.

Davies, Norman. *Vanished Kingdoms: The Rise and Fall of States and Nations.* Penguin Books, 2012.

Deaton, Angus. *The Great Escape: Health, Wealth, and the Origins of Inequality.* Princeton University Press, 2013.

De Backer, Koen, and Sebastien Miroudet. "Mapping Global Value Chains." *OECD Trade Policy Papers,* no. 159, OECD (2013).

de Blij, Harm J., and Peter O. Muller. *Geography: Realms, Regions, and Concepts.* Wiley, 2010.

De Landa, Manuel. *A New Philosophy of Society: Assemblage Theory and Social Complexity.* Continuum Books, 2006.

Derluguian, Georgi M., and Scott L. Greer. *Questioning Geopolitics: Political Projects in a Changing World-System.* Praeger, 2000.

Diamandis, Peter H. *Abundance: The Future Is Better Than You Think.* Free Press, 2012.

Dodds, Klaus. *Geopolitics of Antarctica: Views from the Southern Oceanic Rim.* Wiley, 1998.

Dodge, Martin, Rob Kitchin, and Chris Perkins, eds. *The Map Reader: Theories of Mapping Practice and Cartographic Representation.* Wiley, 2011.

———. *Rethinking Maps: New Frontiers in Cartographic Theory.* Routledge, 2011.

Drezner, Daniel W. *The System Worked: How the World Stopped Another Great Depression.* Oxford University Press, 2014.

Durkheim, Émile. *The Rules of the Sociological Method* (Translated by W. D. Halls). New York: Free Press, 1982 [1895].

Earth Security Group. *Earth Security Index 2014.*

Easterling, Keller. *Extrastatecraft: The Power of Infrastructure Space.* Verso, 2014.

———. "Zone: The Spatial Software of Extrastatecraft." *Design Observer,* June 11, 2012.

Economist Intelligence Unit. *Hot Spots 2025: Benchmarking the Future Competitiveness of Cities.* 2013.

Ehrlich, Anne H., and Paul Ehrlich. *The Population Explosion.* Frederick Muller, 1990.

Ehrlich, Paul. *The Population Bomb.* Buccaneer Books, 1974.

Emmerson, Charles. *The Future History of the Arctic.* PublicAffairs, 2010.

———. *1913: In Search of the World Before the Great War.* PublicAffairs, 2014.

Enriquez, Juan. *The Untied States of America: Polarization, Fracturing, and Our Future*. Crown, 2005.

Escaith, Hubert. "International Supply Chains and Trade Elasticity in Times of Global Crisis." WTO Working Paper, Feb. 1, 2010.

European Union. *Erasmus Impact Study*. European Union, Sept. 2014.

Estevadeordal, Antoni, Juan Blyde, and Kati Suominen. "Are Global Value Chains Really Global? Policies to Accelerate Countries' Access to International Production Networks." Inter-American Development Bank, 2012.

Farole, Thomas, and Gokhan Akinci. *Special Economic Zones: Progress, Emerging Challenges, and Future Directions*. World Bank, 2011.

Featherstone, Mike. *Global Culture: Nationalism, Globalization, and Modernity*. Sage, 1990.

Feldman, Noah. *Cool War: The Future of Global Competition*. Random House, 2013.

Ferguson, Niall, and Moritz Schularick. *The End of Chimerica*. Harvard Business School, 2009.

Finnemore, Martha, and Judith Goldstein, eds. *Back to Basics: State Power in a Contemporary World*. Oxford University Press, 2013.

Fishman, Charles. *The Big Thirst: The Secret Life and Turbulent Future of Water*. Free Press, 2012.

Florida, Richard. *Who's Your City? How the Creative Economy Is Making Where You Live the Most Important Decision of Your Life*. Basic Books, 2008.

Floridi, Luciano. *The Philosophy of Information*. Oxford University Press, 2013.

Ford, Kenneth W. *The Quantum World: Quantum Physics for Everyone*. Harvard University Press, 2005.

Forrester, Jay W. *World Dynamics*. Productivity Press, 1979.

Francis, Diane. *Merger of the Century: Why Canada and America Should Become One Country*. HarperCollins, 2013.

Frank, Malcolm, Paul Roehrig, and Ben Pring. *Code Halos: How the Digital Lives of People, Things, and Organizations Are Changing the Rules of Business*. Wiley, 2014.

Frankopan, Peter. *The Silk Roads: A New History of the World*. Bloomsbury, 2015.

Freedman, Lawrence. *Strategy: A History*. Oxford University Press, 2013.

Freeland, Chrystia. *Plutocrats: The Rise of the New Global Super-rich and the Fall of Everyone Else*. Penguin Books, 2013.

French, Howard W. *China's Second Continent: How a Million Migrants Are Building a New Empire in Africa*. Knopf, 2014.

Friedman, Thomas L. *The World Is Flat: A Brief History of the Twenty-First Century*. Farrar, Straus and Giroux, 2005.

Fukuyama, Francis. *The End of History and the Last Man*. Free Press, 2006.

———. *Political Order and Political Decay: From the Industrial Revolution to the Globalization of Democracy*. Farrar, Straus and Giroux, 2014.

Fuligni, Bruno, and Isabelle Hanne. *Micronations*. Diaphane, 2013.

Galbraith, James K. *The End of Normal: The Great Crisis and the Future of Growth*. Simon & Schuster, 2014.

————. *Inequality and Instability: A Study of the World Economy Just Before the Crisis.* Oxford University Press, 2012.

Garfield, Simon. *On the Map: A Mind-Expanding Exploration of the Way the World Looks.* Gotham, 2013.

Garreau, Joel. *Edge City: Life on the New Frontier.* Anchor, 1992.

————. *The Nine Nations of North America.* Avon Books, 1982.

Gattorna, John. *Dynamic Supply Chains.* Financial Times, 2015.

Gayer, Laurent. *Karachi: Ordered Disorder and the Struggle for the City.* Oxford University Press, 2014.

George, Rose. *Ninety Percent of Everything: Inside Shipping, the Invisible Industry That Puts Clothes on Your Back, Gas in Your Car, and Food on Your Plate.* Metropolitan Books, 2013.

Ghemawat, Pankaj. *World 3.0: Global Prosperity and How to Achieve It.* Harvard Business Review Press, 2011.

Ghemawat, Pankaj, and Steven A. Altman. *DHL Global Connectedness Index 2014.* Deutsche Post DHL, 2014.

Gilens, Martin. *Affluence and Influence: Economic Inequality and Political Power in America.* Princeton University Press, 2014.

Gilman, Nils. "The Twin Insurgency." *American Interest,* July/Aug. 2014.

Girardet, Herbert. *Creating Regenerative Cities.* Routledge, 2015.

Glaeser, Edward. *Triumph of the City: How Our Greatest Invention Makes Us Richer, Smarter, Greener, Healthier, and Happier.* Penguin Books, 2012.

Goldin, Ian, Geoffrey Cameron, and Meera Balarajan. *Exceptional People: How Migration Shaped Our World and Will Define Our Future.* Princeton University Press, 2012.

Goldin, Ian, and Mike Mariathasan. *The Butterfly Defect: How Globalization Creates Systemic Risks, and What to Do About It.* Princeton University Press, 2014.

Goldsmith, Stephen, and Susan Crawford. *The Responsive City: Engaging Communities Through Data-Smart Governance.* Jossey-Bass, 2014.

Goldstein, Avery. *Rising to the Challenge: China's Grand Strategy and International Security.* Stanford University Press, 2005.

Golev, Artem, et al. "Rare Earths Supply Chains: Current Status, Constraints, and Opportunities." *Resources Policy* 41 (Sept. 2014: 52–59).

Gordon, John Steele. *An Empire of Wealth: The Epic History of American Economic Power.* Harper Perennial, 2005.

Gore, Al. *The Future: Six Drivers of Global Change.* Random House Trade Paperbacks, 2013.

Gray, Julia. "Life, Death, or Zombies? The Vitality of Regional Economic Organizations." UCLA, Sept. 2013.

Grewal, David Singh. *Network Power: The Social Dynamics of Globalization.* Yale University Press, 2008.

Guest, Robert. *Borderless Economics.* Palgrave Macmillan, 2011.

Guo, Yvonne, and Jun Jie Woo. *Singapore and Switzerland: Secrets to Small State Success.* World Scientific, 2015.

Gupta, Anil K., Girijia Pande, and Haiyan Wang. *The Silk Road Rediscovered:*

How Indian and Chinese Companies Are Becoming Globally Stronger by Winning in Each Other's Markets. Wiley, 2014.

Hall, Peter. *Cities in Civilization: Culture, Innovation, and Urban Order.* Weidenfeld & Nicolson, 1998.

Hardt, Michael, and Antonio Negri. *Empire.* Harvard University Press, 2000.

Hare, Forrest. "Borders in Cyberspace: Can Sovereignty Adapt to the Challenges of Cyber-Security?" George Mason University, 2011.

Harney, Alex. *The China Price: The True Cost of Chinese Competitive Advantage.* Penguin Books, 2009.

Hartley, Kris. *Can Government Think? Flexible Economic Opportunities and the Pursuit of Global Competitiveness.* Routledge, 2014.

Hausmann, Ricardo, Cesar A. Hidalgo, and Sebastian Bustos. *The Atlas of Economic Complexity: Mapping Paths to Prosperity.* MIT Press, 2014.

Hayes, Christopher. *Twilight of the Elites: America After Meritocracy.* Broadway Books, 2013.

Hayton, Bill. *The South China Sea: The Struggle for Power in Asia.* Yale University Press, 2014.

Hertie School of Governance, Governance Report 2013.

Hobden, Stephen, and John M. Hobson. *Historical Sociology of International Relations.* Cambridge University Press, 2002.

Holsi, Kalevi J. *Peace and War: Armed Conflict and International Order, 1648–1989.* Cambridge Studies in International Relations, 1991.

Hooker, R. D., Jr. *The Grand Strategy of the United States.* National Defense University Press, 2014.

Horn, D. B., and Mary Ransome. *English Historical Documents, 1714–1783.* Eyre and Spottiswoode, 1957.

Hudson, Valerie, and Andrea M. den Boer. *Bare Branches: The Security Implications of Asia's Surplus Male Population.* MIT Press, 2005.

Huntington, Samuel P. *The Clash of Civilizations and the Remaking of World Order.* Simon & Schuster, 1996.

Ikenberry, G. John. *After Victory: Institutions, Strategic Restraint, and the Rebuilding of Order After Major Wars.* Princeton University Press, 2000.

Inglehart, Ronald, and Hans-Dieter Klingemann. "Genes, Culture, Democracy, and Happiness." In *Culture and Subjective Well-Being,* edited by Ed Diener and Eunkook M. Suh. MIT Press, 2000.

Jackson, Patrick Thaddeus, and Daniel H. Nexon. "International Theory in a Post-paradigmatic Era: From Substantive Wagers to Scientific Ontologies." *EJIR* 19, no. 3 (Sept. 2013).

Jacobs, Frank. *Strange Maps: An Atlas of Cartographic Curiosities.* Viking Studio, 2009.

Jacoby, David. *Guide to Supply Chain Management: How Getting It Right Boosts Corporate Performance.* Bloomberg Press, 2009.

James, William. *Essays in Radical Empiricism.* University of Nebraska Press, 1996.

———. *The Meaning of Truth.* Prometheus Books, 1997.

Jayakumar, Shashi, and Rahul Sagar, eds. *The Big Ideas of Lee Kuan Yew*. Straits Times Press, 2014.

Jennings, Ken. *Maphead: Charting the Wide, Weird World of Geography Wonks*. Scribner, 2012.

Jervis, Robert. *System Effects: Complexity in Political and Social Life*. Princeton University Press, 1999.

Johnson, Neil. *Simple Complexity: A Clear Guide to Complexity Theory*. Oneworld, 2010.

Kagan, Robert. *Dangerous Nation: America's Foreign Policy from Its Earliest Days to the Dawn of the Twentieth Century*. Vintage, 2007.

Kagan, Robert A. *Adversarial Legalism: The American Way of Law*. Harvard University Press, 2003.

Kahn, Matthew E. *Climatopolis: How Our Cities Will Thrive in the Hotter Future*. Basic Books, 2010.

Kaku, Michio. *Physics of the Future: How Science Will Shape Human Destiny and Our Daily Lives by the Year 2100*. Anchor, 2012.

Kanna, Ahmed. *Dubai, the City as Corporation*. University of Minnesota Press, 2011.

Kaplan, Robert D. *Asia's Cauldron: The South China Sea and the End of a Stable Pacific*. Random House, 2014.

———. *Monsoon: The Indian Ocean and the Future of American Power*. Random House Trade Paperbacks, 2011.

———. *The Revenge of Geography: What the Map Tells Us About Coming Conflicts and the Battle Against Fate*. Random House Trade Paperbacks, 2013.

Kasarda, John D., and Greg Lindsay. *Aerotropolis: The Way We'll Live Next*. Farrar, Straus and Giroux, 2011.

Katz, Bruce, and Jennifer Bradley. *The Metropolitan Revolution: How Cities and Metros Are Fixing Our Broken Politics and Fragile Economy*. Brookings Institution Press, 2013.

Katzenstein, Peter J., ed. *Anglo-America and Its Discontents: Civilizational Identities Beyond West and East*. Routledge, 2012.

Kavalski, Emilian, ed. *World Politics at the Edge of Chaos: Reflections on Complexity and Global Life*. State University of New York Press, 2015.

Kelly, Kevin. *Out of Control: The New Biology of Machines, Social Systems, and the Economic World*. Basic Books, 1995.

Kennedy, Paul. *Grand Strategies in War and Peace*. Yale University Press, 1992.

———. *The Rise and Fall of the Great Powers*. Vintage, 1989.

Kenny, Charles. *Getting Better: Why Global Development Is Succeeding—and How We Can Improve the World Even More*. Basic Books, 2012.

Keohane, Robert O., and Joseph S. Nye. *Power and Interdependence*. Longman, 1977.

Keynes, John Maynard. *The Economic Consequences of the Peace*. Harcourt, Brace, and Howe, 1920.

———. *The General Theory of Employment, Interest, and Money*. CreateSpace, 2011.

Khan, Mushtaq H. "Beyond Good Governance: An Agenda for Developmental Governance." SOAS, University of London, 2012.

Khan, Mushtaq H., and K. S. Jomo. *Rents, Rent-Seeking, and Economic Development: Theory and Evidence in Asia*. Cambridge University Press, 2000.

Khanna, Parag. *How to Run the World: Charting a Course to the Next Renaissance*. Random House, 2011.

———. *The Second World: How Emerging Powers Are Redefining Global Competition in the Twenty-First Century*. Random House Trade Paperbacks, 2009.

Khanna, Parag, and Ayesha Khanna. *Hybrid Reality: Thriving in the Emerging Human-Technology Civilization*. TED Conferences, 2012.

Kiechel, Walter, III. *The Lords of Strategy: The Secret Intellectual History of the New Corporate World*. Harvard Business Press, 2010.

Kilcullen, David. *Out of the Mountains: The Coming Age of the Urban Guerrilla*. Oxford University Press, 2013.

King, Anthony D. *Global Cities: Post-imperialism and the Internationalization of London*. Routledge, 1990.

Kirshner, Jonathan. *American Power After the Financial Crisis*. Cornell University Press, 2014.

Kissinger, Henry. *World Order*. Penguin Press, 2014.

Knox, Paul, ed. *Atlas of Cities*. Princeton University Press, 2014.

Kolbert, Elizabeth. *The Sixth Extinction: An Unnatural History*. Henry Holt, 2014.

Koolhas, R., O. Bauman, and M. Wigley, eds. "Last Chance." In *All Manakh*. Columbia University Press, 2007.

Kose, M. Ayhan, and Eswar Prasad. *Emerging Markets: Resilience and Growth Amid Global Turmoil*. Brookings Institution Press, 2010.

Krane, Jim. *City of Gold: Dubai and the Dream of Capitalism*. Atlantic Books, 2009.

Krane, Jim, and Steven Wright. *The Gulf Gas Crunch and Qatar: Meeting Regional Needs Versus Feeding Global Markets*. LSE IDEAS, London School of Economics and Political Science, 2014.

Krastev, Ivan. *In Mistrust We Trust: Can Democracy Survive When We Don't Trust Our Leaders?* TED Conferences, 2013.

Krugman, Paul. *Geography and Trade*. MIT Press, 1991.

Kuris, Gabriel. "Remaking a Neglected Megacity: A Civic Transformation in Lagos State, 1999–2012." Princeton Project on Innovations for Successful Societies, July 2014.

Kurlantzick, Joshua. *Democracy in Retreat: The Revolt of the Middle Class and the Worldwide Decline of Representative Government*. Yale University Press, 2014.

Lacy, Peter and Jakob Rutqvist. *Waste to Wealth: The Circular Economy Advantage*. New York: Palgrave Macmillan, 2015.

Lake, David. "Beyond Anarchy: The Importance of Security Institutions." *International Security* 26, no. 1 (Summer 2001).

Lambert, Douglas M., James R. Stock, and Lisa M. Ellram. *Fundamentals of Logistics*. McGraw-Hill, 1998.

Landes, David F. *The Wealth and Poverty of Nations: Why Some Are So Rich and Some So Poor.* W. W. Norton, 1999.

Landry, Pierre F. *Decentralized Authoritarianism in China: The Communist Party's Control of Local Elites in the Post-Mao Era.* Cambridge University Press, 2008.

Lane, David, et al., eds. *Complexity Perspectives in Innovation and Social Change.* Springer, 2009.

Laurent, Clint. *Tomorrow's World: A Look at the Demographic and Socioeconomic Structure of the World in 2032.* Wiley, 2013.

Lee, Ki-baik. *A New History of Korea.* Ilchokak, 1984.

Levinson, Marc. *The Box: How the Shipping Container Made the World Smaller and the World Economy Bigger.* Princeton University Press, 2008.

Levitsky, Steven, and Lucan A. Way. *Competitive Authoritarianism: Hybrid Regimes in the Post–Cold War Era.* Cambridge University Press, 2010.

Lewis, Michael. *Flash Boys.* W. W. Norton, 2014.

Lien Centre for Social Innovation. "Measuring Poverty in Singapore." *Social Space* (2013).

Lin, Justin Yifu. *Against the Consensus: Reflections on the Great Recession.* Cambridge University Press, 2013.

———. *New Structural Economics.* World Bank, 2011.

———. *The Quest for Prosperity: How Developing Economies Can Take Off.* Princeton University Press, 2012.

Longworth, Richard C. *Caught in the Middle: America's Heartland in the Age of Globalism.* Bloomsbury USA, 2009.

Lord, Carnes, and Andrew Erickson, eds. *Rebalancing U.S. Forces: Basing and Forward Presence in the Asia-Pacific.* Naval Institute Press, 2014.

Lovelock, James. *The Revenge of Gaia: Earth's Climate Crisis and the Fate of Humanity.* Basic Books, 2007.

Low, Donald, and Sudhir Thomas Vadaketh. *Hard Choices: Challenging the Singapore Consensus.* NUS Press, 2014.

Luttwak, Edward. *Strategy: The Logic of War and Peace.* Harvard University Press, 2002.

Lynn, Barry C. *End of the Line: The Rise and Coming Fall of the Global Competition.* Crown Business, 2006.

Macdonald, James. *When Globalization Fails: The Rise and Fall of Pax Americana.* Farrar, Straus and Giroux, 2015.

Mackinnon, Rebecca. *Consent of the Networked.* Basic Books, 2012.

Maddison, Angus. *The World Economy.* OECD, 2007.

Mahan, A. T. *The Influence of Sea Power upon History, 1660–1783.* Dover Military History, 1987.

———. *The Interest of America in Sea Power, Present and Future.* Tradition Classics, 2011.

Malik, Yogesh, Alex Niemeyer, and Brian Ruwadi. "Building the Supply Chain of the Future." *McKinsey Quarterly,* Jan. 2011.

Mansel, Philip. *Constantinople.* Penguin, 1997.

Mansfield, Edward D., and Rachel Bronson. "Alliances, Preferential Trading Arrangements, and International Trade." *American Political Science Review* 91, no. 1 (Mar. 1997).

Marber, Peter. *Brave New Math: Information, Globalization, and New Economic Thinking in the 21st Century*. World Policy Institute, 2014.

Martel, William C. *Grand Strategy in Theory and Practice*. Cambridge University Press, 2015.

Mayer-Schonberger, Viktor, and Kenneth Cukier. *Big Data: A Revolution That Will Transform How We Live, Work, and Think*. Eamon Dolan/Mariner Books, 2014.

Mays, Andrew, and Gart S. Shea. "East India Company and Bank of England Shareholders During the South Sea Bubble: Partitions, Components, and Connectivity in a Dynamic Trading Network." University of St. Andrews, Centre for Dynamic Macroeconomic Analysis, 2011.

Mazzucato, Mariana. *The Entrepreneurial State: Debunking Public vs. Private Sector Myths*. Anthem Press, 2013.

McFate, Sean. *The Modern Mercenary: Private Armies and What They Mean for World Order*. Oxford University Press, 2015.

McGregor, Richard. *The Party: The Secret World of China's Communist Rulers*. Harper Perennial, 2012.

McKinsey Global Institute. *Global Flows in a Digital Age*. 2014.

McNeill, J. R., and William H. McNeill. *The Human Web: A Bird's-Eye View of World History*. W. W. Norton, 2003.

McNeill, William H. *The Rise of the West: A History of the Human Community*. University of Chicago Press, 1992.

Meadows, Donella. *Thinking in Systems: A Primer*. Chelsea Green, 2008.

Micklethwait, John, and Wooldridge, Adrian. *The Fourth Revolution: The Global Race to Reinvent the State*. Penguin Press, 2014.

———. *A Future Perfect: The Challenge and Promise of Globalization*. Random House Trade Paperbacks, 2003.

Milanovic, Branko. *The Haves and Have-Nots: A Brief and Idiosyncratic History of Global Inequality*. Basic Books, 2012.

Milhaud, Edgard. "The Economic Reorganization of the World as a Condition of Political Peace." *Annals of Public and Cooperative Economics* 14, no. 3 (Oct. 1938): 561–66.

Mills, Greg. *Why Africa Is Poor: And What Africans Can Do About It*. Penguin Global, 2011.

Mills, Mark P. "The Cloud Begins with Coal: Big Data, Big Networks, Big Infrastructure, and Big Power." Digital Power Group, 2013.

Minter, Adam. *Junkyard Planet: Travels in the Billion-Dollar Trash Trade*. Bloomsbury Press, 2013.

Mirowski, Philip. *Dream Machines: Economics Becomes a Cyborg Science*. Cambridge University Press, 2002.

———. *Never Let a Crisis Go to Waste: How Neoliberalism Survived the Financial Meltdown*. Verso, 2014.

Mishra, Pankaj. *From the Ruins of Empire: The Revolt Against the West and the Remaking of Asia*. Picador, 2013.

Mitchell, Melanie. *Complexity: A Guided Tour*. Oxford University Press, 2011.

Mitchell, William J. *City of Bits: Space, Place, and the Infobahn (on Architecture)*. MIT Press, 1996.

Modelski, George, and William R. Thompson. "The Long and Short of Global Politics in the Twenty-First Century: An Evolutionary Approach." *International Studies Review* 1, no. 2 (Summer 1999): 110–40.

Monmonier, Mark, and H. J. de Blij. *How to Lie with Maps*. University of Chicago Press, 1996.

Montgomery, Charles. *Happy City: Transforming Our Lives Through Urban Design*. Farrar, Straus and Giroux, 2013.

Moretti, Enrico. *The New Geography of Jobs*. Houghton Mifflin Harcourt, 2012.

Morris, Charles R. *Comeback: America's New Economic Boom*. PublicAffairs, 2013.

Morris, Ian. *War! What Is It Good For? Conflict and the Progress of Civilization from Primates to Robots*. Farrar, Straus and Giroux, 2014.

Mufson, Steven. *Keystone XL: Down the Line*. TED Conferences, 2013.

Munoz, Mark. *Handbook on the Geopolitics of Business*. Edward Elgar, 2013.

Murdock, Darryl G., Robert R. Tomes, and Christopher K. Tucker, eds. *Human Geography*. United States Geospatial Intelligence Foundation, 2014.

Murphy, Alexander B., and John O'Loughlin. "New Horizons for Regional Geography." *Eurasian Geography and Economics* 50, no. 3 (2009): 241–51.

Nahmias, Steven. *Production and Operations Analysis*. McGraw-Hill Higher Education, 2004.

Naim, Moises. *The End of Power: From Boardrooms to Battlefields and Churches to States, Why Being in Charge Isn't What It Used to Be*. Basic Books, 2014.

Nasr, Vali. *Forces of Fortune: The Rise of the New Muslim Middle Class and What It Will Mean for Our World*. Free Press, 2009.

National Intelligence Coucil. *Global Trends 2030: Alternative Worlds*. National Intelligence Council, 2012.

Neal, Larry. *The Rise of Financial Capitalism: International Capital Markets in the Age of Reason*. Cambridge University Press, 1990.

Nisbett, Richard E. *The Geography of Thought: How Asians and Westerners Think Differently . . . and Why*. Free Press, 2004.

Nolan, Peter. *Is China Buying the World?* Polity, 2013.

Norbu, Dawa. *China's Tibet Policy*. Routledge, 2001.

OECD. *Interconnected Economies: Benefiting from Global Value Chains*. OECD, 2013.

OECD, WTO, UNCTAD. *Implications of Global Value Chains for Trade, Investment, Development, and Jobs*. OECD, 2013.

Ogilvy, James. *Many Dimensional Man*. HarperCollins, 1979.

Ohmae, Kenichi. *The End of the Nation State: The Rise of Regional Economies*. Free Press, 1996.

————. *The Next Global Stage: Challenges and Opportunities in Our Borderless World*. Wharton School Publishing, 2005.

Olsthoorn, Xander, and Anna J. Wieczorek, eds. *Understanding Industrial Transformation: Views from Different Disciplines*. Springer, 2006.

O'Neill, Jim. *The Growth Map: Economic Opportunity in the BRICs and Beyond*. Portfolio Hardcover, 2011.

Ooi, Kee Beng. *The Eurasian Core and Its Edges: Dialogues with Wang Gangwu on the History of the World*. Institute of Southeast Asian Studies, 2015.

Osnos, Evan. *Age of Ambition: Chasing Fortune, Truth, and Faith in the New China*. Farrar, Straus and Giroux, 2014.

Ostrom, Elinor. "Beyond Markets and States: Polycentric Governance of Complex Economic Systems." *American Economic Review* 100, no. 3 (2010): 641–72.

————. "The Challenge of Self-Governance in Complex Contemporary Environments." *Journal of Speculative Philosophy* 24, no. 4 (2010): 316–32.

Oxford Martin Commission for Future Generations. *Now for the Long Term: The Report of the Oxford Martin Commission for Future Generations*. University of Oxford, 2013.

Padhukone, Neil. *Beyond South Asia: India's Strategic Evolution and the Reintegration of the Subcontinent*. Bloomsbury Academic, 2014.

Pal, Jeremy S., and Elfatih A. B. Eitahir. "Future Temperature in Southwest Asia Projected to Exceed a Threshold for Human Adaptibility." *Nature Climate Change,* Oct. 26, 2015.

Parello-Plesner, Jonas, and Mathieu Duchatel. *China's Strong Arm: Protecting Citizens and Assets Abroad*. IISS Adelphi Books, 2015.

Pelosky, Jay. "Emerging Market Portfolio Globalization: The Next Big Thing." New America Foundation, World Economic Roundtable Policy Paper, July 17, 2014.

Pentland, Alex. *Social Physics: How Good Ideas Spread*. New York: Penguin, 2014.

Perez, Carlota. "A New Age of Technological Progress." Policy Network, Aug. 22, 2014.

————. *Technological Revolutions and Financial Capital: The Dynamics of Bubbles and Golden Ages*. Edward Elgar, 2003.

Pettis, Michael. *Avoiding the Fall: China's Economic Restructuring*. Carnegie Endowment for International Peace, 2013.

Phelps, Edmund. *Mass Flourishing: How Grassroots Innovation Created Jobs, Challenge, and Change*. Princeton University Press, 2015.

Piiparinen, Richey, and Jim Russell. *From Balkanized Cleveland to Global Cleveland: A Theory of Change for Legacy Cities*. White Paper Funded by Ohio City Inc., 2013.

Piketty, Thomas. *Capital in the 21st Century*. Harvard University Press, 2014.

Pillsbury, Michael. *The Hundred-Year Marathon: China's Secret Strategy to Replace America as the Global Superpower*. Henry Holt, 2015.

Pinker, Steven. *The Better Angels of Our Nature*. Viking, 2011.

Pisani, Elizabeth. *Indonesia, Etc.: Exploring the Improbable Nation*. W. W. Norton, 2014.

Polanyi, Karl. *The Great Transformation: The Political and Economic Origins of Our Time*. Beacon Press, 2001.

Porter, Michael E. *Competitive Advantage of Nations*. Free Press, 1998.

"Public-Private Partnerships in Developing Countries: A Systematic Literature Review." Ministry of Foreign Affairs of the Netherlands, Apr. 2013.

Rachman, Gideon. *Zero-Sum Future: American Power in an Age of Anxiety*. Simon & Schuster, 2012.

Raford, Noah, and Andrew Trabulsi, eds. *Warlords, Inc.: Black Markets, Broken States, and the Rise of the Warlord Entrepreneur*. North Atlantic Books, 2015.

Rawls, John. "The Law of Peoples." *Critical Inquiry* 20, no. 1 (Autumn 1993).

Reardon, Thomas, Christopher B. Barrett, Julio A. Berdegué, and Johan F. M. Swinnen. "Agrifood Industry Transformation and Small Farmers in Developing Countries." *World Development* 37, no. 11 (2009): 1717–27.

Rees, Martin. *Our Final Century?* William Heinemann, 2003.

Reich, Robert. *Inequality for All*. Radius TWC, 2013.

Rein, Shaun. *End of Cheap China*. Wiley, 2014.

Rheingold, Howard. *The Virtual Community: Homesteading on the Electronic Frontier*. MIT Press, 2000.

Rickards, James. *The Death of Money: The Coming Collapse of the International Monetary System*. Penguin Books, 2014.

Rieffel, Alexis. *Restructuring Sovereign Debt: The Case for Ad Hoc Machinery*. Brookings Institution, 2003.

Riello, Giorgio. *Cotton: The Fabric That Made the Modern World*. Cambridge University Press, 2013.

Rifkin, Jeremy. *The Zero Marginal Cost Society: The Internet of Things, the Collaborative Commons, and the Eclipse of Capitalism*. Palgrave Macmillan Trade, 2014.

Rivoli, Pietra. *The Travels of a T-Shirt in the Global Economy: An Economist Examines the Markets, Power, and Politics of World Trade*. Wiley, 2005.

Roberts, Paul. *The Impulse Society: America in the Age of Gratification*. Bloomsbury USA, 2014.

Rodin, Judith. *The Resilience Dividend: Being Strong in a World Where Things Go Wrong*. PublicAffairs, 2014.

Ronfeldt, David F. *Tribes, Institutions, Markets, Networks: A Framework About Societal Evolution*. Rand, 1996.

Ronis, Sheila R., ed. *Economic Security: Neglected Dimension of National Security?* National Defense University Press, 2011.

———. *Forging an American Grand Strategy: Securing a Path Through a Complex Future*. National Defense University Press, 2013.

Rosecrance, Richard N. *The Resurgence of the West: How a Transatlantic Union Can Prevent War and Restore the United States and Europe*. Yale University Press, 2013.

———. *The Rise of the Trading State: Commerce and Conquest in the Modern World*. Basic Books, 1986.

Rosecrance, Richard N., and Steven E. Miller, eds. *The Next Great War? The Roots of World War I and the Risk of U.S.-China Conflict*. MIT Press, 2014.

Rosenau, James N. *Distant Proximities: Dynamics Beyond Globalization*. Princeton University Press, 2003.

———. *Turbulence in World Politics: A Theory of Change and Continuity*. Princeton University Press, 1990.

"The Round World and the Winning of the Peace." *Foreign Affairs*. July 1943.

Ruggie, John Gerard. *Just Business: Multinational Corporations and Human Rights*. W. W. Norton, 2013.

Rusk, David. *Cities Without Suburbs*. Woodrow Wilson Center Press, 1995.

Rutherford, Alex, Dion Harmon, Justin Werfel, Alexander S. Gard-Murray, Shlomiya Bar-Yam, Andreas Gros, Ramon Xulvi-Brunet, Yaneer Bar-Yam. "Good Fences: The Importance of Setting Boundaries for Peaceful Coexistence." New England Complex Systems Institute, May 2014.

Ryan, Brent D. *Design After Decline: How America Rebuilds Shrinking Cities*. University of Pennsylvania Press, 2014.

Sagar, Rahul. *Secrets and Leaks: The Dilemma of State Secrecy*. Princeton University Press, 2013.

Saideman, Stephen M. *The Ties That Divide: Ethnic Politics, Foreign Policy, and International Conflict*. Columbia University Press, 2001.

Saideman, Stephen M., and R. William Ayres. *For Kin or Country: Xenophobia, Nationalism, and War*. Columbia University Press, 2015.

Sandel, Michael J. *What Money Can't Buy: The Moral Limits of Markets*. Farrar, Straus and Giroux, 2013.

Sassen, Saskia. *Territory, Authority, Rights: From Medieval to Global Assemblages*. Princeton University Press, 2008.

———. "When the City Itself Becomes a Technology of War." *Theory, Culture, and Society* 27, no. 6 (2010): 33–50.

Schell, Orville, and John Delury. *Wealth and Power: China's Long March to the Twenty-First Century*. Random House, 2013.

Schelling, Thomas C. *Micromotives and Macrobehavior*. W. W. Norton, 2006.

Schmidt, Eric, and Jared Cohen. *The New Digital Age: Reshaping the Future of People, Nations, and Business*. Knopf, 2013.

Schneier, Bruce. *Data and Goliath: The Hidden Battles to Collect Your Data and Control Your World*. W. W. Norton, 2015.

Schubert, Frank N., ed. *The Nation Builders: A Sesquicentennial History of the Corps of Topographical Engineers, 1838–1863*. U.S. Army Corps of Engineers Office of History, 1989.

Schweller, Randall L. *Maxwell's Demon and the Golden Apple: Global Discord in the New Millennium*. Johns Hopkins University Press, 2014.

Scott, James C. *The Art of Not Being Governed: An Anarchist History of Upland Southeast Asia*. Yale University Press, 2010.

———. *Seeing Like a State: How Certain Schemes to Improve the Human Condition Have Failed*. Yale University Press, 1999.

Sehgal, Kabir. *Coined: The Rich Life of Money and How Its History Has Shaped Us*. Grand Central, 2015.

Sennett, Richard. *Together: The Rituals, Pleasures, and Politics of Cooperation*. Yale University Press, 2012.

Senor, Dan, and Saul Singer. *Start-Up Nation: The Story of Israel's Economic Miracle*. Twelve, 2011.

Seung Ho Park, Nan Zhou, and Gerardo R. Ungson. *Rough Diamonds: The Four Traits of Successful Breakout Firms in BRIC Countries*. Jossey-Bass, 2013.

Sharma, Ruchir. *Breakout Nations: In Pursuit of the Next Economic Miracles*. W. W. Norton, 2013.

Sharma, Vivek. "Give Corruption a Chance." *National Interest*, Nov. 2013.

Simpfendorfer, Ben. *The Rise of the New East: Business Strategies for Success in a World of Increasing Complexity*. Palgrave Macmillan, 2014.

Singer, Peter. *One World: The Ethics of Globalization*. Yale University Press, 2004.

Singer, P. W., and Allan Friedman. *Cybersecurity and Cyberwar: What Everyone Needs to Know*. Oxford University Press, 2014.

Slaughter, Anne-Marie. *A New World Order*. Princeton University Press, 2005.

Smil, Vaclav. *Energy in Nature and Society: General Energetics of Complex Systems*. MIT Press, 2007.

———. *Making the Modern World: Materials and Dematerialization*. Wiley, 2013.

Smith, Laurence C. "New Trans-Arctic Shipping Routes Navigable by Mid-century." *Proceedings of the National Academy of Sciences* 110, no. 13 (2013).

Smolan, Rick, and Jennifer Erwitt. *The Human Face of Big Data*. Against All Odds Productions, 2012.

Soll, Jacob. *The Reckoning: Financial Accountability and the Rise and Fall of Nations*. Basic Books, 2014.

Spence, A. Michael. *The Evolving Structure of the American Economy and the Employment Challenge*. Council on Foreign Relations, 2011.

———. *The Next Convergence: The Future of Economic Growth in a Multispeed World*. Picador, 2012.

Spolaore, Enrico, and Romain Wacziarg. "How Deep Are the Roots of Economic Development?" *Journal of Economic Literature* 51, no. 2 (June 2013).

Spruyt, Hendrik. *The Sovereign State and Its Competitors: An Analysis of Systems Change*. Princeton University Press, 1994.

Spufford, Peter. *Power and Profit: The Merchant in Medieval Europe*. Thames & Hudson, 2003.

Standage, Tom. *The Victorian Internet: The Remarkable Story of the Telegraph and the Nineteenth Century's On-Line Pioneers*. Bloomsbury, 2009.

Standard Chartered Bank. *Global Supply Chains: New Directions*. Special Report, May 27, 2015.

———. *Global Trade Unbundled*. Special Report, April 4, 2014.

Starosielski, Nicole. *The Undersea Network*. Duke University Press, 2015.

Stephenson, Neal. "Mother Earth, Mother Board." *Wired*, April 2012.

Stiglitz, Joseph E. *The Great Divide: Unequal Societies and What We Can Do About Them*. W. W. Norton, 2015.

Studwell, Joe. *How Asia Works*. Grove Press, 2014.

Subramanian, Arvind, and Martin Kessler. *The Hyperglobalization of Trade and Its Future*. Peterson Institute for International Economics, 2013.

Sudjic, Deyan. *Hundred Mile City*. Mariner Books, 1993.

Sunstein, Cass R. *Infotopia: How Many Minds Produce Knowledge*. Oxford University Press, 2008.

———. *Simpler: The Future of Government*. Simon & Schuster, 2013.

Taleb, Nassim Nicholas. *Antifragile: Things That Gain from Disorder*. Random House Trade Paperbacks, 2014.

———. *The Black Swan*. Random House, 2010.

Taniguchi, Eiichi, Tien Fang Fwa, and Russell G. Thompson. *Urban Transportation and Logistics: Health, Safety, and Security Concerns*. CRC Press, 2013.

Tansey, Oisin. "Internationalized Regimes: A Second Dimension of Regime Hybridity." *Democratization* 20, no. 7 (2013).

Taylor, Peter. *World City Network: A Global Urban Analysis*. Routledge, 2003.

Tellis, Ashley J., Bibek Debroy, and Reece Trevor, eds. *Getting India Back on Track: An Action Agenda for Reform*. Carnegie Endowment for International Peace, 2014.

Thiel, Peter. *Zero to One: Notes on Startups, or How to Build the Future*. Crown Business, 2014.

Thompson, Grahame. "The Limits to 'Globalization': Taking Economic Borders Seriously." Open University, UCSC, 2005.

Tilly, Charles. *Coercion, Capital, and European States*. Blackwell, 1990.

Timmer, Marcel P., Abdul Azeez Erumban, Bart Los, Robert Stehrer, and Gaaitzen J. de Vries. *Slicing Up Value Chains*. University of Groningen, 2013.

Tompkins, James A. *No Boundaries: Breaking Through to Supply Chain Excellence*. Tompkins Associates, 2003.

Townsend, Anthony. *Smart Cities: Big Data, Civic Hackers, and the Quest for a New Utopia*. W. W. Norton, 2013.

Toynbee, Arnold. *A Study of History: Abridgement of Volumes VII–X*. Oxford University Press, 1957.

Tsai, Shih-shan Henry. *The Eunuchs in the Ming Dynasty*. State University of New York Press, 1996.

Turchi, Peter. *Maps of the Imagination: The Writer as Cartographer*. Trinity University Press, 2007.

Turnbull, C. M. *A History of Modern Singapore, 1819–2005*. National University Press, 2009.

Turok, Neil. *The Universe Within: From Quantum to Cosmos*. House of Anansi Press, 2012.

Turzi, Mariano. "The Soybean Republic." *Yale Journal of International Affairs* (Spring/Summer 2011).

Umunna, C., ed. *Owning the Future*. London: Rowman & Littlefield International, 2014.

Vedral, Vlatko. "Living in a Quantum World." Special issue, *Scientific American*, June 2011.

Viguerie, Patrick, Sven Smit, and Mehrdad Baghai. *Granularity of Growth: McKinsey & Company Report.* John Wiley & Sons, 2008.

Vinogradov, Sergei, and Patricia Wouters. *Sino-Russian Transboundary Waters: A Legal Perspective on Cooperation.* Institute for Security and Development Policy, Dec. 2013.

Vitalari, Nicholas, and Haydn Shaughnessy. *The Elastic Enterprise: The New Manifesto for Business Revolution.* Olivet Press, 2012.

Waldrop, M. Mitchell. *Complexity: The Emerging Science at the Edge of Order and Chaos.* Simon & Schuster, 1993.

Wallace, Jeremy. "Cities, Redistribution, and Authoritarian Regime Survival." *Journal of Politics* 75, no. 3 (2013): 632–45.

Waltz, Kenneth N. *Theory of International Politics.* McGraw-Hill, 1979.

Wang, Chia-Chou. "Political Interest Distribution and Provincial Response Strategies: Central-Local Relations in China After the 17th National Congress of the CPC." *China: An International Journal* 11, no. 1 (2013): 21–39.

Wang, Jin. "The Economic Impact of Special Economic Zones: Evidence from Chinese Municipalities." *Journal of Development Economics* 101 (March 2013).

Watts, Barry D. *Clausewitzian Friction and Future War.* National Defense University, 1996.

Weber, Max. *Economy and Society.* Vol. 1. University of California Press, 1978.

Wedel, Janine. *Unaccountable: How Elite Power Brokers Corrupt Our Finances, Freedom, and Security.* Pegasus, 2014.

Wendt, Alexander. "Flatland: Quantum Mind and the International Hologram." In *New Systems Theories of World Politics,* edited by Mathias Albert, Lars-Erik Cederman, and Alexander Wendt. Palgrave Macmillan, 2010.

———. *Quantum Mind and Social Science: Unifying Physical and Social Ontology.* Cambridge University Press, 2015.

———. *Social Theory of International Relations.* Cambridge University Press, 1999.

Westad, Odd Arne. *Restless Empire: China and the World Since 1750.* Basic Books, 2012.

Williams, Bernard. *Ethics and the Limits of Philosophy.* Routledge, 2011.

Wood, Gillen D'Arcy. *Tambora: The Eruption That Changed the World.* Princeton University Press, 2014.

World Bank. "Special Economic Zones: Progress, Emerging Challenges, and Future Directions." World Bank, 2011.

World Bank Group. *Global Economic Prospects: Having Fiscal Space and Using It.* World Bank, 2015.

World Economic Forum, Bain & Company, and World Bank. *Enabling Trade: Valuing Growth Opportunities.* World Economic Forum, 2013.

World Input-Output Database. http://www.wiod.org/new_site/home.htm.

Writson, Walter B. *The Twilight of Sovereignty: How the Information Revolution Is Transforming Our World.* Scribner, 1992.

Zakaria, Fareed. *The Future of Freedom: Illiberal Democracy at Home and Abroad.* W. W. Norton, 2007.

Zeihan, Peter. *The Accidental Superpower: The Next Generation of American Pre-eminence and the Coming Global Disorder*. Twelve, 2015.

Zetter, Kim. *Countdown to Zero Day: Stuxnet and the Launch of the World's First Digital Weapon*. Penguin Random House, 2014.

Zhang Weiwei. *The China Wave: Rise of a Civilizational State*. World Century, 2012.

Zheng, Y. *De Facto Federalism in China: Reforms and Dynamics of Central-Local Relations*. World Scientific, 2007.

———. "Institutional Economics and Central-Local Relations in China: Evolving Research." *China: An International Journal* 3, no. 2 (2005): 240–69.

Zittrain, Jonathan. *The Future of the Internet—and How to Stop It*. Yale University Press, 2009.

Zogby, John, and Joan Snyder Kuhl. *First Globals: Understanding, Managing, and Unleashing the Potential of Our Millennial Generation*. John Zogby and Joan Snyder Kuhl, 2013.

Zuckerman, Ethan. *Digital Cosmopolitans: Why We Think the Internet Connects Us, Why It Doesn't, and How to Rewire It*. W. W. Norton, 2014.

MAP CREDITS AND SOURCES

1. The New Nodes: Special Economic Zones (SEZs) Mushroom Around the World. Created by University of Wisconsin–Madison Cartography Laboratory; centralamericadata.com; Economist; Embassy of the United Arab Emirates in London; International Labor Organization; Natural Earth; World Bank.

2. China Builds Supply Chain Complementarities Across the Globe. Created by University of Wisconsin–Madison Cartography Laboratory. International Monetary Fund; Natural Earth.

3. International Trade and Investment Volumes Continue to Climb. Created by University of Wisconsin–Madison Cartography Laboratory. United Nations Conference on Trade and Development.

4. FDI Flows and Stocks Rising Among All Regions. Created by University of Wisconsin–Madison Cartography Laboratory. IMF Coordinated Direct Investment Survey.

5. Global Trade Linkages Reveal Rising Connectivity. Prepared by Professor Rahul C. Basole and Hyunwoo Park for Pankaj Ghemawat and Steven A. Altman, DHL Global Connectedness Index 2014. http://www.dhl.com/gci.

6. The Wealth of Continents. Created by Worldmapper. Glen Peters et al.; Global Carbon Project; World Bank.

7. More Than Half of Humanity Lives in Asia. Map from theCarbonMap.org, © Kiln.it. Glen Peters et al.; Global Carbon Project; World Bank.

8. World Poverty Centers on Africa and Asia. Map from theCarbonMap.org, © Kiln.it. Glen Peters et al.; Global Carbon Project; World Bank.

9. Greenhouse Gas Emissions Rising as Populations and Wealth Grow. Map from theCarbonMap.org, © Kiln.it. Glen Peters et al.; Global Carbon Project; World Bank.

10. Asia is the Epicenter of Potential Climate-Related Disasters. Map from theCarbonMap.org, © Kiln.it. Glen Peters et al.; Global Carbon Project; World Bank.

11. Inter-City Networks Flourish with the Rise of "Diplomacity." Created by

University of Wisconsin–Madison Cartography Laboratory. City Leadership Initiative; C40 Cities; University College London (UCL).

12. Europe Fragments as It Grows Together. Created by University of Wisconsin–Madison Cartography Laboratory. Business Insider; European Free Alliance; Natural Earth; Wikipedia.

13. Megacities as the New Economic Geography. Created by University of Wisconsin–Madison Cartography Laboratory. Brookings Institution; International Monetary Fund; Lagos Bureau of Statistics; Natural Earth; Oak Ridge National Library.

14. Africa's Remaining Fault Lines. Created by University of Wisconsin–Madison Cartography Laboratory. Guardian; Natural Earth.

15. Singapore Expands its Economic Geography. Created by University of Wisconsin–Madison Cartography Laboratory. Global Administrative Areas; Indosight.com; Iskandar Malaysia; Natural Earth; Noun Project; OpenStreetMap.

16. Eurasia's New Silk Roads. Map created by Jeff Blossom. Natural Earth; Theodora; Wikipedia; World Resources Institute.

17. *Pax Arabia*. Map created by Jeff Blossom. Desertec; DII; Natural Earth; Theodora; World Resources Institute.

18. *Pax Aseana*. Map created by Jeff Blossom. ASEAN Center for Energy; Asian Development Bank; Natural Earth; Theodora; World Resources Institute.

19. *Pax Africana*. Map created by Jeff Blossom. Africa Energy; African Development Bank; African Union; Natural Earth; Theodora; United Nations Economic Commission for Africa; World Resources Institute.

20. China: Empire of Megacities. Created by University of Wisconsin–Madison Cartography Laboratory. Brookings Institution; Harvard World Map; Kashgar Prefecture Economic and Social Development Report 2011; Lhasa Economic and Social Development Report 2012; McKinsey & Company; Natural Earth.

21. Beyond the Fifty States: America's Next Map. Created by University of Wisconsin–Madison Cartography Laboratory. Joel Kotkin; Forbes Magazine; Natural Earth; Regional Plan Association; U.S. Census Bureau; U.S. High Speed Rail Association.

22. From NAFTA to North American Union. Map created by Jeff Blossom. Canadian Association of Petroleum Producers; Hydro Quebec; Natural Earth; Schiller Institute; Theodora; U.S. Geological Survey; World Resources Institute

23. The South American Union. Map created by Jeff Blossom. Business Insider; LatAm Renewables; Natural Earth; Theodora; Wikipedia; World Resources Institute.

24. Aspiring to Economic Complexity. Center for International Development at Harvard University (CC by-sa).

25. From Complexity to Growth. Center for International Development at Harvard University, Economic Complexity Index 2015 (CC by-sa).

26. Supply Chains are Becoming More Dispersed and Complex. Created by University of Wisconsin–Madison Cartography Laboratory. Natural Earth; Source-Map; thegatewayonline.com.

27. Which Role Model for China? Created by University of Wisconsin–Madison

Cartography Laboratory. *Foundations of the Portuguese Empire, 1415–1580;* Natural Earth; *The Penguin Historical Atlas of the British Empire; The Twentieth Century, The Oxford History of the British Empire Volume IV;* Wikipedia.

28. A Map of Minerals. Map created by Jeff Blossom. BP Statistical Review; CIA World Factbook; Mineral Map of the World; PRIO Diamond Resources; U.S. Geological Survey.

29. World Food Supplies. Map created by Jeff Blossom. USDA; FAOSTAT; CropMapper.

30. Does Russia Have Europe Over a Barrel? Created by University of Wisconsin–Madison Cartography Laboratory. Edison; European Energy Supply Security; Gazprom; International Energy Institute; Natural Earth; Norsk Oljemuseum; OpenStreetMap; Petroleum Economist; U.S. Energy Information Administration; White Stream.

31. The New Arctic Geography. Map created by Jeff Blossom. Arctic Council; Durham University; Grenatec; IBRU; IFT; Ministry of Foreign Affairs of Denmark; Natural Earth; *The New York Times;* Theodora.

32. The World: 4 Degrees Celsius Warmer. © 2009 Reed Business Information—UK. All rights reserved. Distributed by Tribune Content Agency.

33. One Mega-City, Many Systems. Created by University of Wisconsin–Madison Cartography Laboratory. Government of the Hong Kong Special Administrative Region; Global Administrative Areas; Natural Earth; Noun Project; OpenStreetMap; timeout.com.

34. Global Data Flows Expanding and Accelerating. Created by TeleGeography and www.submarinecablemap.com.

35. Global Migration: Origins and Destinations. Created by Mona Hammami. World Bank Migrants and Remittances Database; United Nations Population Division; Migration Policy Institute (MPI) Data Hub; International Labor Office; International Organization for Migration.

36. A World on the Move: Migrants Surge as the World Population Expands. Created by Mona Hammami. World Bank Migrants and Remittances Database; United Nations Population Division; Migration Policy Institute (MPI) Data Hub; International Labor Office; International Organization for Migration.

37. Global Hubs Become Demographic Melting Pots. Created by University of Wisconsin–Madison Cartography Laboratory. American Census Survey; Atlas of Cities; Canada Census Survey; Crown EMEA; Natural Earth; United Kingdom Census Survey; United Nations.

38. Protecting the Planet. Created by University of Wisconsin–Madison Cartography Laboratory. International Union for the Conservation of Nature; Natural Earth; Protected Planet.

INDEX

Page numbers beginning with 413 refer to endnotes.

Abdulla, Abdulkhaleq, 270
Abe, Shinzo, 146
aerial photography, 12
Aerotropolis (Kasarda and Lindsay), 291
aerotropolises, 52
Africa:
 African Development Bank, 97
 aggregation and, 92–95
 civil wars in, 93
 devolution-aggregation dynamic and, 79
 Ethiopia and, 97–98
 foreign investment in, 94–98
 fragile states in, 94–95
 infrastructure development in, 94–98
 Lagos in, 276–78
 mapping of, 46
aggregation:
 Africa and, 92–95
 GCC countries and, 104–6
 geopolitics and, 79–84
 GT Road and, 84–87

Israel and, 105–7
 Southeast Asia and, 87–92
agriculture industry, 155, 165, 213, 218, 287, 360, 376
Alabbar, Mohamed, 263, 265
Alaska, 5, 8, 131–32, 249–50, 378
Alesina, Alberto, 64
Allen, Woody, 63
al Maktoum, Rashid bin Saeed (Sheikh Mohammed), 263
al-Maliki, Nouri, 102
al-Qaeda, 99, 361, 382
al-Rasheed, Fahd, 271
Amazon rain forest, 132, 371, 380
American Dream, 111–12
American Society of Civil Engineers, 10
Andes Mountains, 132–33
Angel, Solly, 24
Anholt, Simon, 7, 305*n*
Annan, Kofi, 35
Antarctica, 27, 251
Antifragile (Taleb), 25*n*
Apple Inc., 57, 149, 152–53, 288, 336

aquaponics, 165

Arab Spring, 99, 102, 104*n*, 206, 264, 295

Arctic:

climate change and, 131, 329

conservation of, 380

deepwater drilling in, 235

energy and food supplies of, 170

global economy of, 248–56

natural gas and, 27, 194

North American Union and, 174

Russia's northern rivers and, 207

shipping industry and, 216, 390

Arctic Ocean, 8, 13, 229, 233, 236, 248, 367

Armenia, 81, 347

Aron, Raymond, 148

Arquilla, John, 56

ASEAN Economic Community, 53, 59, 80, 89–90, 92, 323

Asian Development Bank, 91

Asian Infrastructure Investment Bank (AIIB), 200–201, 317*n*

Asian Tigers, 9–10, 92, 151

Assange, Julian, 56

Atlas of Economic Complexity (Hausmann), 148

Attlee, Clement, 220

automobile industry, 89–90, 116, 130, 166–69, 216, 314

Azerbaijan, 81, 109*n*, 192, 265

Bangladesh garment industry, 301–3, 382–83

Barber, Benjamin, 352

Bashir, Omar, 67

Bauwens, Michel, 339

BCIM (Bangladesh, China, India, Myanmar) forum, 86–87

Beck, Ulrich, 300

Beckett, Samuel, 147

Bejan, Adrian, 31

Bell, Daniel, 354, 385

Berlin, Isaiah, 366

Berners-Lee, Tim, 331

bin Laden, Osama, 221

Blair, Tony, 74, 352

blowback, 221–24

Bolis, Giovanni, 358

border crossings, 12–13, 82–84, 90–91

border fences, 13, 100*n*, 106, 129

borders, political:

India and Pakistan, 12, 144

North and South Korea, 12, 144

Russia and China, 204–5

Serbia and Kosovo, 73

U.S. and Canada, 13

U.S. and Mexico, 12–13, 129–30

Bougainville, Papua New Guinea, 71*n*

Bo Xilai, 115

Boyd, Danah, 339

Braudel, Fernand, 54

Brenner, Neil, 24

Brook, Daniel, 271

Brown, Jerry, 113

Browne, John, 378

Buffett, Warren, 318

Business for Social Responsibility, 304

Byers, Michael, 250

Calatrava, Santiago, 18
call center workers, 159, 344, 382
Cameron, David, 74, 352
Canada:
  Arctic economy and, 248–56
  conservation of, 379
  currency and, 330
  Detroit bankruptcy and, 121
  devolution and, 77–78, 373
  extraction methods and, 166
  immigration and, 124, 351–52, 365
  international trade and, 140–41, 155
  natural resources of, 125–28
  North American Union and, 128–32
Canada Immigrant Investor Program, 124
Castells, Manuel, 56, 341
Central Intelligence Agency (CIA), 179, 221
Chanda, Nayan, 310
Chase-Dunn, Christopher, 35, 50–51
Chiang Kai-shek, 86, 287
children's health, 300–301
China:
  backlash against, 221–24, 232
  checkbook diplomacy of, 221
  "Chinese Dream" and, 286
  Chinese hackers and, 162
  Chongqing as largest city of, 290
  competition with U.S. companies and, 161
  ethnic groups of, 356–57

geologic surveying of Antarctica and, 251
infrastructure provision of, 181–84
investment in Afghanistan and, 209–10
investment in Africa and, 95–98
investment in U.S. and, 122–23
as largest exporter of ICT goods, 153
as maritime sea power, 229
one-child policy of, 124
rare earth minerals and, 163
as self-reliant manufacturer, 162
Silk Road Economic Belt and, 16–17, 198
Taiwan and, 142–45
Tibet and, 144–45
21st-century rise of, 227
transportation systems of, 196–98
Churchill, Winston, 139, 239
cities:
  diplomacy of, 58–60
  mapping of, 49
  megacities and, 49, 143, 291–93
  multi-city corridors and, 49–50
  see also specific cities
civil wars, 70–73, 93, 99–100, 143
Clark, William, 173
Clash of Civilizations and the Remaking of World Order, The (Huntington), 54
Clemens, Michael, 359
climate change, 59, 207, 209, 248, 367, 383
Clinton administration, 179
Clinton, Hillary, 121n

Coase, Ronald, 343

Coca-Cola, 186–87, 212, 282, 344

Collier, Paul, 70

Columbus, Christopher, 227n

competitive connectivity, 6, 172, 187, 210, 216, 238, 390

connectivity:

border crossings and, 12–13

competition over, see competitive connectivity

complex world systems and, 30, 382

flow and friction of, 31–34, 40–41

functional geography and, 15–18, 68

globalization and, 9, 14, 382

infrastructures and, 5–7

intercontinental travel and, 38

measuring connectedness and, 41–44

megacities and, 50–51

SEZs as catalysts for, 280; see also special economic zones (SEZs)

as strategy, 192–93

urbanization and, 19, 24, 223, 280, 286, 291, 312

world travel routes and, 3–5

Connectivity Atlas, xviii

Cook, James, xx

Cook, Tim, 153

Copeland, Dale, 142

corruption, 310–11

Cortés, Hernán, 226

Cowen, Tyler, 318

Cuba, 148, 186–88, 218, 247

currencies, 154n, 330–31, 334

Customs and Border Protection, U.S., 358n

customs barriers, 22, 154, 358n

cyber civilization:

cyber attacks and, 333

cyber war and, 333

digital workforce and, 343–45

Internet and, 327–39

mobile phones and, 328, 340–41

Dalai Lama, 144–45

data sharing, 22–23

Deaton, Angus, 26

de Blij, Harm, 16n

deepwater drilling, 229–30, 234–36

de Lesseps, Ferdinand, 239

Deng Xiaoping, 55, 280, 382

Design in Nature (Bejan), 31

de Soto, Hernando, 296

Detroit bankruptcy, 113–14, 121

devolution:

as check on authority, 19, 66

collapse of Soviet Union and, 64, 72, 192, 197

in Europe, 64–65, 74–78

failure of nation-building efforts and, 64–65

as fragmentation of territory, 63

SEZs and, see special economic zones (SEZs)

terrorism and, 69–70

within United States, 116–21

Yugoslavia and, 73

devolution-aggregation dynamic, 79–80, 86–87

DHL, 22, 57, 156, 187, 363

Diamandis, Peter, 164

Diamond, Jared, 368

diaspora networks, 54–55, 105

digital connectivity, *see* Internet

dilution:

demographic blending and, 19, 347

global genetic dilution and, 347

international migration and, 19, 347–54

international travel and, 357–61

national identity and, 348

diplomacy, 58–60, 174

Dobson, Jerry, 28

Draper, Tim, 120*n*

drone surveillance, 250

Dubai, U.A.E.:

as "center of world", 259

commerce and culture of, 261, 270

connectivity and, 51

expansion plans of, 266–67

governance of, 266

immigrants and, 263, 268–69

independence from Britain and, 260

investors and entrepreneurs in, 264–65

population of, 261, 268

quality of life in, 267

resident rights and, 269–71

success of, 265

trading with China and, 262

Durkheim, Émile, 20, 339*n*, 345, 388–89

Dutch East India Company, 228

Dynamic Supply Chains (Gattorna), 303*n*

Easter Island, 368

Easterling, Keller, 17

Ebola virus, 33, 307

Economic Consequences of the Peace, The (Keynes), 36

economic disparity, 48, 89, 116, 312–16

economics:

comparative advantage and, 20, 148, 389

division of labor and, 20, 90, 96, 182, 388–89

free markets and, 20

supply-demand system and, 19–20, 183

Edelman Trust Barometer, 304

Einstein, Albert, 288, 389

Eisenhower, Dwight, 317

Emanuel, Rahm, 117

emerging markets, 38, 48, 51, 155, 169, 321

Empire (Hardt and Negri), 414

employment opportunities, *see* job creation

energy production, 171, 288

engineering advances, 7–8, 12

environmental safeguards, 306

Escaith, Hubert, 283

Esquel, 89–90

Ethiopia, xxii, 40–41, 93–98, 179

ethnic disporas, 54–55, 105

Europe:

devolution in, 74–78

immigration and, 348–50

inclusive remapping of, 81–82

European Union (EU), 53, 73–74, 78, 82, 380

Ferguson, Mo., riots, 121, 312
financial crisis of 2008:
  de-globalization and, 37
  international migration and, 23,
    111
  job creation after, 75
  multinational corporations and,
    57–58
  urban societies and, 10
  world's billionaires and, 320
  world trade and, 25
Fitzgerald, Keith, 296
flow dynamics, 31–34, 40–41, 92
food industry, 164–65, 300–301
foreign investments, 38–39, 94–98,
    122–23, 211–12, 238–39
Foxconn, 143, 153, 200, 288
Fragile States Index, 71, 295
Franco, Francisco, 64
freelancers, 344–45
functional geography, 15–18, 68

garment industry, 280, 299, 301–3,
    382–83
Gates, Bill, 372, 382
Gates Foundation, 165
Gattorna, John, 303n
Genghis Khan, 197
geo-economics, 28, 138
geo-engineering techniques, 367
geography:
  American education and, 28
  as destiny, 14, 173
  functional vs. political, 14–17, 84,
    294, 379
  Mackinder on, 15

  see also mapping sites and tools
    for; maps
geophysical phenomena, 367
geopolitics, 28–29, 79–84, 138–40,
    175–77
Germany:
  connectedness and, 43–44
  economic master plans and, 119–20
  energy industry and, 171
  as high-tech exporter, 155–56, 160
  immigrants in, 348–50, 355
  infrastructure investments and,
    201
  job creation and, 345
  as part of EU and, 82, 141
  transportation systems of, 314,
    370
  Wirtschaftswunder (economic
    miracle) and, 9
  as world's most admired country,
    43, 163
Ghani, Ashraf, 70, 209
Gilbert, Dan, 121
global competition, 137–39
global financial systems, 319–23
global infrastructure:
  bridges and, 7–11
  flow vs. friction, 19–29
  functional vs. political geography,
    14–19
  satellite images and, 12–14
  supply chains and, 19–29
  world travel routes and, 3–6
globalization:
  Annan on, 35
  beginning of, 35–36

emerging markets and, 38
golden age of, 36–38
hyper-globalization and, 35–41
internationalism vs., 41
Keynes on, 36
mapping power and, 45–58
measurements of, 41–45
peak of, 39–40
surge of, 36
threats to, 37
usage of word and, 37
global power index, 175
global society:
  cyber civilization and, 327–45
  dilution and, 346–66
  nature and, 367–80
  resilience and, 381–91
global supply chains:
  Coca-Cola and, 186–87
  cross-border circuits and, 25
  definition of, 19–20
  Great Supply Chain War and, 28, 151
  hiring low-wage workers and, 151
  infrastructure investments and, 316–19
  maritime network and, 234–37
  measuring footprint and, 377–78
  as spheres of authority, 414
  unbundling production and, 151–52
Global Trends 2030 (NIC), 30, 53, 279
global warming, 207, 255–56, 372
Google, xxiii, 318, 327–28, 329, 331, 335, 336, 362, 364
  Ara project of, 157
  Wi-Fi Zeppelin blimps of, 328
Google Earth, xx
Google Fiber, 341
Google Maps, 332
Google Translate, 340n
Gordon, Robert, 318
Gou, Terry, 143
Grand Trunk Road (GT Road), 84–87
Great Escape, The (Deaton), 26
greenhouse gas emissions, 165
gross fixed capital formation, 9
Grotius, Hugo, 228, 230
Gulf Cooperation Council (GCC), 104–6, 211

Hadid, Zaha, 288
Hardt, Michael, 414, 420
Harper, Stephen, 126, 250
Hausmann, Ricardo, 148–49, 340
Hegel, G. W. F., 79
Hickel, Walter, 132
Himalayan Mountains, 86, 144, 208
Himanen, Pekka, 341
Hobbes, Thomas, 29
Hoffmann, Andreas, 254
Hong Kong, 10, 17, 40, 51, 55, 57, 89, 124, 151, 220, 228, 235, 260, 280, 285, 286–89, 329n
How to Run the World (Khanna), xvi
Huang Nubo, 251
Human Rights Watch, 304
Huntington, Samuel, 54, 180
Husbands and Wives (film), 63

Hussein, Saddam, 68, 104, 210, 343
hyper-globalization, 35–41

Icahn, Carl, 318
illegal immigrants, 13, 354
Imago Mundi, xix
immigrant assimilation, 351–53
imperialism, 173, 197
income inequality, 48, 116–17
India:
    ancient Silk Road and, 16
    diasporas and, 55, 261
    GT road and, 84–87
    as home to Dalai Lama, 144
    independence from Britain and,
        220
    international migration and, 23,
        352–53, 358–62
    Kashmir and, 70, 83, 196
    low-wage workers in, 151
    nuclear technology and, 176
    Pakistan and, 12–13, 66, 85, 144
    technology services and, 33, 281,
        302, 330, 342–43
    water supply and, 208, 374
Indian Ocean:
    China's naval presence around,
        224
    European spice trade and, 243–44
    flow of goods and energy cross-
        ing, 108, 210, 242, 274–75
    underwater Internet cables and,
        329
Indonesia:
    factories in, 89, 143, 158, 168
    Fragile States Index and, 70–71

    international migration and, 177,
        349n
    Jakarta and, 48, 228n
    low-wage workers in, 151
    natural disasters and, 244, 367
    raw materials and, 90, 158, 231–32
Industrial Revolution, 8, 36, 341,
    345
infrastructure:
    China as provider of, 181–84
    connectivity and, 5–7
    economic resilience and, 10
    engineering advances and, 7–8
    global commitment to, 11
    government spending on, 9–10,
        182, 293
    mega-infrastructures and, 8, 19
    privatization of, 17–18
    supply-demand gap and, 10–11
    as tool of influence, 172
infrastructure alliances:
    ideologies and, 178–84
    oil industry and, 192–95
    sanctions and, 186–89
    strategies and, 172–78
    Ukraine crisis and, 189–92
intellectual property, 141, 155,
    161–62, 336
Intergovernmental Panel on Climate
    Change, 368
international law, 29
international media, 266
international migration:
    Australia and, 349n
    Canada Immigrant Investor Pro-
        gram and, 124

climate migrants and, 254–56
Dubai and, 263, 268–69
Europe and, 348–50
financial crisis of 2008 and, 23, 111
illegal immigrants and, 13, 354
immigrant assimilation and,
    351–53
migrant workers and, 308–10, 360
United States and, 32, 116, 349–50
International Monetary Fund (IMF),
    42, 183, 193, 200, 319, 381
international relations:
    21st-century devolution and, 64
    from medieval to modern times,
        20–21
    systems vs. structural change, 30
International Space Station, 191
International Telecommunication
    Union (ITU), 331
international travel, 356–57
International Union for Conserva-
    tion of Nature (IUCN), 379
Internet:
    access to, 214–15
    changing map of, 338
    cyber attacks and, 333–34
    digital censorship and, 332–33
    digital industries and, 289
    digital workforce and, 343–45
    as global brain, 338
    global connectivity and, 44, 56,
        329, 338, 390
    governance of, 331–32
    intellectual property and, 336
    as invisible infrastructure, 327–31
    ISPs and, 331

Schmidt on, 327
social network analysis and, 339n
supply chains and, 20
surveillance and, 332, 336
Internet Corporation for Assigned
    Names and Numbers (ICANN),
    331
Iran, 42, 86, 101, 103, 104, 109n,
    112, 143, 176, 178, 187, 189, 200,
    205, 210–14, 219, 221, 234, 243,
    262, 272, 275–76, 349n, 370, 372
ISIS, 30, 47, 54, 102–3, 224, 334, 361
Israel, xx, 13, 55, 69, 103, 105–9,
    143, 188n, 333, 342, 370, 372

Jacobs, Frank, 205
Japan:
    "Abenomics" and, 291
    aging population of, 160, 350
    agriculture industry and, 376
    as Asian Tiger, 92
    China and, 145–46
    high-tech industry and, 160, 169
    investments and, 8, 201, 238–39
    Tokyo as megacity, 49–50
    World War II and, 224, 233
Jeddah, Saudi Arabia:
    African visitors to, 274
    "Dubai effect" and, 271
    employment and education in, 272
    as gateway to holy cities, 273
    Gulf of Oman and, 274–76
    King Abdullah Economic City
        (KAEC) in, 271–73
    King Abdullah University of Sci-
        ence and Technology in, 272n

Jefferson, Thomas, 173
job creation:
    Bangladesh garment industry and,
        301–3, 382–83
    elections and political parties vs.,
        297
    high-employing sectors and,
        318–19
    high-skill jobs and, 152–53
    Mexico's auto industry and, 130
    migrant workers and, 308–10
    near-shoring and, 168
    public works investment and,
        9–10
    in the United Kingdom, 75
    youth bulge and, 296

Kaku, Michio, 19
Kant, Immanuel, 388
Kasarda, John, 291
Keegan, John, 66
Kelly, John, 129
Kennedy, Paul, 174
Kenny, Charles, 295
Kent, Muhtar, 187
Keynes, John Maynard, 9–10, 36
Kieran, Tom, 127
Kim Il Sung, 219
Kim Jong Il, 219
Kim Jong Un, 186, 217–19
Kissinger, Henry, 387
knowledge industry, 43–44, 288,
    362
Koolhaas, Rem, 267, 269
Kotkin, Joel, 120
Kublai Khan, 205

labor regulations, 304–6
Lanier, Jaron, 338
Lee Kuan Yew, 87, 244, 353
Lerner, Jaime, 353
Levinson, Marc, 22
Lewis, Meriwether, 173
Li, Daokui, 115
Li Keqiang, 183
Lin, Justin Yifu, 292, 317
Lindsay, Greg, 291
Little, Brad, 123
Lochard, Itamara, 47
Locke, Gary, 179
Locklear, Samuel, 147
London:
    England and, 59
    international migration and, 348,
        352
    Lloyd's and, 237
    London School of Economics
        (LSE) and, 341
    as megacity, 259–60, 291
    United Kingdom and, 75–76
    as world financial center, 25, 40,
        212, 220
Longworth, Richard, 118
Louis XIV (king of France), 369
Lovelock, James, 378
Low, Patrick, 152
Luttwak, Edward, 66
Lynn, Barry, 170

Mackinder, Halford, 15, 28, 73, 197,
    208–9, 226
McKinsey Global Institute, 43, 51,
    294, 362

Connectedness Index of, 43, 260

Macmillan, Harold, 222

McMillon, Douglas, 23

Macomber, John, 272

Mahan, Alfred Thayer, 229

Major, Eric, 365

Malaysia:

ease of doing business in, 311

energy markets and, 238–39

mining industry and, 159

SEZs in, 26

Singapore and, 87–89

solar industry and, 284

Thailand and, 232–34

virtual private networks (VPNs)
and, 333

World Responsible Accredited
Production and, 302

Mansel, Philip, 101

manufacturing industry, 40–41,
89–90, 114–16, 217, 287

mapping sites and tools:

AJD Geospatial Concepts, 393

Anthropocene, 401

ArcGIS, 393

Atlas of Economic Complexity,
393–94

CAGE distance framework, 394

Carbon Map, 394

ChronoAtlas, 394

coastal sea level calculator, 395

Esri's Mapping Center, 395

Esri's Story Maps, 395

First Mile Geo, 395

FleetMon, 396

Flight Radar, 396

Gapminder, 396

Gateway House, 396

GDELT project, 397

GeoFusion, xxii, 397

Global Spatial Data Infrastructure
(GSDI), 397

Globaïa, 397

Google Earth, xxiii, 398

IMF's Direction of Trade Statistics, 398

Instaar Data Sets, 398

McKinsey Global Cities, 399

Map Projections, 398–99

Maps-of-War, 399

MapStory, 399

MIT's Immersion, 398

NASA's Global Change Directory,
399

National Geographic Intelligence
Agency, 400

Norse Attack Map, 400

OpenStreetMap, xxiii, 400

Planet Labs, xxiii, 400

Sourcemap, 401

Visual Literacy, 401

World Bank's PUMA, 401

WorldMap, 394

Worldmapper, 402

World Migration, 402

maps:

21st-century, xx

cartographic history and, xxi

early world, xix

evolution of, xx–xxi

Gall-Peters projections, xx

globalization and, xxv

maps *(Cont.)*
  Google Maps and, 332
  Hobo-Dyer projections, xx
  labeling natural resources on, 380
  Mercator projections, xv
  political maps, xx
  satellites and, xxii–xxiii
  software and, 44
  techniques in, xix
  technology and, xxii–xxiv
  telegeography maps, 328
  world maps, xix
Mare liberum (Grotius), 228, 230
marijuana legalization, 119
maritime history, 226–29
maritime network, 234–37
Ma Ying-jeou, 143
Middle East:
  al-Qaeda and, 99
  civil wars in, 99–100
  GCC countries and, 104–6
  ISIS and, 102
  Israel and, 105–7
  oil industry and, 103–4, 107–10
  refugees and, 103
  water scarcity in, 107
Midler, Paul, 302
migration, *see* international migration
Milanovic, Branko, 384
military expenditures, 175, 182, 413
mining industry, 24, 201–3, 217
Minnikhanov, Rustam, 72
mobile phones, 328, 340–41
Modi, Narendra, 85, 144

Mongolia, 26, 201–3, 209, 214, 222, 223, 286, 295n, 308, 347
Monnet, Jean, 82
Moretti, Enrico, 152
Moss, Mitchell, 296
multinational corporations:
  American multinationals and, 152, 180, 315
  Beck on, 300
  Dutch East India Company and, 228
  financial crisis of 2008 and, 57–58
  global citizens and, 362–64
  social responsibility and, 304–5
Musharraf, Pervez, 261

Napoleon I, emperor of France, 197, 369
Napoleonic Wars, 387
National Geographic, 346
National Geospatial-Intelligence Agency, 102–3, 400
National Intelligence Council (NIC), 30, 53, 175, 279
nationalism, 222–23, 354
national personality, 64
national security, 332, 361
National Security Agency (NSA), 332, 334, 336, 337n
National Security Council, 295n
National Union of Metalworkers, 314
nature:
  coastal civilizations and, 367–70
  natural disasters and, 90, 367, 370, 374

natural geography and, 14, 85, 370

natural resources and, 27, 70, 369, 380

river borders and, 369–70

see also climate change; global warming

near-shoring, 129, 168

Needham, Joseph, 127

Negri, Antonio, 414

Nenshi, Naheed, 126

New England Complex Systems Institute (NECSI), 68*n*

Newton, Isaac, 29

New York, N.Y.:

global connectedness and, 58, 113, 259–60

as megacity, 49–51, 291

Occupy Wall Street movement in, 313

terrorist attacks in, 37, 69

as world financial center, 25, 40, 115–17

9/11 terrorists, 37, 69, 221

Nolan, Peter, 39

Nordism, 254

North American Free Trade Agreement (NAFTA), 128–32

North American Union, 53, 54, 128–32, 173–74

North Atlantic Treaty Organization (NATO), xxi, 84, 180–81, 190, 193, 203, 252

North Korea, 32, 42, 146, 186–87, 210, 214–20, 335

North Pole, 249–51, 329

Norway, 17, 43, 233, 249–55, 378, 385

Novosseloff, Alexandra, 14

Obama, Barack, 142, 154, 176, 187, 211, 250, 349, 380*n*

Obama administration, 175

Occupy Wall Street movement, 30, 313

oil industry, 24–25, 103–4, 107–10, 125, 164, 192–95

Oman, 104, 243, 274–76, 391

O'Neill, Jim, 76

Organisation for Economic Co-operation and Development (OECD), 317*n*, 351, 359

Orwell, George, 139–40

Osborne, George, 179*n*

Pahlavi, Reza, 210

Pakistan, 12, 13, 47, 48, 52, 66, 69–70, 71, 100, 84–85, 144, 179, 208, 209, 213, 221, 225, 242–43, 244, 296, 309, 349*n*, 370, 371

Pan-African Infrastructure Development Fund, 97

Panama Canal, 229, 235, 237, 240–41, 249

expansion of, 227, 234*n*, 245–46

pan-Asian Regional Comprehensive Economic Partnership, 53

Park Geun-hye, 219

Paulson, John, 247

Pentland, Sandy, 339

Perez, Carlota, 341

Philip II (king of Spain), 76, 226

Piraeus Container Terminal (PCT), 184–86

Pirtle, Charles, 197

political geography:
mapping cities and, 49–52
mapping commonwealths and, 53–54
mapping communities and, 54–56
mapping companies, 57–58
mapping countries and, 45–48

Polo, Marco, 287

Poorly Made in China (Midler), 302

population growth, 49, 255, 261, 272, 281, 291

port cities, 241–43, 280

Porter, Michael, 303*n*

Portugal, 132, 222*n*, 238, 243, 348, 364

power, new map legends and:
cities and, 49–52
commonwealths and, 53–54
companies and, 54–56
countries and, 45–48
"diplomacity" and, 58–59

Protected Areas Categories System, 379

Putin, Vladimir, 190, 205, 216, 361

Putnam, Robert, 340

Rafaelsen, Rune, 255

Raffles, Stamford, 238

Rajapaksa, Mahinda, 244–45

Rajaratnam, S., 353

Rawlings, Michael, 117

Rawls, John, 384

refugees, 66, 103, 296, 308, 348, 371, 379

religious fundamentalism, 85

remapping:
administrative vs. sovereign space, 82
exclusive remapping and, 80, 83
frozen conflicts and, 83
inclusive remapping and, 81–83

Rhodes, Cecil, 172

Ricardo, David, 20, 148, 149

Rio Tinto, 71*n*

Rise and Fall of Great Powers (Kennedy), 174

Rockefeller Foundation, 375*n*

Rodman, Dennis, 186

Romer, Paul, 297

Rosenau, James, 414

Rovaniemi, Finland, 253

Runnion, Timm, 362

Russett, Bruce, 83*n*

Russia:
border with China and, 204–5
droughts and crop failures in, 206
exports to China and, 207
hydro-engineering in, 208
as largest country in world, 42, 46
North Korea and, 216
North Pole and, 250
Ukraine and, 81, 158, 188

Sandel, Michael, 383

São Paulo, 8, 49, 58, 291, 374

Sassen, Saskia, 25, 51

satellite images, xxiii, 12, 99, 103, 232, 400

Satyarthi, Kailash, 363

Schmidt, Eric, 164, 327

Schroeder, Chris, 264

Schuman, Robert, 147

Schwarzenegger, Arnold, 113

Scott, James, 66

Sechin, Igor, 249–50

Second World, The (Khanna), xvi, 140n, 192

Seed Vault, 255

Selden, John, 230

SelectUSA program, 122

self-determination, 67–68

Seward, William, 131

sex traffickers, 309

Sharif, Nawaz, 85

Shi, Yingtao, 227

Shiller, Robert, 10

shipping industry, 22, 159, 184–86, 236–37, 248–49

Silicon Valley, 25, 32, 48, 50, 57, 116, 120n, 152, 288, 337n, 343, 351, 388

Silk Road Economic Belt, 16–17, 198

Singapore, xxi, 4, 9, 26, 32, 40, 43, 45, 59–60, 69, 87–90, 91, 92, 151, 158, 163, 165, 217, 232, 236, 238–39, 244, 260, 263, 268, 269, 280, 285, 288–89, 297, 342, 352, 353, 358, 361, 373, 375

Sirisena, Maithripala, 244–45

Skidelsky, Robert, 22

Smil, Vaclav, 15, 46

Smith, Adam, 20

Snowden, Edward, 336

social network analysis, 339n

solar industry, 122, 293, 373

South America:
    Amazon rain forest and, 132, 371, 380
    Andes Mountains and, 132–33
    São Paulo and, 374

South China Sea, 230–38

Southeast Asia:
    aggregation and, 87–92
    cross-border railways and, 90–91
    devolution-aggregation dynamic and, 79
    financial investments in, 90
    natural disasters in, 90
    strategic waterways and, 237–41

sovereignty wealth funds (SWFs), 321

Soviet Union collapse, 64, 72, 192, 197

Sparks, Mike, 116

special economic zones (SEZs):
    aerotropolises as, 52
    China and, 228–29
    competition among, 299
    connectivity and, 280
    in Dominican Republic, 281
    in Dubai, 265–66
    in Ethiopia, 41
    in North Korea, 216–17
    rise of, 26–27
    in Saudi Arabia, 271
    in undeveloped countries, 281
    United Nations promotion of, 280
    in Vietnam, 283

Spence, Michael, 8

Spufford, Peter, 58

Sri Lanka, 70, 228, 244–45

Standage, Tom, 329n, 341

Startup Rising (Schroeder), 264

Stephenson, Neal, 329

Stiglitz, Joseph, 313

Suez Canal, 7, 108, 185, 235, 239, 241–42, 249, 271, 274, 390

Sun Tzu, 240

supply chains:
  corruption and, 310–11
  economic inequality and, 312–16
  global financial systems and, 319–23
  infrastructure investments and, 316–19
  lack of laws and regulations in, 305–8
  low-paid workers in, 308–10
  shared management of, 300–305
  see also global supply chains

Switzerland, 69, 77, 160, 194n, 264, 369, 385
  economic complexity and, 163
  infrastructure of, 68n
  SOCAR gas stations in, 192–93
  trans-Alpine tunnels of, 8n
  water pricing in, 373

Taleb, Nassim, 25n

Taliban insurgents, 47, 84, 221, 225

Taobao (Chinese eBay), 300

Tata, Jamsetji, 282

technology companies, 57, 281, 288, 291, 328, 336, 344

telecommunications industry, 328–29

terrorism, 37, 69–70, 221, 277, 348, 390

Thailand:
  Burmese immigrants in, 92
  drug traffic from, 32
  energy markets and, 233–34, 239
  Japan's investment in, 239
  manufacturing industry and, 89–91, 151
  Thai Canal and, 239

Thakkar, Ashish, 262

Tibet:
  China's relations with, 144–45, 197–98
  Himalayan plateau and, 208
  Lhasa as capital of, 196
  U.S. relations with, 179

time zones, 160

Tito, Josip Broz, 73

topographical engineering, 231–32

Toynbee, Arnold, 172–73

Toyota, 89, 146, 168

transportation systems, 10, 15–16, 196–99

trash recycling, 167

Trutnev, Yury, 207, 216

Turkle, Sherry, 340

Turzi, Mariano, 183

Ukraine crisis, 81, 158, 180, 188–93

underwater resources, *see* deepwater drilling

United Arab Emirates (U.A.E.), 69, 165, 176, 259–71, 275, 276, 361
  see also Dubai, U.A.E.

United Auto Workers union, 116, 314

United Nations:
  membership in, 64
  UN Convention on Law of Sea, 231
  UN Industrial Development Organization, 280
  UN relief agencies, 371
  UN Security Council, 41, 179

United States:
  American Dream and, 111–12
  China's investment in, 122–23
  counterterrorism pledges of, 182
  devolution within, 116–21
  education levels in, 116
  employment in, 122–23
  failing cities in, 113–14
  financial system of, 42
  food security in, 375
  foreign policy of, 175–77
  global incomes and, 365
  immigration policy and, 32, 116, 349–50, 354
  infrastructure investment and, 10–11
  long-term jobless rates in, 313
  migration from, 23, 111
  national pride and, 365
  outsourcing jobs and, 114–16
  political borders and, 12–13, 16
  Puerto Rico as tax haven and, 247
  as rich, safe, technologically advanced, 112–13
  Tibet and, 179

transportation systems of, 10, 199, 317–18
urban revival and, 121–22
Upwork, 343–44
urbanization, 19, 24, 223, 280, 286, 291, 312
USA*Engage, 211

van Agtmael, Antoine, 169
Venkatesan, Ravi, 172
Victor Emmanuel II, king of Italy, 64
Vietnam:
  garment industry in, 90
  PetroVietnam and, 230
  SEZs in, 283
  UN Convention on Law of Sea and, 231
  Vietnam War and, 175
von Neumann, John, 288

Waiting for Godot (Beckett), 147
Walsh, Sam, 184
Wang Jing, 246
Wang Yilin, 230
water supply, 107, 126, 206–7, 372–75
Weber, Max, 383
WikiLeaks, 30, 56
Wilson, Woodrow, 67
workers' rights, 300
World Bank, 11, 95, 200, 223, 274, 298, 317–18, 380–81
World Cup championships, 350
World Economic Forum, 22, 154, 192, 201, 381

World Expo, 260
World Food Programme, 103
World Happiness Report, 265
world population growth, 256
world trade:
  cross-border flows and, 8–9
  financial crisis of 2008 and, 25
  manufacturing networks and, 148;
    see also global supply chains
  restrictions on, 153–54
  services and, 148, 155
  trade agreements and, 140–42
World Trade Organization (WTO),
    37, 152–54, 161*n*, 200, 322
world travel routes, 3–5
world wars:
  arms supplies during, 210
  European trade before, 148

Japanese railways and, 224
Norway's conflict resolution and,
    255
security provided by U.S. military
    and, 181
strategic waters and, 233
Western dominance and, 37
World Wide Web, 20, 327, 331
World Wildlife Fund, 380
Wowereit, Klaus, 355
Wriston, Walter, 159–60

Xi Jinping, 141–44, 183, 198, 205

Yakunin, Vladimir, 132

Zhang Weiwei, 386
Zheng He, 228, 243–45

PARAG KHANNA is a global strategist, world traveler, and bestselling author. He is a CNN Global Contributor and a Senior Research Fellow at the Lee Kuan Yew School of Public Policy at the National University of Singapore. Khanna is the co-author of *Hybrid Reality: Thriving in the Emerging Human-Technology Civilization* and author of *How to Run the World: Charting a Course to the Next Renaissance* and *The Second World: Empires and Influence in the New Global Order.* He has been a fellow at the New America Foundation and the Brookings Institution, advised the U.S. National Intelligence Council, and worked in Iraq and Afghanistan as a senior geopolitical adviser to U.S. Special Operations Forces. He holds undergraduate and graduate degrees from the School of Foreign Service at Georgetown University and a Ph.D. from the London School of Economics. He serves on numerous governmental and corporate advisory boards and is a councilor of the American Geographical Society, a trustee of the New Cities Foundation, and a Young Global Leader of the World Economic Forum.

paragkhanna.com
Facebook.com/DrParagKhanna
@paragkhanna

blog and newsletter

For literary discussion, author insight,
book news, exclusive content,
recipes and giveaways, visit the
Weidenfeld & Nicolson blog and
sign up for the newsletter at:

www.wnblog.co.uk